THE COMPLETE BOOK OF
MODEL AIRCRAFT
SPACECRAFT
AND ROCKETS

Airborne! The great moment of triumph when a working model airplane goes into flight, in this case, a radio-controlled monoplane powered by a miniature internal-combustion reciprocating engine. One hobbyist launches the model while at the rear another holds and keys the radio transmitter that directs the model's course in the sky.

Hobby Industry Association of America, Inc.

THE COMPLETE BOOK OF
MODEL AIRCRAFT
SPACECRAFT
AND ROCKETS

LOUIS H. HERTZ

BONANZA BOOKS   •   NEW YORK

OTHER BOOKS BY LOUIS H. HERTZ
THE COMPLETE BOOK OF MODEL RACEWAYS AND ROADWAYS
THE COMPLETE BOOK OF MODEL RAILROADING
NEW ROADS TO ADVENTURE IN MODEL RAILROADING
ADVANCED MODEL RAILROADING
COLLECTING MODEL TRAINS
MESSRS. IVES OF BRIDGEPORT
RIDING THE TINPLATE RAILS
THE HANDBOOK OF OLD AMERICAN TOYS
MAKING YOUR MODEL RAILROAD
MECHANICAL TOY BANKS
MODEL RAILROAD CONVERSION MANUAL
MINIATURE RAILROAD SERVICE AND REPAIR MANUAL

TO G. WILLIAM HOLLAND
Good friend, model builder and collector,
and a master of the photographic art

CONTENTS

INTRODUCTION

With the publication of this, the writer's third *Complete Book of,* each devoted to an entirely different broad category of models and model-making, a more or less definite pattern of purpose and scope appears to have firmly established itself. There seems little doubt that it is this particular concept and approach that accounts for the very gratifying reception that has been accorded *The Complete Book of Model Railroading* and *The Complete Book of Model Raceways and Roadways.* No doubt each of these books, including the present volume, can be said to operate at once on several levels, each with varying appeal and value to major elements of the entire spectrum of enthusiasts in the hobby to which it is directed. Of course, it is to the beginner, to the enthusiast who is just approaching a new and fascinating hobby for the first time, that these books in particular have been intended to appeal in order to provide both a rational introduction to and a comprehensive coverage of a particular model hobby.

Basically, however, the endeavor of *The Complete Book of Model Aircraft, Spacecraft, and Rockets,* as with its counterparts on model railroading and on model raceways and roadways, goes somewhat well beyond this in an effort to provide the following: (1) An introduction to the hobby that will enable the newcomer to understand what it is all about; what paths are open to him; what types of equipment and components are available and how to make use of them; the customs, standards, and nomenclature of the hobby —in short, to bring together all that the hobbyist need to know to understand the framework of his chosen hobby and to be able to function intelligently therein. (2) As complete a coverage of *all* aspects of the hobby, both major and minor, as is consistent with avoiding devoting a disproportionate amount of space to certain sidelines and byways of (at the moment, at least) comparatively limited popularity. Here, of course, a conscientious author must endeavor to guard against unwittingly providing an imbalance by possibly overemphasizing his own personal tastes and preferences. (3) To provide a book of useful permanent reference and a source of new and stimulating ideas that will be of continued usefulness regardless of what particular point of experience, sophistication, or seniority a given individual may reach within the hobby. (4) A history of the hobby—material that invariably proves extremely interesting in itself, as well as a source of prideful background to the state to which the hobby has attained, and that very often also is of practical value in relationship to present-day matters as well.

When originally projected, some time ago, this volume was conceived to fill the need for a practical and comprehensive book on model aircraft. The writer is indebted to Brandt Aymar for his bringing the idea into the space age, as it were, by suggesting that it be expanded to include spacecraft and rockets, as well as for his thoughts and counsel in general, and in particular regarding the arrangement of the historical material.

There is one further matter of which notice should be taken. It is often interesting and surprising to observe how much certain people are capable of reading conclusions into the presence of certain visual material, or the lack thereof. There is no particular significance to the presence or absence of pictures of certain given models or equipment. In preparing a book of this type every effort is made to secure pictorial material covering commercial products from as many different sources as possible. For one reason or another, some firms do not respond at all, some simply do not have the required type of material available, while still others provide a superabundance. In any event the matter finally comes down to a problem of selection and balance in terms both of attaining the greatest possible variety of typical or pertinent examples and, within this framework, as equal a division as possible among the various sources of the material. While every manufacturer can, of course, immediately recognize his own products—as also can a substantial number of advanced hobbyists, as well as most of those engaged in any way in the hobby business—to many individuals, for example, one model of a particular prototype airplane may look much like another; one engine much like another; one radio transmitter much like another, and so on. An effort is accordingly made to select typical examples among the pictorial material available. To do otherwise would be more to essay an attempt at the compilation of an exhaustive catalog rather than of a practical book. The fact that a photograph of a particular item is included certainly does not carry any implication that the author regards it as necessarily superior to a competitive unit; neither does the absence of any particular unit carry a converse implication.

The author is profoundly grateful to all those who have so generously assisted in the preparation of *The Complete Book of Model Aircraft, Spacecraft, and Rockets*. If any of their names have been omitted from the following list, it is entirely inadvertent:

To G. William Holland, whose skill with the camera and willingness to travel far in his enthusiasm again have played a major role in the creation of a book on models; Howard G. McEntee, Charles Hampson Grant, Commander Paul M. Boyer, USNR, and Lieutenant (jg) W. S. Turner, USNR, of the United States Navy, Shelby Thompson and George Gardner of the National Aeronautics and Space Administration; John Worth of the Academy of Model Aeronautics; G. Harry Stine of the National Association of Rocketry; Mark Haber, Victor G. Didelot, Charles A. Stenman; I. Warshaw of the Warshaw Collection of Business Americana; Harold H. Carstens and Naomi Drake of Carstens Publications; Irwin, Nathan, and Lewis Polk, Marguerite Hubert, Lee Fox, Anne D. Podell, Eva Feist, Jerry Spevak, Milton Plaut, William Merklein, Mary Walsh, John Breheney, Joseph Bamberger, Cliff Crane, and the late Charles Binder of Polk's Model Craft Hobbies, Incorporated; William MacMillan, Walter Caddell, John T. Lillis, Ginny Scott of the Hobby Industry Association of America, Incorporated; Frank A. Taylor, Paul E. Garber, Robert B. Meyer, and Mereve Beldon of the Smithsonian Institution; G. W. B. Lacey and T. E. Lillywhite of the Science Museum, South Kensington, London; H. H. G. McKern of the Museum of Applied Arts and Sciences, Sydney, Australia; Joe Miller, Jr., and Bobbi Jenkins of the National Hobby Institute; Richard H. Palmer of Rich's Hobbytowne, Incorporated; Leon Shulman, Helen C. Harris, Bernard and Cecil Tassler, Aubrey Kochman, Joseph and Katharine Daffron; Walter L. Schroder and Betty Morelli of *Model Airplane News;* William J. Winter of *American Modeler;* Joseph J. Hardie and Don McGovern of *Flying Models;* Albert L. Lewis and Rose Borello of *Air Progress;* Dr. G. A. Robinson, Charles A. Arens, Captain Ralph S. Barnaby, USN (Ret.); Harry D. Graulich, Russell Holderman, Charles W. Meyers, George A. Page, Jr., Jean Alfred Roché, Armour Selley; Alfred W. Dater, Jr., of the Stamford Historical Society; Timothy J. Dannels of *The Engine Collectors' Journal;* William L. Effinger, Jr., Frank Zaic, Douglas Rolfe, Merle C. Gillette, M. L. Weiss; Lloyd W. Rittenhouse and R. S. Allen of the Emerson-Rittenhouse Company, Incorporated; Mrs. Leslie Lord of the Honeoye Falls, New York, Public Library; C. H. Burk, William E. Eckhardt.

Also: Herman A. Ecker, John Mebane, Carter Tiffany, Norman Shavin, J. H. Elliott, Mel Anderson, John Hart Krickel; F. H. Smith of the Royal Aeronautical Society; Emmett J. Glazer of the Wingfoot Lighter-Than-Air Society; J. Howard Bushway; Emily M. Schossberger of the University of Notre Dame Press; Joseph Kane, John G. Steenken; Richard Miller of the Soaring Society of America, Incorporated; R. S. Wood of the Kendrick and Davis Company; Jerome D. Smith of Horsman Dolls, Incorporated; Harold E. Morehouse; A. C. Kalmbach and Willard V. Anderson of the Kalmbach Publishing Company; Pan American World Airlines, Incorporated; United Airlines, Incorporated; the Federal Communications Commission; Mrs. M. E. Haben of the General Post Office Radio Services Department, London; F. G. Nixon of the Air Services of the Department of Transport of Canada; George E. Parry of the Model Aeronautics Association of Canada; Myrtle B. Coad of the Western Associated Modelers, Incorporated; Elmo N. Pickerill of the Early Birds of Aviation, Incorporated; Max E. Ripken; Donald Lockwood of the Illinois Model Aero Club; Joseph Wagner, Dr. R. E. Nichols, Harrison Cady, K. Krause; C. Thomas Dean of Long Beach (California) State College; the staffs of the New York Public Library and of the Social Sciences Department of the Chicago Public Library; George Boon; Ben McCready, W. Voorhees, Ted Erickson, and R. A. Berger of *Playthings;* Herman Reid, Louis Retzkin, Gilbert Rose, Melvin Weiss, Gil Ross, Lloyd W. Ralston, Alice Ives, Edward C. Ives, Joseph Finelli, Carl Schmaedig; Lennie Goodman and Stephen Ditta of America's Hobby Center; E. P. Lott, Julia Gunsbury, Alexander H. Weinberg, H. Walter Maass, Harry W. Aitken, William Dean, Riley Wooten, John Pond; Jack Levine of Lee's Hobby Supplies, Incorporated; Edward P. Fickeissen; Michael F. Spielman of *Toys and Novelties;* Henry Struck, Charles Werve, Edward B. Miller, D. F. Grout, Carl Sotscheck, Dr. Richard H. Walden, William H. Van Precht, Ethel K. Sidney, and Bud Hollzer of *Craft, Model and Hobby Industry;* N. L. Mead of the Curtiss-Wright Corporation; E. J. Banks, Robert Larsh, John Lorence, Basil Hiotakis, Louise Swan Harworth, Charles Ragot, Richard G. Berger, E. S. Lincoln; Ralph Bush and Allan W. Fink of the Pasadena (California) City Schools; Carl Dangel of the Goodyear Tire and Rubber Company; Monroe Drew, Jr., of the Aereon Corporation; Warren Potter, Alan V. Denham; Michael G. Tager and Joseph Malcolm of Michael G. Tager Associates; Ernest P. Doclar, Jr., of the Boy Scouts of America; P. H. Spencer, W. D. Guthrie, David Newmark, Ben Shereshaw; Samuel Bradford of the Connecticut Electric Equipment Company, Incorporated; Ann T. Sokol of the Connecticut Telephone and Electric Corporation of Meriden; Rudy Funk; Harry Adler; Dr. S. G. Weiss.

Also: Paul F. Runge of Ace R/C, Incorporated; the Acme Model Engineering Company; Walter T. Cusack of the Aldine Paper Company; Arthur E. Laneau of the Ambroid Company; Lloyd E. Kennie of the Airfix Corporation of America; Robert D. Strock of the AMF Wen-Mac Division of the American Machine and Foundry Company; Eugene Horvat of Aristo-Craft Distinctive Miniatures; John R. Cuomo, William Silverstein; John Tillotson, Sam Komarow, and Layle Eiden of the Aurora Plastics Corporation; W. Clyde Austin of the Austin-Craft Company; Babcock Controls, Incorporated; R. H. Fuller of Bassett-Lowke Limited; Russell LaValla of the Borden Chemical Company; the Burgess Battery Company; Peter Cabrol of C & L Developments Limited; Jim Adams of C & S Electronics; the Centuri Engineering Company; Virginia G. King of the Citizen-Ship Radio Corporation; Edward T. Packard of the Cleveland Model and Supply Company; M. B. Shamberg of the Comet Model Hobbycraft Corporation; Arthur Hasselbach of Consolidated Models, Incorporated; William H. Selzer, Bob Wallach, and Dale Kirn of the L. M. Cox Manufacturing Company, Incorporated; Loisjean Blasser of the Curtis Dyno-Products Corporation; J. K. Moore of Davies-Charlton Limited; Harold F. deBolt of the deBolt Model Engineering Company; J. V. H. Robins of Derritron Limited; Stanley A. Johnson of Dynamic Models, Incorporated; Vernon Estes and Norman Avery of Estes Industries, Incorporated; F & M Electronics Incorporated; D. Reece, I. R. Francis, and J. Holdaway of Flight Link Controls Limited; Flyline Models; Duke Fox of the Fox Manufacturing Company; William D. Perry, Marshall H. Frisbie, and Maurice H. Romer of the A. C. Gilbert Company; C. F. Gladen of Gladen Enterprises, Incorporated; Carl Goldberg of Carl Goldberg Models, Incorporated; John Murray of Paul K. Guillow, Incorporated; Phil Thompson of the Hawk Model Company; N. B. Winick and B. G. Coplin of the Hi-Flier Manufacturing Company; A. V. Duffill of the Humber Oil Company Limited; Ted Scarlet of Imprint Art Products; Prem Gary and S. Greenhouse of the International Balsa Corporation; E. Keil and Company Limited; Sheldon M. Ostrowe of the K & B Manufacturing Corporation; Dick Nelson of Lindberg Products, Incorporated; Jean Zeiler of Walter Kidde and Company, Incorporated; Norman H. Wyner and Bernard Saydol of Lines Brothers, Incorporated; Pat Papa of the Lionel Toy Corporation; Marown Engineering Limited; Frank S. Garcher of the Midwest Products Company, Incorporated; Robert C. Schmidt of Min-X Radio, Incorporated; T. Smith of Model Aircraft (Bournemouth) Limited; Augustus Wildman of Model Hobbies; P. L. Keller of Model Missiles, Incorporated; Jack M. Besser of Monogram Models, Incorporated; William Eccles and Anthony Iato of the MRC-Enya Company, Incorporated.

Also: LaVerne Klipp of the North American Plywood Corporation; R. B. Zimmerman of the North Pacific Products Company; Orbit Electronics, Incorporated; Charles A. Dolbier of the Park Plastics Company; Charles Eifflaender of the Progress Aero Works; Burt Zollo of the Public Relations Board, Incorporated; Remcon Electronics; Arthur H. Rosenbloom, Louis S. Wetzel, Edward Wetzel, Ruth Cohn, and George Harte of Renwal Products, Incorporated; Joel K. Rubenstein of Revell, Incorporated; Mr. and Mrs. E. Nedrow of the J. Roberts Manufacturing Company; Irving S. Wait of the Rocket Development Corporation; John D. Frisoli of the Scientific Model Airplane Company; Glen Sigafoose of the Sig Manufacturing Company, Incorporated; R. T. Fuller of Solarbo Limited; Everett R. Atkins, Jr., of Superscale; Ed Manulkin of Sterling Models; Matthew A. Sullivan of Sullivan Products; John Tatone of Tatone Products; the Teleradio Company (Edmonton) Limited; J. E. Petit of the Testor Corporation; Robert Gordon Britt of Turbocraft; Ida Guild of the Universal Powermaster Corporation; H. E. Hoskins of L. W. Vass Limited; Gilbert Henry of the Veco Products Corporation; Westee Hobby Imports; Christine Zaic of the C. A. Zaic Company, Incorporated.

LOUIS H. HERTZ
Scarsdale, New York
June, 1966

CHAPTER 1

Preliminary Considerations

The designer and builder of flying models frequently finds it necessary or at least advisable to depart from either absolute fidelity to the proportions of a specific real airplane or even from the general design of actual aircraft. In some instances these changes are quite minor and, unless specifically pointed out, often pass unnoticed by most observers. At other times, a search for certain desired flight characteristics in a flying model results in a ship that flies and maneuvers superbly, but has a radical or even somewhat grotesque appearance when compared to the customary forms of the prototypes. It might be added parenthetically that in many instances these changes have been experimented with in the past by designers of real planes, and for one reason or another have not been used. On the other hand, some features developed for models have eventually found their way into real aircraft; still others are practical for models but cannot be translated to the real thing, or at least means have not yet been found for adapting them.

When model aircraft design substantially follows that of a real airplane but departs from being an exact model in certain details or proportions, these changes generally are made for one or both of two reasons. One is that the weight distribution of the model varies from that of the prototype. To illustrate, let us take any prototype airplane and reduce it to an exact scale model, building our model of the usual lightweight ma-

terials. So far, we have a model that looks exactly like the real airplane. However, when it comes to making the model, which is an excellent static reproduction, into a flying model, we may well run into problems.

When we add the mechanism for driving the propeller (and the propeller itself will have to be substantially larger than scale size for a flying model), we are certain to alter and very likely destroy the balance of the miniature aircraft as contrasted to the real plane. This holds true whether we install a rubber-powered mechanism or an internal-combustion reciprocating engine, although each will alter the balance somewhat differently. Even the way model materials are employed will produce a different balance. The model may look the same whether a balsa framework covered with tissue is employed throughout or if the fuselage is covered with plank balsa, but both the overall weight and the balance will differ. The expert model plane designer will compensate for these differences by skillful changes in proportions and contours. He may find it desirable to move the wings forward or backward; he may find it necessary to increase the size of the wings and elevator, and thereby of the lifting surfaces.

The result may be an excellent flying model, but it is no longer in most cases a true scale model. Hard as the designer may try, he will find that certain prototype airplanes do not make for wholly satisfactory flying models. This is par-

1

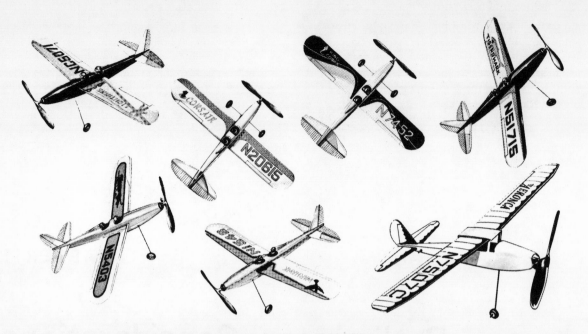

Fig. 1. A variety of completely assembled, inexpensive, ready-to-fly rubber-powered model airplanes are available. These models have plastic fuselages and aluminum foil covered balsa-wood wings. Other types of simple flying models are so fully prefabricated that they snap together in a matter of seconds.

Comet Model Hobbycraft Corp.

ticularly true of many low-wing monoplanes. This is not a hard-and-fast rule, but generally speaking, model high-wing monoplanes perform much better than do low-wing models. This is the reason that in many excellent flying models the wing is mounted on a structure on top of the fuselage that positions it much higher proportionately than would ever occur in a real airplane.

Still other factors enter into these necessary changes and compromises. The wind, for example, obviously cannot be scaled down as is the model airplane. Of course, a hobbyist would not attempt to fly a plane in a high wind, but what might seem an almost unnoticeable breeze reacts on a model plane far more than it would on a real airplane, and can affect its flight characteristics and maneuverability. A number of models have been improved aerodynamically by substituting a double rudder that, while having the same over-all surface as a single large rudder, presents only half as much surface to a breeze coming in from the side.

THERE IS NO PILOT IN THE COCKPIT

The second reason why many, probably most, flying models are compromises stems from the fact that there is no live pilot in the cockpit. This is not belaboring the obvious. Whatever air conditions he runs into that affect the stability of his plane, the pilot instinctively corrects at once by manipulating his controls; when the nose dips

or rises, the pilot is there to correct it, and so on. A model airplane, and especially one designed for free flight, must be so designed that insofar as is possible the plane will automatically trim itself when it runs into variations in the air currents. Model aircraft designers have achieved amazing results in producing planes that will thus, in effect, fly themselves, but this usually is accomplished at the expense of departing either from scale proportions and general prototype design or from both.

While with control-line model airplanes, the hobbyist does have a certain measure of control over the model while it is in the air, this control even in expert hands still does not equal that of a live pilot in the cockpit, and certain compromises still are necessary. Further, in control-line flying, planes designed for different types of competitive events must be designed to provide the best possible performance in the type of flying desired, and again changes and compromises are required; a model plane designed purely for speed will differ from one intended to be flown in events where maneuverability is the requisite, such as stunt and combat contests. Both of these categories are similar in that they call for maneuverability and for being able to fly as well upside down as in the normal position (this affects not only the design of the plane itself but also that of the engine and fuel feed system) However, each of these two classes also has certain individual needs that may affect design. The basic requirement in a stunt model is maneuverability—effective flying in either a regular or inverted position usually is attained in both stunt and combat models by using a symmetrical wing cross section. That is, both the top and the bottom surfaces of the wing present the identical curve or airfoil.

Combat models, on the other hand, being flown against another plane in the air, frequently collide with the opposing plane, or crash merely as a result of the hobbyist's losing control of the craft in the heat of trying to cut the tissue streamer on the other plane. Consequently, combat models usually are designed with strength in mind, as well as a simplicity of design that permits ease of repair after an accident. At the same time, combat models often are designed for quicker response to control commands than are stunt models, although many commercial models supplied in kit form are classified as dual combat/stunt designs.

As the preceding paragraph suggests, the ease and speed with which a control-line model airplane responds to control are factors that can be regulated by the designer of the model—again usually at the expense of fidelity to real airplane design. A beginner learning to manipulate a control line almost invariably tends to overcontrol his model. Therefore it is desirable to provide him with a model plane that flies somewhat slowly, has a maximum of stability, and will react slowly to the novice's instinctive overcontrol manipulations. There is a special class of plane designed for this purpose, known as a trainer. The point to emphasize here is, once again, the need for a departure from exactly following real aircraft design and merely scaling down a prototype and expecting to produce a perfect flying model.

Only with radio-controlled model aircraft does the hobbyist fully begin to approach a parallel to real flying; of being able to control a plane high in the air much the same as if he

actually were in the cockpit. The more sophisticated the system of radio control used, the closer the model enthusiast comes to duplicating real flying—when he can exercise control over the rudder, elevator, ailerons, and motor speed. Yet even here he does not actually feel the changes in air current as does a pilot in a real airplane, and his responses to what he sees as his plane is in the air must necessarily be somewhat slower than if he were in the cockpit. Accordingly, even when model airplanes are specifically designed for radio control they too must often make compromises with absolute scale fidelity in the interests of flying ability. There are, in fact, separate competitive events for radio-control models as such, and for radio-control scale models. In the latter event, the contestant must establish to the satisfaction of the judges that his model is a scale replica. He is awarded points on fidelity to scale and workmanship; he may also gain points on what are known as scale operations. This covers such things as the ability to retract and extend landing gear and to lower and raise flaps. In addition the plane competes for points by performing in a flight pattern similar to the performance pattern that makes up the entire regulation radio-control contest event.

Having broadly discussed scale and prototype fidelity in connection with the compromises that may be required in flying models, it is time to turn to the meaning of scale more specifically. Nothing that has been said so far in this chapter should be taken to mean that scale fidelity is not important in a flying model. It most certainly has a definite place in flying models, wherever and to what extent it can be retained without sacrificing flying ability; and in the realm of nonoperating display or static models, it is all important.

Fig. 2. Nonflying display models, built from kits of easily assembled precision-molded plastic parts, are built and collected by millions of model airplane enthusiasts. Shown here are two such models of jet airplanes, the U.S. Air Force's X-15 rocket plane and the U.S. Navy's F8U Crusader.

Aurora Plastics Corp.

Fig. 3. The United States Navy is very active in promoting model aviation, and often participates in national competitions.

Official Photograph, U.S. Navy

SCALE

Regardless of how far practical flying considerations may impel the designer of a flying model to depart from absolute scale fidelity to a prototype, the original and basic frame of reference in all types of models is that of scale. Most model airplanes that attempt in any measure to reproduce a prototype are built to easily used and conventional modelmaking scales. The scale to which a model is built refers properly to the physical dimension on the model that represents a given unit of measurement—usually one foot—on the prototype. With the exception of a few old scales that now are widely used on model airplanes built from construction kits of plastic parts, the common scales used in model airplane building (and which are almost invariably used for flying models) are ⅛ inch to the foot, 3/16 inch to the foot, ¼ inch to the foot, ⅜ inch to the foot, ½ inch to the foot, ⅝ inch to the foot, ¾ inch to the foot, and 1 inch to the foot. Larger scales sometimes are used, but even a scale of ¾ inch to the foot or 1 inch to the foot usually results in a pretty large model. However, generally speaking, engine-powered flying models today tend to average much smaller in size than they did in the 1930's because of the ready availability of small engines.

If we assume a real airplane with a wingspan of 40 feet, translated into aforementioned scales, this 40-foot dimension would result in an actual wingspan on the models as follows: ⅛-inch scale, 5 inches; 3/16-inch scale, 7½ inches; ¼-inch scale, 10 inches; ⅜-inch scale, 15 inches; ½-inch scale, 20 inches; ⅝-inch scale, 25 inches; ¾-inch scale, 30 inches; and 1-inch scale, 40 inches. Every other prototype dimension will vary accordingly; a 2-foot-wide cabin window will reduce to an actual ½ inch on a ¼-inch scale model

and to ¾ inch on a ⅜-inch scale model. If one of the scales larger than 1 inch to the foot were used, the 40-foot wing would reduce to 60 inches in 1½-inch scale. In 2-inch scale it would be 80 inches. Such a model might fly beautifully and be the envy of all who viewed it, but carrying it to and from the flying field would present some difficulties, although these usually are decreased by making the wing detachable in such a huge model. Some such large models—and even larger ones—are still at times built and flown. One reason such model planes are so seldom seen now is that the present-day contest regulations—which classify plane size according to engine size—exclude such giants from taking part in conventional competitions.

If we were going to be purists, we would always refer to scale as the expression of one fixed dimension in relation to another fixed dimension, such as ¼ inch to one foot. However, in day-to-day normal usage hobbyists generally designate scale simply by the first dimension—⅛-inch scale, ¼-inch scale, and so on—and assume everyone knows that these figures represent one foot on the prototype. This system of reference passes satisfactorily in most model building hobbies other than model airplanes. As we shall observe in a moment, there exist some notable and often confusing designations in plastic kit model airplane practice that depart from this norm.

SIZE AND PROPORTION

First, however, both because it is important in itself and also because it is absolutely vital to an understanding of these exceptions to normal model usage, it is necessary to comment on proportional references to scale and size. If a model is built to a scale of ⅛ inch to the foot, it is 1/96th the size of the prototype; if built to a scale of ½ inch to the foot, it is 1/24th the size of the prototype, and so on. These proportions are readily ascertained by multiplying the dimension of the scale—the denominator of the fraction that represents the scale—by one foot or rather, for the purpose of the arithmetical problem, by 12 inches. Thus, with a scale of ⅛ inch to the foot, you multiply 8 by 12, and the result is 96.

Sometimes kit manufacturers refer to a model in terms of its proportion or size. To determine the actual scale of a model referred to only by its proportion or size, you reverse the aforementioned procedure and divide the denominator of the proportion into 12 inches. Thus if you are told a model is built to 1/96th proportion or size, you can establish the scale by dividing 96 into 12 inches. The answer is .125 inch, which is the same as ⅛ inch. With a model designated 1/48th proportion or size, you divide 48 into 12 inches and get an answer of .25 inch, or ¼ inch. The 12-inch dimension has to be carried out beyond the decimal point, of course; what you actually do is to divide the denominator of the proportion into 12.00 or 12.000 inches.

Unfortunately, a considerable area of confusion often is added to what should really be comparatively simple by some hobbyists and even some manufacturers when they refer to the factor or proportion or size as "scale" and give us designations such as "1/96th scale," "1/48th scale," and so forth. These are properly the designations of proportion or size, and should correctly be referred to as 1/96th size, 1/48th size—that is, 1/96th and 1/48th the size of the prototype— which correspond, of course, to ⅛-inch scale and ¼-inch scale respectively. When properly used, the smaller the scale, the smaller the model, and at the same time the larger the denominator in the fraction indicating proportion or size. As can be seen from the following, there is a world of difference in the physical size of a model built to ⅛-inch scale and of a model of the same prototype built to ⅛th proportion.

SCALE PER FOOT	PROPORTION
⅛ in.	1/96th
3/16 in.	1/64th
¼ in.	1/48th
⅜ in.	1/32d
½ in.	1/24th
¾ in.	1/16th
1 in.	1/12th
1½ in.	1/8th
2 in.	1/6th

This is where much of the confusion about

scale, size, and proportion occurs to confuse hobbyists, particularly the beginners, who are most in need of an accurate frame of reference and point of departure. Scale and proportion (usually rendered as "size") are two entirely different measurements, although both refer to the physical size of the model as compared to that of the prototype. After a while hobbyists become familiar with these designations and immediately understand what is meant, even when the terminology is misused. Likewise, in time, hobbyists are able to visualize immediately the approximate size of a proposed model with whose prototype dimensions they are familiar merely upon hearing the scale in which it is to be built.

As noted, there are some scales now widely used in nonoperating plastic model airplane kits that depart from the normal practice of an easily worked fraction of an inch being used as the scale reduction that represents one foot on the prototype. The oldest and most frequently encountered of these is the 1/72nd size, which actually works out to a scale of 1 inch representing 6 feet, or to give it in the customary terminology of scale to the foot, it is 1/6 inch to the foot. Inasmuch as our rulers in English linear measurement are divided into units based on the quarter inch and the eighth inch, one may well wonder why such an odd scale should ever have found acceptance. The answer is that this is the scale established during the Second World War as the standard to be used in the construction of aircraft-recognition models used in the training of the Armed Forces and of civilian airplane spotters. Presumably it already had been established as the standard for the same purposes in Great Britain. It was calculated that when a 1/72nd-size model was viewed at a distance of 35 feet, it provided the same effect as an actual plane seen at a distance of one-half mile. Initially the plan was

Fig. 4. For the hobbyist who wishes to start by flying a model powered by an internal combustion reciprocating engine, there are complete outfits, such as this one, containing everything required, including fuel and battery. The airplane model is a ready-to-fly molded plastic model of a P-51 Mustang.

L. M. Cox Mfg. Co., Inc.

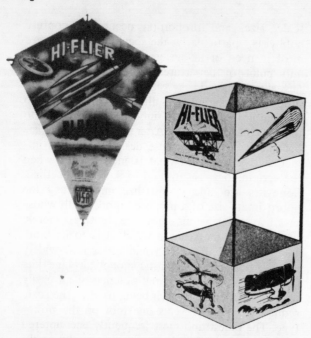

Fig. 5. Kites are not model aircraft in the sense that they are miniatures of actual prototypes, but kiting can play an important part in learning about air currents as a step toward more skillful flying of model gliders and airplanes. Pictured here are a conventional kite and a box kite.

Hi-Flyer Mfg. Co.

for great quantities of these 1/72nd-size models to be made by high school manual-training classes, the Boy Scouts, patients in veterans' hospitals, and model airplane hobbyists. The models were to be painted a uniform dull black, without insignia or detailing, so that they could serve their intended purpose as silhouette recognition models. The plan was widely successful as a patriotic exercise, but for one reason or another the United States Government contracted for the commercial manufacture of enormous quantities of solid molded plastic models of all types of planes, friendly and enemy, and in actual practice it was these models that generally were employed for aircraft-recognition training.*

Even before the war was over, so many of these plastic models had been made that the United States Government permitted quantities to be released to the civilian hobby trade. Accordingly, many model airplane enthusiasts became familiar with the 1/6th-inch scale, and employed the same scale in some of their own model plane construction activities. Some manufacturers determined to follow suit and to produce kits built to the 1/6-inch scale, 1/72nd-size wartime

---

*Aside from its value in making innumerable hobbyists, young and old, feel they were making a valuable contribution to the war effort, the program may never have been intended as other than a stopgap measure. The writer recalls being told at the time that a great percentage of the models built in this fashion had to be rejected because they were out of scale or exhibited crudities that made them useless for the purpose intended.

standard instead of using the more familiar pre-war scales, and the practice continues.

"CONSTANT SCALE"

With increasing frequency, the term "constant scale" has been heard in the vocabularies of model airplane enthusiasts who build static models from kits. When a given manufacturer's entire line or a specific series of model airplane kits are said to be built to "constant scale," it means that all the models in the series are designed in the same scale. The term originated with a postwar line of 1/6-inch scale models. This does not mean that "constant scale" is always 1/6-inch scale, 1/72nd size, although frequently this is the case. Nor, for this reason, is each manufacturer's "constant scale" the same as every other maker's "constant scale," although the fact that so many fabricators of a "constant scale" line employ the 1/72nd size has given many people this impression. Some manufacturers have created another scale; another "constant scale," simply by halving the 1/72nd size, with the result of a 1/12-inch-to-the-foot scale, 1/144th-size group of model kits. This smaller scale is favored for models of larger prototypes. Recently still another "constant scale" has been announced. This is a scale of .24 inch to the foot; the proportion of the models is 1/50th. This scale is so close to the long-established conventional scale of ¼ inch to the foot, 1/48th size, that its purpose and usefulness seem somewhat obscure other than that "1/50th" has a nice round sound to it.

There is an obvious advantage in assembling a collection of display model airplanes all built to the same scale—each plane is in exact proportion to each other. When a sufficiently large and varied collection in a given scale is lined up, it provides a graphic display of airplane development. A model of a prototype with a 100-foot wingspan has a wingspan exactly 2½ times that of a model of a real plane with a 40-foot wingspan. On the other hand, a series of "constant scale" models may result in models of small planes that are perfectly miniscule in size, while the models of the largest craft are comparative giants. Some hobbyists, of course, followed the principle of "constant scale" in their model-building activities (whether from rough materials or from selected kits) long before the term "constant scale" came into use commercially, in an effort to promote carefully related historical series of models.

In contrast to the "constant scale" idea, there are many model airplane hobbyists who feel that there is a more or less "proper" size for a model

Fig. 6. A great many model airplane hobbyists build their flying models from easily assembled kits, which are available in an extremely wide variety, many at extremely low cost. Four such models are shown here, the two upper ones being rubber-powered, while the lower two are designed for use with small internal-combustion reciprocating engines.

Scientific Model Airplane Co.

airplane and who seek to build and display models all more or less in the size that is most personally attractive to them. Some may prefer models with about a 6-inch wingspan, others an approximately 10- or 12-inch wingspan, while still others may like all their models to be quite a bit larger. The factor of detailing, which will be discussed in a moment, may also enter this picture of the choice of a preferential size.

There is another term that is used in the manufacture of model airplane kits and that is sometimes heard among hobbyists. This is, simply, "scaled to price." There is nothing derogatory in this expression, for it does not imply a reduction in quality but merely in scale. A manufacturer may wish to produce a series of model airplane kits uniformly packaged and priced; say a line of fifty-nine-cent kits or seventy-five-cent kits or six-shilling kits. It is desired that from each kit may be built a model plane of approximately the same size. Therefore, although perhaps most of the models will be built to the same scale, and very likely one of the standard ones, there may be certain models of larger prototypes in the series that must be reduced to another and smaller scale in order to conform to the general size of the series. They are therefore "scaled to price," perhaps to a smaller regular scale, perhaps even to a purely arbitrary scale. Similarly, models of smaller proto-

types may be built to a larger scale than most of the other models in the series.

SCALE AND SIGHT

Before leaving the subject of scale, there is still one more point to take up, one essentially peculiar to flying model aircraft. That is, when a model airplane is in action—in flight—there is no surrounding territory of other models that serves as a standard of comparison. This is not

Fig. 7. A plastic display model of a historic airplane. This is a model of the Vickers Vimy, the first airplane to fly nonstop across the Atlantic Ocean in 1919, piloted by John Alcock and navigated by Arthur W. Brown from Newfoundland to Ireland. The model is built to a scale of 1/6 inch to the foot, and is, accordingly, 1/72 the size of the original.

Lines Bros., Inc.

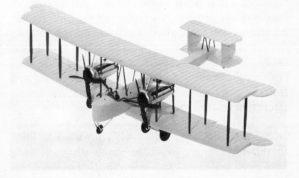

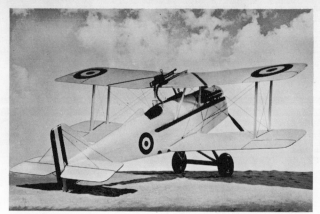

35 feet gives the effect of seeing the prototype from a half mile away, a model half the size (1/12-inch scale, 1/144th size) viewed from 35 feet would simulate a real plane one mile away. Or if the size of the original model were doubled to a 1/3 inch, 1/36th-size model of the same prototype, and it were viewed from the basic 35-foot distance, the effect would be that of seeing a real plane from a distance of a quarter of a mile.

The foregoing examples are based on static

Fig. 9. Interest in building model airplanes extends over all ages and deep into the ranks of airmen themselves. At the top, W. D. "Jim" Guthrie, aviation pioneer and famous manager of Roosevelt Field, Long Island, New York, holds a model of a 1908 Antoinette. In the second picture a member of the U.S. Navy's "Blue Angels" exhibition team examines a model of one of their jets. A close-up of the latter airplane is shown at the bottom.

Renwal Products, Inc.
Official Photograph, U.S. Navy
Lindberg Products, Inc.

Fig. 8. Model airplanes can be designed as working flying models and still retain an astounding realism, as these photographs demonstrate. The upper model is a 32-inch wingspan, rubber-powered model of the famous British World War I plane SE-5. The lower model has a wingspan of 30¾ inches and is an internal-combustion-reciprocating-engine-powered model of a United States F-51M Mustang. Note that the engine is mounted in an inverted position so as to be as inconspicuous as possible.

Sterling Models
C. A. Zaic Co., Inc.

literally true, for in certain cases, such as racing and combat competitions, more than one model plane may be in the air at the same time and in close proximity to another model. For the most part, however, flying model planes occupy their own miniature world in the sky, and scale is not so important as it is in, for example, model railroading or model racing, where not only the moving units themselves but their accompanying scenic surroundings usually all have to be in the same scale so as to provide a realistic and reasonable setting.

In connection with the 1/6-inch scale, 1/72nd-size model airplanes used as recognition models during the Second World War, the fact was mentioned that when viewed from a distance of 35 feet, models provided the effect of real aircraft at a distance of one-half mile. It therefore follows that if the models were viewed from a distance of 17½ feet, they would represent full-size aircraft at a distance of a quarter mile, or if viewed from 70 feet, the effect would be that of actual aircraft seen from one mile away.

By the same token, it follows that the distant effect would be varied by viewing models built to different scales from the same distance. If a 1/6-inch scale, 1/72nd-size model viewed from

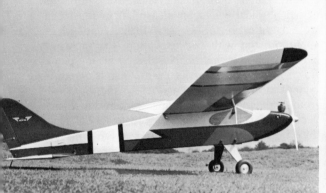

Fig. 10. Four large and handsome flying models designed primarily for radio control, with wingspans of 34 inches, 36 inches, 45 inches, and 54 inches respectively, built from British kits. The second and third models are two different size versions of the same basic design. The fourth model, shown with radio transmitter, is a replica of a Cessna Skylane.

Model Aircraft (Bournemouth, Ltd.)

models, but the same principles apply to flying models as well. Let us suppose we construct three models of the same prototype airplane, one model in ¼-inch scale, one in ½-inch scale, and one in ¾-inch scale. If all three models are lined up on the ground, or all three are flying overhead at the same height, the differences in size are immediately apparent. If we fly the same planes at different heights, however, the size differentials become unimportant. The ¼-inch scale model flying at a height of 50 feet will look as large as the ½-inch scale model at 100 feet and the ¾-inch scale model at 150 feet. At a height of 100 feet the ¼-inch scale model will appear two-thirds the size of the ¾-inch model at 150 feet, although the smaller plane actually is only one-third the size of the larger. If we keep the ¼-inch scale model at 100 feet and the ¾-inch scale model climbs to 300 feet, they again will appear to be the same size model.

When we fly only one model at a time, the size comparisons are of no consequence. The experienced hobbyist, knowing the size of the model in flight, can, to be sure, approximately gauge its true flying height. Similarly, either from recognizing a specific model in flight, or by comparison with some surrounding objects, such as treetops, the experienced hobbyist probably can tell us the actual size of the model in view. How-

ever, the point is that, for all practical effect, a scale model airplane in flight loses its relationship to any objects on the ground. It is essentially an airplane—or a model airplane, if you will—in flight. Consequently, while as much scale fidelity as can be built into a flying model airplane may be desirable in itself when the model is viewed on the ground, and such fidelity does count for points in the judging of scale model flying events, this does not have the inherent importance when the model is in action that it does in other types of models.

When in action, a flying model airplane is tied neither to ground-level viewing, as are other types of working models, nor to a track in relation to other models and model surroundings, as are miniature trains and racing cars. Model boats are not tied to a track, but they do function at ground level and often in company with other boats. While some factors of distance of viewing and perspective can enter the picture at times with boats, the situation is never quite parallel to that of viewing a model airplane in flight. Only model airplanes and other types of flying models are freed from this constriction of ground-level viewing, with the consequent optical phenomena that makes the precise size of the model in action of somewhat lesser importance than with other types of models.

Fig. 11. Three control-line monoplane models, available in completely assembled, ready-to-fly form. Top to bottom: 17½-inch-wingspan Super Cub 150; 22-inch-wingspan PT-19 flight trainer; and 20-inch-wingspan Curtiss A-25 bomber. (This last was the U.S. Army's version of the Navy's SB2c bomber.)

L. M. Cox Mfg. Co., Inc.

CLASSIFICATION OF MODEL AIRPLANES

As a matter of fact, unlike most other working models, including trains and racing cars and, of course, static model airplanes—for all of which the basic classification is that of scale—flying model airplanes, even scale flying model airplanes, are not divided and classified according to scale. Flying model airplanes are classified primarily according to the area of the lifting or supporting surfaces (gliders and rubber-powered models), the capacity of the engines (non-radio-controlled models with internal-combustion reciprocating engines and jet engines) and, in the case of radio-controlled models, by the amount of control.* Many people unfamiliar with the intricacies of model aircraft competition classification assume that, if not scale itself, then the actual physical wingspan measurement must control classification. This is a logical enough assumption, but with one exception it is incorrect. The exception is that of the rules governing planes flown in the Navy Carrier event. This is a specific type of model competition where planes are flown from and landed on a miniature aircraft carrier deck. Any size engine or any scale model plane may be entered in this event, but the wingspan of the model may not exceed 44 inches.

Model aviation is filled with confusing and overlapping terms. The Navy Carrier event described above is a specific classification of model aircraft competition. It should not be confused with model airplane contests of various types that are annually held in the United States under the sponsorship of the United States Navy and take place on the flight deck of an actual aircraft carrier.

As noted, the primary means of classifying gliders and rubber-powered model airplanes for competitive events is according to the area of the supporting surfaces of the model. Thus, to take indoor rubber-powered flying models as an example, there are four size classes: Class A, models with a total area of the supporting surfaces not more than 30 square inches; Class B, more than 30 square inches but not over 100 square inches; Class C, more than 100 square inches but not over 150 square inches, and Class D, more than 150 square inches but not exceeding 300 square inches.

In the radio-control classes, Class I planes are those controlled about the yaw axis by rudder control only. Class II planes are controlled about the yaw and pitch axes by rudder and elevator control only. Class III planes are controlled about the yaw, pitch, and roll axes by rudder, elevator, and aileron control. (See Chapter 3 for the explanation of these terms). Engine speed control also may be used in any of the three classes. Class I planes may be entered in either Class II or Class III events, and Class II planes may be entered

---

*Those interested in pursuing the subject of model plane classification in depth should obtain the official regulations of the Academy of Model Aeronautics, or of its counterpart organizations. See Appendx I.

Fig. 12. Great interest exists in models of early airplanes. Here are six ¼-inch scale (1/48th-size) plastic models of the immortal "crates" of World War I. Left to right, top row: British Sopwith Camel, SE-5 and French Breguet; second row: Sopwith triplane; German Fokker monoplane and triplane.

Aurora Plastics Corp.

in Class III events if the hobbyist so wishes. Thus radio-controlled model airplane classification is based in no way on the size or scale of a model plane itself or on the power of the engine. However, in the special event for scale model radio-controlled planes, points are awarded for the scale fidelity of the model, and these points are incorporated in the overall total scoring.

It is in the field of flying models with internal-combustion reciprocating engines that the beginner usually is most interested and that at the same time he initially finds the most confusing. Such models are divided into four basic classes according to the size of the engines. More precisely, the division is on the basis of engine cylinder capacity or, as it usually is expressed, displacement, meaning the displacement of the piston. That is, the volume swept by the piston during one stroke. Most model airplane engines are single-cylinder engines; the displacement therefore is that of a single piston. On occasions where a model aircraft engine has more than one cylinder, the capacity of the engine is calculated by totaling the displacement of all the cylinders. Actually, the capacity of the engine, the displacement, may not truly reflect the amount of fresh vaporized fuel retained in the cylinder by the compression stroke. Depending on the design of a given engine, a varying but small amount of fresh fuel may be sucked out of the cylinder along with the gases remaining from the previous firing. The factors that affect this are

the design of the engine porting and of the baffle usually placed on top of the piston to divert fresh fuel coming from the intake port away from the exhaust port. Manufacturers' engine specifications therefore give the correct displacement; any loss of fresh fuel from a new charge is a variable. In almost every case, what with the perfection of modern engine design, such loss is comparatively minute.

For those interested in such details, the formula for determining the displacement of an engine is Stroke $\times$ Bore^2 $\times$ 11/14. Stroke represents the distance the piston travels; bore is the diameter of the inside of the cylinder.

In the United States, engine capacity or displacement is measured in cubic inches. In countries where the metric system of measurements long has been standard, engine capacities are rendered in cubic centimeters (cc.). In Great Britain both systems of engine measurement appear to be in more or less equal use at the present time.

There are four classes of internal-combustion reciprocating engines recognized for model airplanes: ½ A, A, B, and C; the ½ A being an addition to the original classification, added after smaller engines became commercially practical. Confusingly, the measurements of the engines in each class differ according to the rules of specific types of events. Thus a .19 engine (an engine with a displacement of .19 cubic inches) is not always a Class A engine.

Fig. 13. Leading model airplane flying competitions are conducted with great care and precision; a new record may be set at any time. At the left, officials equipped with scale, stopwatches, and camera confer at an Academy of Model Aeronautics meet in Florida. At right, an official timer keeps tabs with a stopwatch as a free-flight model takes off.

National Hobby Institute, Cape Coral, Florida

CLASS	FREE FLIGHT	CONTROL LINE SPEED	CONTROL LINE ACROBATIC
½ A	.000 to .050	.000 to .050	No Class ½ A
A	.051 to .200	.051 to .1525	.000 to .200
B	.201 to .300	.1526 to .300	.201 to .300
C	.301 to .650	.301 to .650	.301 to .650

It should be noted that these classifications represent the total capacity or displacement of all the engines on a given model, if a model has more than one engine. Thus, a model plane with two .020 engines would have a total displacement of .040 cubic inches and would still remain a Class ½ A plane in the free-flight and control-line speed categories. A model with two .049 engines would, however, have a total displacement of .098 cubic inches and would thus rate as a Class A plane in these events. Bear in mind always that it is the engine displacement that always determines the class of a model airplane

Fig. 14. All nine of these display model airplanes, built from kits of plastic parts, are built to the same scale of 1/6 inch to the foot (1/72nd size), and accordingly proportionately reflect differences in the size of the various originals. Note, for example, the comparative size of the Vimy Vickers at the bottom center to that of the World War II bombers on either side of it. The older craft would by no means be considered a small one at any era.

Lines Bros., Inc.

powered by an internal-combustion reciprocating engine, not the wingspan or the area of the supporting surfaces. This is the explanation of why you will sometimes see a model airplane kit cataloged or advertised as a "½ A or A Class." If you put an engine of .050 cubic inch displacement or less in the model built from that kit, the plane competes as a ½ A model. If you put an engine of more than .050 cubic inch in the same plane, it becomes a Class A model. Similarly you will at times find kits that build an "A or B" model, or even, depending on the engine used, that can give you an "A, B, or C" plane from the same kit.

The foregoing table will also explain to beginners why so many engines are manufactured in certain seemingly odd sizes such as .049, .19, and .29—these represent the largest and most powerful engines that can be used within a given class for certain events. Similarly, some sizes, such as the .051, are the smallest engines that can be used in certain classes for certain events.

In some events the admittable engine sizes are not divided into alphabetical classes. These

Fig. 17. This photograph makes clear the comparative sizes of working model internal-combustion reciprocating engines of the smaller sizes. The displacements of these engines in cubic inches are .010 for the tiny engine in the hand and, left to right, bottom row: .020 and .049; upper row: .051, .09, and .15. All engines are of the front rotary-valve type.

L. M. Cox Mfg. Co., Inc.

events either have a maximum engine size set for them or specify a given range of engine sizes as acceptable. In the free-flight scale event the maximum engine size is not over .200 cubic inch; in the control-line combat event the maximum engine size is .36 cubic inch. In the control-line endurance competitions the range is .190 to .360; in control-line team racing it is .140 to .300; in rat racing it is .15 to .40. In the control-line scale event the maximum engine size is 1.25 per engine (not, note, total displacement of all engines if the plane is multimotored). Hence we get other popular engine sizes commonly manufactured that seem at first glance to be rather odd sizes for anyone to choose to make.

Always be careful to watch the decimal point in engine displacements, whether measured in cubic inches or centiliters. An .020 is always a smaller engine than an .049; an .049 smaller than a .15; a .15 smaller than a .29, and so on. At times manufacturers and others will leave out the decimal point when describing engines, which also can be confusing to novices. There are engines on the market that can be used in giant model aircraft, although they are far beyond any of the usual sizes and those recognized for the various established classes that have a displacement of close to 2.0 cubic inches. A 2.0 cubic inch engine is quite a different proposition from a .200 cubic inch engine, much less from an .020 cubic inch unit. At the present time there appears to be some movement to the possible commercialization of engines somewhat larger than the .650 cubic inch, however. It may be that .750 cubic inch engines intended specifically for model airplane use, or models at least approaching that displacement, will be on the market soon. Such engines would

Fig. 15. Most flying model airplanes are built much as are real airplanes. This is what the balsa-wood framing of a 17-inch-wingspan rubber-powered model of a Cessna 180 looks like before the covering material is applied. The rubber is already in place within the fuselage. Note the instrument panel with miniature dials in the cockpit.

Sterling Models

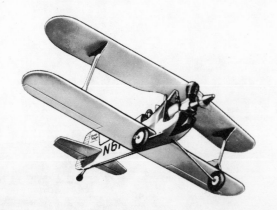

Fig. 16. Here is an interesting 16-inch-wingspan internal-combustion reciprocating engine powered balsa-wood biplane model, easily built from an inexpensive kit. Most of today's flying models are monoplanes, but biplanes also maintain considerable popularity, both for the type itself and also as replicas of historic older airplanes.

Carl Goldberg Models, Inc.

Fig. 18. Models of three famous airplanes of World War II: the Hawker Hurricane, the B-17 Flying Fortress, and the B-24 Liberator. These models were built from kits of molded plastic parts. All three models are built to the same scale of 1/6 inch to the foot, making them 1/72nd the size of the originals.

Revell, Inc.

be intended for radio-control use, which is not currently limited by the .650 cubic inch ceiling. Yet there also is some talk of efforts to raise the .650 limit so that larger engines can be used for competition in certain categories other than radio control.

INCHES, CENTIMETERS, AND HORSEPOWER

The foregoing engine-size regulations are taken from the *Official Model Aircraft Regulations* of the Academy of Model Aeronautics. As an American organization, the AMA rules naturally measure engine displacements in cubic inches. The AMA functions as part of the international network organized under the overall regulation of the Fédération Aéronautique Internationale (FAI), which is the governing body, not for model aviation alone, but for all aviation matters, including rules and records for real airplanes. The requirements for engine displacement limits in all international events are calculated in cubic centimeters.

For example, in FAI team racing competitions, the maximum engine size is 2.5 cubic centimeters, which is .1526 cubic inches. The American regulations here, as in some other events, allow much larger engines. AMA team racing-engine sizes may range from .140 cubic inch to .300 cubic inch. In international competitions, for international records, planes must, of course, accord with FAI regulations. The British regulations may also at times show differences from the American, again usually disclosing a tendency to allow bigger motors in given AMA events. Thus, as we have seen, the AMA control-line combat regulations permit engines with a maximum displacement of .36 cubic inch (approximately 5.81 cubic centimeters) whereas the British regulations limit such planes to 3.5 cubic-centimeter engines. A 3.5 cubic-centimeter engine corresponds approximately to a .201 cubic-inch engine.

All this points up the importance of a model enthusiast consulting the rules set up by his own national organization. There are often very definite variations between national classifications in the

Fig. 19. Prizewinning airplane designs, often the original creations of individual hobbyists, frequently are commercialized and made available in kit form. Two examples of this are the 58-inch-wingspan Shark "45," twice the open-line stunt champion, designed by Lew McFarland (left), and the 48-inch-wingspan radio-control Charger. Designer Milt Boone is shown with the plane, his transmitter, and some of the prizes the model garnered.

C. A. Zaic Co., Inc.
Ambroid Co., Inc.

various countries, as well as between national classifications and the FAI international classifications. There is a national model airplane organization in almost every country. In some cases the national airplane club organized under the FAI handles model aviation affairs directly. In other countries a special subsidiary model aircraft governing body has been set up, as in the United States the Academy of Model Aeronautics, and in Great Britain the Society of Model Aeronautical Engineers. A number of these clubs will be found listed in Appendix I. In other countries the national body governing real aircraft under the FAI should be consulted for information on the source of model regulations.

The following table showing the displacement of various popular-size engines in terms both of cubic inches and cubic centimeters will be of value in visualizing the comparative size of engines. It is based on the size of American engines as accurately measured in cubic inches. In some cases the corresponding measurements in cubic centimeters have been worked out exactly by manufacturers. In other sizes the calculations are, while close enough for all practical reference, somewhat in the nature of approximations. Within a given engine size there may be slight variations among different makes. Authorities differ, for example, as to whether the proper metric equivalent for a .60 cubic-inch engine should be 9.9 cubic centimeters or 10.0 cubic centimeters.

Cubic Inch	EQUALS	Cubic Cent.	Cubic Inch	EQUALS	Cubic Cent.
.010		.163	.201		3.42
.020		.327	.29		4.9
.049		.819	.35		5.75
.051		.835	.36		5.91
.06		.99	.40		6.495
.07		1.21	.45		7.33
.09		1.48	.59		9.75
.15		2.499	.60		9.9
.19		3.25			

It will be seen that the .15 cubic-inch engine has a metric equivalent of exactly 2.499 and therefore falls just within the international limit to engines for a maximum displacement of 2.5 cubic centimeters for certain events.

What of the horsepower of these miniature engines? As we have seen, horsepower plays no part in the assigning of classification levels. Indeed, it could not play such a part, for depending on various factors of engine design, fuel, and so on, varying engines of the same displacement could produce different horsepowers—of course

almost all horsepower in relation to model airplane engines is fractional horsepower. Nevertheless, the matter of actual potential horsepower is always of interest, both as a subject of curiosity to beginners and casual observers and as a technical point to more advanced hobbyists. Actually, the hobbyist who delves into engine technicalities is more interested in the potential revolutions per minute (rpm) of a given engine than in horsepower. In the early days of internal-combustion reciprocating model aircraft engines, the horsepower delivered by a given engine usually was regarded of as more importance in estimating the potential of an engine than it is today.

As a matter of interest, here is a table giving the horsepower of a number of typical modern American and British engines, as taken from the manufacturers' specifications:

Displacement	Horsepower
.07 cu. in.	.08
.09 cu. in.	.176
.15 cu. in.	.28
.15 cu. in.	.34
.19 cu. in.	.4
.29 cu. in.	.5
.35 cu. in.	.6
.45 cu. in.	.7
.59 cu. in.	.95

There are various factors that operate here. Radio-control engines with throttle and exhaust regulators usually put out less horsepower than similar engines without these controls. For ex-

Fig. 20. Every year sees numerous prizes awarded for the top performing model aircraft, as well as some special awards such as the Connie Mack Jr. Sportsmanship Trophy, seen here being presented by Joe Miller, Jr., of the National Hobby Institute, to James L. Juliano.
National Hobby Institute, Cape Coral, Florida

Fig. 21. Six more models of World War II airplanes, built from kits of plastic parts. Top row: P-40 Flying Tiger, British Spitfire, and B-25 Mitchell bomber; center row: P-51 Mustang, Martin Marauder bomber and P-38 Lockheed Lightning. Except for the P-40 and the Spitfire, which are ¼-inch scale, these models are built to varying scales.

Aurora Plastics Corp.

ample, on a given .29 engine, the horsepower is .8 without speed control and .5 with throttle valve; on a .35 engine the horsepower is .8 without speed control and .6 with the control. However, the above table will be of some value as a matter of interest and of roughly gauging the potential horsepower of model airplane engines. Any of the largest engines generally available today probably come close—as the table indicates—to delivering one horsepower under optimum operating conditions. That is indisputably a lot of power for a little engine that you easily can hold in your hand!

In a later chapter we shall return to the subject of internal-combustion reciprocating engines and go into the intricacies of the subject at greater length. For the moment, the material presented here will suffice to make the intervening chapters more readily understandable.

Rocket engines for solid-fuel rockets also are classified into ½ A, A, B, and C categories. However the categories are on an entirely different basis than the internal-combustion reciprocating engines, and we safely can reserve the discussion of these units for the chapter devoted to solid-fuel rockets.

TERMINOLOGY

Model aircraft has a language of its own, based to a large extent on real airplane termin-ology and in part on special terms relating only to models. The beginner often is greatly confused by this terminology, especially when he finds it used in books or magazine articles without any preliminary explanation. There also is some over-lapping of terminology where meaning can be determined only by context. Take the word *pylon,* for example. A pylon may variously be a starting derrick, a tower that marks the limits of an air-field or racecourse, the central post to which a tethered flying model is connected, or an actual part of the structure of an airplane, specifically the mounting above the fuselage to which a high wing is attached on a high-wing monoplane or glider.

Without attempting an exhaustive glossary, which could fill many pages, it is appropriate that we now examine a few of the specialized terms widely used in real and model aircraft so that not only the pages that follow but also the general run of current model airplane literature will be more understandable to the average reader and particularly the newcomer to the hobby:

A *pusher airplane* is one with the propellers mounted behind the wing or wings, as in the orig-inal Wright biplane. A *tractor airplane*—beginners usually assume the term has something to do with the wheels or landing gear—is simply a plane in which the propellers are mounted in front of the wing or wings. Most readers will already be famil-iar with the fact that a *monoplane* has one wing

Fig. 22. Wherever possible, communities, clubs, or hobby dealers endeavor to provide suitable areas for the outdoor flying of model airplanes. This is an aerial view of one such establishment, with several flying circles for control-line model airplanes, located alongside a major highway.

and a *biplane* has two, but many younger ones may be unaware that there also is a definite *triplane* classification as well, with three wings, and planes have been built with even more than three wings.

In the field of lighter-than-air craft, a *dirigible* or *zeppelin* is a rigid airship, completely framed within the outer covering. The *semirigid airship* has a metal keel running the length of the ship and reinforced at the nose and tail. The *blimp,* or *nonrigid airship,* is essentially an elongated balloon without any framing. The popular name *blimp* derives from the British system of classification during World War I, that is, "Class B—Limp."

To turn to words referring to particular parts of an airplane, the *airfoil* is any lifting surface, such as a wing, and refers more particularly to the profile or cross-section shape of that surface. *Dihedral* refers to the angle obtained by raising the wingtips above the level of the center of a wing. *Empennage* is not a synonym for the tail of an airplane, as often is thought, but rather a general term embracing all the tail surfaces—fin, rudder, stabilizer, and elevator. The *firewall* is a protective bulkhead placed behind the engine; in model practice it is usually made of plywood. *Fuselage* is a term probably understood by everyone. It is the essential body of the airplane, to which the wings and other appendages are attached. On the other hand, the term *airframe* refers not only to the fuselage but also to the entire structural makeup of an airplane, fuselage, wing, and tail.

Polyhedral is a modification of dihedral wherein two or more separate angles are used in raising a wing from its central level to the higher angle at the tips. The *leading* and *trailing edges* of a wing or tail are the front and rear edges respectively. A *horn* or *control horn* in real or model aircraft is a lever or plate attached to a control surface, such as a rudder or elevator, to which the control wires that move that surface are attached. A *thermal* is a rising air current—warm air rises, hence the name. By somewhat illogical extension, a *dethermalizer* is a device that spoils the flight of a plane and causes it to glide to earth after a certain period of flight, in order to prevent it being carried away and possibly out of sight by rising air currents.

Stick is another multimeaning word. It can refer to the control stick or joy stick (sometimes said to be a contraction of its inventor's name, Joyce) of a real or model airplane; also to a miniature replica used with certain types of radio-control apparatus to transmit signals to a model plane. *Stick* also refers to the fuselage of very simple model airplanes and gliders wherein the fuselage consists of a single stick of wood—or, in certain cases, more than one stick—hence the term *stick model.* Or, further, *stick* also means an internal stick within the fuselage of a contoured and covered rubber-powered model on which the rubber motor is mounted, that is, a motor stick.

ROG is an abbreviation for "rise off ground." A ROG model is one whose design is such that it will take off from the earth when the power is released; it does not have to be hand-launched to become airborne, as do many models. There are also some models that will ROG under certain wind conditions, but must be hand-launched at other times. A true ROG model should, however, take off by itself under any weather conditions not too severe as to preclude successful flight of the model altogether. A *ROW* model, similarly, is a model seaplane or flying boat that will take off from water by itself without the aid of an artificial launching impulse. In the 1930's, there also was frequent mention of *ROS* models, models that would rise off snow. As model airplane contests generally are held at times and in places where good weather conditions exist, it would be difficult to include ROS classes in the standard competition categories. On the other hand, there is no reason why the enthusiastic hobbyist who lives in areas where winter snow is the norm and who wishes to pursue flying through-out the year cannot continue to build and fly ROS models as a personal interest.

Last, to cover an area wherein most beginners find confusion, what is the difference between an *autogiro* and a *helicopter,* and what is an *ornithopter?* The helicopter as a plane must be distinguished from the rather old flying toy of the same name, although both operate on the same principle. Many earlier model aviation references defined autogiro and helicopter as the same thing, and many people still are confused as to where the difference, if any, lies. Both rise almost vertically by means of horizontally rotating vanes or planes. An *autogiro,* however, is a plane whose lift, but not its entire sustenance in flight, is provided by the rotating blades; it also has wings. A *helicopter,* on the other hand, is sustained and maintained in flight entirely by the rotating mechanism or mechanisms.

An *ornithopter* is an aircraft that obtains flight by beating its wings as does a bird. As with autogiros and helicopters, there also are recognized competition classes for ornithopters. All three types of craft may be designed for indoor or outdoor flight, and compete accordingly.

CHAPTER 2

Non-flying Display Models — and Other Matters

There are many subjects that relate almost equally to nonflying and flying models—reading plans, superdetailing, tools and materials, and so on. These must now be considered, although in some cases certain points regarding them as applying only to flying models will be expanded upon later. Also to be covered now is the selection of the most embracive yet techincally correct term to describe nonflying model aircraft and, within the limitations of flying possibility already defined, model spacecraft. Upon much consideration *display models* appears to provide the best description, although some may argue that if a hobbyist builds a model and, instead of actually displaying it— possibly because he simply lacks space—packs it away in a box the miniature in question manifestly is not a display model. However, no other term appears to fill the bill as adequately and as accurately. The old favorite, *solid models,* may be understood and, indeed, still be used by many older hobbyists, but it obviously is inaccurate when applied to models built from modern construction kits made up of molded plastic parts. Two other descriptions, *nonoperating models* and *static models,* fall by the wayside when it is considered that a considerable number of models built from plastic kits, while manifestly nonflying, are far either from being nonoperating or static in the fullest sense, for they can provide a host of operating or operatable features, such as doors and bomb bays that open and close, landing gears that extend and retract, wings that fold on carrier-based planes, movable controls, canopies that open and close, propellers, and other action parts powered with small, low-voltage battery-operated electric motors, and so on. Indeed, there is available a veritable galaxy of such action parts, although the practice is usually to limit the inclusion of such action features to one or two on any given model. At times some fans and manufacturers tend to separate such models into a category of their own, *action models,* as distinct from display models on which virtually nothing moves, except perhaps that the propeller may be attached so that it may be spun by hand. There are also so-called remote-control plastic model planes where the control surfaces are arranged to move in accord with the directions transmitted from a miniature joy stick located outside of and a slight distance from the model itself. Not only do the control surfaces move, but their movement causes the plane to assume different flight positions or attitudes similar to those that would be taken by a real airplane upon similar control movements.

PLASTIC KITS

Perhaps the most important point to make is that kits of plastic parts for model airplane building have reached a position of such perfection, multiplicity, and acceptance as to continue to amaze those who witnessed their first tentative

Fig. 23. Models of passenger-carrying jet airplanes built from kits of plastic parts: Convair 880, Boeing 727, and DC 8.

Aurora Plastics Corp.

introduction following World War II. It should also be noted that the use of molded plastic components is not confined to nonflying display models. There are kits of plastic parts for building flying models, some of fairly considerable size, both rubber- and internal-combustion-engine powered. It goes without saying that the engines employed in such models are of conventional construction and are not built of plastic parts. Molded plastic also is used for making many ready-to-fly model airplanes, mainly powered by internal-combustion reciprocating engines, but in some cases employing rubber power. Again, particularly in relation to the kits that build flying models, it will be seen that many of the remarks in this chapter, while primarily relating to nonflying models, apply to certain flying models as well.

Kits of plastic parts for nonflying model airplane construction vary greatly in cost and in the size of the model that they build, and the matter of scale has already been discussed. One great attribute of plastic molding is the amount of detail that it permits to be molded directly into any part. External parts in virtually all kits are highly detailed, within the scope of the size model involved, although not unnaturally there

are variations in the type and degree of the detailing that different manufacturers feel to be desirable and practical. Most plastic model airplanes are intended to be painted and decorated after assembly. In some cases this is not necessary if the hobbyist does not want to undertake this additional work, as the parts are molded of colored plastic. In certain kits some of the parts are supplied in a metalicized finish closely simulating the surface of real planes of this type, so in such cases further painting of these parts is neither necessary nor desirable.

Generally speaking, the smaller the finished model and the less expensive the kit, the fewer the number of separate parts that will be supplied and required to build the model. In a rough way, the number of parts in a kit serves as a denominator of the time and skill required to assemble a kit, and to a certain comparative extent at least of the detailing and intricacy of the completed replica. Many manufacturers mark the boxes in which their kits are packed with the number of parts. A kit comprising, say, seventy-five parts obviously represents a somewhat more demanding job of assembling than one with, say, twenty-five parts. It will probably but not necessarily build a

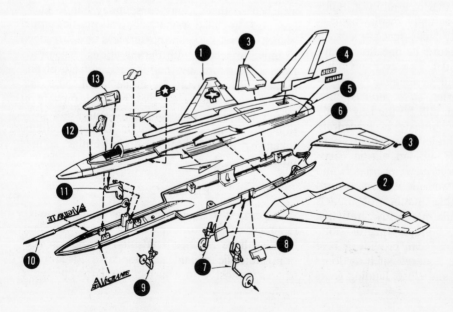

Fig. 24. A drawing from the instruction sheet from a kit of plastic parts, showing an exploded view of the molded components that are assembled into the complete ⅛-inch scale model of a Vigilante A3J-1, a United States carrier-borne airplane.

Universal Powermaster Corp.

Fig. 25. An assembled plastic model of the A3J airplane. Note that while the model pictured here is of the same prototype as the drawings in Fig. 24, this is built from another kit and is a larger model, built to ¼-inch scale.

Monogram Models, Inc.

larger and more detailed model. It would be a mistake to assume, as unfortunately too many do, that there is little or no real work or skill required to assemble a model airplane—or, indeed, any kind of model—from a kit of plastic parts. The introduction of these kits did enable many individuals to produce acceptable models with greater ease; it allowed many persons who might never have felt themselves competent to build an attractive model to do exactly this. On the other hand, the plastic kit, no matter how simple a one it may be, does not eliminate the need for modelmaking skill. There is a world of difference between a model that has been sloppily assembled and finished and one that is the result of careful workmanship, a difference that can be apparent even to the casual observer.

Everyone's skill improves as he progresses. The novice's second job of kit assembly usually shows a great improvement over his initial effort, and while subsequent improvements may not show so marked a variation between the twentieth and twenty-first kit assembled as between the first,

second, and third, the factor of ever-increasing skill is nevertheless inexorably in operation. Many hobbyists after successively assembling a number of different model airplane kits purchase duplicate kits of their earlier models, the comparative defects of which have become noticeable, and assemble replacement models employing their enhanced skills.

Usually the parts in a kit relate exclusively to the model airplane itself. In some cases, however, kits include a few additional parts that can be used to help create a realistic display scene for the model, such as miniature figures of members of the ground crew, posed in realistic positions, or accessory equipment. Many kits also include material for building a display stand, usually of transparent plastic, that poses the model plane as if in flight.

ASSEMBLING PLASTIC KITS

Assembling a model airplane from a kit of plastic parts is usually not a difficult matter—

Fig. 26. Five 1/6-inch scale models reproducing some of the fascinating flying machines that helped usher in the airplane age. These models are built from kits that combine plastic parts with a special new covering material for wings and other surfaces designed to simulate perfectly the original fabrics. See also Fig. 29. The models are, respectively, of the 1909 Curtiss Golden Flyer, 1903 Wright Kitty Hawk Flyer, 1908 Voisin Farman, 1909 Blériot, 1909 Avro triplane.

Renwal Products, Inc.

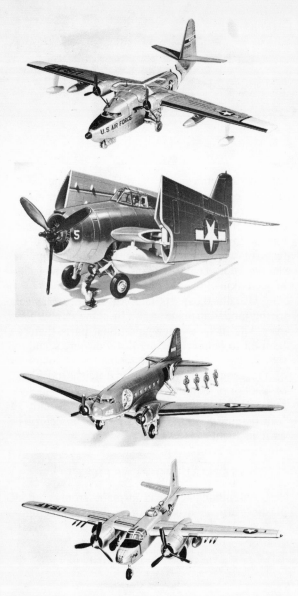

Fig. 27. Four interesting model airplanes crafted from kits of plastic parts. Top to bottom: an SA-16B Albatross rescue flying boat and a Grumman F4F Wildcat with working folding wings; bottom, a C-47 Skytrain and a B-26 Invader bomber. The F4F and C-47 show miniature accessory figures such as are sometimes included wih model airplane construction kits.

Monogram Models, Inc.

These cavities are gated or connected by means of small passages so that when the liquid plastic is injected into the mold at one point, it will be forced through the various passages until it completely fills every cavity. The resulting molding, when it is solidified and thrown out of the mold, consists of the plastic parts themselves, connected by a network of thin runners of surplus plastic that filled the connecting passages. If we compare the actual parts to fruit, the surplus runners to the branches, and the main lead of surplus plastic from the point of injection to the trunk, it is easy to visualize these parts and the analogy to a tree becomes obvious.

In most cases the manufacturers do not separate the parts from the runners, but pack entire trees in the kits. The reason for this is twofold First, separating and trimming the parts would involve labor that would necessitate increasing the cost of the kit—and at the same time would reduce the amount of work that the hobbyist himself would have to perform and presumably enjoys performing. Second, there is far less chance of small parts being lost when the trees are packed complete in the kit. The possibility that one or more parts may be missing is always an unpleasant prospect. Occasionally this may be due to a fault at the factory, as when an incomplete or damaged tree accidentally is included and overlooked by the vigilant eyes of the inspectors. Manufacturers will always replace missing or damaged parts resulting from such oversights, but it is still annoying to discover the need for this and to have to wait for the needed component. On the other hand, the chief cause of missing parts is that someone has yielded to an impulse that so many hobbyists find irresistible, and examined the contents of the kit while it was in stock at a hobby shop. With the best and most honorable of intentions it is difficult to examine kits without having a part lost or broken. The manufacturers' attempts to prevent this by sealing kits with tape or with a complete transparent wrap are all too frequently frustrated by hobbyists insisting they be allowed to see what is in a given kit, and by the store owner yielding to these entreaties.

Most present-day kits of plastic parts are provided with instruction sheets lavishly illustrated, particularly with what is known as exploded drawings, or photographs. In these illustrations all the parts that make up a completed model are shown, successively converging from different directions and in the order of their subassembly and assembly toward a central point where the finished model emerges. It would be well-nigh impossible to build a model from rough

there are those enthusiasts who delight in intricate model building who would say that it is far too simple. As already observed, skill is required, albeit it is skill devoted to finishing and assembling parts rather than in constructing the parts themselves. Finishing parts in a kit of this type involves separating and trimming the various components. The parts, or at least the small parts, are not supplied each as a separate unit, but in groups or "trees" of parts just as they come from the injection molding machines. A mold may contain the cavities for ten or twenty or more small parts.

Fig. 28. Plastic, ¼-inch scale models of two famous United States biplanes of the 1930's, the Boeing F4B-4 (left) and the Boeing P 12 E. Note that the detailing of these models includes the retarding hooks under the tails used for carrier landings.

Aurora Plastics Corp.

materials from plans of this type, but they are ideal for use in assembling the plastic parts provided in kits of this type. Copious and easily understood instructions usually accompany these pictures, although in many cases the drawings are so clear and so completely rendered that the written instructions may appear superfluous. Nevertheless the manufacturers' instructions should be studied and followed, particularly in regard to the preferred order in which the various parts are to be assembled. Two major points apply in the assembly of all plastic kits: the removal of the parts from the trees and their trimming and smoothing, and the proper technique of cementing the various units into place.

TRIMMING AND CEMENTING

There probably is no model-building hobby in which fewer tools are absolutely necessary for the average constructor than that of model airplanes. This applies not only to the assembling of plastic models but to model airplane building in general. For many years the author constructed numerous model airplanes, both display and flying models, with no equipment other than a jackknife, a penknife, a fine file or two, and a pair of pliers. The jackknife and penknife could be replaced today by a modelmaker's knife, and the pliers, which the author subsequently learned were of the variety known as gas pliers, should be improved upon by substituting regular long-nosed pliers. Indeed, about the only tools or equipment required for assembling modern plastic components are a knife—which can be a modelmaker's knife, a penknife, or simply a single-edge razor blade—and fine sandpaper. For working kits of plastic parts the modelmaker's knife probably is preferable, although later it will be explained why this may not always be the best type of knife

for working with soft wood.

In addition to these tools, there are a number of little gadgets that the average model airplane builder can devise or adopt for himself: toothpicks and cotton-tipped swabs for applying cement, spring clothespins and various homemade clamping devices—including ordinary rubber bands—for holding parts in position while cement is drying, tweezers or ordinary pins for lifting and positioning small parts, and so on.

The tools and equipment mentioned above are for the actual building operations. The requirements of the painting and decorating process will be taken up a little later.

Many plastic components are slotted or keyed both for ease in assembling and in securing perfect alignment. In removing parts from the trees, and in trimming and cleaning them up, care must be exercised not to damage or remove any of the smaller keying segments. Other than this, the basic procedure is to cut each part free of the tree and remove all surplus plastic and then free the edges of all parts from molding burrs, especially the fine continuous lines that occur at the parting line of the molds. These operations may be accomplished by cutting or scraping with a knife or by the use of very fine sandpaper, or glasspaper, as it is known in Great Britain. The important thing to bear in mind in performing these operations is to take your time and proceed with care. The old adage that it is very easy to remove too much material but almost impossible to put it back on aptly applies here. It is indeed much more difficult to correct too much cutting on molded plastic parts than it is on wood. At times serious overcuts in molded plastic parts can be rectified by the judicious application of model automobile body putty or actually by welding a bit of surplus plastic to the damaged piece, using the heat of a match, but this quite ticklish pro-

Fig. 29. Steps in the assembling of a 1/6-inch scale model of the 1908 Antoinette from a kit incorporating a special new covering material (see also Fig. 26). Top left, the outline of each part to be covered is traced on the covering material, using the corresponding plastic part as a guide. The traced portions are then cut out with about ⅛-inch clearance. Top right, the covering material is placed over the matching plastic part and bonded to it with plastic solvent. Center left, the excess covering material is carefully trimmed off with an emory board or nail file. Center right, the individually covered components are assembled into the complete airframe. Lower left, the model is rigged, using black thread. The final illustration shows the completed model.

Renwal Products, Inc.

cedure is usually unsatisfactory. Inasmuch as the parts for plastic model airplanes usually are molded in groups, plus the overall low cost of the units, it is not often practical to order a single replacement for a damaged component from the manufacturer. The only satisfactory solution in such cases may be to purchase another kit of the same type.

CEMENTING PLASTICS

The material generally used in the molding of plastic parts for model airplane kits is polystyrene, although at times high-impact copolymer styrene may be used in model aircraft components. In any event, a special type of adhesive must be employed in assembling and repairing these parts. Ordinary "model airplane cement," which is a cellulose adhesive used in constructing wooden models, cannot be employed, nor can ordinary household or workshop cements or glues.

What must be used for bonding styrene components is what is known as a "solvent adhesive." That is, a cement that actually dissolves a small portion of the surface of the two moldings that are being joined. Such adhesives may be called plastic cement or styrene cement or some other but similar name by the various manufacturers, and are available both in jars and in tubes. Some of the manufacturers of kits of plastic parts for model airplane construction market a brand of plastic cement for such models under their own name, while others commonly found on the hobby market are sold under the brand names of specialized paint and adhesive manufacturers. Some hobbyists swear by a favorite brand; others express a feeling that they all are pretty much alike and equally good; in some cases the identical cement probably is being merchandised under more than one label. Care must be maintained at all times in employing any of these solvent adhesives in model building.* Inasmuch as a solvent adhesive acts by melting a little of the surfaces of the parts to be joined, it follows that if any quantity, no matter how minute, is dropped on a surface other than those to be joined, or if excess cement is squeezed out of a joint onto such a surface, the cement even if removed almost immediately will act upon and somewhat disfigure the surface. Most hobbyists, and especially beginners, apply more cement to joints than actually is necessary. It admittedly is difficult to control the amount of cement when applied directly from a tube or brushed or swabbed on from a jar. Only really large surfaces call for brushing or swabbing on the styrene cement. For most of the small joints an ideal mode of application is to apply a drop or two from a toothpick that has been dipped in the adhesive.

The modern practice in the design of kits of plastic parts is to arrange as many of the points of juncture between components as internal joints, so as to reduce the danger of excess cement falling or being squeezed onto surfaces that will stand exposed in the completed model. In the case of most models, however, some external joints become necessary somewhere along the line, if only in the final steps in assembly, and especial care must be taken in cementing these joints. It is good practice, however, to try to make all your joints, whether visible or invisible in the finished model, with care and neatness, so as to acquire experience in the technique of applying plastic cement. In time it will become second nature.

At times surfaces damaged by plastic cement can be somewhat restored by the methods suggested previously in the event that too much material has been cut away by a knife, but this is seldom completely satisfactory. The repair may pass muster from a distance, or if the entire model is painted, but it often is impossible to conceal such a defect from close examination if the plastic is left in its original molded-in color. Some enthusiasts have reported relative success, however, by polishing cement-damaged areas with a very mild abrasive such as toothpaste, automobile rubbing compound, or silver polish. This requires great patience on the part of the model builder and is accompanied by the danger that the physical pressure, no matter how slight, of the polishing process will misalign or break delicate moldings.

A common failing in all model cementing processes is to proceed from one joint to another without giving each connection sufficient time to harden and set fully. The result is that junctures made earlier are distorted or broken. While most model airplane cements and glues will superficially set within a minute or two—this relates not only to styrene cements but to cellulose model airplane cement and all other types of bonding materials— joints may not actually be completely bonded for several hours. No handy rule or time chart can be given for this, because the length of time required for a cemented joint fully to set depends

---

*The usual model cements, glues, solvents, paints, thinners, and similar materials are generally quite safe if properly used in a well-ventilated area. However, some are highly toxic if breathed or taken internally. Others are highly inflammable. In all cases they should be used only in a properly ventilated area, and away from any spark-producing equipment (including, obviously, any operating internal-combustion model airplane engines) or open flames or units with pilot lights, such as stoves or heating equipment. They should always be stored so as to be inaccessible to very young children.

Fig. 30. Three plastic models of jet airplanes. The Hawker Hunter (left) was used by the Black Arrow flight demonstration team of the Royal Air Force. The center model is the Douglas F4D-1 Skyray, a United States carrier-based plane; while at the right is the Douglas X-3 Stilleto, a hypersonic jet plane of exceptional speed.

Lindberg Products, Inc.

to a certain extent on the sizes of the area joined with the accompanying amount of adhesive required, and on the relative degree of clamping and supporting aid needed by and furnished to a particular joint. Model builders often grow impatient to proceed to the next step without waiting an adequate period of time. This is one reason it is sometimes wise to assemble several different kits simultaneously. With such an arrangement the hobbyist can proceed to work on Kit No. 2 while a joint on Kit No. 1 is hardening; then perhaps to Kit No. 3 and Kit No. 4, before returning to the next step on Kit No. 1.

Some model airplanes built from kits of plastic parts are so simple to build that they almost literally snap together with a minimum of cementing. Such kits may be assembled in a very short period of time. In most instances, however, when you hear a model builder boast of putting together a model airplane kit in a seemingly startlingly short span of time, you usually can feel assured that this has been accomplished at the expense of waiting to allow the joints to set properly. Such a hastily assembled model may be a good one. On the other hand, it may well show signs of poor alignment and structural weakness. A display model is not normally, of course, called on to undergo much stress and handling. Nonetheless, the sturdiest construction possible is, naturally, the best.

COVERED MODELS

So far in this chapter the subject of non-flying models has been dealt with entirely in terms of kits of molded plastic parts. The surface or skin of the prototype airplane, whether of fabric or metal, is reproduced, and usually reproduced with more than merely creditable accuracy, in the plastic moldings. There is, of course, nothing to stop the builder and displayer of non-flying model planes from assembling such kits for flying models as meet his requirements for scale fidelity and using the completed model—often with the motor omitted and with a scale-size propeller substituted for the oversized flying-model propeller—as display models. Indeed, as most models built from kits of plastic parts are, in the eyes of many, comparatively small, such usage of flying model kits often is the only way that the devotee of larger-sized display models can achieve the type of collection he desires, short of building each model from scratch.

Recently a new type of kit, basically a plastic one but with one important innovation, has appeared on the market and has met with widespread favor. This type of kit involves the use of a non-plastic material for covering the wings and other surfaces. This form of construction is particularly suitable to the building of models of very early types of planes, including, indeed, the earliest, although it obviously is adaptable to many types of model aircraft representing fabric-covered prototypes. The first kits of this general type appeared in France, and employed nylon for the covering material.

More recently an American manufacturer has introduced a line of kits for classic flying machines that appears to refine the process still further, employing a preprinted paper covering of special composition to simulate the fabric covering of these early types of airplanes through the application and bonding of the paper to the plastic surfaces of the model. The plastic parts

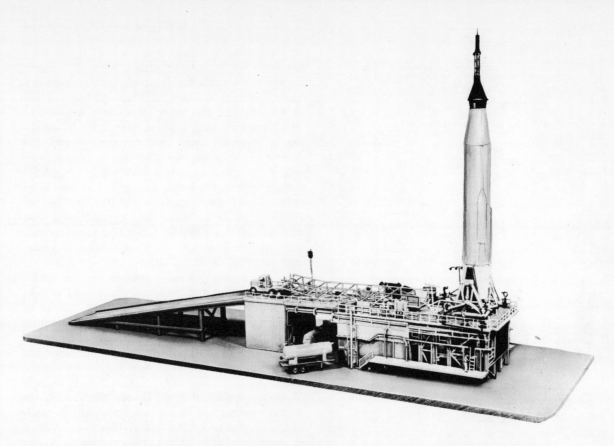

Fig. 31. As history is made in space, models become available mirroring in miniature the achievements that capture the world's attention. These are plastic models of the Friendship 7 Mercury Capsule in which Lieutenant Colonel John Glenn, Jr., made three earth orbits, together with its Atlas booster rocket and launching base, ramp and pad, and of the Mercury capsule with the Redstone booster rocket that carried the United States' first astronaut into space.

Revell, Inc.

Fig. 32. Further models of space vehicles built from kits of plastic parts. The rocket at the left is a close replica of the old Convair Atlas, although now renamed the Saturn. At the right is a ¼-inch scale model of the Jupiter. The model in the center is a 1/5th actual size replica of the Vanguard satellite.

Hawk Model Company

with one side or other areas made of transparent plastic so that the interior detailing is visible. There is even one kit that builds a completely transparent model through the skin of which all the internal equipment and machinery is visible. Any model of an open-cockpit airplane lends itself to detailing or superdetailing. This may include such refinements as complete instrument panels with dummy gauges that can be read only under a magnifying glass! Similarly, any model of an older type of airplane usually lends itself to further detailing as to the struts and bracing with wire and thread; some builders substitute more in-scale construction of this type for the molded components furnished with the kit.

There really is no practical limit to which the imagination and skill of a deft model builder can carry him when it comes to the matter of detailing. However, there is one basic point in regard to detailing that applies to all scale models, not only to display and flying model airplanes, but to all types of models as well as planes—trains, automobiles, ships, and so on. At first thought it would appear that the larger the model, the more detailing can be applied, and that this really is the only determining factor. However, there is a counterpoint to this that newcomers to any model-building hobby often fail to note, namely, that the larger the model, the more detailing will be required to make it look, if not "complete," then at least "worked on." The smaller the model, the less detail is, broadly speaking, required to achieve the same effect. For example, the absence of imitation glass in the cabin windows of a very small model may well pass unnoticed; on a larger model this might show up as a glaring omission. Furthermore, once you start to detail some models, the lack of similar detailing on other models displayed with them, which may previously have passed unnoticed, will at once become apparent to almost all viewers. In short, once you start to add minor detail to some models you will probably want to bring all of your models up to a similar level of perfection.

While a small model often will pass muster without much of the detail that might be required on a larger one, this fact should not be taken to mean that, given sufficient skill and patience, almost any amount of detail can be worked into a model no matter how small the size of the model itself or how extraordinarily minute must be some of the construction of the detailing. The day is long past when anything that modelmakers achieve in the way of tiny detail on a relatively small model is considered strikingly unusual, although the skill and workmanship involved therein

are ribbed out precisely to duplicate the structure of the protoypes. The outline of each part to be covered is traced out on the special paper finishing material, using the assembled plastic unit as a guide. For example, the wing covering is traced, using the molded wing as a guide, and the paper then cut out, leaving a little clearance on all sides. The paper is then bonded to the plastic wing molding with solvent adhesive and the excess clearance paper is trimmed away with an emory board or nail file. The result is an extremely realistic model, which may further be detailed by rigging to the correct design with thread.

DETAILING

As a matter of fact, many model airplanes constructed from kits of plastic parts present opportunities for further individual detailing by the builder. Some kits of this type now provide for much detailing by providing molded parts in the kit for highly detailed mechanical features, or for complete interior fittings. In some cases the kits are designed to allow the model to be opened, or is certainly always appreciated fully by those acquainted with the modeling art.

AUTHENTICITY

All operations leading up to the completion of a display model replica of a specific prototype should aim for authenticity. In the process of assembling a kit of parts, the hobbyist generally can rely on the manufacturer to provide him with authentically prepared components, although some specialists may find erroneous or at least debatable points. If so, these are usually of a very minor nature. Time and again it has been found that such so-called errors merely reflected the fact that the manufacturer had designed and tooled his kit from drawings and photographs of a specific plane at a given time and that other examples then or at other times showed variations in detail. There probably is no class of prototype from which models are built that shows more individual variation in design and finish than airplanes, or concerning which it is more difficult as a general rule to obtain accurate information even a few years after the real plane has been built and flown.

Yet such data, difficult as it may be to obtain, must be the very meat on which the man feeds who goes beyond basic kit formulations and detailing and strives to add additional detailing. Equally, such data is important in the painting and decorating stages, often even of standard kit models. There is little merit in superdetailing a model plane if the detailing is unauthentic—at least if the builder professes to be making a scale replica of a particular prototype. Without authenticity such a model might be considered to be little more than an exercise in modelmaking techniques. The writer recalls both with nostalgia and regret how he detailed and overdetailed some of his first display models (balsa-wood solids) with unauthentic and superfluous struts and bracing and other impedimenta when he was a boy. It was some time before he realized that the art was to add the things that appeared on the real airplane but were not included in the kits, not to hum away and put on as much extra equipment as could be fitted in the space available.

A case in point is the authenticity of camouflage. Many people are of the opinion that the camouflage of warplanes was invariably a hit-and-miss affair; that any colors were mixed in any pattern and, lo and behold, the plane became invisible, or at least somewhat more difficult to see at a distance. Actually, this is not true at all. Even in World War I, camouflaging was a carefully thought-out and scientific process. The famous

Fig. 33. Examples of variations in British World War II camouflage as applied to 1/6-inch scale plastic models. Note that one of these models (third from top) is a glider, the Hotspur II, not an airplane. The Blackburn Skua bomber (bottom) entered service in 1938 and was the Royal Navy's first monoplane with folding wings.

Lines Bros., Inc.

Fig. 34. Kits of plastic parts are available today for virtually every major classification of aircraft. Here are three examples of helicopter models constructed from such kits, the Hiller Hornet ramjet helicopter, the Sikorsky S-55, and the Piasecki H-21.

Aurora Plastics Corp.

lozenge camouflage used on some of the planes of the Central Powers was based on a selection of definite colors and involved a very definite repetition of each color in relation to every other color. There was more than one lozenge pattern in use. To model a camouflaged plane of this type authentically, the hobbyist must not only know the colors and arrangements of the patterns; he must also know which pattern was used on the particular plane at a given time.

Obviously the model builder interested in advanced model aircraft detailing and decorating must become somewhat of an airplane historian as well. He must obtain photographs, drawings, and information on the planes he intends to reproduce. He must learn not only where to locate this information—and much of it may be extremely difficult to find—but also how to evaluate and interpret it when he does find it, for much that he will succeed in finding will be vague and contradictory. Nevertheless, gathering this material and translating it into the form of tangible models is a rewarding and fascinating aspect of the hobby of model aviation.

SPACECRAFT MODELS

In comparison with the mass of kits for building model airplanes, the selection of spacecraft kits is fairly limited at the present time. Thus the enthusiast for this type of model building must to a large extent rely on his own constructions from scratch rather than on kits.

Interested government agencies, however, are today doing all they can to encourage the building of models of the various devices connected with the space program. Obviously, certain highly classified details are withheld, but the external forms and general designs of most of the equipment are made readily available to individual model builders and to manufacturers who desire to produce kits for their construction in miniature. In the United States the National Aeronautics and Space Administration has done much to encourage both the building of display models of rockets, spacecraft, and satellites, and of working model rockets. They have, in fact, published an excellent report, *Model Spacecraft Construction,*[*] with photographs (some of them reproduced here), drawings, and explicit instructions for the construction of models of such devices as the Saturn rocket and Apollo capsule, the Explorer satellite, the Orbiting Solar Observatory (OSO), the Relay satellite, and the Mariner spacecraft. Revised editions and new documents will no doubt make available additional and subsequent material.

The Academy of Model Aeronautics, also taking full cognizance of the space program, has expanded its activities and engaged in an extensive project, in collaboration with NASA, that eventually will result in the publication of an extensive series of plans for building scale-model spacecraft. The first of these plans to be published were those of the Mars Mariner, coincident with the launching of the prototype in late 1964. The AMA at the same time undertook to organize competitive modeling of the Mariner, and offered a special Academy membership that supplied plans and instructions for building the model and allowed for entry and participation in the special AMA Mariner contests. The AMA now is working on further spacecraft projects, and expects to engage fully in the promotion of spacecraft modeling on a continuing basis. Speaking of the future of this

*Model Spacecraft Construction, 1964, United States Government Printing Office, Document 1964 0—741—996, obtainable for $2.00 from the Superintendent of Documents, United States Government Printing Office, Washington 25, D.C.

Fig. 35. An unusual plastic model built from a kit. All the outer parts of this model of the P-51 Mustang are molded in clear plastic so as to reveal all the interior details of the craft, including the engine and cockpit. This is a ⅜-inch scale model.

Monogram Models, Inc.

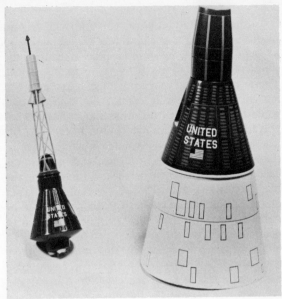

Fig. 36. Models of the Mercury (left) and Gemini space capsules, built to a sufficiently large scale to reveal the details of the historic capsules themselves. These models were built from kits of plastic parts. The Mercury (left) is ¼-inch scale; the Gemini is built to a scale exactly twice as large, ½-inch to the foot.

Revell, Inc.

program and the eventual building of flying model spacecraft, the AMA noted in the November, 1964, issue of their magazine, *Model Aviation*: "The chances are excellent that all our regular activity with working and flying models will provide an attraction to take over when his space model become only an ornament on the shelf. Just as the X-15 is half airplane and half space ship, the initial space interest probably will shift somewhat to accommodate what wings can do for liftless body . . . a whole new world, with the best of both—lift *and* thrust!"

From time to time newspapers will run a sensational story to the effect that all spies need to do to secure secret information is to walk into a hobby shop and for a modest sum buy a kit and its accompanying plans. Such stories are of course absurdities. All kits and plans available to model builders are based on information released and supplied by the appropriate branch of the government, and contain nothing of a classified nature. The United States Government is anxious to promote model building and to cooperate with model builders and manufacturers in every way possible, but obviously their enthusiasm does not extend to releasing anything that should be kept secret.

THE USE OF PLANS

The hobbyist who builds a model from a kit is provided with a complete set of plans and assembly instructions. When an enthusiast turns to building a model on his own, the situation becomes somewhat more complex. Suitable plans for older types of aircraft may often be found in old books and magazines, but very little plan

material has been prepared for those who wish to construct their own nonflying replicas of the latest types of aircraft. In many instances the builder in this field will have to locate and adapt plans published for constructing flying models of these prototypes.

It is characteristic of most plans published for the individual construction of airplanes—and this applies both to display and to flying models—that regardless of the scale of the plans, drawings seldom are provided for the complete airplane. Rather, because of space limitations on the printed page, the drawings of the front and top elevations usually are truncated. In many instances only the fuselage and half of the wing will be shown. For example, if the right half of the wing is shown, the left half must be built by ear, so to speak. Similarly, in many plans, the full stabilizer and elevator assembly will not be shown, but only one half and perhaps a portion of the other. If the wing section were simply a solid flat block with right-angle edges, it would be simple to build two wing halves over the drawing for the right or left half, as the case might be, and then flip one finished wing to serve as the opposite wing on the model. However, as the wing involves tapered leading and trailing edges, a profile representing the correct airfoil, and the dihedral or upward sweep of the wing, such a shortcut approach, while it might produce results not displeasing to the eye of noncritical observers in the case of certain prototypes, hardly can be commended to anyone wishing to produce a really accurate and acceptable model. What must be done is to reverse; to produce a mirror image, of one half of the wing or stabilizer assembly for the other half.

Many model builders can and will accomplish this by eye, particularly as the obtaining of a proper and precise reverse plan is neither the simplest nor the least costly thing in the world. There are two ways to accomplish this, however. An ordinary photostat cannot be used because while there is both a negative and a positive involved in the conventional photostat process, the true photostat negative is not a mirror image of the original and of the positive, but is identical except for the reversal of the positioning of the black-and-white areas. However, there are types of office copying machines of the chemical type (not the electrostatic) that in making a positive print identical to the original produce a mirror-image negative. Customarily this mirror negative is discarded after printing the positive. In the case of model airplane plans the negative is dried and retained, for it provides the precise mirror-image plan that is being sought. This method is not only less expensive than the alternate to be described in a moment, but has the advantage of automatically providing a mirror drawing in the exact size of the original. In fact, if the negative and the positive prints carefully are trimmed and pasted together on a sheet of artist's board, the result will be a perfect and complete working plan of the entire airplane, although half of the plan will be made up of black lines on white and the other half of white lines on black.

Not every hobbyist will be able to obtain access to the use of an office copying machine of this type. The alternative way of making a mirror-image print is to make a regular photograph of the half of the wing or other part. The negative is then printed so as to produce a reverse-image print, by turning the negative so that what was at the right of the picture in the original photograph now is at the left of the print. Furthermore, the print must be an enlargement, blown up so that the print will be exactly the same size as the original drawing.

ENLARGING AND REDUCING DRAWINGS

In the process described above, the object has been to secure a mirror print that will render the missing portion of the incomplete plans. It cannot be assumed, however, that the original plans will be drawn to the size in which the model is to be built, whether the builder intends to use them as is as far as completeness of the drawings is concerned, or to fill in the missing wing and other areas with mirror-image prints. On the contrary, it is more than likely that the plans at hand will be drawn to either too large or too small a scale. The plans as found in a book or magazine, or perhaps taken from a kit for a flying model of the same prototype, probably will be drawn full sized to one of the conventional scales such as ⅛th inch, ¼th inch, ½ inch to the foot. This is not always a safe assumption because at times plans originally drawn in a larger scale have been reproduced in books in a reduced size, often including the original and now incorrect notation as to the size of the drawings or an actual miniature scale ruler showing inches and fractions. At times special scale rules have had to be included in books of model aircraft plans so that model builders could compensate for the variations caused by reprinting plans in a smaller size.

Furthermore, some slight and unintentional variations from intended size may occur through shrinkages during the photographic and plate-making process preliminary to printing. The vari-

Fig. 37. Animated display model airplanes built from kits. The Marine attack fighter at the top has a propeller driven by an electric motor, similar to that shown in the inset. The B-58 Hustler (center) and the Handley Page Victor jet bombers have remote-control sticks that put them into various flight positions.

Lindberg Products, Inc.

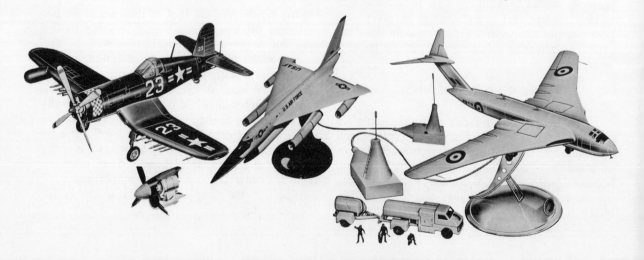

Fig. 38. Although this is a photogaph of a flying model, it provides an idea of the type of interior superdetailing that can be attained on many model airplanes, including some of the larger display models if the hobbyist is willing to expend the time and effort necessary to attain such an achievement.

Tatone Products

ous parts of the airplane will remain in correct proportion to each other, but the plans as printed may be slightly under the designated scale. In all likelihood the variation will be very small, but may be compounded in further reduction or enlargement. It is always desirable therefore, if possible, to check the accuracy of any plan that is being worked, and especially one that is to be enlarged or reduced, in order to ascertain just how close it is to the specified scale.

The method usually advocated for enlarging or reducing plans is to divide the original into squares and then divide a large sheet of paper into enlarged or reduced squares. For example, if the original plans are drawn to ¼-inch scale, and you wish to build a model in ½-inch scale, you divide the original drawings into ¼-inch squares and the sheet for your new drawing into ½-inch squares. Taking each square one by one, you redraw the lines in the smaller squares into the corresponding larger square. If you wish to reduce a plan, the process is reversed. It is difficult to see why this method is so often recommended. It is not impossible to do, but it is extraordinarily difficult for the average hobbyist to obtain a decent enlarged or reduced plan by this process. An individual experienced in drafting can attain a commendable plan with this method, in combination with the instruments with which he is familiar, but such an individual does not require the grid of squares anyway to achieve satisfactory results. The only method that can wholeheartedly be recommended to the amateur is to have the original plans photostated up or down to the enlarged or reduced size in which the model itself is to be built. The photostating must be done carefully and the finished photostats checked to assure there are no distortions caused by shrinkage in drying the negative or positive; this checking should be done at several positions on the finished print because it is possible for one portion of a photostat to hold its accuracy while shrinkage occurs at another spot on the print.

However, if you explain your purpose and need for accuracy to the photostat operator in advance, he will undoubtedly produce such accurate prints for you. In the case of large plans that are to be reduced, it may be necessary to photostat the original plans in sections and then trim and paste together two or more sections of the reduced-size prints in order to secure a complete drawing.

This chapter is devoted to nonoperating display models, but the preceding remarks on the use of plans and their enlargement and reduction apply to all model airplane work, including flying models. By this time the reader should be aware of the possible difficulties that may arise in attempting to build a flying model airplane in a size other than that of the original design, although the enlargement or reduction of the plans themselves will present no difficulties. For many reasons, a plane that makes an excellent flying model in ½-inch scale may provide an entirely different story when built to exactly the same plans in ¼-inch or ¾-inch scale.

WOODEN MODELS

There is little doubt that wood is the ideal material for the hobbyist who wishes to build his own display model airplanes, although some very fine models have at times been made of other materials, including metal. The wood involved in display-model airplane building does not have to meet any particular requirements of relative strength or lightness as does the wood employed in flying models. Nevertheless, balsa wood has become so universally associated with model aircraft that it naturally comes to mind when a wooden airplane model is projected.

Balsa wood is an extraordinarily light wood with a relatively high tensile strength, hence ideal for flying model airplanes. Balsa wood weighs about half as much as cork. Its extreme lightness comes as a surprise to those first using it. Balsa wood has been widely used for model aircraft only since the 1920's. Its introduction no doubt had a prodigious effect on advancing and popularizing model aviation. It comes from Central and South America and is supplied to the hobby trade in the form of strips, sheets, planks, or blocks in innumerable sizes, usually in 36-inch lengths, although longer pieces also are available. The wood usually comes completely dressed and polished; if you require a strip of, say 1/16th inch by ⅛th inch balsa you order a strip of that dimension and find it a true and accurate measurement. It also is possible for builders of flying models to procure balsa strips already shaped to provide leading or trailing edges for wings.

The selection and grading of balsa as to strength, weight, and suitability for certain purposes is a somewhat complicated business. Some processors grade and color-code their balsa according to hardness. However, not all handlers of balsa follow the same grading or coding. Some grade three degrees of hardness: soft, medium and hard; others, to five grades and still others to as many as seven. Quarter-grain balsa is cut at right angles to the growth rings. It shows a distinct flecked pattern in the grain. It is not so easy to bend as the ordinary cut but at the same time has considerably greater resistance to warping and is ideal for certain applications where this is of great advantage, such as wing edges and ribs. The variations in balsa are of course of the greatest interest to the builder of flying models and will be described further in that section of the book.

For the builder of display models, the softer grades of balsa may well be avoided altogether; bear in mind that even the hardest grade of balsa is relatively speaking a very soft wood compared even to pine. In general woodworking, pine is considered a soft wood. Pine is, in fact, an ideal wood for use in making nonoperating display models. It is somewhat harder to work than balsa, although this is not necessarily a disadvantage, and it will produce a stronger model that will stand up under a lot more handling and moving around than will balsa. A number of other woods also are quite practical for display models, such as ash and poplar, but in most instances the choice will be between balsa and pine. The relatively light weight of balsa is of no advantage in a display model, except perhaps that the finished model may be hung by a very light and almost invisible thread. While balsa is traditional for model airplanes, its very softness may be somewhat of a disadvantage in carving a display model, for it may cut much too easily, especially if a regulation modelmaker's knife is used. For this reason, in working solid blocks of balsa in building display models, an ordinary pocket knife or a sloyd knife may well be preferable to the usual modelmaker's knife.

WOOD SHAPING AND FINISHING

Correctly contouring the various wooden parts that go to make up a display-model airplane or spacecraft is the chief problem in model building of this sort. In the days when many plans were being published for building nonoperating models, they frequently included outlines of various cross-section points on the fuselage that could be used as guides to make cardboard templates to be employed in checking the carving work as it progressed. Whether such templates for the fuselage and for other parts as well really are useful is open to question. Many experienced model airplane builders feel that it is more work to prepare such templates than to do all the carving freehand; there is also a considerable feeling that if a model builder cannot carve a satisfactory section freehand he is not likely to do much better with the supposed aid of templates. This, obviously, is a matter for the individual builder to determine to his own satisfaction. In many instances today, however, plans with templates simply will not be available anyway. In essence, constructing a display model is a matter of whittling, and the final results will depend to a large extent on just how good a whittler is the builder of the model.

The wooden blocks for the main parts should be obtained in sizes as close to the finished dimensions as possible. Here balsa wood holds a certain advantage, for it usually is possible to obtain balsa blocks and planks already close to the required dimensions. Most model builders find it a substantial help to transfer the outlines of the finished part to the wood by placing a piece of carbon paper over the wood and under the plan and, holding everything firmly in place, go over the outlines of the unit as they appear on the plans with a pencil, thereby producing an outline on the wood itself. Some builders find it necessary to put the outline of a fuselage only on one side of the block. It is somewhat difficult to align tracing on two sides of a block correctly, and almost impossible to put tracings in the exactly proper position on all four sides of a block, except as a rough guide to the most preliminary carving of the block.

It is much easier to carve the basic fuselage and then to carve any unusual formations or ap-

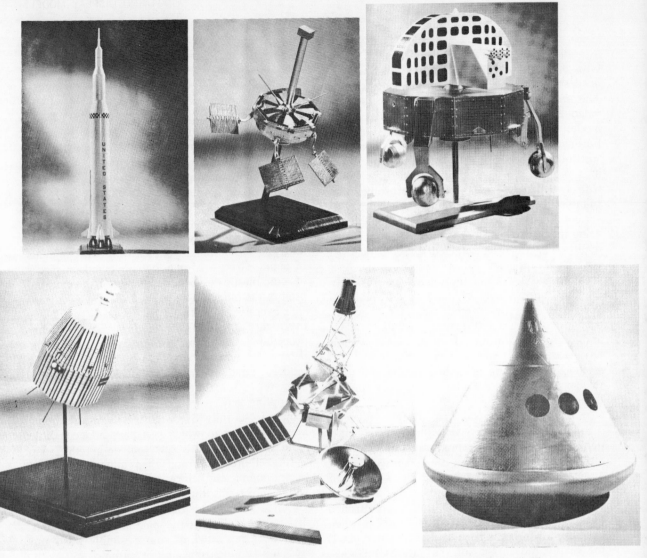

Fig. 39. Six spacecraft models, constructed largely of wood in combination with a few other readily obtainable materials, developed as projects by the National Aeronautics and Space Administration, which publishes a booklet containing detailed plans and instructions for their construction. The six models are: top row, Saturn V rocket and Apollo capsule, Explorer XII satellite and orbiting solar observatory; lower row, relay communications satellite, Mariner II exploratory spacecraft, and Apollo moon capsule.

National Aeronautics and Space Administration

pendages separately and glue them to the fuselage rather than to incorporate them in a single main carving. Until the model builder gets accustomed to the feel both of his carving tool and of the wood itself, slow and easy should be the watchword. It is easy to cut away wood; it is impossible to restore it, although sometimes damaged work can be saved by gluing in a patch or by the judicious used of plastic wood. A common failing is to attempt to take off too much in a single cut, especially in the rough carving work at the beginning. At all times it is best to remove material with a series of gradual, shallow cuts. Remember to leave sufficient material to allow for the final finishing and cleaning up to be done with sandpaper, or glass paper, as it is known

in Great Britain. Many experienced modelmakers leave much of the final work to be done with sandpaper, first using a coarse paper, then a finer paper, and, for the last step, an extremely fine paper that leaves the model almost glass smooth and ready for painting.

Balsa-wood models may be assembled with regular model airplane cement; some modelers run reinforcing pins through delicate parts to produce a more solid construction. Models built of pine and similar woods may be constructed by using white glue for the joints. However, for superior construction, some hobbyists prefer using a waterproof glue on their models, although for a proper joint this usually requires curing for ten or twelve hours under pressure.

PAINTING MODELS

Plastic models require the use of a special type of paint in their decoration, just as they need special plastic cement in their construction. The paints suitable for plastic models are designated as such and should not be confused with model airplane dope. Wooden models may be finished with almost any type of paint or lacquer; softwood will soak up paint like a sponge, and it is preferable first to prime coat such models with two coats of clear lacquer or some other suitable sealer. However, the technique may be varied according to the type of airplane that is being modeled. Some hobbyists feel that the most realistic effect can be obtained if they sand modern metal airplanes to as smooth a finish as possible and seal them thoroughly before applying the thinnest layer of paint that is practical. With older, fabric-covered airplanes, however, they prefer to leave the wood a little rougher and apply the paint directly to the wood, without any lacquer or sealer. Those who follow this method feel that the procedure results in a more realistic simulation of the fabric covering of the old planes.

Paint may be applied to models either by brush or by spraying. Several methods of spray painting are available: spray cans of paint, an airbrush, or the use of a small sprayer outfit, either an elaborate conventional rig with an air compressor, or a small self-contained unit wherein the propellant gas is supplied from a can attached to the spray gun and replaced by a fresh can when exhausted. Much has been said and written about the relative advantages of the various methods, but actually the caliber of the resulting paint job depends more on the skill of the hobbyist than on the method by which he applies the paint; an unskilled workman can soak a model almost beyond saving as readily with a spray as with a brush. Many beginners' paint jobs are spoiled simply because they have applied the paint too thickly. If they are brushing it on, they have failed to thin the paint sufficiently so that it will flow on smoothly. If they are using a spray, they have held the nozzle too close to the model being painted. Beginners often go astray in the belief that they must completely cover the surface with the first coat of paint. Actually, two or even perhaps three thin coats will produce a better finish than one thick one, especially on plastic models. When models are molded in a dark-colored plastic and a light-colored paint is being applied, two or three successive thin coats are almost a necessity to achieve satisfactory results.

In any case, never hesitate to thin the paint with the proper thinner advised by the paint manufacturer so that it will flow freely and smoothly from the brush.

Lastly, be sure to give the paint plenty of time to dry before you handle it or before you put on a second or a third coat. Don't touch the paint so see if it is dry yet. Many model paints will appear dry to the touch in a comparatively short time, but the paint will not be truly dry and hardened for quite a few hours. It is well to experiment in advance as to the precise characteristics and capabilities of the paint you intend to use on a model so that you will know exactly how long it actually does take to dry and how long you should make yourself wait between coats of paint. These tests may be conducted on pieces of scrap plastic or wood, depending on the material used in the model to be painted. However, a good safe overall rule is to let each coat of paint dry overnight before applying another coat. Two other procedures, both time-consuming but worth the delay, are recommended when painting plastic models. First, allow at least twenty-four hours after the assembling work is completed before attempting any painting in order to allow the cement to set fully. Second, wash the entire model in warm water to which you have added a little hand soap—but not a detergent or laundry soap—rinse thoroughly, and then allow the model to dry completely before starting to paint it. This will remove oils that have been transferred to the model from the builder's hands and which may adversely affect the painting. Do not soak the model in a bowl, of course; simply wash and rinse it carefully, using a bit of cotton or soft cloth.

DECORATING MODEL AIRCRAFT

The usual method of decorating small model airplanes, applying the proper numbers and insignia, is by means of decalcomanias. Decalcomanias, or "transfers" as they sometimes are called, are printed in the appropriate colors on transparent paper that is provided with an adhesive backing and a protective backing sheet. Suitable decalcomanias for the particular plane to be built customarily are included with kits of plastic parts. A wide variety of aircraft decalcomanias also are obtainable separately for those who build their own models from scratch. In applying decalcomanias, the desired number or insignia is cut from the sheet, soaked in warm water for a few seconds in order to loosen it from the backing sheet, and then carefully slid from the backing sheet into the correct position

Fig. 40. While most kits of plastic parts build a single model airplane, there are some kits available that build groups of related models that mount in flight positions on a single base. Here are two such groups: five different U.S. fighter planes and a midair refueling scene.

Monogram Models, Inc.

on the model. When in position, the decalcomania is pressed gently but firmly in place and any excess water dabbed away with a piece of clean cloth.

While a very great variety of separate decalcomanias are available for model builders, embracing most of the standard insignia in various scales, it is not impossible that the builder of individual display model planes will not be able to locate precisely what he needs for a particular model among the stock designs readily available. A possible solution is to purchase an inexpensive kit of plastic parts for a similar plane just in order to obtain the decalcomanias supplied in the kit. Decalcomanias can be had made up to special order from decalcomania manufacturers; the price is not necessarily prohibitive, but it is at best a rather costly method of obtaining transfers for one or even a small group of models. On the other hand, hand painting of the requisite insignia is, except in the hands of a real expert, likely to produce a rather rough and unsatisfactory effect and may well spoil the appearance of an otherwise extremely satisfactory model. Suggesting that the model airplane builder confine his construction efforts to models for which decalcomanias readily are available is hardly a satisfactory solution, although the thought is not entirely without merit. There really is no overall answer that will completely satisfy the requirements of every model builder in every situation.

DISPLAYING MODEL AIRPLANES

The hobbyist who starts to acquire a number of completed display models of aircraft or spacecraft soon is faced with the problem of what to do with them. More specifically, the question is how to display them. Not that display is absolutely necessary; it is possible to conceive of a model builder who would be satisfied to pack his handiwork away, gaining his satisfaction solely from the pleasures of the construction process. In the main, however, the builder of display models produces them for that purpose. Shelves or cases are an obvious solution to the housing and showing off of a collection of display-model aircraft; some modelers like to suspend model airplanes from thread or cord in flight positions. At times the balance of models must be altered

by inserting a small weight of modeling clay in order to adapt them to a position other than that for which they originally were intended; models originally designed for use on display stands, for example, often must have the balance changed when used in another manner. Ideally, the change in the center of balance should be made before the model is assembled and painted, but this is not always practical, at least until the model builder has acquired some experience as to what the exact balance requirements are for the purpose he has in mind. As a result, makeshifts often are resorted to, such as taping a small piece of metal to the underside of a model, or to the side that will be out of sight facing a wall when the model is placed in its permanent display position.

Of late, two new trends have been noted in the display of model aircraft. The first is the use of the models as purely decorative articles in various rooms of the home, with the models either on shelves or suspended. There are limitations, of course, to the number of models that can be used effectively in this manner, but within these limitations well-built aircraft models make extremely attractive and acceptable decorative articles, with the older planes, especially, appearing to be favored for this purpose.

The second new trend is toward the construction of special diorama or shadow boxes involving model aircraft in a complete miniature scene. The number of models of a given scale that can be displayed in the same area is considerably less when dioramas are employed than when the models simply are shelved side by side, but the overall attraction and effect are enhanced considerably. Dr. G. A. Robinson, a figure well known in model circles, told of his dioramas in a recent letter:

"You asked me to describe the dioramas or shadow boxes I am building to display my ¼-inch scale models of World War I airplanes. Each box is about 2 feet long and 18 inches high and deep. They are lighted with small bulbs powered by a heavy Ives toy train transformer.

"In one box for example the brave pilots of the Lafayette Escadrille are lined up in front of one of their planes being decorated by a French general. The soldier figures are ⅜-inch scale which, with the ¼-inch scale plane behind them adds to the effect of depth and perspective. In another diorama we see a section of the Allied trenches in the foreground, occupied by the Princess Pats. Behind the trench (actually it is in front of the trench in no man's land) a ¼-inch scale Fokker is positioned nose-down into the earth. The fuselage has been blackened with paint and a tube let into it and up into the tail gives off smoke. The smoke is provided by the smoking mechanism from a toy locomotive mounted behind the diorama and also powered by the Ives transformer. This diorama provides an extraordinarily realistic effect . . . The most difficult thing to make are clouds for scenes of actual flight. So far, the best thing still seems to be cotton but I hope to be able to improve on this eventually."

Obviously such constructions take the hobbyist out of the field of model aviation alone and into the realms of miniature figures, scenery, stagecraft, and lighting. They are very striking in appearance, however, and appear well worth the effort required, adding as they do an entirely new dimension to the display of miniature aircraft.

CHAPTER 3

Flying Models

Because the airplane is heavier than air, it is necessary for it to remain in continuous motion in the air, to sustain itself. Two factors are involved, thrust and lift. The propeller provides the thrust. Whether mounted at the front of the plane (tractor) or behind the wing or wings (pusher), the propeller spirals its way forward through the air just as an ordinary woodscrew spirals into a piece of wood. In fact, in Great Britain, the propeller generally is known as an airscrew, a somewhat more descriptive and possibly more accurate name for the device when applied to aircraft.

Lift is the second factor. It is provided by the lifting surfaces, or airfoils: the wing or wings and stabilizer ("tailplane" in British terminology). If you move a sheet of cardboard with the front edge angled slightly upward into the wind, it will have a tendency to lift further. Similarly, if you mount the cardboard in such a way that the front and rear edges are free to move, and play a strong current of air toward it, the principle of the wind tunnel, the front edge likewise will lift. In somewhat the same way the front of a surfboard will lift when it is rapidly towed through the water.

The lift of a surface, whether the experimental piece of cardboard or the wing of a real or model airplane, when moved through the air comes both at the top and bottom of the surface. In an airplane the top of the wing is rounded so that the air going over the top of the wing has a greater distance to travel in passing the wing than has the air going under the wing. Inasmuch as the air pressure behind the air going both over and under the wing at any given moment is the same—that is to say, the air pressure in front of wing; the air into which the airscrew is thrusting the airplane—the air passing over the greater distance created by the curve, or camber, in the top of the wing must move faster than the air passing under the wing in order to traverse the same overall wing width distance in the same amount of time. This reduces the downward air pressure on the top of the wing. The corresponding pressure on the bottom of the wing, an upward pressure, therefore is greater and tends to lift the wing even more. In fact, the greater the comparative curve on the top of the wing or wings, the greater the amount of lift. However, too great a curve on the top of the wing is not desirable, for the greater the curve, the greater also will be the drag or resistance of the wing. Basically, however, when the air passing over and under the wing is sufficient to provide a lifting force equal to the overall weight of the airplane with its pilot or crew and cargo, an airplane, real or model, will fly and will continue to fly as long as the propeller provides sufficient thrust to drive the craft forward into the wind and thus sustain the needed lifting force on the wing. This is the reason an airplane always take off facing *into* the wind.

Fig. 41. The lines of several of the Piper airplanes make the designs suitable for adaptation as scale flying models. The 1-inch scale, 36-inch-wingspan Piper Super Cruiser model (top) is suitable for free-flight, control-line, or radio-control flying. It may also be mounted on floats in a manner similar to that shown on the smaller, ½-inch scale, Piper model (right). Both models are designed for use with internal-combustion reciprocating engines.

Sig Mfg. Co., Inc.
Scientific Model Airplane Co.

Two other major factors operate on the flight of an airplane: drag, or air resistance, already mentioned, and the pull of gravity. Both are negative factors; they do not help the airplane to achieve flight, but, rather, must be overcome by lift and thrust for an airplane to fly.

It all sounds rather simple, but a great many years passed before these principles could be put to use in practical man-carrying heavier-than-air flight, and a great many men lost their lives in the subsequent development of the art of flight —and still do in its further enhancement.

UPS AND DOWNS

Another pertinent point is the angle at which the main supporting surfaces of an airplane approach or attack the wind: the tilt of the wings. To a certain extent, the greater this tilt, the greater the amount of lift provided by the wings. However, there is a point beyond which increasing the angle starts rapidly to destroy the proper related upward and downward air pressure on the wing; in short, to destroy the lifting property of the wing. This point of no return may be caused by inherently faulty design in a plane; it may be caused by improperly adjusting a good design; or with a plane that flies well under most con-

ditions, it may be caused in the air by attempting to make the plane climb at too great an angle for its capabilities. In a model airplane such a failure is likely to occur for the first or second reason; in a real airplane it generally is the result of the third reason, although a similar condition may take place with certain model planes with normally excellent flying qualities by attempting, by means of control lines or radio control, to put them into too steep a climb while airborne. In any event, such a failure is known as stalling, or a stall. Most people who are interested in real or model airplanes have heard this expression, but usually those who have only a cursory knowledge of the subject assume that it refers to the engine stalling in a real plane or in an engine-powered model, just as at times the engine in an automobile will stall. This type of stall can, of course, occur with the engine of an airplane. However, aeronautically speaking, stall refers to a failure, not of the engine, but of the balance of pressures that provide the lifting power of the wing or wings of an airplane. The plane starts to climb sharply, then suddenly loses its lift, and dives. Thus, a rubber-powered model airplane can stall in this aeronautical sense just as readily as can an engine-powered model. When a real airplane stalls, which seldom occurs with a quali-

Fig. 42. Launching a free-flight model airplane powered by an internal-combustion reciprocating engine. This is a Class B model, built by Ray A. Van De Walker. The scene is a national meet where approximately 1,000 contestants competed, held at the U.S. Naval Air Station at Dallas, Texas, July 21, 1964.

Official Photograph, U.S. Navy

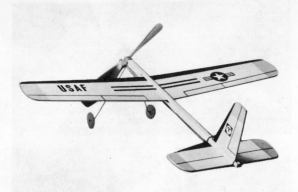

Fig. 43. Inexpensive, easily assembled rubber-powered balsa-wood flying model airplanes. The model at the left is essentially the traditional stick model, while in the case of the model at the right there is a semblance of a profile fuselage.

Testor Corp.
Paul K. Guillow, Inc.

fied pilot at the controls, if the plane is sufficiently high at the time the pilot usually can safely pull it out of the dive. With a model airplane the situation is somewhat different, and a stall usually results in a crash, unless the plane has been properly designed, and properly adjusted before flight, first to eliminate the possibility of a stall insofar as possible and, second, to assure that in the event of a stall the model will go, not into a disastrous dive, but rather into a gentle glide that will bring it safely back to earth. By the same token, the design of the model plane should be such that when in any flight the power is cut off or exhausted, the model will glide down.

Bear in mind that what is being referred to here is not someone's home-design plane, in the creation and building of which all these problems multiply manyfold, but expertly designed and fully tested patterns of model airplanes built from kits. Yet keep in mind also that even with such planes built from kits—and it is safe to say that virtually every flying-model kit on the market today will build an excellent flying miniature—the success of the resulting model depends to a large extent on the skill and care of the builder. A certain amount of adjustment is almost always necessary to the finished model. Slightly changing the contour of the airfoil, perhaps by just a little too much sanding of an edge or by a slight warp in a wing can, if undetected and either not corrected or compensated for, completely change and destroy the flying qualities of any model airplane. Precisely the same remarks apply to models built, not from complete kits, but from plans provided in model airplane magazines and books.

If a plane stalls, the result is a dive. Yet dive may also be considered as in itself the opposite of stall. A dive in itself, as distinguished from a dive resulting from a stall, may be described simply as too abrupt and steep a glide.

In the average model, assuming the basic angle of the wing or wings is correct for the specific design in hand, a stalling condition immediately upon launching usually is the result of the nose of the plane being too light toward the front in its overall distribution of weight, and usually can be corrected by adding weight or ballast to the nose (customarily in the form of a little modeling clay). If a model tends to dive immediately upon launching, the plane probably is too light toward the rear, and this condition can be compensated for by adding weight in the tail.

MODEL AERODYNAMICS

Any airplane, if it is to fly satisfactorily, must possess and be capable of sustaining its equilibrium; it must possess a certain measure of stability. The factor of stability should not be confused with that of controllability, although in a model airplane, and particularly in a free-flying model airplane, these two things must to a considerable extent at least be intertwined. Stability relates to the ability of the plane more or less automatically to counteract forces that act to upset the balance and general attitude of the plane in flight. Controllability relates to the degree of ease and speed with which the pilot can maneuver the airplane in response to his regulation of the controls. Neither stability nor controllability are absolutes; in fact, each has its own proportionate role to play in real aircraft design and usage. Stability, for example, would be particularly desirable in a plane designed for a novice or for personal use, whereas greater controllability, that is to say, quicker maneuverability, even at the sacrifice of some stability, would be sought in a fighter plane.

Much of this is reflected in model airplane design; in control-line models there are the more

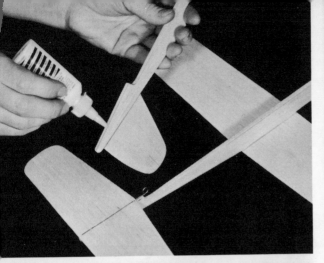

Fig. 44. This step-by-step sequence pictures the assembly of a simple rubber-powered flying model biplane from the kit shown at the upper left, through cutting out, sanding, and pinning and gluing the various parts, to the completion of the model. Note the use of simple cardboard jigs to assure the correct alignment of the wings. Two different styles of flying model monoplanes may optionally be built from the same basic kit, as shown in the last photograph. (Photographs read from top to bottom.)

North Pacific Products Co.

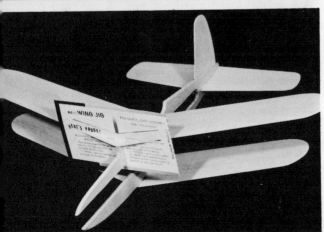

stable and less quickly responsive to control-command trainers and there are the highly maneuverable and responsive stunt and combat designs. Basically, however, stability plays a much larger proportionate role in all model airplane design than it does in the design of real planes, and this is true especially in the area of free-flying model planes where there not only is no real pilot at the controls, but the modeler has no control whatsoever over the plane once it is launched—again, as compared to control-line and to radio-controlled models.

Mention was made in Chapter 1, in outlining the classes of radio-control contest models, of three axes: the yaw axis, the pitch axis, and the roll axis. These are the three axes that affect real and model airplane stability. Just as the earth revolves around an imaginary axis, an airplane in flight has these three axes or imaginary lines around which it normally balances and around which it can and does actually move. The roll axis, or more properly the longitudinal axis, is the long, or fore-and-aft, axis of the airplane. It runs from the front to the rear of the airplane at right angles to both of the other axes. A plane rolls around its longitudinal axis.

The pitch, or lateral, axis runs in a straight line across the wings, again at right angles to both of the other axes. The lateral axis might also be called the climbing axis; when an airplane is directed up or down from a level flying position, it is then in effect turning on its lateral axis. The yaw, or vertical, axis is the turning axis, and is a line extending perpendicularly from the intersection of the longitudinal axis and the lateral axis. When an airplane turns right or left, it is revolving about its vertical axis. The sudden forces

Fig. 45. Flying models built from a series of four kits of balsa-wood parts designed to form a sequential beginner's course in model airplane building, starting with the glider at the upper right and working through three rubber-powered kits of 14½-inch, 18-inch, and 21⅜-inch-wingspans respectively.

Comet Model Hobbycraft Corp.

that can affect an airplane in flight may make it turn on any of its three axes. The more stable the design of the airplane, the less, comparatively speaking, will these forces act upon the plane and the more will the plane resist the play of these forces and the more readily and actively will it resist and equalize the power of these forces. The flying model plane must perform in much the same manner, only, as it were, even more so proportionately because of the absence of a live pilot in the craft, and the free-flying model must possess the desired characteristics of stability to an even greater degree than the other broad general classes of models. (Keep in mind that basically there are three types of flying model airplanes: free flight, control line, and radio control.)

STABILITY

The radio-control contest rules list the axes in the order that they do—yaw, pitch, and roll—because the simplest form of radio control is rudder control only, control of the yaw, or vertical, axis. In considering these axes in terms of model airplane design in general, however, it appears more desirable in the interest of relating a connected story to reverse this order and to discuss first roll, then pitch, and finally yaw. To a certain extent these movements of an airplane are analogous to similar movements of a ship or boat in water. However, it is wise not to allow ourselves to become too bemused by such comparisons as, even though air may be considered a

gaseous liquid and often is so considered for certain experimental and theoretical purposes, the actions and reactions of an airplane obviously are in many ways entirely different from those of boats.

Longitudinal stability and lateral stability should actually be considered together. It should be made clear that while there are a longitudinal axis and a lateral axis, longitudinal stability depends on the lack of or the correction of movement along the lateral axis, and lateral stability depends on the lack of or the correction of movement along the longitudinal axis. In short, when a plane rolls, it rolls around its longitudinal axis. One wing tip goes up and the other wing tip goes down. What is affected and what automatically works to correct this condition is the lateral stability of the given airplane. When a plane pitches, it moves around its lateral axis; the nose goes up and the tail goes down or the nose goes down and the tail goes up. What is affected and what automatically works to correct this condition is the longitudinal stability of the real or model plane in question. Failure to grasp this at first seemingly confusion of terminology is the chief cause of so many hobbyists finding it difficult to understand something that is essentially simple and basic.

Longitudinal stability depends to a large extent on the stabilizer (now the particularly apt usage of this name for this particular part becomes apparent), or tailplane. The lifting surface of the stabilizer is designed to meet the wind at a

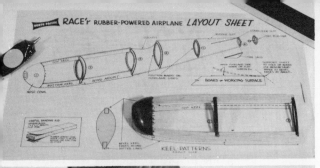

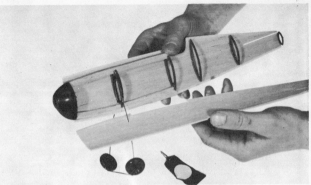

Fig. 46. Four steps in assembling a simple rubber-powered flying model with sheet balsa-wood sides assembled over a plastic nose cowl and bulkheads. The first photograph shows how most model airplanes are assembled directly over the printed plans. Pins are used temporarily to hold components in position while the glue is setting.

North Pacific Products Co.

different angle from that of the wing, and this tends to create a compensating force that helps to stabilize the airplane against the force of sudden gusts that would otherwise tend materially to tilt the plane up or down along the lateral axis. In simple flying models wherein the elevator is not moveable but rather the design of the aircraft is such that the stabilizer and elevator form a single unit, one of the most effective and widely used methods of correcting a tendency in the model to stall or dive is to adjust the rear edge of the stabilizer-elevator by bending it slightly downward to correct for stalls or slightly upward to correct for dives.

Lateral stability, that is, the correction of unwanted movement or roll around the longitudinal axis, is primarily dependent on the dihedral of the wing or wings. This, as noted in Chapter 1, represents the angle at which the wing tips are raised above the center of the wing, or the point where the wing on a low-wing monoplane meets the fuselage. Speaking more precisely, now that the matter of the axes has been explored, dihedral represents the angle that obtains between the wing or wing halves and the lateral axis, an angle known as the dihedral angle. Usually, on monoplanes, the lower the wing, the greater the dihedral angle. Also, generally speaking, the greater the dihedral

angle, the larger should be the vertical surfaces of the empennage; a large fin and rudder assembly tends to balance a large dihedral angle and add to the craft's stability. Also, as a general rule, the faster a model flies, the larger in proportion should be the area of the fin and rudder. The dihedral adds to the stability of the plane and serves to right it when the airplane rolls on its longitudinal axis in this manner: when the plane rolls, the lifting power of the lowered wing is

GUILLOW'S
BRITISH SE-5A KIT 202

GUILLOW'S
NIEUPORT 11 KIT 203

GUILLOW'S

Fig. 47. As in the case of display models, flying models of the historic airplanes of World War I are extremely popular with hobbyists. These are 24-inch-wingspan models of, top to bottom, the British SE-5A, the French Nieuport, and the American Thomas Morse Scout. These models may be built powered either by rubber or by ¼ A Class internal-combustion reciprocating engines.

Paul K. Guillow, Inc.

Fig. 48. Essentially a glider for soaring, this interesting British design has auxiliary power in the form of an internal-combustion reciprocating engine mounted on a pylon with a pusher propeller. The fuselage is constructed of solid balsa wood, hollowed out inside.

Model Aircraft (Bournemouth) Ltd.

increased and that of the raised wing is decreased. As a result there is a natural tendency of the plane to restore itself to the proper flight position as the lowered wing is moved upward and the raised wing pushes downward. Similarly, when a model banks in making a turn, the dihedral serves to act automatically to restore the proper flight position of the wing or wings.*

The vertical, or yaw, axis is the turning axis, about which the plane may be said to revolve to right or left when making a turn. To a certain extent stability around the vertical axis, or directional stability as it is called, is attained in much the same manner as the tail or fin of a weathervane keeps the arrow or other indicating device pointing always into the wind. Remember that the rudder is in a fixed position on a free-flight model, just as is the tail or fin of the weathervane. When the plane tends to be blown out of course momentarily by a sudden gust, compensating pressure is exerted in the direction that is opposite to that of the yaw or turn, causing the plane to return to its course. This compensating pressure always is exerted behind the line of the vertical axis; the mounting standard of a weathervane may be regarded as identical with the vertical axis of an airplane for purposes of comparison. The wings also play a part in maintaining directional stability. When a plane yaws, the wing side that leads into the wind automatically tends to develop a greater amount of drag or resistance than the other side of the wing, thereby creating a compensating force that tends to bring the wings and thereby the plane back into position, not unlike

*It is interesting to note that the dihedral, which was well known at the time, was disdained by the Wright brothers. Writing in *The Century Magazine* in September, 1908, they stated: "After considering the practical effect of the dihedral principle, we reached the conclusion that a flyer founded upon it might be of interest from a scientific point of view, but could be of no value in a practical way." The dihedral quickly was restored to airplane design by subsequent inventors.

the manner in which the dihedral angle restores the equilibrium of a plane that is rolling around its longitudinal axis, although in the former case we are dealing with drag and in the latter with lift.

Another factor enters the picture of directional stability, however. This is the adjustment of the thrust of the propeller, and this is a factor with all propeller-driven models, whether free flight, control line or radio control, and whether powered by rubber, internal-combustion reciprocating engines, or some other device. If the propeller were mounted with its shaft absolutely parallel to the longitudinal axis, the torque of the propeller would cause the model plane to pull to the left in flight. This torque must be compensated for by offsetting the propeller so that it thrusts a little to the right. In rubber-powered models all that usually is required is to offset the nose block a little. With engine-powered models the entire engine is offset. This is necessary with both free-flight and control-line models, and the principle often is applied to radio-

Fig. 49. Two 24-inch-wingspan flying models, suitable for either rubber power or internal-combustion reciprocating engine power. Or they may, as shown here before the covering material is applied be built as nonoperating display models; a World War I British SE-5A (top) and an Aeronca Champion 85.

Paul K. Guillow, Inc.

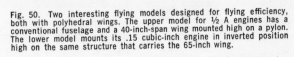

Fig. 50. Two interesting flying models designed for flying efficiency, both with polyhedral wings. The upper model for ½ A engines has a conventional fuselage and a 40-inch-span wing mounted high on a pylon. The lower model mounts its .15 cubic-inch engine in inverted position high on the same structure that carries the 65-inch wing.

Carl Goldberg Models, Inc.

Fig. 51. A highly prefabricated kit for a control-line trainer plane, including solid balsa-wood wing with finished airfoil section and solid balsa-wood fuselage. The checkered material is a decalcomania sheet for decorating the finished model. The picture shows a diesel engine in position, but this is not included in the kit.

Model Aircraft (Bournemouth) Ltd.

controlled models as well, although there is some question as to whether it is needed or desirable, as even the simplest of radio-control models provide rudder control. In all types of models, propellers usually are mounted so as to thrust downward a bit, either by adjusting the nose block on rubber-powered models, or the entire engine on other types of powered model aircraft. This downthrust serves to prevent stalls when launching models and also to help provide a slow, safe glide back to earth after the power cuts off.

BALANCE

A real airplane must be designed so as to balance under all reasonable loading conditions of passengers and freight. The location of the center of gravity in a plane, whether real or model, does play a substantial part in longitudinal stability. With a model the computation of the balancing is by no means so difficult as in a real plane, for, with the possible exception of model aircraft that may be called upon to carry a payload in certain competitive events, the balance can be established for the ship itself as it is to be flown, without the necessity of taking into consideration

the weight of the pilot or crew or of possible loadings. However, the center of gravity in a model airplane should vary somewhat, depending on the type of plane. For example, the balance point usually is located considerably further back from the leading edge of the wing on free-flight and radio-controlled models—and also on nonpowered gliders—than on control-line models. Furthermore, while naturally one would normally expect to find the center of gravity or balance point somewhere on a line down the center of the model, the balance point of control-line models usually must be located off center, toward the side of the model on the outside of the circle (usually the right-hand side of the model, standing behind the plane) in order to compensate for the weight and drag of the control lines. This is by no means the only departure from free-flight model plane design practice that is required in the case of control-line models, as described in the following chapter.

Enough has now been said to provide the necessary information for a flying model enthusiast to understand the basic principles and workings of his models, as well as to provide a measure of insight into the very real and com-

Fig. 52. Four balsa-wood, rubber-powered flying models are shown here, framed and ready for the application of the covering material, along with a matching picture showing the appearance of the completed plane. The models shown have 22- to 24-inch wingspans. Top to bottom, a French Nieuport 17, a Stearman PT-17 crop duster, a P-51D Mustang, and a Beechcraft Bonanza.

Sterling Models

plex problems that must confront the designer of any flying model airplane. While a number of control-line models of molded plastic are available in assembled, ready-to-fly form, the majority of these models, as well as virtually all of the free-flight models on the market, are to be had in the form of assembly kits based largely on balsa wood. A few very simple ready-to-fly free-flight model planes and gliders also are available. In virtually

every case, from the simplest stick model to the largest and most complicated jobs, a model plane requires a certain amount of trim and adjustment before a successful flight. In view of what has been said concerning some of the things that enter into the design of model airplanes, it is hoped that the reader will understand the reasoning behind the suggestion now made, that he begin his flying activities either with a ready-to-fly model or with a model built from a standard kit of parts. Designing his own model airplane is, frankly, not for the beginner, fascinating as such a project may be.

Successful model airplane design is not merely a job of drafting a design. It also involves the proper choice of materials; for example, the best type and weight of balsa or other wood for each part. It is an entrancing and complicated subject throughout, for one thing leads to another, and may often, in turn, interact.

For example, in designing a wing for a model airplane, whether to be built as an individual model or as the basis for a successful kit of which many, many thousands may be sold, the serious designer is confronted with the selection of the best grade of wood for each part that will provide the requisite strength and yet produce as light a weight wing as possible. Balsa wood, for example, runs in density from six to sixteen pounds per cubic foot; the heavier the wood, the stronger; the lighter the wood, the softer. The best weight and cut must be ascertained for each part. The wing tip, for instance, may account for a substantial portion of the total volume of wood in a tissue- or fabric-covered wing. yet the weight may be kept down here by using the lightest balsa wood available. On the other hand, strength is required in the spars, and that means a heavier wood. The ribs when totaled also account for a considerable proportionate bulk and should be rigid, so quarter-grain cut balsa, as explained in Chapter 2, may be called for here, but at the same time they should be light lest their total volume bring an excess of weight to the wing. Having concluded his calculations along these lines, the model airplane designer may then take under consideration whether another type of wing construction may not be more desirable for the model in question; perhaps a smaller mainspar with the entire leading edge of the wing covered with thin sheet balsa wood instead of covering the entire wing with tissue or fabric. Careful analysis of the suggested revised design may reveal that such a wing is as strong as, or even stronger than, the original design and may (although at first glance it appears to have far more volume of wood in it) actually be as light as, or even lighter than, the original conception.*

Much the same thinking in other instances

*Solarbo Ltd. of Great Britain have worked out and published some of the most stimulating and helpful data on the use of balsa wood in model airplane design, including elaborate balsa weight charts, and the writer is indebted to them for many of the thoughts expressed here. Their material has appeared in advertisements in the British periodical *Aero Modeller*, but unfortunately, as far as is known, never has been compiled and published in more permanent form.

Fig. 53. Two views of an internal-combustion reciprocating-engine scale model of the Goodyear racer "Buster," suitable for free-flight, control-line, or radio-control flying. This model has a wingspan of 48 inches and is built to a scale of 3 inches to the foot, the prototype having a wingspan of only 16 feet. The photographs clearly show the construction, embodying a molded plastic nose cowl and cheeks.

Sig Mfg. Co., Inc.

would be applied to the relative merits and selection of other woods, to the possible use of balsa in combination with other woods, and so on. The design of a successful model airplane kit, or rather a kit that will build a successful model airplane, is, as can be seen, far from a hit-or-miss game or an exercise in mere intuitiveness. It is a very serious and complex exercise in engineering.

THE MERITS OF KITS

This brings the discussion back once again to the merits of kits of parts for constructing flying model airplanes. With the exception of a certain limited number of kits that contain plastic parts for the major elements of the airplane (many kits today contain some plastic moldings for small parts such as propellers, pilots' canopies, and so on), the typical kit will involve basically wooden materials. In some cases, depending on the type of plane or the designers' particular concepts, the wood will provide only the framing for the plane, and is to be covered with tissue or other suitable material. This is true of most free-flight rubber-powered models. At other times the kit will involve an essential overall wooden construction; sometimes, in smaller planes, a formed or in effect molded wooden construction; sometimes wood to build a profile model; in larger ships usually planking to be applied to a wooden understructure. In most cases the wood in kits will be the model airplane builders' old and familiar friend balsa; in kits for some larger planes of various types there often will be found elements of harder woods, such as spruce, and in some kits, plywood components. The slogan often heard now is "Balsa Flies Better." That is, better than plastics. While indubitably an advertising slogan, this conception may

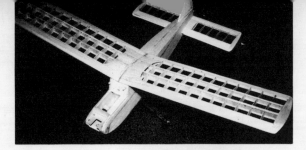

Fig. 54. Constructional details of heavier model airplanes, in this case both radio-control jobs and both with planked balsa-wood fuselages. The upper model has a 48-inch wingspan. The lower pictures show a 38½-inch-wingspan model with wide, solid leading edges on the wings. The finished models are shown below the structural photographs.

Ambroid Co.
C & S Electronics

not be without a considerable measure of truth, particularly when applied to free-flight model airplanes. Certainly it appears that for some time to come, barring the possible unexpected discovery of some more suitable wood or other material, balsa will continue to figure as the primary and most popular material in flying model airplane kits.

Upon first opening a typical construction kit for a free-flight model airplane, the novice's first reaction may well be one of surprise at the small amount of material in the kit from which a plane of fairly substantial size can be constructed. There likely will be a few sheets of balsa, balsa strips, some light tissue paper, a propeller, rubber strand, a tube of cement, a plan and instruction sheet, decalcomanias, and a few odd parts of wood, metal, or plastic. Yet from this seemingly negligible supply of material, if the instructions are followed, can be built a beautiful and competent flying model, a model that will fly great distances and, barring an accident, give indefinite pleasure to its builder. The resulting model will seem, of course, almost feather light. It will, especially to beginners, appear to many to be an astoundingly weak and fragile object. Yet it is a flying model that will perform gloriously in the air, and every spar or brace in its design is purposeful; none have been omitted that are needful; not one of those present is superfluous; none are lighter or weaker than they should be; none are too thick and heavy. The average kit is, in fact, a work of art on the part of the designer.

Meritorious as the kit and the model built from the kit may be for sport flying or for casual flying fun, the question must arise in the minds of many as to the relative value of a model built from a kit in organized contest flying. Does not the fact that a number of models built from the same design kits may compete against each other in a contest rather take all the uncertainty out of any such event, and would not the man who designed his own and possibly superior model stand a better chance of winning? In the main, the answer is No. For one thing, there will almost always be variations in models built by different hobbyists from identical kits. Indeed, there may well be variations in two models constructed from similar kits by the same individual. There are differences in skill in building, differences in the way the model may be trimmed—"trimmed" being used here not as referring to decoration but in its aeronautical sense as pertaining to the balancing and adjusting of a model plane for flight—and differences in flying ability and technique, although the latter factor naturally plays a somewhat bigger role in control-line and radio-control planes that in free-flight models, although not by any means absent from free-flight endeavors. Variations beyond the control of any individual—in the wind and temperature, for instance—may also add to the uncertainties of competition flying.

As for the man who can design his own competitive plane having the best chance in a contest, there may be times when this holds true. How-

Fig. 55. An internal-combustion reciprocating-engine flying model airplane under construction. The fuselage is largely planked. The wing held in the hobbyist's hand has already been covered. The matching wing on the table has not yet had the covering material applied.

Academy of Model Aeronautics

Fig. 56. A largely planked radio-control model, completed and ready for decorating (shown with transmitter). Note how the wing is held on by rubber bands so that in the event of a crash landing it will give way and suffer a minimum of damage. The wing in the upper model in Fig. 54 is also secured by rubber bands.

Aristo-Craft Distinctive Miniatures

ever, it is far from uncommon to find the flyers of models built from kits coming in ahead of the field; in fact this happens far more often than not. One need only examine the lists of wins by given model airplanes built from kits that the manufacturers frequently proudly print in their literature and on the kit boxes to realize how often such planes do win, even in the top competitions. Furthermore, and lastly, if an individual hobbyist designs and builds a new model airplane that proves itself an outstanding contest performer, it is almost certain that the design quickly will be purchased by a manufacturer of model airplane kits and put into production so that kits for building the same model will be on the market and available to all in a fairly short time.

KIT COMPONENTS

There really is no such thing today as what might be termed a "typical kit." Model airplane kits vary greatly not only in the design of the plane they provide the parts for building and in the choice of various kinds and qualities of materials for the various parts but also in the ease with which the kit can be assembled. This in turn depends to some extent on what might be termed the amount of prefabrication that the manufacturer puts into his parts and materials. While the day is past where the kit buyer is supplied with a block of wood and told to carve his propeller from it (although as will be seen shortly certain individuals insist that to get the right propeller they must make it themselves), there is a wide variation in the form in which parts are supplied in kits and in the amount of work that the hobbyist must put into the construction of the model airplane.

Furthermore, inasmuch as building the model is to many as much or almost as much pleasure as flying it, having a kit with only a limited amount of prefabrication is by no means considered a drawback. For many, their chief pleasure lies in the construction of flying models rather than in flying them. The degree of prefabrication of the parts within a kit is therefore in the main not so vital a factor as it might appear at first glance. A highly prefabricated kit can be built up in less time than one in which the individual builder must cut and shape almost everything himself. But there probably is no kit on the market today that is so highly prefabricated that it does not require at least some measure of skill to build a successful flying model from it; there probably is no kit on the market today that requires so much skill to build that the average hobbyist will experience difficulty in constructing a good model from it.

The most important component in every kit is the plan and instruction sheet, or sheets in some of the largest and most elaborate kits. In the case of flying models, the elements of the plane are intended to be built directly over the corresponding drawings on the plan sheet, as will be described shortly. Two very important directions should be followed when using these plan and instruction sheets: *Read everything* on the plan and instruction sheet before taking the first step toward doing any actual assembly work or even any preparation of parts; if the instructions indicate that a certain order should be followed in the assembly of individual parts into units, or of such units into the completed plane, *follow this rotation carefully.*

At times the instructions for assembling a kit will leave certain details or dimensions to the choice of the hobbyist. For example, with a rubber-powered model airplane, it may be optional whether the nose block be cemented permanently in place or made removable so that the rubber may be stretched out before winding, a procedure that allows more turns to be put into the rubber and, consequently, longer flights. On

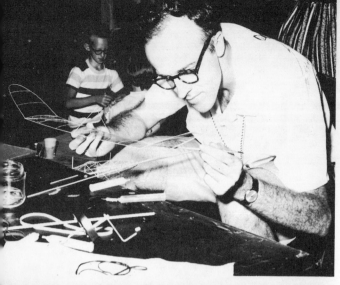
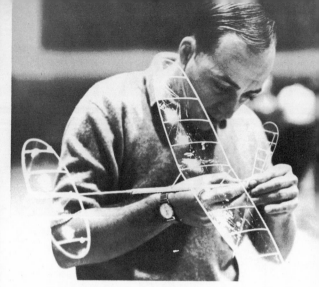
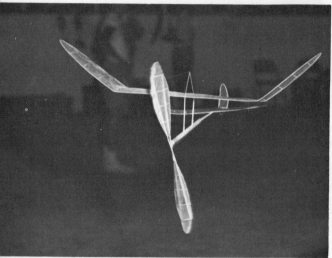

Fig. 57. Microfilm models are rubber-powered models used for flying indoors, with the lifting surfaces and the propellers themselves covered with a specially prepared delicate transparent film. The upper photographs show such a model being assembled and a completed model; at the bottom is a model in flight.

Academy of Model Aeronautics
Hobby Industry Association of America, Inc.
Official Photograph, U.S. Navy

models powered by internal-combustion reciprocating engines the positioning of the engine mounts may require some adjustment in order to accommodate certain engines. Usually any such possible options or adjustments are noted in the instructions or on the plan sheets.

PUTTING KITS TOGETHER

It is unwise to depart, no matter how slightly, from the prepared design. Changes during the construction process can be the cause of stalling and diving. Any distortion or warp acquired during the construction process is a potential hazard, whether the model is the smallest and simplest or the largest and most elaborate. Such things as an incorrectly shaped leading edge on a wing; too small or too large a dihedral angle; a wing on one side that does not match the wing on the other—all these and many similar things can cause trouble. Sometimes faults may be inevitable—for example, no one can wholly guard against warps occurring during the covering process—but many faults can

be avoided during the construction process if due care is exercised.

It is best to proceed methodically and without haste. Also, there is no doubt that many flaws might be avoided during the construction process if the model builder used certain jigs and fixtures to hold and align parts during assembly. Such helps may range from things such as angled hardwood blocks to regulate exactly the dihedral angle in mounting the wings (the value of such devices depends of course on having a smooth and square working surface on which to build the model) to elaborate precision metal devices that can be leveled properly and adjusted to various angles. Sometimes magnetic blocks are used in conjunction with such metal surfaces to hold the various parts in accurate alignment during the construction process. Many expert model airplane builders do make use of aids of this type. The average hobbyist, however, particularly the novice who is interested in turning out a few inexpensive model planes for sport flying, usually does not care to take the time to make such equipment or is in a position to buy the commercial varieties. He relies on his own unassisted dexterity when assembling a model airplane.

Generally, much of the measuring of the material and the actual cementing of various small pieces will be carried out directly on the drawings supplied in the kit. Unlike plans furnished in model-airplane magazines and books, which so often must be either reduced in size or truncated, sometimes full-size drawings for a large assembly, such as a wing or fuselage, must be spread over a number of pages; the plans supplied in kits for assembling flying model airplanes almost invariably are on large sheets that allow each unit to be rendered as a complete full-size drawing. The plan sheet being worked on should be carefully smoothed out and pinned or thumbtacked to the working surface. To protect the plan from picking up cement and also to prevent parts assemblies from sticking to the plan, the surface of the drawings should be covered with waxed paper, carefully pinned or tacked over the plan. Waxed paper has a sufficient transparency to allow the model builder to see all details of the plan clearly.

It is advisable not to do any actual cutting of wood or other materials over the plan in order not to chance cutting the waxed paper and even the plan itself. Material to be cut should be marked carefully for the cuts while held over the plan and then transferred to a separate cutting board to make the actual cuts. Model-building tolerances are so close that the marking should be done whenever possible by making a shallow cut with the knife on the upper surface of the wood rather than attempting to mark with a pencil as one would be likely to do in conventional woodworking. However, many model builders assert that no matter how careful the hobbyist attempts to be in marking for cuts, it is much more accurate to make the cuts over the plans, particularly when cutting strip balsa wood to needed lengths and angles, and that the plans should simply be regarded as expendable in the process.

Unless the flying model is one that uses large areas of preformed or plank balsa as a covering, or in a few cases some other covering material such as metal, the usual means of covering and completing a flying model airplane is with paper or cloth. It is during this covering process that the airframe, no matter how precisely built and aligned, can be subject to warping due to stresses set up in the necessary process of shrinking the covering material to the structure of the airplane.

One further word in regard to the construction of the airframe before proceeding to the matter of covering. This concerns the need of temporarily holding parts to each other, or to the work surface during construction. If tape is called for, this should invariably be artists' masking tape, not electricians' tape or ordinary adhesive tape. If pinning is required, as is more often the case, great care must be exercised so as not to split delicate balsa-wood members during the pinning process, and preferably the pins should be of the thinnest variety obtainable, although most model builders make do quite well with common household pins.

THE COVERING PROCESS

The covering material largely will vary according to the size and purpose of the model. For rubber-powered free-flying models where lightness of overall weight is of the utmost importance, special model airplane tissue that combines relatively great strength with lightness is the standard material. This material is known by various names: Japanese tissue, rice paper, and so on. One important characteristic of this paper is that it has a very definite and noticeable grain. This grain should be taken into account when cutting the tissue for application to the model airplane; the grain should always run parallel to the length of the fuselage and parallel to the leading and trailing edges of the wing. It is quite true that some individual model builders prefer to apply the tissue to the wings with the grain of the tissue running parallel to the fuselage because they feel that when so applied it conforms better to the curves of the airfoil when drying, but this definitely is not recommended practice. The only time it is advisable is when two layers of tissue are applied to a model, which is seldom necessary or desirable. When two layers are used, however, they are applied so that the grain of one layer always runs at right angles to the grain of the other layer. Tissue usually is supplied with the grain running parallel to the long edge of the sheet.

It is difficult to say what is the best material for applying the tissue to the balsa-wood framing. Some model builders and manufacturers advocate using clear model airplane dope just as it comes from the bottle; others to thicken the dope with glue; still others to use the dope as is but to apply dope thinner *over* the tissue at the doped spots and allow it to soak through. Not that model airplane dope is the only substance suggested for applying tissue, but it is so standard and satisfactory that most departures from it must be regarded more or less as conscious efforts to be different. In any case, the dope is applied only to

Fig. 58. The capabilities of rubber-powered model airplanes should not be allowed to be overshadowed by the popularity of models powered by internal-combustion reciprocating engines. This 3-foot-wingspan rubber-powered model is capable of flying a mile in free flight!

Scientific Model Airplane Co.

the wooden members that are to be covered with tissue, gently pulling the tissue taut to eliminate wrinkles and to cover as great an area as possible with a given amount of tissue. A second coat of dope may be applied around the tissue edges. After drying, the excess overlapping tissue is cut away with a modelmaker's knife or razor blade.

The next step is to shrink the tissue by gently spraying on plain water. This should be done once, and to all tissue surfaces at the same time. Because strength of the tissue lies in its dryness, the spraying must be done very carefully and lightly lest it result in breaking the tissue. When the tissue has dried, it will be found that in shrinking it has pulled quite tight and eliminated any remaining minor wrinkles. Never underestimate the power of the shrinking tissue to warp portions of the model, especially wings and tail surfaces. Such warping seriously affects the flying caliber of the model, and the plane should be carefully examined after applying tissue in order to detect such warps. The accepted procedure for removing such warps is to hold the model over a teakettle under which the heat has just been turned down from a full boil so that the steam is just lazily flowing out of the spout. When the tissue covering is seen to relax, the warped portion is very carefully twisted by hand until the warp is removed and then held in position in the hands and away from the steam until the tissue is taut again. While this procedure might seem makeshift, making as it does the accuracy of important surfaces depend entirely on the eye and hand, it is the best solution that the model airplane hobby has been able to come up with in all these years, and, when carefully carried out, it works.

After the tissue has been applied, shrunk, and dried and any warps presumably corrected, the entire tissue surface of the model should be covered with clear dope to protect the tissue from moisture. Again there is a vast area of disagreement as to the state in which the dope should be applied: exactly as it comes from the bottle or thinned, and if thinned, how much, and whether there should be one or more than one coat; if more than one, how many? When in doubt, fol-

low the recommendations of the manufacturer in his instructions. However, it should be noted that the purpose of doping in a flying model is to produce a comparatively strong and moisture-resistant surface. In a rubber-powered model dope applied, the more weight will be added. If desired, colored dope may be applied to such models in place of clear dope. The newcomer to the hobby, having seen beautifully finished model airplanes of various types, including nonoperating display models and control-line models, frequently is discontented with the somewhat bare and bleak appearance of rubber-powered models finished with clear dope, with much of the ribbing and skeleton of the plane showing through. He should bear in mind that the prime requisite of such models is their performance in the air, which is enhanced by doping as lightly as possible to attain the desired sealing.

From the lightest tissue used on rubber-powered models and on some very small models powered by internal-combustion reciprocating engines, the model builder can work up through various other covering materials customarily used on larger models. Silk has for many years been held in perhaps the highest esteem, although nylon has also become a favorite in recent years. Then there are available a number of paper and fabric covering materials, usually merchandised under a trade name that ends with the word "span." Some of these materials are intended to be applied dry; others can be applied wet or dry.

Whatever covering material is applied, and whether it is put on wet or dry, constant vigilance is necessary to guard against warping as the covering material dries and shrinks. One way to cut down on this is never to dope one side of a wing or tail surface completely before doping the other side, but rather to work alternately on each side of the model. For example, dope a certain area on the right-hand side of a wing, and then immediately dope the corresponding area on the left-hand side before applying more dope to the right-hand side. Dope also is applied to wooden surfaces to act as a sealer, although there are special wooden filler and sealer materials available for the job. With many large models that may involve both fabric-covered and planked areas, model builders often cover the planked areas as well with silk or other covering material to produce an attractive, uniform, and airworthy finish. Again, the manufacturer's own instructions and suggestions on finishing a given kit may well be regarded as the best guide by the builder, especially the novice. To convey an idea of just how many steps and processes may be necessary or desirable on some of the larger flying models, the following is drawn, with some slight modifications to eliminate trade names, from the instructions for a sixty-inch wingspan stunt model suitable for engines up to the largest size currently recognized for regular competitions:

1: Apply one coat of balsa fillercoat to the entire model.

2: Sand with No. 320 wet or dry sandpaper (use dry).

3: Apply one to three coats of fillercoat over hinges and rough places, sanding with 320 W or D between coats.

4: Cover wing surface with heavy paper and the remainder of the model with a lighter-weight paper (cover wet).

5: Allow paper to dry completely; then dope with clear dope until paper begins to gloss (about three coats).

6: Sand rough spots, edges, and blemishes with 400 W or D sandpaper.

7: Brush on one coat of clear dope (add ten drops of castor oil to a pint to prevent excessive drawing).

8. Add one or two balsa fillercoats to entire model (thinned down) and sand smooth with 400 W or D between coats.

9: Apply additional coat of clear dope.

10: Add one or two coats of colored dope to entire model.

11: Mask areas to be trimmed and clear dope inside edge of trim to prevent color seepage.

12: Add one to three coats of colored trim as required.

13: Apply three to eight coats of clear dope (the more, the better).

14: Sand with 600 W or D after dope has dried at least overnight or longer.

15: Rub out with a fine grit rubbing compound and then wax the entire model with automobile wax.

The result? Undeniably an exceptionally beautifully and handsomely finished model, equally undeniably attained only at the expense of a great deal of effort. In employing any combination of finishing materials on a job of this type—clear dope, colored dope, fillercoat—it is of vital importance for the model builder to make sure that all these things are compatible. Dopes and related liquids vary as to type and base. To use one type of clear dope (type, not necessarily brand) and another type of colored dope may produce chemical reactions that will endanger a good finish and may cause one coat to "lift" and not properly adhere to another coat. The builder of rubber-powered models does not have to be concerned with the type of dope used so long as two incompatible types are not overlaid, which seldom would occur in the construction of such models anyhow. In the case of building model planes powered by internal-combustion reciprocating engines, another element enters into the picture, namely, the damage that can be done to a finish by engine fuel splattering or otherwise reaching the covering, a condition that virtually is impossible to avoid when a model airplane is flown. The builder of such models must therefore be careful to employ fuel-proof dope, generally known as "hot fuel proof" or else a separate fuel proofer applied over ordinary dope.

MICROFILM MODELS

It is a far cry from the tough, enduring covering and finish attained with the fifteen steps outlined above to the most delicate of all forms of covering, microfilm. The fragility of microfilm covering is such as to make the lightest of

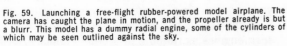

Fig. 59. Launching a free-flight rubber-powered model airplane. The camera has caught the plane in motion, and the propeller already is but a blurr. This model has a dummy radial engine, some of the cylinders of which may be seen outlined against the sky.

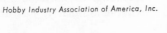

Hobby Industry Association of America, Inc.

tissue coverings seem almost as of sheet metal in strength by comparison. Yet countless microfilm model airplanes are built, handled, and flown, and this is the preferred mode of covering modern models used in indoor flying, although its use goes back to the early 1930's at least. Actually microfilm is perhaps only half the weight of the lightest tissue, but it is so thin that it cannot be touched by hand and at first the process of making and applying it appears so delicate and difficult as to present problems that might appear akin to attempting to remove a spider's web intact. However, with a little practice, any hobbyist can become quite adept in the techniques of microfilm.

Microfilm is made by allowing chemicals to set on top of water and form a film. The film is then transferred to an extremely light balsa-wood framework, either by having the frame under the water in which the microfilm is formed and lifting the frame upward so as to bring it forth covered with the microfilm, or by using a wire loop to lift the microfilm and bring it to the framework. Microfilm is not made from any one substance or combination of substances. Acceptable microfilm may be made by floating any number of substances or combinations on the water: rubber cement, clear lacquer and castor oil, wood alcohol, and so on. Two specific formulas are a 3:1 ratio of collodion and liquid ether or one drop of castor oil to each quarter ounce of clear metal lacquer. Of critical importance in most microfilm production is the temperature of the room in which the work is performed and of the materials, water and microfilm solution proper. An ideal mode of procedure would be to place the water and the solution in the room where the work is to be performed some hours beforehand so that everything will be at the same temperature. In removing microfilm from the surface of the water, it should not be lifted straight up but rather slowly slid off sideways. Because microfilm has the tendency to cling to the surface of the water and to require this sliding motion to minimize the possibility of this adhesion to break the microfilm, present-day practice leans toward removing the microfilm with a wire loop and then applying it to the framework of the plane that previously has been moistened with water or with a solution made up of a teaspoon of sugar dissolved in a pint of water to receive it. The easiest answer to the problem of microfilm solution is to purchase it in prepared form as supplied by model airplane supply houses.

The propellers on microfilm models designed for endurance flights customarily are not made of solid stock (although very light balsa-wood propellers often are used for training or sports flying)

but are built with a framework of extremely thin balsa-wood strips that are overlaid with microfilm. The propellers for microfilm models, which are of course always powered with rubber, usually are extremely large in proportion to the model—far larger than would be propellers on outdoor models of similar wingspans. The drag of such large propellers tends to slow down the unwinding of the rubber. The result is that microfilm models fly very slowly and often stay up in the air what seems, comparatively speaking, as astounding length of time.

PROPELLERS

Essential to the efficient operation of any airplane is a propeller or propellers of the proper size and design. As already observed, the propeller long has been known in Great Britain by the more descriptive name of airscrew. Thus the function of the propeller is to the screw forward through the air and convert the energy of the power source, which is delivered in the form of rotary motion, into forward motion or thrust. Much confusion exists, and is not necessarily confined to beginners, concerning right- and left-hand propellers and the terms some manufacturers use in regard to their propellers of "tractor" and "pusher" types, that is to say, propellers that are used at the front and at the rear, respectively, of aircraft.

Such confusion can quickly be dispelled once three important facts are understood. One is that right- and left-hand and clockwise and counterclockwise are always relative terms. When two men stand facing each other, what is right-hand to one is left-hand to the other: what is a clockwise direction to one is counterclockwise to the other. The second is that what properly is the right-hand side of any vehicle is determined by the right-hand side of the driver—in the case of an airplane the pilot—as he sits facing the direction of travel. The third is that while a rubber-powered model airplane can be wound in either direction, so that when unwinding the propeller will revolve in a direction opposite to winding, most miniature internal-combustion engines will operate in one direction only. When mounted in an airplane, the engine usually operates in what is a right-hand or clockwise direction as viewed from the pilot's seat. However, as the miniature engine usually is started by someone standing in front of the engine and flipping the propeller, instructions usually are given to flip it in a counterclockwise direction, and consequently it is common practice to speak of such engines as running in a counterclockwise direction. Similarly, instructions for flying rubber-powered models usually indicate that the engine be wound by moving the propeller in a clockwise direction, while the man doing the winding is looking at the model. This means that when the propeller is released, it runs in a counterclockwise direction when one faces the model, the same as the aforementioned internal-combustion reciprocating engine. From an aeronautical standpoint, both of these propellers are running in a right-hand, or clockwise direction when viewed from the pilot's seat, and both propellers would be right-hand propellers. Whether a propeller is right- or left-hand always is determined by the direction in which it moves when viewed from the rear or concave side. Properly speaking, propellers can be classified only as right-hand or left-hand, not as "tractor" or "pusher"; the reason is this:

Take a rubber-powered model with a right-hand propeller. Stand facing it, wind the rubber by turning the propeller in a clockwise direction as before; release it and it moves counterclockwise when viewed from the front but in a right-hand or clockwise position when viewed from the pilot's seat. Take a rubber-powered pusher-type airplane and mount the same right-hand propeller. The winding position now is behind the plane, and the hobbyist who does the winding is facing in the same direction as the imaginary pilot; the hobbyist's right hand now is on the same side as the pilot. The rubber in this case is wound by moving the propeller in a counterclockwise, or left-hand, movement; release the propeller and it moves in what is a clockwise, or right-hand, movement both to the imaginary pilot and to the hobbyist.

You cannot do quite the same thing with miniature internal-combustion reciprocating engines, however, because such engines have a shaft at only one end and in most cases the engine will run in only one direction: counterclockwise as you face it. In comparison it might be said that the rubber-power mechanism represents an engine with a shaft at each end. When the internal-combustion reciprocating engine is placed in a tractor position, the shaft turns in the correct direction for a right-hand propeller to thrust. When the same engine is placed in a pusher position, the shaft will turn only in the opposite direction; a right-hand propeller will not screw forward into the air. In fact, its tendency will be to thrust toward the rear. Consequently, with an internal-combustion reciprocating engine mounted in the pusher position, a left-hand propeller is necessary in order to attain the required forward thrust, hence the custom of designating propellers for internal-combustion-engine use as "tractor" and "pusher" propellers respectively, actually right- and left-hand. Within a

framework of reference confined to internal-combustion reciprocating engines the "tractor" and "pusher" terminology is adequate, but only within such limitations. The terms have no validity within model aviation as a whole. With a rubber-powered model you can just as readily put a left-hand propeller in a tractor position; and so long as the hobbyist remembers to wind his rubber by turning the propeller in a counterclockwise position while he faces the plane, it will upon being released screw forward into air just as efficiently as would a right-hand propeller. As a matter of fact, when twin propellers are used on a rubber-powered model, a situation not met with too often nowadays but one quite common in an earlier era of model aviation, one right-hand and one left-hand propeller almost always are used, regardless of whether the propellers are in a tractor or a pusher position. In this manner the directional pull of each propeller exactly compensates for that of the other.

PROPELLER SIZES AND PITCH

A propeller may be regarded essentially as a screw having a very large helical dimension. The diameter of any propeller is an obvious dimension, but a second measurement always is given in describing propellers: pitch. Pitch represents the distance a given propeller will move forward in one complete revolution if operating at 100 percent efficiency, and obviously depends on the contouring of the curved portions of the blades. A propeller with a 4-inch pitch would theoretically move forward 4 inches in one revolution, regardless of whether the diameter was 4 inches, 6 inches, or 8 inches. In actual practice the stipulation is only theoretically important because few if any model airplane propellers ever are operated at 100 percent efficiency, and many model propellers, especially on rubber-powered models, probably normally operate at substantially less than 50 percent efficiency. However, as pitch is an important factor in the selection of a proper propeller for a model aircraft, it is necessary to take the figures for what they are worth, as computed, as the only practical yardstick available. In any event, in model airplane propeller designations the first figure indicates the diameter in inches and the second figure the pitch in inches. Thus a 4-2½ or 4×2½ propeller would be one with a diameter of 4 inches and a pitch of 2½ inches; an 8-5 or 8×5 propeller would have a diameter of 8 inches and a pitch of 5 inches.

The selection of the best size and pitch propeller for a given plane always presents difficulties and very often can be satisfactorily solved only

Fig. 60. Putting more power into a rubber model by stretching the rubber out while winding. This is a two-man job, made easier in this case by employing a hand drill as a winding tool.

Official Photograph, U.S. Navy

through experimenting with propellers of different sizes and pitches until the best propeller for a given plane and purpose is determined. Of course, the purpose for which a given model airplane is to be used is usually determined by the design of the model itself. In the case of ready-to-fly models and kits for building rubber-powered models that include a propeller, it may be assumed that the manufacturer has provided a satisfactory and perhaps the best all-around unit. A great deal can, however, be learned about propellers, flying, and model airplane performance by experimenting with different propellers. In kits designed for internal-combustion reciprocating engines the manufacturer of the kit may suggest recommended propeller sizes and propeller and engine combinations. The makers of engines also may make recommendations of their own. However, there are so many variables in connection with both plane and engine design, as well as in combining a given engine with a given plane, that such recommendations often must be regarded more as a starting point for experimentation than as a final solution.

Propeller diameter and pitch may vary considerably according to the type of flying that is to be done, as well as the type of power, and not all hobbyists agree on the precise sequence and degree of variation, although in a general way the more powerful the type of engine, the smaller the propeller diameter and pitch. Thus, models powered by internal-combustion reciprocating engines use smaller diameter and pitch propellers than do out-

door rubber-powered models, and outdoor rubber-powered models usually have smaller diameter and pitch propellers than do indoor rubber-powered models. In the case of internal-combustion reciprocating engines, if running in on a bench is advocated before any attempt to use the engine in flight, a larger-diameter propeller usually, but not always, is employed than when the engine is flown in a plane. Simply to give an idea of how recommended propeller diameter and pitch may vary, one manufacturer of an .09 (1.49 cubic centimeter) diesel engine recommends the following propellers:

Running in 9×4
Free flight 8×4
Control line 7×5

On a similar .06 (1 cubic centimeter) diesel, an engine of approximately two-thirds the displacement of the one above, the same manufacturer's recommendations are:

Running in 8×3
Free flight 8×4
Control line 7×5

Only the propeller size for running in is changed, and the reduction is slight. It is possible to learn a great deal about engines, flying, and propellers merely by studying these two set of figures. They tell us that while the power varies substantially between two engines, it does not follow that it is either necessary or desirable to regulate propeller size and pitch solely on the basis of engine power.

MORE ABOUT PROPELLERS

What does more importantly affect propeller size and pitch is the purpose for which the engine is to be used. These figures follow the usual conception that with a given engine a control-line model-airplane would have a propeller with a smaller diameter and a greater pitch than with a free-flight model, but this too can never be regarded as a hard-and-fast rule. It should be noted also that a 7×5 or an 8×4 propeller would be regarded as having a more or less medium pitch for these diameters when used with internal-combustion reciprocating engines; for rubber power the pitches would run much higher and the propellers would still be rated as having a medium pitch, say, 9- or 10-inch pitches for propellers of these diameters. On indoor models the pitches would rise much higher and still be considered medium; in fact a 7- or 8-inch-diameter propeller would be rather unusual on an indoor model, where diame-

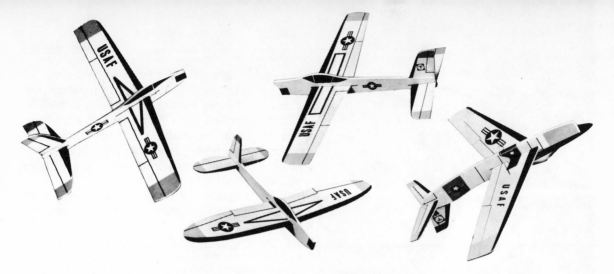

Fig. 61. Inexpensive solid balsa-wood gliders. These brightly decorated models are readily assembled, and require putting together only a few pieces of wood. The model at the lower right is intended for operation on a control line.

Testor Corp.

ters might run up to 20 inches or more and pitches perhaps to 40 inches or even more.

Let us return to the aforementioned .09 (1.49 cubic centimeter) diesel and see if we cannot learn something more about propellers from the engineering data supplied by the manufacturer in the form of a copy of a report that appeared in the British magazine *Aero Modeller,* where the engine was tested as to revolutions per minute with propellers of various diameters and pitches and of various makes. Using propellers of the same diameter and pitch, but of different makes, there is one instance where two propellers of the same diameter and pitch but of different makes ran at the identical rpm. However, there are several instances where using a propeller of different make but of the same diameter and pitch gave variations of from 200 rpm to as much as 1,000 rpm. Obviously, then, diameter and pitch alone are not the only things to be considered in propeller selection —the general form of the propeller, the shaping of the airfoil (this same word applies to propeller sections as well as to airplane lifting surfaces)— and material from which the propeller is made and the caliber of the workmanship, particularly the accuracy with which a propeller is balanced, all must be taken into consideration in propeller experimentation and selection.

Some hobbyists attempt to test every propeller for balance and to balance any that are found to some degree wanting in this respect. A poorly balanced propeller can vibrate in flight, creating serious problems. Like any object that revolves at a high rate of speed, it should be balanced. However, any sort of balancing job, whether of a model airplane propeller, an electric motor armature, or any other device, is a ticklish job for most hobbyists and one in which there usually is more chance of worsening than of improving the situation.

Ready-made model airplane propellers are supposedly checked for balance at the factory and any that are found wanting withheld from sale. Upon finding he has somehow received a propeller that is badly out of balance, the average hobbyist is advised to return it to his dealer or stock list and exchange it for a good one rather than try to balance it himself either by attempting to shave material from a blade that is too heavy or by adding weight in the form of paint or dope to a blade that is too light. The expert model builder; who may in some cases prefer to make his own propellers and must therefore of necessity balance them, can be left to make his own decisions regarding attempts to balance commercial propellers. The trouble with all modelmaking balancing processes is that the act of balancing always has a certain aura of the spectacular about it, especially when performed before an audience, and carries with it such an air of professionalism that many hobbyists are attracted to making the attempt rather than undertake the far easier and logical course simply of exchanging a poorly balanced propeller.

In continuing the discussion of propellers, it should be mentioned that pitch plays still another role in free-flight model airplanes in addition to that already mentioned. To a certain extent whether a high- or low-pitch propeller is used affects the turning radius of a model airplane. Assuming that right-hand propellers are employed, with a free-flight model that is adjusted normally to turn to the right, a high-pitch propeller will increase the turning radius and a low-pitch propeller will reduce the turning radius. With a plane adjusted normally to turn to the left, a low-pitch propeller will increase the turning radius and a high-pitch propeller will reduce it. Remember, this is with a right-hand propeller. With a left-hand propeller the exact reverse would hold true. While

Fig. 62. Molded plastic gliders representing jet airplanes (a Chance Vought F7U-3 Cutlass in the upper photograph and a Convair F102) that are designed to be launched from rubber slings.

Gladen Enterprises, Inc.

most model airplane propellers have a fixed pitch, it also is possible to obtain adjustable or multipitch propellers for models powered by internal-combustion reciprocating engines. Such propellers allow the blades to be loosened, turned to any desired pitch as marked on indexes on the hub, and then locked in the new position. Such propellers allow the hobbyist to adjust the propeller until the pitch is matched to the plane and engine combination so as to secure the best possible performance.

Most model airplane propellers are made of wood or molded plastic and have two blades. A certain number of three-blade propellers also are available in ready-to-use form as well. It is quite possible to have a practical propeller with only one blade, but then it is necessary to have a metal counterweight to the blade, and such devices can be quite dangerous, are outlawed at all regular meets, and should be left strictly alone, as should all-metal propellers. There exists considerable debate in model airplane circles as to the relative merits of wood and plastic propellers. Plastic propellers, being more flexible, are less likely to break in imperfect landings. There always exists a considerable danger of breaking or at least damaging a propeller when a model airplane lands, and the prudent flyer will always provide himself with extras. When wood is used, balsa wood generally is employed for rubber-powered models, but harder woods are used for the propellers of models

powered by internal-combustion reciprocating engines; in both types suitable plastic propellers provide a satisfactory alternative for many hobbyists. Plastic propellers must be molded of more substantial plastic material for internal-combustion-reciprocating-engine power than for rubber, as the number of revolutions per minute is much higher with the former than with the latter.

Some builders of rubber-powered models go in for folding propellers or free-wheeling propellers, in order that when the power store in the rubber runs out the propeller cannot possibly stop in a position that would destroy the balance of a delicately balanced craft and send it into a dive instead of the desired gradual glide to bring it down. Such devices are ingenious but usually tricky and delicate, both in construction and in performance. As far as is known, nothing of this nature is available ready made, and the hobbyist who wishes such a device must construct it on his own. A folding propeller must be arranged so that when the rubber power ends, the force of the wind will be sufficient to push and hold the hinged blades back along the fuselage. With a freewheeling propeller, a clever device automatically declutches the propeller from the rubber-powered drive shaft when the power is exhausted, and the propeller is then free to turn harmlessly as the wind directs while the model descends in a glide.

Little need be said here concerning the art of the hobbyist making his own propellers. Years ago propeller making was an almost universal practice among model airplane enthusiasts, and the hobbyist accounted himself fortunate when he was provided with a roughly preshaped propeller blank on which to do his final shaping and smoothing. With the advent of plastic propellers, practically every kit, even the simplest and most inexpensive, is provided with a ready-to-use propeller, and a very wide variety of finished propellers are available separately. In a way this is unfortunate, for propeller making was never quite so arduous a task as it may seem to those who have never essayed it. On the other hand, in former days a good part of the time involved in building a model might well go into the making of a satisfactory propeller. Today propeller making is largely confined to those who wish to experiment with special shapes, to those who take pleasure in making as much of a model themselves as is possible, and to a group of enthusiasts who feel, rightly or wrongly, that an individual hobbyist can produce a better propeller than a factory. In making a propeller the essential points are not the shaping and finishing of the blades—for most hobbyists can produce a propeller that will fly a model, after a fashion at least—so much as to be sure that the shaft hole is drilled square and is exactly centered in the hub.

RUBBER POWER

The rubber strand in a rubber-powered model airplane (never refer to it in the hearing of a model enthusiast as a "rubber band") has for decades proved itself a highly satisfactory mode of powering model aircraft. Theoretically it will put out as much energy as has been stored up in it in the winding process. Undoubtedly some of this energy is lost, but the fact remains that the rubber can be made to deliver a very satisfactory amount of power and that to a large extent this power varies both with the care with which the rubber is treated and the method by which the power is put into it. On the other hand, care must be used not to put too much power into the rubber so as to go beyond its inherent limit of elasticity. Rubber also has its natural enemies and must be protected from them: heat, oil, dust, sunlight. It goes without saying that the use of the best grades of model airplane rubber will always pay off in performance. Model airplane rubber today usually is furnished in the form of strips of different widths, ⅛th inch, 3/16th inch, and so on, but the thickness more or less remains constant and does not increase with the width. A single length of rubber seldom is used in a model airplane, but rather the length of rubber is looped back and forth several times in loops between the holding hook at one end of the fuselage and the hook on the propeller at the other. Thus, if the distance between hooks is 15 inches, a length of rubber a little more than 30 inches long, looped once, will provide two strands; a 60-inch-long piece of rubber will loop twice to provide four strands, and a 90-inch-long piece will loop three times, making six strands. Years ago model airplane builders frequently looped enormous lengths of rubber into great multiples of strands, but this seldom is done nowadays and with today's model airplane designs seems uncalled for. While the ends of the rubber can be pierced so as to slip over the hook, this is not a very satisfactory method, and the best procedure is to tie the ends of the rubber to the hook, or to the round dowel that is used in place of a rear hook in many modern models. A little slack should always be left in the rubber strands as installed in the airplane.

The rubber should never be wound to its full capacity on the first windings. Rather, the rubber should be broken in gradually, say, 25 turns on the first winding, 50 on the second, 75 on the third, and so on, until the maximum safe number has been reached. A great many more turns, with re-

Fig. 63. The proper method of hand-launching a typical balsa-wood model glider. The glider is, in effect, thrown. It shou'd be held in a banked position of 45 degrees or more, with the nose pointed up at an angle of from 45 to 40 degrees.

North Pacific Products Co.

sulting greater power and longer flights, can be put into the rubber if it is stretched before winding after it has been broken in. This type of winding can be performed if the model airplane has been built with a removable nose block. One hobbyist holds the airplane while a second faces it and steps back holding the propeller and nose block assembly until the rubber is stretched to two to three times its normal length. It is then wound, with the hobbyist doing the winding slowly moving toward the model as he winds, until the maximum number of turns have been put into the rubber and the nose block is back in its flight position. When the rubber is thus stretched for winding, it is usual and far more convenient to use a special model airplane rubber winder, or a device converted from a hand drill or an eggbeater, than to wind by moving the propeller around by hand; in addition, more turns can be put into the winding with such a mechanical device.

The rubber should be lubricated so that the various strands will slip over each other easily in winding and unwinding. Oil or grease, which deteriorate rubber, should obviously never be used as a lubricant for model airplane rubbers, although a drop of oil may be placed on the propeller thrust washer, positioned between the propeller and the nose block and not in contact with the rubber. Nor, even with the propeller lubricant for rubber, should any lubricant ever be allowed to go on the knotted

Fig. 64. This is called a "Glite," or gliding kite. It may be flown on a string as a kite, either with or without a tail. It may also be flown as a glider, or may be operated on dual-control lines as an aerial stunter in a manner similar to the method employed with control-line model airplanes.

North Pacific Products Co.

ends that hold the ends of the rubber to the hook or post, lest they allow these knots to slip and open. The usual lubricants for model airplane rubber are glycerin and soap, or a combination of both. Household cleaning soaps or detergents should never be used. Shavings of hand soap may be boiled in a little water to make a thick solution to be mixed with glycerin, but green soap may be purchased in liquid form to eliminate this process. The usual mixture of soap and glycerin is 50:50, although some enthusiasts advocate increasing the proportion of glycerin to as much as two parts of glycerin to one of soap when the weather is warm; others use glycerin only. It also is possible to obtain prepared lubricant for rubber models from hobby shops and model airplane supply houses. The lubricant is applied by rubbing a few drops into the rubber, and wiping off any excess.

A great deal has been said and written concerning the further care of model airplane rubber. It should be remembered that the requirements of the hobbyist who regularly engages in contests, as well as the time he is prepared to put into the care of rubber, may differ materially from those of the average sports flyer. Some fans wash and dry the rubber strand after every use, remove it and store it in special light-proof containers and, in fact, often possess multiple rubber assemblies for a given model airplane. At the time the writer built his first flying models it was the custom to advise that the rubber always be removed from the model and stored away in a dark box after dusting it with talcum powder. The average hobbyist seldom is inclined to go to these lengths, and if we are to be candid about the matter, in most cases the rubber is allowed to remain in the plane and receives no attention other than lubrication. Naturally, in time all rubber deteriorates or tires and must be replaced with new rubber. The prudent hobbyist will examine his rubber frequently for signs of deterioration that might result in breakage either during the winding process or in flight. Actually, when rubber goes it is more likely to break during winding than in flight, but the results of a wildly flapping rubber strand released inside a lightly constructed model can be disastrous.

Another form of rubber, rubber bands, is often used to properly align and secure the wings of model airplanes. In examining the illustrations in this book it will be observed that a number of the models pictured employ this construction. The purpose is to protect the model in the event of a rough landing or an outright crash. In such cases a wing permanently secured to the fuselage might well break and perhaps damage the fuselage at the same time. With the wing held by rubber bands—which if employed in a properly designed assembly provide a quite secure structure for flight, even with fairly heavy planes—the wing gives rather than breaks, and if the crash is accompanied by considerable force the rubber bands will break, releasing the wing, before the wing itself is seriously damaged. At times a similar rubber band mounted assembly will be used in small internal-combustion-reciprocating-engine planes for the entire engine mounting assembly. Again the idea is that in a crash the rubber bands will take the stress and give or break, protecting the engine assembly and plane from major damage.

LANDING GEAR

In a good landing, a model airplane should of course come down in its glide in such a way as to alight on its landing wheels (or on its floats, if a seaplane), the front wheels hitting the earth first and taking up the shock of landing. One factor that tends to act against this ideal condition taking place, and the cause of so many broken propellers, is that the propellers on many models are so oversized in comparison to the plane that if the propeller stops in or near a vertical position the lower tip of the propeller is likely to strike the ground before the front wheels touch or the tail goes down. (Here, again, just how perfectly the model has been balanced and adjusted plays a part.) The landing gear on smaller models is usually very simple, formed of springy wire that serves as a

shock absorber and wheel mount in one unit. Another point to be mentioned is that frequently the
wheels on such landing gear do not turn freely
upon making contact with the ground, sometimes
because the bearings have become clogged with
dust and grime, but more often because the force
with which the model touches down after a slow
glide is not sufficient to force the wheels to overcome the resistance of rough earth or grass. The
landing effect then is that of the model sliding as if
on skids, and indeed many early models were built
with skids for landing instead of wheels. This is not
to say that there are not many models that repeatedly make perfect three-point landings, with the
wheels functioning just as they should. The small
tail wheel is more likely to become stuck than the
larger wheels and to act simply as a skid. Consequently many models are built with a tail skid instead of a tail wheel. There also are models whose
design calls for a single large wheel at the front, almost under the nose, which takes the initial landing
shock, and two fairly large wheels somewhat
farther back, usually under the wing.

Larger and heavier models often are built
with more prepossessing landing gear, including
units with coil springs and sometimes even real
miniature working brakes. Rubber tires are employed, including sponge wheels, semipneumatic
wheels, and even inflatable air wheels. The tire and
wheel usually are made as a single unit, hence the
terminology designating these parts as wheels rather than as tires alone. On the most elaborate radio-
control models, extremely interesting and realistic
things sometimes are done with the landing gear.
In some cases it is made steerable by radio control,
so that the model airplanes can be made to taxi

over the field in any direction desired. At times
radio-controlled retractable landing gear is installed, so that the wheels and landing gear are
drawn up into the plane when it becomes airborne,
and are lowered into position again preparatory
to landing.

Several types of models customarily are made
without any landing gear whatsoever. These include some of the very simplest and most inexpensive rubber-powered models, control-line speed
models, and all types of gliders and sailplanes.

GLIDERS AND SAILPLANES

It has long been customary, and it is a good
custom, to suggest that anyone interested in flying
models undertake his (or her) first experiments
with a simple glider. This is excellent advice, but
unfortunately it has been heard so often that it has
to some extent conveyed to many an erroneous idea
that all model gliders are simple and that their use
is confined solely to preliminary steps in model
flying. Nothing could be further from the case, for
building and flying model gliders can be and is to
many a rewarding hobby in itself on a highly advanced level, and there are several recognized
classes of glider competition, both indoors and
outdoors. A glider is a craft similar in general
design to an airplane, but without any source of
power, whose climbing ability depends on finding
and taking advantage of rising air currents, or
thermals. It is more difficult to define accurately
the differences, if indeed there properly be any,
between a large glider, a sailplane, or what sometimes is known as a high-performance glider. Suffice
it to say that these may for practical purposes be

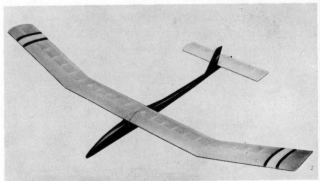

Fig. 65. Two prepossessing model gliders of balsa wood with tissue-
covered lifting surfaces. The wings on both models are detachable and
are secured in position with rubber bands. The model on the left has a
wingspan of 47 inches and the towline glider below has a 41-inch
wingspan.

C. A. Zaic Co., Inc.
Ambroid Co.

considered substantially the same thing, usually launched with a towline and constructed with a tissue-covered wooden framework to a large extent resembling that of most rubber-powered models.

Inasmuch as it is desirable that every free-flight model airplane, once the power is exhausted, descend to earth in a gentle glide, it is apparent that every would-be model flyer can learn much that is practical in reference to powered models by building and studying gliders. The glider or powered airplane in a glide is attracted toward earth by gravity. The path it follows down is known as the glide path, usually in properly adjusted models a fairly wide circle, and the distance covered in the glide from the moment the model goes into its glide until it touches ground is known, somewhat confusingly, as the radius of glide. Ratio of glide refers to the ratio of the radius of the glide to the height at which the plane was when it started its glide. Thus if a model started to glide at an altitude of 200 feet and glided for 1,000 feet (radius of glide) before it landed, the ratio of glide is 5 : 1. If a plane started to glide when at an altitude of 200 feet and the radius of glide was 1,500 feet, the ratio of glide would be 7½ : 1.

It is desirable that a powered model glide back to earth as soon as the power ceases; it is conceivable that a model might glide so well and run into such thermals that its glide could carry it in the air for a considerable length of time and a considerable distance. However, the balance of most powered models is such that they usually glide down fairly directly and rapidly; the choice usually is between a proper glide and, if luck runs ill or the plane was not properly balanced, a dive that will crash the plane. With a glider per se, on the other hand, the object is to catch the thermals as much as possible and climb on them as high as is possible before the glider is brought down. Usually in competition, the object is not the altitude reached by the glider but the length of time it will sustain itself in the air.

Gliders are launched by one of three methods: hand-launching, catapult, or towline. The first two usually are employed for the small, solid-wing gliders of balsa wood or molded plastic. In hand-launching the glider is held as level as possible and thrown into flight from the hand of the hobbyist. In catapult launching a glider is launched by stretching a rubber launcher attached to the nose of the model as far as possible and then releasing the glider. Larger model gliders must be launched from a towline. Such models may have a solid balsa construction, but more often the wing is of tissue-covered construction, sometimes with a stick fuselage; sometimes with a built-up and tissue-covered fuselage. A towline glider is launched with a string, much as is a kite, but is arranged so that the string detaches after the model becomes airborne. For the best results it is desirable that two hobbyists participate in the launching, although towline gliders have at times successfully been launched by a single individual. In the usual procedure, one hobbyist holds the glider facing about 20 degrees to windward. The towline, usually 100-foot length in the United States and 50 meters (a little over 150 feet) in Great Britain, is attached to the keel of the glider by an open hook. The free end of the towline is taken in the hand of the second hobbyist, who then moves forward at a brisk speed. The man holding the glider releases it as the cord is played out and the man holding the cord continues forward, turning the glider so that it heads into the wind. When the glider is almost overhead the man with the towline slows down and allows the line to go slack so that it automatically disengages from the hook on the glider and falls to earth, while the glider, it is hoped, soars away. All types of gliders may require considerable adjustment, balancing, and likely the addition of ballast before they perform at a peak level.

The glider should never be sold short. It has an enduring allure and attraction of its own, entirely apart from its value as a preliminary step in gaining valuable flying experience. Large and elaborate gliders have been built containing radio control receivers so that if they glided so high or so far as to be lost, a radio signal could be dispatched to trigger a mechanism to alter the balance of the craft and force it to glide back to earth.

By the same token, the smaller, simpler, and least-expensive rubber-powered model airplanes, whether furnished ready-to-fly or in kit form, never should be underrated. Not only are they capable of providing almost endless pleasure in themselves, but flying them provides knowledge and experience that will prove of the greatest value in all further ventures in model aviation, whether free flight, rubber, or internal-combustion-reciprocating-engine power, control line, or radio control.

FLIGHT LIMITATION AND MODEL RECOVERY

No one wants to lose a model airplane on which time and effort have been lavished and which has provided the builder with a substantial amount of enjoyment. Paradoxically, to some extent the better the model and the better adjusted and trimmed, the greater the chance of losing it if the right air currents catch it after the power is exhausted and it glides away. It is difficult for many

Fig. 66. Old-timer flying events are devoted to the efforts of hobbyists who construct model airplanes from designs published up to the early 1940's. Here Tim Dannels (left), shows Carl Goldberg a model built from a 1937 Goldberg design. At the right, John Pond readies another old-timer for flight.

Engine Collectors' Journal

who are not fairly familiar with model flying, and particularly with gliders, to visualize just how potent are the thermal currents and how far away they may carry a properly balanced and trimmed model airplane. In many cases models have been found miles from their starting point, if they were found at all. Even when found they are sometimes in quite inaccessible places. In any event it certainly is no fun to have to try to cover a considerable area of ground looking, as if for a needle in a haystack, for a model airplane. Accordingly, many free-flight models are provided with some sort of time-limitation device, or dethermalizer as they usually are called. Actually, such systems comprise two basic units, the timing device proper and what might be called a flight spoiler, which is tripped into play when the timing device operates.

Both the timing device and the flight spoiler may take different forms. In the case of gliders and rubber-powered models, the purpose of the flight spoiler is literally that. With model planes powered by internal-combustion reciprocating engines, what is needed is a device that will shut off the fuel supply to the engine. With the ignition engines formerly so widely used, all that was necessary was a device that would break the ignition circuit. With glow-plug and diesel engines, however, the fuel supply must be disconnected, usually by releasing a clamp that pinches the flexible fuel-supply tube so that no more fuel passes to the engine. In the case of pressurized fuel tanks, another method usually is used whereby the timer releases fuel into the venturi, or air intake, of the engine, thereby flooding the engine and instantly stopping it without the sputtering that accompanies bringing the engine to a halt by stopping the fuel supply. Timers for internal-combustion-powered reciprocating engines usually are of the spring-operated type and can be adjusted so as to operate to cut off the engine in any time desired up to twenty-five or thirty seconds. The usual length of time permitted

free-flight internal-combustion-reciprocation-engine planes to fly under power is fifteen seconds after launching for hand-launched models and twenty seconds for rise-off-ground or rise-off-water models. When these time limits are set down in black and white, as they are here, they seem quite short; much shorter in fact than they seem when witnessing an actual flight, but they have been found to be the time periods most suitable and safe for today's highly developed and efficient model engines and planes. Some hobbyists attempt to limit the time the engine operates by doing away with a fuel tank and using a fuel supply tube of sufficient length to hold a premeasured quantity of fuel, just enough fuel for a fifteen- or twenty-second engine run, but this method is not very certain or satisfactory.

In the case of gliders or rubber-powered models, the best type of timer again is a spring-operated device, adjustable for the desired length of flight, whereupon a mechanical actuator is released to motivate the flight-spoiling device. Such timers may weigh about three-quarters of an ounce and are suitable for all but the very lightest of aircraft. The flight spoiler itself may be one of many forms, although a pop-up tail that sends the plane into a downward glide is the most popular. Other forms involve disturbing the wing, shifting weights, or even releasing a parachute. The alternate way to actuate such devices, as opposed to a proper timer, is the use of a slow-burning fuse that puts the flight spoiler into operation when the fuse burns through a rubber band that holds the dethermalizer in normal flight position. It must be manifest that any scheme which, regardless of supposed safety precautions that may be taken, sends a lighted fuse into the air on a glider or free-flying model airplane is something to avoid.

Various schemes have been suggested as aids in locating planes that have flown out of sight, including tinfoil or aluminum broiler foil on sections of the model that will catch the rays of the sun. Of course, the best thing is for the hobbyist to keep his eye continually on the model in an effort to see where it comes down, or at least the direction in which it was heading when last seen. One suggestion has been the arrangement of a lighted fuse on the model that will ignite a smoke bomb after a certain interval so that the model will send up a column of smoke from its eventual landing place. This idea makes no more sense than a fuse used on a model for any other purpose. Furthermore, fortunately, it is illegal in many localities. A more commendable scheme, used on some large models, is a battery-powered red blinking light that is mounted on the model. This is not much help during daylight hours, but can be seen a considerable distance at night and consequently may result in the location and recovery of a model plane after dark.

FLYING ANTIQUE MODEL PLANES

The latest development in free-flight model plane flying, and one that evidently is attracting considerable interest and undergoing rapid growth, is the building and flying of what are known as Old-Timers, or antique model airplanes. These are newly constructed planes built from designs and plans created originally in an earlier era of model aviation. Of course, in model aviation "antique" is a relative term. Any model airplane designed and flown prior to 1943 is considered an antique for the purposes of these events. The planes must be constructed exactly as they were designed and built originally. The only alterations permitted are to strengthen known weak spots in a given design and the use of dethermalizers. The planes in some

events are flown with actual old engines of the period. In other events more recent or current engines may be used. The latter is a necessary concession in the interests of the continuing growth of this branch of the hobby. Otherwise the number of participants would be limited by the quantity of antique engines available. However, a substantial number of these old engines are known to exist and others are continually being unearthed by enthusiasts for use both in historical collections of old engines and for actual flying purposes in the antique model planes. The Old-Timer events at model airplane meets tend to become more and more popular, and there is a Society of Antique Modelers devoted to this facet of model aeronautics (see Appendix I), as well as a publication, *The Engine Collectors' Journal* (Appendix III), which supports but is independent of the SAM.

It is true that the old engines and planes usually do not possess the power and zip of current models, although in many cases if alterations in the light of today's knowledge and techniques were allowed, the performance of the antiques would be substantially enhanced. This, however, is not at all in line with the purpose of the antique model enthusiasts, which is to build planes just as they were designed and built in the earlier era. Many of these planes represent excellent designs and provide superb performance; at times and under certain weather conditions they can outperform many of the latest designs, but this is not the object. If anything, aside from nostalgic and historical interest, the purpose of those who build and fly the old models is to create a low-pressure flying event, as contrasted to the tension that often attends hot competition in many modern events. In short, the purely competitive element is secondary in these Old-Timers events.

CHAPTER 4

Control-Line Models

The practice of flying a model airplane tied to a cord or cable goes back to the early dawn of real and model aviation. From the days of World War I, flying model airplanes with various forms of power have been demonstrated in store sales areas and at model exhibitions by anchoring them to a central post or pylon and letting them fly around an area of limited diameter. On various occasions prior to the introduction of control-line model flying as such in 1940, hobbyists have flown what were essentially free-flight model airplanes on lines of varying and often quite considerable length. Today control-line flying is very well known and practiced in hundreds of areas far too small to permit free flight.

Also well known in a considerable area is tethered-model flying which is not control-line flying. Indeed, if anything, this noncontrol-line tethered flying is more popular now than in the not too distant past, and shows indications of continuing growth. A control-line model airplane is, of course, a form of tethered model, but not all tethered, models by any means are control-line models. The vital word in control-line models, or its alternate, U-control models, is "control." A control-line model is one in the flying of which the hobbyist exercises a measure of actual control over the model, most particularly control of the elevator of the model; at times also of the engine speed or some other special function, such as ejecting a miniature pilot and parachute. Control-line models thus are all in a sense tethered models, the line or lines being in most cases today tethered to a control handle that the hobbyist holds in his hand, and manipulates. Usually when the designation "tethered model" is applied what is meant is a model airplane tethered to a post or other fixture rather than tethered to a control handle, although this does not always necessarily hold true.

VARIATIONS

In truth, the whole field of tethered and control-line models embraces so many possible variations and overlappings, even seeming contradictions of terms, that it is not at all an easy task to clearly define and classify all its possibilities and variations. Since it is the newcomer to model aviation who needs such a clarification, the best way to survey the field might well be to divide the models into certain definite groups according to the method by which they are flown. The following categories are admittedly arbitrary. They have been created for the purposes of this book and have no standing or counterparts in the regular competition classes of organized groups such as the AMA. As a matter of fact, only the fourth group includes models that would be eligible for competition in regular AMA events at the present time.

Group 1: Tethered models without any power. This group is best exemplified by the so-called "whipping" type of model airplane; a model

Fig. 67. A group of internal-combustion-reciprocating-engine airplanes of 21- to 24-inch wingspan equipped to be flown in tethered flight or, optionally, as control-line or free-flight models. The models are a Douglas C-47 transport, a Fairchild PT-19 open monoplane, a Mustang F-51, and a Fairchild cabin monoplane.

Sterling Models

without any engine that is attached to a flying line that in turn is attached to a rod. The operator holds the rod in his hand and more or less whips the model airplane into and through the air, making it loop or perform other acrobatics as he wishes. Whipping planes are frankly regarded primarily as devices for very young enthusiasts.

Group 2: Tethered models with engines driven by a power source outside the model aircraft itself. This group is comprised of the models that appear almost periodically with an electric motor driving the propeller and the electric power coming from a battery contained in the control handle. The flight line seemingly is a single flexible cable. Actually, because electricity requires two wires for a complete circuit, there must be two lines, even though the external appearance of the flying line may give the impression of a single line. The outer cable itself may provide one of the requisite electrical lines, with the second insulated line within, or the cable may contain two internal wires providing the electrical circuit. Theoretically such model planes become airborne and fly themselves by the electric power alone and the cable is manipulated only as a control; in many instances what actually is involved is a combination of both the thrust of the electrically operated propeller and a mild whipping or sustaining action with the cable. The cable itself naturally presents considerable added weight and resistance to the air. In the eyes of most model aircraft hobbyists, planes of this type are chiefly of interest to the younger fans.

Within this group also should be included models of lighter-than-air craft with electric motors taking current from a power source located on the ground. Although the wires that convey the current to the model are in effect flight lines, and considerable precise control can be conveyed to the model by regulating the various motors from controls located on the ground, these are considered neither tethered nor control-line models in the usual sense. They are true flying models, however, for despite the weight and drag caused by the wires from the ground to the model, the helium in the model sustains it in the air. Such models are of course limited as to their practical height and range by the length of the attached wires.

Group 3: Tethered models with engines and power sources completely contained within the model aircraft. The models in this group, like those in the preceding two groups, may be flown indoors or out, although obviously no one should attempt to operate any sort of combustion engine indoors without providing ample ventilation. In actual practice, it usually works out that, except at occasional public exhibitions, combustion-engine-powered models in this group are flown outdoors, while rubber-powered models are flown both indoors and out, although usually tethered rubber models are operated indoors. In any event, the models in this category are flown in a circle; the flying line is tethered to a post or other fixture, and other than starting the engine or releasing the rubber at the appropriate moment, the hobbyist exercises no control whatsoever over the model. The model airplane flies by itself until the power is exhausted. It is to this group of models that most model aircraft enthusiasts refer when they speak of tethered models. Models flown in this manner make up an important and worthy segment of serious model aeronautical endeavor.

Group 4. Models with engines and power sources completely contained within the model aircraft, but controlled by the hand of the hobbyist operating through the flying line or lines. This group comprises the control-line models proper, usually powered by internal-combustion reciprocating engines. In many cases, however, the models are powered by jet engines instead. The main control is the elevator of the model airplane, which may be effected by one line, although this system is not used too often today. The customary control is by means of two flying lines from the plane to a handle held by the hobbyist. For additional control functions, a third line may be used. In most cases the supplementary control is a mechanical one, working entirely through the third line. At times, however, the supplementary control is an electrical one, one side of the circuit being carried through the flying lines and the other side of the electrical circuit through the third line. Actually, additional lines and control functions could be added, but models with more than three lines are seldom in use nowadays. In any case, the main control function, elevator control, is the basic control and is always carried out entirely by mechanical means.

TETHERED MODELS

Having thus covered the subject in general, it is now advisable to examine the types of flying performed by the third and fourth groups in more detail. In the case of any tethered or control-line model, the weight and drag of the flying line or lines is a material factor that must be taken into consideration. With rubber-powered tethered models, a sturdy thread should prove ample, and its comparatively light weight will add materially to the flying caliber of the model. With any sort of engine-powered model, a sturdier line material

Fig. 68. Two profile trainer models for control-line flying. Both are profile models and ideally suited to the purpose of learning the fundamentals of control-line flight. The upper model is shown fitted with an engine with separate fuel tank, while the lower model is equipped with an engine with integral tank.

Paul K. Guillow, Inc.
Carl Goldberg Models, Inc.

is an absolute must. Fishing line may pass muster for lighter and less powerful models, but ideally the line material should be a tough material like Dacron or, for really large and powerful models, steel wire. Whatever material is used, the lines should be inspected periodically for kinks, defects, or signs of deterioration, and replaced as soon as anything shows amiss. Control-line flying is not a dangerous sport, but it takes little imagination to picture the possible danger should a line holding a fast-moving model break during flight, especially if there is a crowd nearby. All control-line models and many tethered models are balanced to offset the effect of the weight and drag of the line or lines. Sometimes this is accomplished by adding weight to the tip of the outboard wing; the wing farthest away from the center of the flying circle. Another method is to increase the size of

Fig. 69. Four control-line models of various types, ranging from the 24-inch-wingspan trainer model at lower left to the 54-inch-wingspan Piper Cub J-3 at the lower right. The latter is also suitable for free flight or radio control. At the upper right is an interesting twin-engine, double-profile fuselage model of the Lockheed P38 Lightning.

Sterling Models

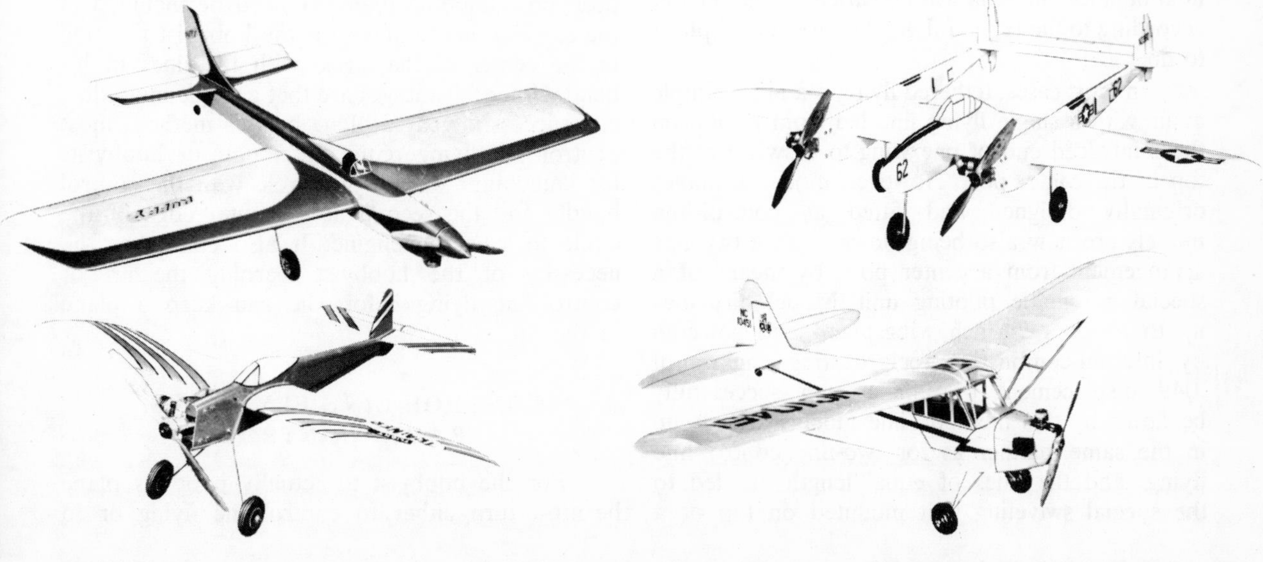

Fig. 70. Two interesting control-line scale models. At the top is a ¾-inch scale, 31-inch-wingspan North American AT-6. The lower model is a 32½-inch wingspan model of the Stearman P-17 crop duster, for engines of .19 to .35 cubic-inch displacement. This plane was widely used as a World War II trainer.

Sig Mfg. Co., Inc.
Sterling Models

post, usually about 3 to 4 feet high. The elevator of the model plane should rest in a neutral position when the model is held at the same height from the ground as the swiveling control unit. With such an arrangement the model resists any tendency to climb higher or lower than the level determined by the height of the post. If it starts to climb, the elevator is automatically adjusted to bring it down again to the desired flight height; if the plane begins to descend, the device automatically compensates, adjusts the elevator as required, and brings the plane up again to the proper level. In short, the model airplane automatically resists all tendencies to depart from the predetermined altitude until the fuel becomes exhausted. When the engine power then fades, the model airplane goes into a glide and safely lands.

While the hobbyist exercises no control over the model airplane in flight with this system, it has certain inherent advantages. For one thing a plane can be flown on much shorter lines by this method and therefore in a much smaller circle than in the usual control-line usage. Most control-line models are flown with lines anywhere from about 25 to 70 feet in length. These measurements represent the radius, not the diameter, of the flying circle; the diameters would be a little more than 50 to 140 feet respectively. The addition to the actual double length of the lines is caused by the allowance for length of the arm of the turning hobbyist standing in the center of the flying circle and holding the handle to which the lines are attached in one hand. With tethered models, lines of 10 feet or less can be used in many cases, and the length of the lines used even when flying an internal-combustion-reciprocating-engine-powered model with two lines run about 12 to 15 feet, or an optimum flying circle diameter of about 30 feet. As the lines pivot around the post, no additional diameter need be included in the calculations to allow for the hobbyist pivoting in the center of the circle with the lines in his hand. Other advantages are that a single individual can successfully fly a plane by this method, most control-line flying requiring a pair of hobbyists for launching: one in the circle with the control handle and the second at the outer edge of the circle to start the engine. It also eliminates the necessity of the hobbyist learning the art of control-line flying before he can keep a plane in the air.

the wing—that is, to increase the lifting area—nearest to the center of the circle. At times both methods are employed in combination. Other aids to successful tether and control-line flying are to offset the thrust of the engine and to offset the rudder. Various combinations of these four things are used at times. Models to be flown from a line balance somewhat differently from those intended for free flight, and in most cases the center of gravity is not at a point along the center line of the plane but rather a little away from it toward the outside of the flying circle. There are kits available that build model airplanes suitable for free-flight, tethered flying, or control-line flying; final balance and trim will be varied by the builder according to the type of flying he intends the plane to do.

In most cases, tethered flying is a fairly simple affair with a single flying line led from a loop on the reinforced end of one wing to a swivel at the top of the center post. However, model airplanes originally designed and fitted as control-line models are now also being flown, with a two-line arrangement from a center post, by means of a special automatic piloting unit. Model airplanes up to about a 24-inch wingspread and powered by internal-combustion reciprocating engines of .049 displacement or smaller can successfully be flown by this method. The models are set up in the same manner as for two-line control-line flying, and the lines of equal length are led to the special swiveling unit mounted on top of a

CONTROL-LINE FLYING VS. RADIO CONTROL

For the hobbyist to actually pilot his plane he must turn either to control-line flying or to

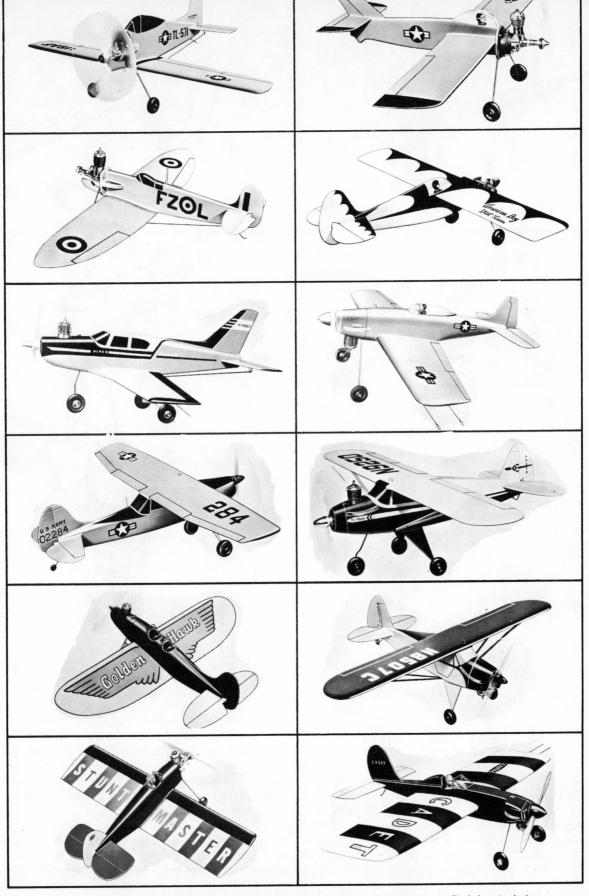

Fig. 71. A variety of control-line models for which inexpensive kits are available, ranging from profile trainers to stunt models. Most of these models measure 18 inches in wingspan, and all of them are suitable for small internal-combustion reciprocating engines.

Scientific Model Airplane Co.

Fig. 72. A group of six scale model molded plastic control-line airplanes, available in completely assembed, ready-to-fly form. Wingspans range from 16 to 23 inches. The prototypes are SB2C Helldiver (with remote-control pilot bail-out and parachute), L-4 Grasshopper, P-40 Warhawk, R.A.F. Supermarine Spitfire, P-51 Bendix Trophy Racer and R.A.F. Kittyhawk.

L. M. Cox Mfg. Co., Inc.

radio control. Of the two, control-line flying is the simplest by far to master and the least expensive in terms of cost of equipment. As a matter of fact, control-line flying is entirely different from radio-control flying. In control flying the hobbyist retains a direct physical or mechanical contact with his model airplane itself; the control runs from his hand to the control-line handle, through the lines to the model airplane and the bell crank therein, through the bell crank to the elevator horn and thence to the adjustment of the elevator itself. In a measure the effect is much as if the hobbyist were sitting in the pilot's seat and directing the movement of the elevator while at the same time standing at a distance from the plane in midair and watching it respond to his control directions.

Actually there is little comparison between control-line and radio-control flying. Each presents an entirely different type of model flying and neither is necessarily superior. In control-line flying the hobbyist is comparatively close to his

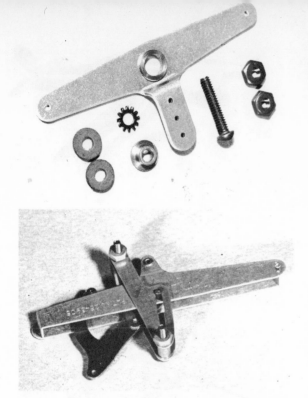

Fig. 73. The heart of any control-line model airplane is the bell crank, which converts the pull on the lines parallel to the wings into an elevator-controlling movement parallel to the fuselage. At the top is a typical bell crank as used in two-line control. Below is a special bell crank for three-line control, the third line regulating the speed of the engine.

Polk's Model Craft Hobbies, Inc.
J. Roberts Mfg. Co.

However, there is nothing to stop the same hobbyist from pursuing both branches of model aviation if he so wishes.

Let us then enter the exciting miniature flying world of control-line models and examine the various systems, components, techniques, and plane categories.

HOW MANY LINES?

It is vital in control-line flying for the line or lines to be kept taut between plane and operator so that he can maintain constant control over the model. If the lines go slack, control contact is lost and must be recovered immediately. The balance and design of the model airplane itself, plus the action of centrifugal force while the model is in circular flight, serve to help keep the lines taut, but in the final analysis all depends on the skill of the operator. The great advantage of the single line would appear to lie in the fact that there exist only the weight and drag of a single flying line. Consequently the system often is preferred by those flying in competitive speed events where everything possible is done to gain the utmost speed.

In all systems there must be a transmission of movement from the operator to the elevator of the model plane, and a translation of this move-

model plane while it is in flight. In radio-control flying the plane is mainly at a considerable distance from the operator; the control is purely electronic between pilot and plane. The effect is that of standing on the ground, watching a real plane in flight, and having the power to bridge the gap between observer and plane and cause the plane to move and perform as the observer wishes. Consequently, if cost is not a factor, it becomes a matter of personal preference.

Fig. 74. Control-line flying details. The top left drawing shows how the lines are connected to the bell crank in the model airplane. At the lower left is shown how the elevator moves in accord with up-and-down control commands from the arm of the operator. The right-hand drawing illustrates the positioning of the model airplane for takeoffs.

L. M. Cox Mfg. Co., Inc.

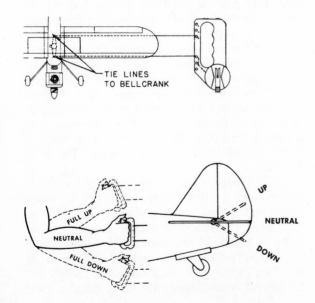

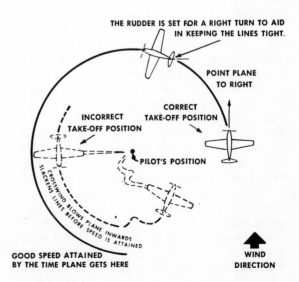

Fig. 75. Three scale model plastic control-line models available as kits or in assembled, ready-to-fly form; models of Goodyear Trophy racers: a 13¾-inch wingspan Bonzo; a 17-inch Denight Special; and a 16½-inch Little Toni. At the lower right is an unusual, ready-to-fly twin-engine model of the B-25 bomber.

K & B Mfg. Corp.

ment, which starts as one parallel to the wing, into one parallel to the fuselage center line and finally into an up or down movement of the elevator.

The lines in the basic two-line system start from the control handle held in the hobbyist's hand. Much confusion exists among beginners concerning handles, reels, and combined handles and reels. The handle is the control implement; the reel merely is a storage device for the lines when not in use and, if combined with the handle, an aid in adjusting the lines to the desired length for a given flight or series of flights. However, once the lines are adjusted so that both are of exactly the same length, the reel as such plays no further part in the operation of the plane. It does not come into play again until the hobbyist wishes to change the length of his lines or to reel up his lines completely at the conclusion of a session of control-line flying. Actually, the so-called reel, whether integral with the control handle or an entirely separate unit, consists of two reels or spools, one for the storage of each of the two lines. Aside from its use as an aid in easily adjusting the length of the lines, the reel serves to protect and preserve the stored control lines. Consequently the use of a reel is strongly recommended. For the average flyer the combined

handle and reel will prove the most convenient. Some advanced enthusiasts, however, prefer separate handles of special designs that do not incorporate reels in their construction, and consequently use separate reels.

All actual control is obtained and maintained solely through the manipulation of the handle, which is normally held in the hand in a vertical or neutral position. Pulling the top of the handle back slightly causes the elevator in the model airplane to rise from its neutral or level position, and in turn causes the model airplane to climb. Pulling the bottom of the handle back slightly causes the elevator in the model airplane to descend from its neutral or level position, and in turn causes the airplane to descend. In setting up the model, care must be directed to making certain that the "up" line is at the top of the control handle and the "down" line is at the bottom.

What happens when the control handle is manipulated so that either the upper or lower line is pulled back? With a normal slight control movement (beginners invariably make too pronounced backward and forward movements with the handle), the model airplane, influenced by its offset rudder and other balancing factors and centrifugal course, continues in its circular flight

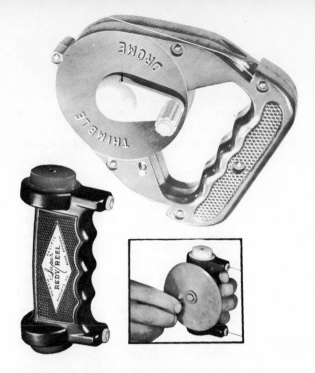

the hobbyist, causing the elevator control wire to move toward the front of the plane and lower the elevator.

That, basically, is the operation of two-line control line flying. The hobbyist can learn the actual technique of flying only through experience. Experience alone can show how far back the top or bottom of the control handle should be drawn for the desired response on the part of the plane, how much control should be exercised by the hand alone moving the control handle, and how much movements up and down of the entire arm should enter the picture. Control-line planes differ widely both in speed and in responsiveness to control. For this reason, the beginner should start flying with a comparatively slow plane, one that is not too responsive to control movements. A special class of trainer planes is available for those who are learning the art of control-line flying. Later, as the flyer gains experience, he can go on to faster, more responsive ships and to more specialized types of control-line models. The hobbyist who wishes to build his own trainer plane from a kit should obtain a kit specifically advocated by its manufacturer as suitable for use as a trainer.

Later, as the hobbyist gains experience, he can go on to faster, more responsive ships and to more specialized types. It is truly amazing what can be done in the way of complicated flying maneuvers and aerial acrobatics by a trained and experienced control-line flyer. Almost nothing seems to be too complicated for him. To watch such a performance one almost forgets that the model airplane is connected to the hobbyist's hand and is not being flown by a miniature pilot in the cockpit.

In most control-line models the control is over the elevator only. However, in some more advanced models, control also is attained over supplementary elevators on the wing or ailerons as

Fig. 76. Combination control-line handles and reels for standard two-line operation. The model at the top stores the lines when not in use on special reels ahead of the handle. The lower type stores the lines on reels within the handle itself. A special snap-on friction winding disk is attached when the lines are to be wound.

L. M. Cox Mfg. Co., Inc.
North Pacific Products Co.

path. The control-line handle movement is not sufficient to pull the plane from its course. Upon reaching the fuselage, the control lines are attached to the two ends of a bell crank that is mounted on the plane so that it is free to respond even to very slight movements of the control line.

BELL CRANKS

A bell crank is a device for transmitting motion and force at a right angle. A typical model airplane bell crank is pictured in Fig. 73. Each of the two control lines is attached to one of the holes at the extremities of the bell crank, the bottom line on the control handle, the down line, to the hole on the bell crank nearest the front of the airplane, and the top, or up, line to the hole on the bell crank nearest the tail of the airplane. A third line, or push rod, is attached to the third or offset hole in the bell crank and thence runs backward in the model airplane where it is attached to the control horn that raises or lowers the elevator. Thus, pulling back the top of the control handle pulls the rear of the bell crank toward the hobbyist, causing the elevator control wire to move toward the rear of the plane and raise the elevator. Returning the control handle to neutral puts the bell crank to neutral and, in turn, the elevator returns to a neutral or level position. Pulling back on the bottom of the control handle pulls the front of the bell crank toward

Fig. 77. A plastic, ready-to-fly control-line scale model of the Boeing P-26. This 20-inch-wingspan model is available optionally with a special third-line controlled throttle that permits the operator in the center of the flying circle to adjust the speed of his engine without touching the airplane itself.

AFM Wen-Mac Division

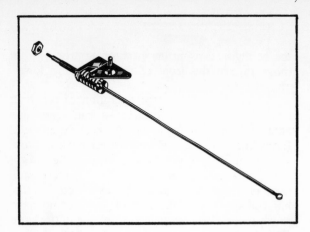

Fig. 78. Single-line control of model airplanes is attained by means of a twisting rather than a pulling motion. This illustrates a control unit for installation in the model, where it substitutes for the bell crank of two-line control. Twisting the control arm turns the worm in either direction, which in turn transmits motion to the crank that is attached to the elevator.

Polk's Model Craft Hobbies, Inc.

well, their up and down movements being connected to the same bell crank action so that they raise and lower simultaneously with the movements of the elevator.

The first question that a control-line flyer usually asks is whether he will get dizzy as he keeps turning around to follow the flight of the model plane. Probably at first, even though he follows the customary advice to keep his eye on the model plane and not on the surroundings. If he does this he should soon overcome any sensation of dizziness.

One advantage of control-line flying is that it is much easier to fly accurate and perfectly proportioned scale models of certain prototype aircraft than in free flight. The tethered status of the model provides considerable stability in itself, and the hobbyist has the means immediately to correct any faults in flight as soon as they start to occur. Unlike free-flight models, control-line models are not launched into the wind. That is to say, they are started with the wind at their back, or at least approaching that position. In this way the model will have gathered enough speed by the time it is in a crosswind position to resist the power of any crosswind to push the plane in toward the center of the flying circle and slacken the control lines. Remember that regardless of the direction in which a control-line model might be launched, it rapidly encounters all possible winds as it moves around its flight circle: upwind, crosswind, downwind, and crosswind again in fairly quick rotation. The menace in control-line flying in any fairly high wind is that a crosswind will drive the plane in toward the center of the circle and control will be lost because of the lines slackening. Thus beginners should start flying with comparatively short lines, about 20 to 25 feet in length, and not attempt to fly if there is an

appreciable breeze blowing. This raises the question of exactly what is an "appreciable breeze." In terms of miles per hour for the wind, an appreciable breeze might be considered anything much over seven or eight miles per hour. Local weather reports usually give the wind forecasts for the day.

Since the beginner will experience a number of faulty if not downright bad landings it is a good idea to use flexible plastic propellers and, if possible, select a soft grassy field to learn on. However, takeoffs are much easier from hard-packed surfaces. In most cases, especially when using an area especially set off for model airplane flying, the beginner will have to accept the surface as he finds it. Ideally, however, he would put in his initial flights on ground that would permit the plane to take off on a fairly hard surface and the flyer then to step back so that if the model crashes it will come down on grass.

Taking a quick step back when and if the flying lines slacken for any reason is the standard procedure for regaining control of a model in flight. The beginner must take care that his movements do not take him all over the area, thereby moving the flight circle so that the path of the plane endangers either spectators or the plane itself. It is a good idea when possible to mark a definite circle on the flying field within which the operator should remain while his model is in flight.

SAFETY PRECAUTIONS

As a preliminary to flying, it is wise to have an assistant walk the model plane all around the proposed flying circle after the control lines have been attached, while the operator, or pilot, if you will, holds the control handle and turns with the plane. This will give an accurate check on the proposed size of the flying circle as well as an opportunity for the assistant to spot any stones or obstructions that may lie in the path of the takeoff and landing of the plane. In most cases an assistant will be needed for successful control-line flying to help in launching the plane properly, although the usual control-line launching process is a rise-off-ground one, and hand-launching is not employed.

The size of the flying circle available will of course determine the length of the lines that can be used. Spectators should be kept back an additional 20 to 30 feet from around the actual flying circle. Of course, at a regular model airplane meet this will be taken care of by the organizers of the event, but if you are flying by yourself with a few friends the entire responsibility will rest on you. This means that if you are flying with 25-foot lines you will want to find a flying area about 95 feet in diameter. With 70-foot lines you will want an area about 200 feet in diameter. Never under any circumstances fly near any kind of overhead electrical lines, telephone, telegraph, light, power, or what-have-you, regardless of how well insulated they appear or you have been assured they are. It is quite possible for the hobbyist to electrocute himself if his flying lines become entangled in overhead power lines.

Examine your flying lines periodically and replace them immediately if they show any signs of deterioration. It is also imperative that the flying lines be tightly secured both to the connections on the model plane and to those on the control handle. Since lines must be of exactly the same length, new hobbyists often loosen knots to readjust the length of one line or the other, then fail to tighten the knots properly before flying. In some cases the tightening of a knot may pull one line out of mate with the other, so perhaps the flyer may feel that it is just as well to let things go as they are and get to flying. The essential point when flying with lines that must be measured and adjusted by hand is to be willing to give attention not merely to attaining the correct matched length but equally to seeing that the lines are securely fastened.

AVOIDING OVERCONTROL

Until the beginner learns exactly how little motion with the control handle is actually necessary, he will find himself repeatedly in difficulty even in simple around-the-circle flying. He must master the art of controlling his plane in simple flight before attempting any further maneuvers, even of the simplest sort. The physical properties of the control handle are such that the farther apart the lines are mounted on the handle, the greater will be the pull transmitted to the plane by pulling back the top or bottom of the handle a given amount. Many control handles have a number of holes to provide a choice of wire-mounting position. The beginner with a comparatively slow-responding trainer type of plane may mount the wires the greater distance apart; with a more responsive plane he would do well to arrange his wires with a closer spacing so that less movement is transmitted to the plane with a given movement of the handle. No matter how little he thinks he moves the handle, the novice is almost invariably going to overcontrol the plane by moving the handle back too far for the maneuver.

There are means available of limiting the

Fig. 79. A control-line model employing a special system of three-line control, using the special bell crank illustrated in Fig. 73 for control of engine speed by means of the third line. This particular model airplane is designed for use in Navy Carrier and racing events. The inset shows the special three-line control handle employed with this system, the inside trigger actuating the third line.

J. Roberts Mfg. Co.

movement of the elevator on a learner's model or for automatically correcting overcontrol movements when they are made. The most favored method is to have a limiting device attached to the bell crank. The limitation of movement must be made at the bell crank. There obviously is no way of limiting the movement of the beginner's hand and arm at the other end of the control lines. When the hobbyist has begun to fly his model successfully, the limiting device then can be removed. Flying without it will at first present some problems again, but the beginner will at least by then have a better idea of just how little movement is required with the handle and be better able to control the model.

A way for the plane to correct itself automatically is now being included with certain models built from kits, which also permits comparatively small control-line models being flown on longer lines than previously had been customary. If the lines are allowed to go slack and line tension is lost, this device, in company with an unusually heavy weight in the outboard wing tip, causes the model airplane automatically to bank outward, and, as it were, fly out to the end of the control lines and thus allow the hobbyist to regain complete control of the ship.

Learning control-line flying may seem a comparatively slow process at first. After a little time, however, the hobbyist usually suddenly finds that he is learning much more rapidly and becoming quite proficient. Continued practice still is needed, and it would be a mistake at this point to abandon the training ship in favor of something

Fig. 80. Control-line models designed especially for use in the Navy Carrier event, where models take off from land on a miniature aircraft-carrier deck. At the left is a 34-inch-wingspan Douglas Sky Shark with profile fuselage. The center model is a 36-inch-wingspan scale model Grumman Guardian; and the right-hand plane is a 34-9/16-inch-wingspan scale model Corsair AU-1.

Sterling Models
J. Roberts Mfg. Co.

considerably more responsive or larger. The ideal is to attain more or less complete mastery over a training plane before trying something else. It is possible to have a great deal of enjoyment with a training model, and many sport and stunt activities that generally are thought of as requiring special types of airplanes—and to require special aircraft when entered in organized competitive events—can be performed in similar or slightly modified form with a trainer in purely-for-fun flying, for example, racing and combat.

As the hobbyist becomes more and more experienced in control-line flying, he will learn to automatically make those very slight movements with the control handle needed for perfect control over the model in flight. There are no hard-and-fast rules or recommendations pertaining to the spacing of the lines on the type of control handle that offers several alternate settings. Once the enthusiast becomes accustomed to the use of the control handle and to the response of various models, he can adjust the spacing of his lines as

he prefers, even using the outermost line mounting holes on the control handle, which provide the greatest leverage from any given movement of the handle, on highly responsive models. Once the basics of flying around the flight circle have been mastered, the control-line enthusiast can go on to simple stunts, such as wingovers, loops, and inverted flight, and then to more complicated stunt or acrobatic maneuvers. There are, in fact, a whole series of recognized maneuvers used in competitions, including such seemingly exotic ones as consecutive outside square loops, square horizontal eights, vertical eights, and four-leaf clovers.

THREE-LINE AND ONE-LINE CONTROL

So far the discussion of control-line flying has confined itself to the most widespread form, flying with two lines. The alternates are one-line and three-line control. Inasmuch as three-line control systems simply add a third line to the

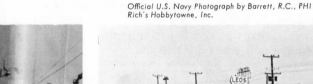

Fig. 81. Real and model aircraft-carrier decks. At the left is a scene on the flight deck of the USS Lexington, where a model plane is being fueled for a control-line competition held under the auspices of the U.S. Navy. At the right is shown the "USS Morris County," a model aircraft-carrier flight deck built to the specifications required by the Navy Carrier control-line event.

Official U.S. Navy Photograph by Barrett, R.C., PHI
Rich's Hobbytowne, Inc.

standard two-line system, all that has been said so far regarding the latter is equally applicable to three-line control. Three-line control simply adds a third control line to enable the hobbyist to perform a second remote-control function, usually but not always the regulation of engine speed. One-line control on the other hand is a complete departure from the principles employed in the other methods. Its essential difference is in the method by which movement is transmitted from the hand of the hobbyist to the elevator of the model plane. In all such matters of safety, the importance of keeping the lines taut, plane types, maneuvers, and so on, these are substantially as applicable to one-line control-line flying as to flying with two or three lines.

At the time control-line models first became popular, the internal combustion engines used in flying models were almost all of the ignition type. A change from high to low speed, or back again, could be obtained by the use of a special engine timer having both high and low speed points.

apparatus, the engine automatically went to low speed. It must be borne in mind that the model airplane itself carried ignition batteries for the engine, and the engine ran from these batteries regardless of whether or not current was received from the battery in the operator's pocket.

This system, although workable, had several drawbacks. The flying lines had to be of enamel insulated wire; and wires with excess length to accommodate the changing position of the bell crank had to be mounted on the bell crank and led to the relay. Consequently a three-line system was developed which, although adding the weight of another line, somewhat simplified things electrically. Only the third line had to be insulated, and it ran directly to the relay. The flight lines provided the other side of the electrical circuit, and the metal bell crank itself was in this circuit, a single wire running from the bell crank to the other terminal of the relay coil. When the relay was energized, the two-speed system worked in the same manner as described in the preceding para-

Fig. 82. Three combat-stunt models of the flying-wing type, with wingspans of 19 inches (for .049 cubic-inch engines), 29 inches (for .15 to .19 cubic-inch engines) and 36 inches (for .19 to .35 cubic-inch engines) respectively. Combat models are liable to suffer considerable damage in use, as indicated in Fig. 83.

Carl Goldberg Models, Inc.

High speed was obtained by the use of a relay, an electrically operated switch, which when energized disconnected the low speed points. When the relay was not energized, the slow speed points were in the circuit and served to delay the firing time and hence the speed of the engine. The use of this device in a control-line model necessitated the hobbyist carrying a battery to energize the relay, usually tucked in a pocket, and a special switch to put the battery into series with the insulated control lines. When the switch was thrown, current from the battery traveled to and from the relay along the insulated control lines, the relay was energized, and the low-speed points were cut out of the circuit so that the engine ran at high speed. If anything went wrong with the

graph. Other systems were proposed or tried, including the use of a bell crank made of a nonconductor such as fiber or plastic, and using only two lines, but the three-line system seems by far to be the best. However, the rapid climb to popularity of glow-plug and diesel engines shortly after World War II quickly changed the problem from one of electrical control to that of mechanical control, and made the third line an absolute necessity in many cases.

With glow-plug or diesel engines, speed control can be attained by moving a choke either on the intake or the exhaust, or both, or, for a purely two-speed engine, by the use of a double needle valve with two fuel feed lines. When both lines are in use, the engine runs slow; when one line is cut off the engine runs fast. The details of these devices are discussed in the following chapter. If desired, these devices could be operated in control-line flying by a relay and electrical means, using either two insulated flying lines or the three-line system described above. However, relay operation is not required except when two needle valves are used. Almost all modern variable-speed engines rely on manipulating intake and exhaust chokes. Therefore, the control can be purely mechanical and nowadays is customarily accomplished by means of the third line, often used in combination with a special handle that includes a special trigger device for manipulating the engine speed control line. In its simplest form the third line is connected to a second bell crank that is spring-loaded against the pull of the third line. In practice this usually provides only a two-speed control. In a more elaborate form a special single unit combines both bell cranks (Fig. 73) and, when used with the special control handle mentioned above, it is possible for a skilled operator to attain a truly variable engine speed control. The system relies on the centrifugal force of the flying model to move the engine speed control lever when the third line is released, rather than on the action of a spring opposing the pull of the third line. In common with other three-line methods, this system can be used, if desired, for the control of functions other than motor speed control, such as ejecting a pilot and parachute or retracting and lowering landing gear.

Nowadays, simpler three-line systems are used in smaller planes, including some ready-to-fly models, either for engine speed control or for other actions. Although various methods have been proposed from time to time to enable a single hobbyist to launch and fly a control-line model without the aid of another enthusiast in the actual launching, few have attained widespread popularity or, indeed, been very successful except in expert hands. With a third-line throttle control, one-man launching becomes an actuality, for the flyer can set his plane in position at the edge of the flying circle, start the engine and allow it to idle and then walk to the center of the circle, take up the control lines and then pull the third line to open the throttle for the takeoff. While in flight, the engine can be speeded up by pulling on the third line; if the line is allowed to slacken, the engine slows down.

Three-line flying appears to be headed for many further developments in the not too distant future, and should enjoy a much greater popularity than at present. The whole outlook of control-line stunting would be changed if hobbyists had an easy means to regulate the speed of their engines while going through the maneuvers and were able to match the performance of the miniature engines with that of a real airplane as it went through similar acrobatics. A number of enthusiasts are working on these and other improvements in control-line engine speed control. The three-line method seems to have the edge over other methods in this direction.

Now a word as to single-line control. With a single control line, the control action on the line must be a turning or twisting one, not a pulling one. The external control details are not radically different from two-line control other than in the manipulation of the control line. However, the apparatus inside the model airplane itself must of necessity differ and usually is considerably more complex. Two-line control involves only a simple bell crank for the transmission of pulling actions. Single-line control translates the turning or twisting action between control handle and model plane to a pulling action somewhere between the point that the control line enters the plane and the elevator, not simply a change in the direction of the same action. Various methods have been developed for this change from a twisting to a pulling action, including the use of a worm at the airplane end of the line, with a portion of a special bell crank threaded onto the worm itself or the worm working a gear segment attached to the bell crank. In any event, the two-line system is now so universally popular that most beginning hobbyists will start with and stick to this system. The single-line system may justly be regarded as a somewhat advanced and specialized form, of interest primarily to those who wish to fly speed models where the reduction of drag to that of a single line may be of crucial importance.

Apropos of this point, however, it might be noted that advocates of such three-line systems wherein all three lines are under tension at all times have advanced the theory that overall line drag is not increased by the use of a third line. Their reasoning is that since all three lines are always sharing the tension, each line can safely be lighter than with a two-line control on the same given model airplane. If the same reasoning is followed in the case of a one-line system, it might appear that a single line would have to be twice as strong as each of the two lines used in a two-line system with the same given model aircraft and that there is less reduction in drag through the use of only one line than might appear at first thought. An added advantage of two-line control would be that if one line should break, the second

Fig. 83. At the left, two control-line fliers maneuver their planes in an aerial combat event during which each attempts to cut the streamer hanging from the opponent's model. At the right, a photograph taken after another combat reveals one plane with only a broken propeller but the opposing plane in quite bad condition.

Official Photograph, U.S. Navy
Rich's Hobbytowne, Inc.

line still would secure the plane (although the bell crank and elevator might move wildly under such circumstances if no safety stops were provided) and provide an added element of safety. If a model plane is flying on a single line and the line breaks, the results can be disastrous. A table of wire sizes is available through association membership, and should be consulted and followed so that a proper margin of safety can always be maintained. It is customary to test lines prior to any organized flying event.

CONTROL-LINE PLANE TYPES AND EVENTS

What are the various specific types of competition usually recognized and the specialized types of model aircraft that have been developed for them? Even if the hobbyist does not intend to engage in organized competitions, he will find the answer to this question useful as a guide in understanding the various types of models that are used and in making selections for his own purposes.

First, of course, there is the ubiquitous trainer, designed primarily as an easy-to-control, crash-resistant, comparatively slow-moving and unresponsive (to compensate for the beginners' inevitable tendency toward overcontrol) craft with which to learn the art of control-line flying. Trainers may be obtained in ready-to-fly form or can be built from kits of molded parts or—and far more frequently—from wooden components. Optionally, of course, a control-line trainer could be constructed from plans appearing in model airplane magazines. The trainer may be a full fuselage model, and likely will be if of molded plastic, or it may well be a profile model. Aside

from their use as literally a training ship, just as real pilots are trained in special trainer-type airplanes, the model airplane trainer also is literally, as already pointed out, a fun plane. There are no specific competition classes in which trainers are flown, but hobbyists can employ their trainers in carrying out many contest-type events when they engage in sport flying.

Control-line sports models may be regarded as an advance upon trainers. They admittedly are purely fun models, designed for so-called sport flying as opposed to competitive flying. Sometimes models are designated as trainer-sports models. Among molded plastic models where a full fuselage and the attempt to model a specific prototype are customary, there is little difference between trainers and sports models. Among models built from kits of wooden parts there is likely to be a noticeable difference, with the sports models more closely resembling real aircraft with full fuselages (although there also are kits that build full-fuselage trainer models from wooden parts).

Between control-line sports models and control-line scale models there again often is very little difference and some overlapping. Scale models, whether built from kits or from scratch, are accurate models of particular prototype aircraft, much easier to fly successfully in most cases with control line than in free flight. Again there is a certain overlapping of the ready-to-fly plastic models, for many of these are accurate scale models and with some justice may be regarded as filling a combined role of trainer, sports, and scale model. There are, however, organized competitive events for control-line scale models. The models entered in these contests often are fairly large, and points are awarded for fidelity to scale and

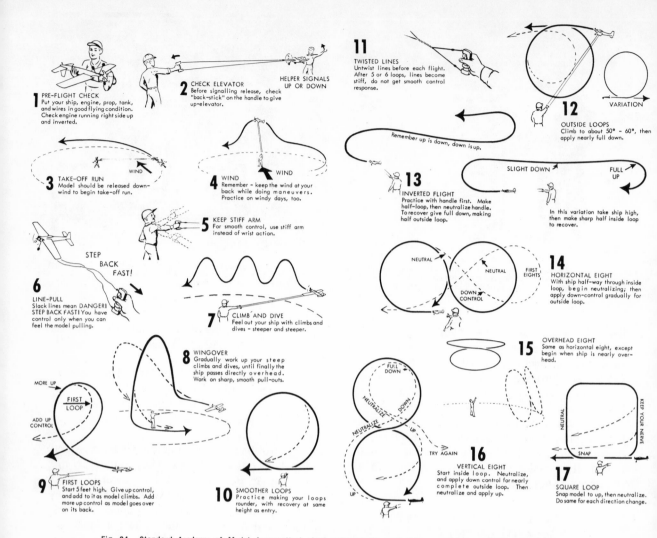

1 PRE-FLIGHT CHECK
Put your ship, engine, prop, tank, and wires in good flying condition. Check engine running right side up and inverted.

2 CHECK ELEVATOR
Before signalling release, check "back-stick" on the handle to give up-elevator.

HELPER SIGNALS UP OR DOWN

3 TAKE-OFF RUN
Model should be released downwind to begin take-off run.

WIND

4 WIND
Remember – keep the wind at your back while doing maneuvers. Practice on windy days, too.

WIND

5 KEEP STIFF ARM
For smooth control, use stiff arm instead of wrist action.

STEP BACK FAST!

6 LINE-PULL
Slack lines mean DANGER! STEP BACK FAST! You have control only when you can feel the model pulling.

7 CLIMB AND DIVE
Feel out your ship with climbs and dives – steeper and steeper.

8 WINGOVER
Gradually work up your steep climbs and dives, until finally the ship passes directly overhead. Work on sharp, smooth pull-outs.

MORE UP
FIRST LOOP
ADD UP CONTROL

9 FIRST LOOPS
Start 5 feet high. Give up control, and add to it as model climbs. Add more up control as model goes over on its back.

10 SMOOTHER LOOPS
Practice making your loops rounder, with recovery at same height as entry.

11 TWISTED LINES
Untwist lines before each flight. After 5 or 6 loops, lines become stiff, do not get smooth control response.

12 OUTSIDE LOOPS
Climb to about 50° – 60°, then apply nearly full down.

VARIATION

Remember up is down, down is up.

SLIGHT DOWN   FULL UP

In this variation take ship high, then make sharp half inside loop to recover.

13 INVERTED FLIGHT
Practice with handle first. Make half-loop, then neutralize handle. To recover give full down, making half outside loop.

NEUTRAL

NEUTRAL   FIRST EIGHTS

DOWN CONTROL

14 HORIZONTAL EIGHT
With ship half-way through inside loop, begin neutralizing; then apply down-control gradually for outside loop.

15 OVERHEAD EIGHT
Same as horizontal eight, except begin when ship is nearly overhead.

FULL DOWN
NEUTRALIZE   DOWN
NEUTRALIZE
UP
TRY AGAIN
UP

16 VERTICAL EIGHT
Start inside loop. Neutralize, and apply down control for nearly complete outside loop. Then neutralize and apply up.

NEUTRAL   KEEP YOUR NERVE
SNAP

17 SQUARE LOOP
Snap model to up, then neutralize. Do same for each direction change.

Fig. 84. Standard Academy of Model Aeronautics' stunt patterns for control-line precision acrobatic competitions. Some of the patterns are quite complicated, but hobbyists who are interested in these events usually master them through continuous practice in less time than at first seems possible.

Carl Goldberg Models, Inc.

special scale operations, such as retracting and lowering landing gear and variable-speed throttle control, as well as for flying ability. Needless to say, the models entered in these contests are of a fairly elaborate type and a considerable remove from the ready-to-fly plastic model no matter how accurate a scale replica the latter may be.

Another organized event is the endurance contest where the object is to remain in the air the greatest length of time. Only models powered by internal-combustion reciprocating engines are admitted to these events, and the engines must have a displacement of from .190 to .360 cubic inches. There are no particular rules as to the type of plane that must be entered in these contests. Obviously an important part of preparing for an event of this type lies in tuning up the engine so that it will perform at its greatest efficiency. The .190 to .360 cubic-inch range is that of the AMA rules; the rules of the Western Associated

Modelers, Inc., provide a broader range of .001 to .650 cubic inches in their endurance-contest regulations. While the WAM rules are to a large extent similar to those of the AMA, there are variations within similar events, and each group has certain recognized events not duplicated by the other organization. In this book the AMA rules are those cited unless specific notice is made to the contrary. Those interested in a further exploration of the matter, and especially those residing in the western part of the United States, are advised to obtain and study the official rules of both organizations (see Appendix I).

THE NAVY CARRIER EVENT

Control-line Navy Carrier events are among the most interesting and popular of all control-line flying contests. In these events a model of a naval aircraft carrier is used, the model, or at

Fig. 85. Two control-line stunt models of conventional model airplane design. The 31-inch-wingspan model at the top is a combat-stunt model with profile fuselage. At the bottom, Bill Werwage holds his 52-inch-wingspan Ares, with which he three times became the National Stunt Champion.

Ambroid Co.

least the flight deck, being curved to conform to the radius of the control-line flying circle (Fig. 81). The deck is 44 feet long and 8 feet wide. The object is to take off from the carrier deck and, after flight, successfully land on the rear portion of the deck. Arresting cables are suspended across the landing area approximately 1 to 1½ inches above the deck and 2 feet apart, and model planes are fitted with an arresting hook for use in landing. While any type of model plane with up to a maximum wingspan of 44 inches may be used in the carrier event, inasmuch as extra bonus points are awarded for any scale model of a United States Navy carrier aircraft, the planes used in this event customarily are of this type. They may be powered either by internal-combustion reciprocating engines or by jet engines. All the ground area is considered water, and if after the model is released for takeoff and before it has landed on the deck again any part of it comes in contact with the "water" it is considered that the model has crashed in the "water" and the flight has ended.

The actual contest involves takeoff, a high-speed flight, a low-speed flight, and landing. The event therefore necessitates the use of a two-speed or variable-speed engine. Kits are available for building models specifically designed for the Navy Carrier event, or other models may be adapted for the purpose. The emphasis in the design of special planes for this event is, of course, on the reproduction of a scale model of a Navy carrier-based plane, embracing flight characteristics of quick takeoff, high speed, stability at low speeds, and a fuselage and landing gear (fixed or retractable) sturdy enough to take the shock of the arrested landings on the carrier deck.

The control-line Navy Carrier event has proved so popular among both hobbyists and spectators that plans are proceeding for additional AMA event classifications of this general type, including at least one reserved for somewhat smaller models and restricted to smaller engine sizes. The initial AMA Navy Carrier event regulations put no limit on the size of the engines and called for 60-foot-long flying lines. The WAM has two carrier-event classifications, one known as the ½ A event for engines from .001 to .050 cubic inches, which is flown on 30-foot lines, and an ABC event for engines from .051 to .650, which is flown on 60-foot lines.

COMBAT PLANES AND EVENTS

Kite fighting long has been popular in the Orient, with kite strings dipped in paste and covered with ground glass or porcelain. The object is to cut the string of an opponent's kite. Control-line combat flying is the mechanized version of this ancient sport, the object being to cut a long crepe or tissue paper streamer hanging from the tail of an opponent's plane as many times as is possible during a five-minute flight period. The cuts must be made by the propeller or the model itself; cuts made by the control lines are not counted. Under AMA rules the streamers are of crepe paper, 8 feet long and 2 inches wide, with an approximately 2-inch-square string leader of cardboard attached to the head of the streamer and the whole attached to the model plane with a 5-foot-long string. Sometimes more than two contestants are called for the start of the event, and the first two to get their engines started are allowed to launch their planes while the others are pulled back from the flying circle to await the next flight. The AMA has a single combat classification using 60-foot lines. The WAM divides combat competitions into three classes: ½ A with .001 to .050 engines and 35-foot lines; A with .051 to .200 engines and 52-foot lines, and BC with .201 to .360 engines and 60-foot lines.

The planes used in model combat events are not, as some might expect, scale models of prototype warplanes, but, rather, highly specialized designs created for model airplane combat service. Combat models must fly fast, be highly maneuverable and capable of flying equally well in regular

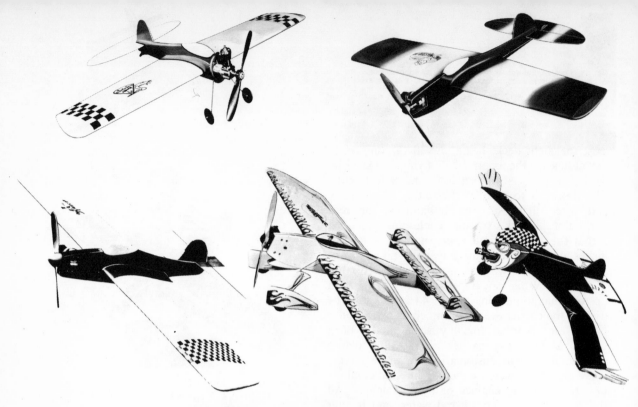

Fig. 86. Variations on a theme. These are all modifications of essentially the same stunt model design, the first three being primarily size variations with 21-, 30-, and 42-inch wingspans. The last two models are customized versions built from a special customizing kit that permits construction of models of over 50-inch span, with numerous variations in wing tips, tails, landing gears, fuselage, and so on, including the "Flying Man."

Sterling Models

and inverted flight. The exigencies of combat flying call for much of the same maneuvering that goes into stunt flying, and combat and stunt planes often are very similar in design. Sometimes kits are offered for what are called combat/stunt models. Generally speaking, however, combat models are required to have a sturdiness not vital to purely stunt models, for collisions and crash landings are not uncommon in combat flying, although any attempt in the eyes of the judges for any contestant deliberately to make his plane collide with that of his opponent or cause his opponent's plane to crash immediately disqualifies the offender. Like stunt planes, combat planes are made with symmetrical wings so as to fly equally well in any position; indeed, many combat models are in effect simply flying wings. Using an especially sturdy leading edge aids in combat and is a characteristic of most special combat planes, but anything savoring of a special device for cutting an opponent's streamer or the roughening or sharpening of any surface for that purpose is not allowed.

Combat flying now is one of the most popular forms of control-line flying. To be successful at it requires a considerable degree both of flying skill and agressiveness, combined with good judgment and the ability to make split-second deci-

sions. The combat flyer should remain primarily on the offensive and study an opponent's techniques. Many flyers have pet maneuvers that they like to use over and over again. The combat contestant must watch for these maneuvers by his opponent and try to take advantage of them, while at the same time trying to avoid repeating his own favorite maneuvers lest he give the opponent a chance to know what to expect. Cutting the streamer of an opposing plane counts for additional points each time it is accomplished. Cutting the leading string itself, so that no part of the opponent's streamer or cardboard string leader remains, counts as a "kill."

The writer has on several occasions been asked for the names of suitable mythical countries that can be attached to planes used in combat competitions; many combat enthusiasts frown on the idea of attacking a model airplane that bears the markings of or is designated a plane of their own country. Actually, any such designations and markings are entirely unnecessary. A model airplane combat should be regarded simply as a sporting event between two individuals and their individual planes. However, in recent years there appears to be a growing inclination among many model aeronautical enthusiasts to provide designations for their combat planes. Here, therefore, is such a list of mythical or fictional countries: Graustark, Ruritania, Utopia, Erewhon, Atlantis, Lilliput.

STUNT PLANES

Model airplanes for stunt or, as it sometimes is more officially termed, precision acrobatic flying, form an extremely extensive and varied range of models, including both profile and full fuselage types. The main requirements are maneuverability and capability of flight in any position. Extra-large elevators are usually employed, sometimes in combination with additional and interlinked elevators on the wings themselves, making such models extremely sensitive and responsive to control directives emanating from the control handle. Like combat models, stunt planes have symmetrical wing sections so as to fly equally well inverted. Stunt models come in all sizes and accommodate the entire range of engine displacements. Many stunt models are built with landing gear, some without, whereas combat models are never provided with landing gear. While most stunt models are more or less freelance designs, created and built for their flying ability alone, some stunt models attempt to reproduce, either in profile or in fuel fuselage models, specific prototype air planes. A manufacturer may produce kits for a design that has proved especially good in several sizes for engines of different displacements—this practice is not confined to stunt models alone but is followed with other types of models, notably radio-control planes.

The regulations for organized precision acrobatic events are quite elaborate, and require the performance of a definite series of maneuvers within a set time period. In addition, points are awarded on the appearance of the model. The event is not, therefore, purely one of performance, although this is its chief object. By far the greater number of points are awarded on the ability with which the contestant takes his plane through each of the prescribed maneuvers. Little more can be said here relating to specific advice to the stunt flyer, except that it is always best to dive into the wind and to climb with the wind. This applies to all types of control-line flying, although such advice pertains particularly to combat and stunt flying.

TEAM RACING

Team racing involves from two to as many as six semiscale models flying at the same time in the same flying circle, each operator or pilot seeking to achieve the fastest time for a race over a definite distance: 1½ miles, 2½ miles, and 5 miles in the preliminary heats; 10 miles in the grand finals. These distances are translated into terms of so many flaps around a given flying circle (not less than that provided by the use of 60-foot-long lines). The planes must land during the races if and when the fuel supply they are carrying is exhausted or they require repairs. They must be refueled and otherwise serviced as rapidly as possible and sent into the air again. This is where the team comes in. The team for each plane customarily consists of three members; the pilot, who must stay within special areas designated at the center of the flying circle and who does the actual flying; and two mechanics, who must refuel and service the plane when it lands and start the engine again for another takeoff. The time required to refuel and service the model

Fig. 87. Full-length and part-length cast-metal speed pans used under control-line speed model airplanes to provide a landing skid as a substitute for conventional landing gear.

Tatone Products

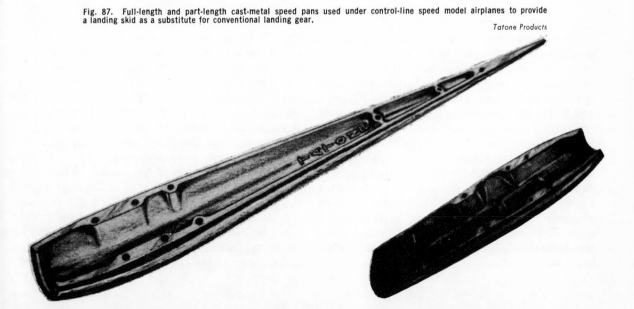

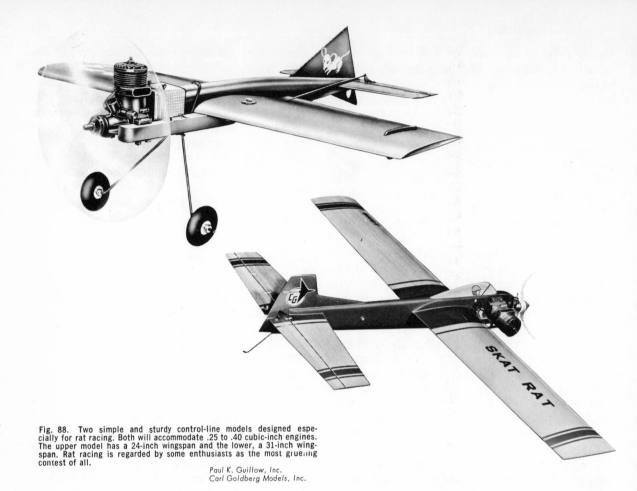

Fig. 88. Two simple and sturdy control-line models designed especially for rat racing. Both will accommodate .25 to .40 cubic-inch engines. The upper model has a 24-inch wingspan and the lower, a 31-inch wingspan. Rat racing is regarded by some enthusiasts as the most grueling contest of all.

Paul K. Guillow, Inc.
Carl Goldberg Models, Inc.

is counted in the overall time required to complete the assigned number of laps that determines the order of the winners. The mechanics must therefore be as quick in getting about their business as possible, while conforming to very definite regulations governing their conduct and procedures, most of them relating to field safety requirements.

One may question how two planes (much less more) can possibly race each other around a control-line flying circle, their operators pivoting and turning to follow the craft in flight, with one plane passing the other, without the control lines from one plane becoming hopelessly twisted with those of the other, let alone collisions between operators. The fact is that in racing, the field and techniques both are somewhat different from regular control-line flying and, unless only a single plane is in the air at one time, no pilot is allowed to pivot in one spot. Rather, each plane is followed by its pilot in flight by walking around the inside edge of what is known as the pilot's circle. The pilot must keep abreast of his plane at all times, flying with the controlling arm fully extended and being careful that he merely follows and does not lead or whip his plane.

The flying area is laid out in four concentric circles around a common center. The inner and smallest circle is the pilot's circle, within the bounds of which the pilot must remain when walking his plane around in the race. The next circle is used only by pilots who are landing their planes for refueling or at the end of a race. The pilot moves out of the pilot's circle and into this next circle, sometimes known as the pilot's ready circle, only when he is going to land. The third circle is the actual flying circle as such, the widest of all the circles, and is bordered by a fourth, narrow circle that provides the landing and take-off zone. Thus, when the control-line pilot steps out of the pilot's circle and into the second circle, his plane is moved out of the flying circle and into position for a landing on the fourth circle. Outside the limits of this fourth circle is the pit area, where the teams of mechanics await to refuel and service the plane after it has landed. When it is ready to take off again, they start the engine and the pilot makes the takeoff and then moves back into the central, or pilot's, circle so that his model plane now is flying within the confines of the third, or flying, circle. With 60-foot flying lines, the outer border of the fourth and last circle is at least

80 feet from the common center of all the circles.

If all the regulations are adhered to, the entire performance of racing, landing, refueling and servicing and taking off again should proceed smoothly. With each of the pilots walking his plane around the edge of the inner circle, passing either over or under another plane readily can be accomplished with the cooperation of the pilot whose plane is being passed. Passing over another plane is preferable to passing under it. In any case, the pilot who desires to pass informs the other pilot of his intention. The rules for team racing are detailed and complex and, as in the case of any organized event, potential contestants should carefully study the regulations of the organization under whose sponsorship and regulations an event will be run.

RAT RACING

Rat racing merely is a simplified form of team racing. Almost any type of plane may be raced against planes of similar type if desired, although kits are available for sturdy, somewhat bare models specifically designated as rat racers. The AMA has two distinct sets of rules for team racing and rat racing respectively; the WAM has a single set of rules for what they call the 10 Mile Race. Many regard the term "rat racing" as a somewhat unfortunate selection, and its origin and meaning are often misunderstood by novices both in the United States and elsewhere. The name definitely does not imply that any sort of unsportsmanlike behavior is tolerated in a rat-race event, any more than in team racing or any other competition category. Indeed, in any organized model airplane contest, any deliberate interference with another plane, or unsportsmanlike or improper behavior of any kind will result either in penalization or outright disqualification from the event and possibly from future events as well. The name "rat race" derives from the idiomatic expression implying running around in circles and getting nowhere, as does a pet rodent on the exercise wheel of its cage.

SPEED MODELS AND CONTESTS

Speed models, far from everybody's dish, have their own ardent and enthusiastic following. There also is a considerable body of opinion that regards the speed model events not so much as a form of control-line flying (as opposed, for example, to precision acrobatics) as a display of the working of centrifugal force! The object of flying a speed model is, of course, speed, and to set a new speed record within a given class if possible. Truly tremendous speeds are attained at times; as much as close to 200 miles per hour; real miles per hour, not any sort of scale miles per hour or special model miles per hour. Except when designed to follow in a general way a particular prototype for entry in special speed proto events, most speed models are highly streamlined and individualistic in design, and are built without landing gear, or with a landing gear that drops off automatically immediately after takeoff. When no landing gear is fitted, the models are launched from a special wheeled vehicle or dolly which they leave behind as they become airborne. In order to protect the model in landing without the benefit of landing gear, it is customary to fit what is known as a speed pan to the bottom of the model or, rather, to build a speed model around such a speed pan. The speed pans are cast of lightweight metal, such as aluminum or magnesium, or alloys involving these metals. Although these pans serve to provide a rigid structure and a solid point of mounting for the high-speed engine, their primary purpose is to provide a landing aid in the form of a metal skid cast integral with the pan. Speed planes do not, therefore, really land on the belly of the fuselage as it may appear to casual onlookers, but on a skid, which is, after all, a long-accepted form of landing gear for aircraft.

Speed planes frequently are built of more or less solid construction, with fuselages carved from a solid block of balsa wood or even pine, and then sawed down the middle and carefully hollowed out inside. At times wings may be covered with sheet aluminum. Either internal-combustion reciprocating engines or jet engines may be used in speed models. While it is quite true that many speed models could not sustain themselves in flight at other than the extremely high speeds at which they are flown, those who tend to belittle the amount and skill of control required are doing the models and their builders an injustice. The very high speeds involved make these models quite difficult to control; the operator must respond instantly to any need for control correction, and at the same time all control movements must carefully be limited so as to avoid an overcontrol that would be very difficult or entirely impossible to recover from with a craft going so fast. In regard to control, the speed plane is at the extreme opposite end of the control-line spectrum from the position occupied by the trainer.

CHAPTER 5

Internal-Combustion Reciprocating Engines

When today's hobbyists follow the common custom and refer to internal-combustion reciprocating engines for model aircraft as "gas" engines, they are technically correct only insofar as they understand this to refer to the fact that the liquid fuel used in these engines is vaporized into a gaseous state before combustion. "Gas engines" does not, however, apply in the sense in which many new enthusiasts or casual onlookers at model airplane events understand it; that is, that the fuel employed in most engines is regular gasoline similar to that used in real automobiles. In Great Britain, where gasoline is known as petrol, these engines generally are called "petrol engines." Again, this term is now a misnomer, enduring from the earlier days of miniature internal-combustion reciprocating model airplane engines.

At one time most internal-combustion reciprocating model airplane engines did use a fuel compounded of unleaded white gasoline and automotive oil. These engines were of the spark ignition type. The use of combined fuel and lubricating oil was dictated by the fact that most of these engines were of the two-stroke cycle type—this point will be enlarged upon shortly. More recent developments in miniature spark ignition engines permitted and even made desirable the use of high-test gasoline combined with oil. While any statement to the effect that spark ignition engines are for all practical purposes now more or less obsolete for small model aircraft would not be precisely

accurate and would no doubt raise a storm of protest from a very active and enthusiastic body of aficionados of this type, the fact is that the average hobbyist of today probably never will encounter this type of engine during his entire experience in building and flying model airplanes unless he deliberately sets out to find it. For all practical effect, as far as model aviation as a whole is concerned, the ignition engine now has been replaced by either the glow-plug, or glow-head, engine (which a few enthusiasts of simplified spelling insist on writing as "glo plug") or the diesel engine.

The basic fuel of the glow-plug engine is a mixture of menthanol (a form of alcohol) and castor oil. That of the miniature diesel engine is ether, kerosene (known as paraffin oil in Great Britain), and castor oil. In both cases the castor oil serves as the lubricating oil called for by the two-stroke cycle engine design, and the other substances are the actual primary fuels. The castor oil is of the commercial, not the medicinal, type. It is derived from the castor bean, grown in the Far East, the kernel of which resembles a half-size pecan. If these basic mixtures of fuel and castor oil were all there was to the matter of miniature internal-combustion reciprocating model airplane engine fuel, engine operation and the requisite operator's know-how would be greatly simplified. Unfortunately, this is not the case. As will be seen later, the subject of engine fuels and their relation to performance is an extremely complex one, with almost endless ramifications. First, however, to the subject of the engines themselves:

ENGINE TYPES

Much confusion exists among beginners as to the working of miniature internal-combustion reciprocating engines and particularly concerning the term "cycle." Internal-combustion reciprocating engines, regardless of their size, are divided into two basic types, correctly designated two-stroke cycle engines and four-stroke cycle engines. However, common usage has long confusingly abbreviated these terms. This is particularly true in the United States, where they generally are called two-cycle and four-cycle engines, although "stroke" is actually the crucial word in understanding the terminology and the actual working of these engines. "Stroke" refers to the movement, upward or downward, of the piston and connecting rod; each such movement, regardless of its direction, is one stroke. Each stroke moves the crankshaft, to one end of which the propeller is attached. The cycle of an internal-combustion reciprocating engine refers not to the number of times the crankshaft turns or makes its mechanical cycle, but to *the number of strokes of the piston and connecting rod required to obtain one complete power cycle of the engine.* Regardless of whether there are two or four strokes to the power cycle, there is only one power stroke, the downward stroke caused by the combustion of the fuel driving the piston downward in the cylinder.

Thus, in a two-stroke cycle engine, the power cycle consists of two strokes, one up and one down, causing the crankshaft to revolve once. In a four-stroke cycle engine, the power cycle consists of four strokes, two up and two down, and the crankshaft makes two complete revolutions for each power stroke. The common terms "two-cycle engine" and "four-cycle engine" are therefore completely erroneous and meaningless. The use of these common but incorrect and confusing designations cannot be blamed either on model aircraft hobbyists or on model engine manufacturers, for they were already in common use in the United States long before the advent of the first miniature engines specifically designed for model airplanes in the first decade of the twentieth century. In Great Britain the common short form of engine designation is two-stroke and four-stroke, which retains the essential word "stroke" and is therefore much more understandable to the novice.

Another point that often causes some confusion among beginners is the supposed relationship between the method of exploding the vaporized

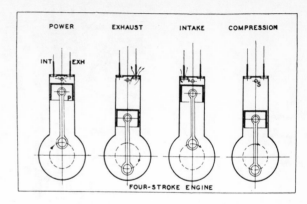

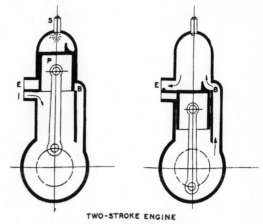

Fig. 89. The working of typical four-stroke cycle (top) and two-stroke cycle internal-combustion reciprocating engines is diagrammed here, and fully explained in the text. The two-stroke cycle design (bottom) is that used in virtually all model airplane engines today.

Carstens Publications

charge of fuel and the number of strokes in the cycle. Many fans who have recently entered the hobby have somehow acquired the erroneous conception that model airplane spark ignition engines, fired by means of a miniature spark plug (or "sparking plug" as it is often termed in Great Britain) similar to the spark plugs in an automobile engine are, like most automobile engines, four-stroke cycle engines, and that a change was made in model aircraft engines to the two-cycle design with the introduction of glow plugs. This is not the case. The glow plug, or more precisely, the "hot wire" idea, which is substantially the same, goes back to the earliest days of model aircraft internal-combustion reciprocating engines. While a fairly limited number of four-stroke cycle engines for model airplanes have been individually built from time to time by model craftsmen, and a few models have been put into commercial production, the two-stroke cycle design has been so widely followed that it might well for all practical purposes be described as the generally accepted practice since the beginning. The two-stroke cycle engine is in fact a very old and basic design that once was extremely popular for all sorts of gas engines of

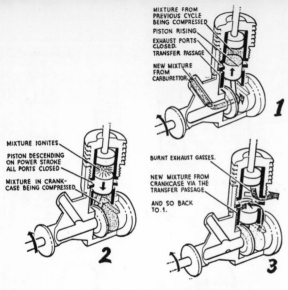

MIXTURE FROM PREVIOUS CYCLE BEING COMPRESSED

PISTON RISING

EXHAUST PORTS CLOSED.

TRANSFER PASSAGE.

NEW MIXTURE FROM CARBURETTOR.

1

MIXTURE IGNITES.

PISTON DESCENDING ON POWER STROKE ALL PORTS CLOSED.

MIXTURE IN CRANK-CASE BEING COMPRESSED.

2

BURNT EXHAUST GASSES.

NEW MIXTURE FROM CRANKCASE VIA THE TRANSFER PASSAGE.

AND SO BACK TO 1.

3

Fig. 90. These drawings show the internal construction and working cycle (two-stroke cycle) of a model airplane diesel engine (more properly, a compression ignition engine). Note the adjustable compression plate or contra piston below the cylinder head. This is found in most, but not all, miniature diesel engines.

Davies-Charlton Ltd.

varying sizes up to quite large ones, for home electric plants, stationary farm engines, light manufacturing work, small boats (including the so-called vapor or naphtha launches that were so popular in the early years of the twentieth century), automobiles, and so on. While we generally tend to think of the modern automobile engine as a prime example of the four-stroke cycle design, there are, in fact, some automobiles being manufactured today with two-stroke cycle engines.

Whether a two-stroke cycle or a four-stroke cycle design is best depends of course to a large extent on the application and in a more particular sense on the engineering thinking involved in a given case. The fact that the two-stroke cycle engine is simpler in design, with fewer moving parts and generally of overall lighter weight than a comparable four-stroke cycle engine, and capable of driving a propeller mounted directly on its crankshaft at high speed, has commended this type of engine to model airplane builders. Above all, because it is simpler than the four-stroke cycle type, it should not be thought of as inherently a less efficient or less refined mechanism.

Incidentally, while attempting here to clear up some common basic points of confusion, it should be observed that a mechanism that produces rotary movement through a reciprocating action, usually through pressure acting on a piston—whether that pressure is steam, air, or that resulting from the explosion of a vaporized fuel—properly is an engine, not a motor. This holds true despite the fact that there are countless historical references to such devices as motors, even to the extent of the inclusion of the word "motor" in company names of manufacturers of such engines for model aircraft, and the fact that we almost all on occasion

indulge in the very common misapplication of terminology of referring to the engine of an automobile as the motor. On the other hand, an electrical machine that produces rotary motion through magnetic attraction and repulsion acting directly on the turning portion of the mechanism (the armature) is a motor. There also is admittedly a gray area concerning electrical devices, for there are mechanisms that create rotary motion through a reciprocating action powered by magnetic attraction and repulsion of a moving segment or segments (again termed the "armature" or "armatures") that are at times called motors on the basis of their electrical motivation and at times designated as engines because of their use of a reciprocating motion to create rotary motion. Again, jet or rocket power devices generally are termed "engines." On the other hand, a clockwork can stand alone by that name, or the description can be expanded by calling it a clockwork motor or a spring motor.

FOUR-STROKE CYCLE ENGINE OPERATION

Although the two-stroke cycle engine is simpler in design and operation, and is the type almost universally used today in model aircraft, the four-stroke cycle engine will be described first in order to make the comparison of the two-stroke cycle type more readily understandable. The four strokes that make up the complete cycle of operations are as follows:

No. 1: *Intake or Suction.* The piston is at the top of the cylinder from the previous exhaust stroke. The piston starts to move downward, and as it does, the exhaust valve is closed and the intake valve opens and admits the vaporized fuel

Fig. 91. A cutaway illustration of a two-stroke cycle internal-combustion reciprocating model airplane engine, in this case a spark ignition engine with timer (on propeller shaft behind the propeller drive washer) and spark plug, but internally similar to many glow-plug engines. This particular engine has a rear intake and vertical needle valve.

Carstens Publications

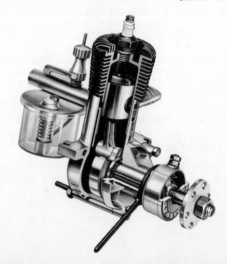

Fig. 92. Typical modern internal-combustion reciprocating engines for model airplanes. A glow-plug engine is pictured at the left and a diesel engine at the right. At the top centers of the respective cylinders may be seen the glow plug and the compression adjustment lever.

Testor Corp.
Progress Aero Works

from the carburetor into the upper part of the cylinder.

No. 2: *Compression.* The piston, having reached the bottom of its travel, starts to move upward in the cylinder; the intake valve closes, and the piston continues to move upward toward its position nearest the top of the cylinder.

No. 3: *Power.* When the piston has reached almost to the top of the cylinder and the compression of the fuel is at the optimum, the fuel is ignited by means of a timed spark in a spark ignition engine, by means of the glow plug in conjunction with the greater volatility of the compressed fuel in a glow-plug engine, or entirely by the volatility of the compressed fuel in a diesel engine. The fuel explodes, and the pressure exerted by this explosion drives the piston downward on its power stroke.

No. 4. *Exhaust.* When the piston reaches the end of its downward power stroke, the exhaust valve opens and the burnt gas escapes from the cylinder into the outer air. As the piston travels upward again it completes the exhaustion of the burnt gas, and the exhaust valve closes. The engine then starts to repeat the cycle of four strokes again with the intake or suction stroke.

In the four-stroke cycle engine there are, therefore, two separate valves opening into each cylinder. (Most model airplane engines are of the single-cylinder type, although two- and four-cylinder engines also have been built both individually and commercially.) The intake valve opens because when the piston moves downward it creates a partial vacuum in the cylinder above the piston. The pressure of the air outside the cylinder therefore forces open the intake valve and the fuel moves into the cylinder. The intake valve then closes on the compression stroke. In fact, both valves are closed during the compression and power strokes. The exhaust valve is opened on the exhaust stroke by mechanical means properly timed to open the valve at the correct moment. In some engines mechanical means also are employed to open or assist in opening the intake valve.

It will be observed that in the four-stroke cycle engine the fuel is always above the piston; it enters, is compressed, exploded, and exhausted

above the piston. While in small four-stroke cycle engines, oil is mixed with the fuel in order to provide lubrication for the cylinder itself, the lubrication of the crankcase is entirely independent.

Fig. 93. A view of the parts that go to make up an internal-combustion reciprocating two-stroke cycle glow-plug engine, together with a picture of the assembled engine. This particular engine incorporates an adjustable throttle valve and exhaust baffle to be operated by radio control, and the cylinder has a separate liner, shown in the center with the piston.

Aristo-Craft Distinctive Miniatures

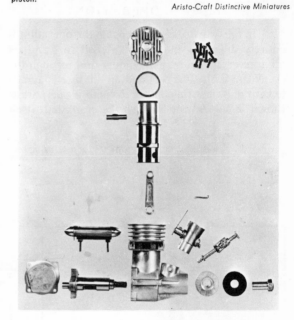

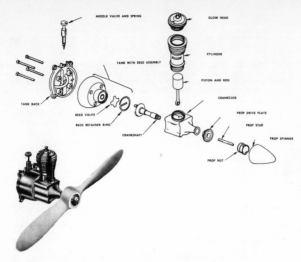

Fig. 94. An .020 cubic-inch (.327 cubic-centimeter) reed valve internal-combustion reciprocating two-stroke cycle glow-plug engine with reed valve and integral fuel tank, together with an exploded drawing of the engine showing the parts that make it up.

L. M. Cox Mfg. Co., Inc.

TWO-STROKE CYCLE ENGINE OPERATION

In the two-stroke cycle engine the operation is entirely different, and the combined fuel and oil mixture enters below the cylinder and through the crankcase itself. The fuel and oil mixture is admitted at the proper time either through a side port as shown in Fig. 95, or through the crankshaft itself by means of a rotary disk valve operating on the crankshaft, or by means of a reed valve that vibrates in resonance to the stroke of the engine. The two strokes are the compression stroke and the firing stroke. On the compression stroke the piston is moving upward, the piston itself serving to open and close the exhaust valve and what is known as the bypass, which serves for the actual intake of fuel into the cylinder, the fuel bypassing the piston through this channel as it goes from the crankcase below the piston into the cylinder above the piston. The fresh fuel in the crankcase has already been somewhat compressed by the downward movement of the piston on the power stroke, and rushes through the bypass and into the cylinder, being directed toward the top of the cylinder by means of the baffle on top of the piston at the same time that the exploded gas is being exhausted through the exhaust port. As the piston continues to rise, it closes off both the exhaust port and the bypass and compresses the new fuel in the top of the cylinder. The fuel is then fired when the piston is at the top of its upward stroke, and drives the piston downward again on the power stroke, whereupon the engine starts on its next cycle. An added factor in the operation of a two-stroke cycle engine is that

Fig. 95. Rotary valve engines. The model at the left has a rear intake; that at the right, a front intake. The exploded view shows the parts that go into the makeup of an engine similar to the latter. The displacements of the engines shown are .15 and .35 cubic inches respectively.

K & B Mfg. Corp.

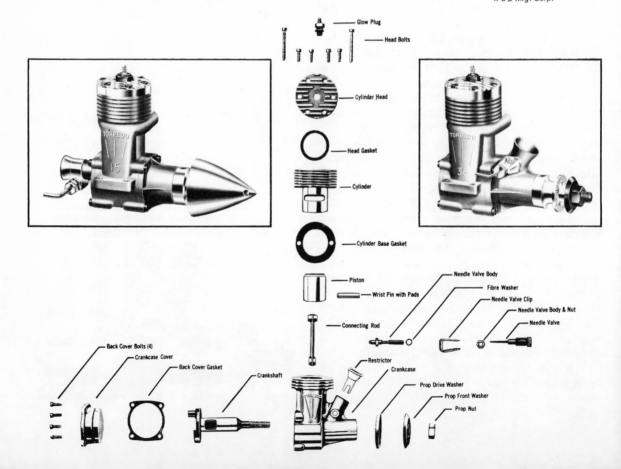

as the piston rises on its compression stroke, it creates a vacuum or at least a partial vacuum in the crankcase, and this vacuum serves to suck the fresh charge of fuel into the crankcase.

The value of an engine depends of course to a large extent on its efficiency in compressing the fuel charge. The lubricant in the cylinder serves both as a film on which the piston rides up and down and as a final seal between the piston itself, or the piston rings (pistons with rings are not too often used in modern model aircraft engines), to increase the efficiency of compression. When and if an engine loses its proper tight fit between piston and cylinder wall, the compression efficiency is lowered to the detriment of operation, and when the compression drops beyond a certain point the engine is useless. Compression ratio refers to the ratio between the volume of fuel admitted to the cylinder when the piston is in its bottom position to the volume within which the fuel has been compressed when the piston is in its highest position; that is, the volume of the space between the top of the piston and the bottom of the cylinder head. Thus an engine that compresses its charge of fuel into an area one-sixth the size of the area of the cylinder over the piston when the piston is at its bottom position is said to have a compression ratio of 6:1. In the main, the tendency today is to build model airplane engines with greater compression ratios than those common in recent years. This has the effect of making a given-size engine more powerful, or, to put it another way, it has the effect of increasing the size of the engine. This is one reason many of today's small engines are used satisfactorily to fly planes of considerably larger size than once would have been practical. Increasing the compression ratio also affects the type of fuel and the precise mixture of ingredients that may efficiently be used, just as automobile engines with a high compression ratio require special high-test fuels for their efficient operation.

While it is true that the basic design of the two-stroke cycle model airplane engine has changed little since the very first engines, the refinements of design have been almost beyond measure and are an ever-continuing process. Model internal-combustion reciprocating engine design now is largely the province of highly skilled professional engineers who make a full-time job of designing ever better engines for the model engine manufacturers with the result that still further improved engines are reaching the market almost continually. This situation no doubt will continue in the years ahead. It is also worth noting, however, that this process of development, coupled with ever-increasing demand and the economies of mass-production manufacturing, has resulted in the availability of efficient engines at extraordinarily low prices, both actual and comparative.

At times a two-stroke cycle engine will fire only on alternate compression strokes; that is, it fires on every fourth stroke, as does a four-stroke cycle engine; in fact, this condition is known as "four-cycling." The term derives from the American custom of referring to the engines as two- or four-cycle engines; more properly of course what the engine is doing is "four-stroking." This condition is the result of too much fuel being introduced into the cylinder for the proper compression of the fuel. Consequently some of the excess unexploded fuel is discharged through the exhaust port on what should be the power stroke, and the engine fires on the completion of the next compression stroke. Four-cycling generally has been regarded as a malfunction with two-stroke cycle engines ex-

Fig. 96. A radio-control internal-combustion reciprocating glow-plug engine, in this case of .40 cubic-inch displacement. This photograph clearly shows the moving exhaust baffle (left) and throttle, which are linked so that they move together as directed by the commands transmitted to an actuating device.

Testor Corp.

Fig. 97. A front view of two .45 cubic-inch-displacement glow-plug engines. The model at the right is a standard engine; that at the left is the same model equipped for radio control, in this case with an adjustable throttle valve and two needle valves. No exhaust baffle is employed in this particular design.

MRC-Enya Co. Inc.

Fig. 98. A radio-control-actuated engine speed adjustment available as an accessory unit to convert certain standard model engines to radio control. It consists of a throttle control linked to an exhaust baffle control so that both move at once when actuated, and is available in several sizes to match particular engines.

L. M. Cox Mfg. Co., Inc.

cept when it might occasionally be induced deliberately to provide a second speed; the engine does not run smoothly when four-cycling. Recently at least one new design of two-stroke cycle engine has been introduced that will run smoothly when four-cycling, and it is possible that additional designs will be brought out, or perhaps the efficiency of existing models will be brought to the attention of modelers, so that four-cycling will no longer have the same connotations as in the past.

METHODS OF FIRING

As noted, the number of strokes in the power cycle of an engine bears no relation to the method of firing. When glow plugs were first introduced commercially after World War II, they were initially offered as substitutions for spark plugs in the same engines. At first they were regarded with some curiosity and a certain trepidation by many enthusiasts who regarded them as being somewhat in the nature of a departure from the natural order of things. The advantages of glow plugs over the then conventional spark-plug ignition were, however, so quickly manifest that the glow plug rapidly emerged triumphant. It should be noted here that all remarks pertaining to glow-plug engines relate equally to glow-head engines. The design of the firing element and the method of operation are the same. Some engines are designed with the glow element integral with the cylinder head; when a new firing element is required the entire cylinder head is replaced by a new one. Separate glow plugs, on the other hand, are screwed in or out of a cylinder head just as are spark plugs.

There are two main advantages to the glow plug: First, the system is less complicated than spark-plug ignition. The second advantage hinges on the first; by doing away with certain adjuncts to the spark-plug ignition engine that had to be car-

ried on the model airplane itself, considerable weight, comparatively speaking, is eliminated. If desired, a larger and more powerful glow-plug engine can be installed in a given model plane than is possible with a spark ignition engine, because of this saving of weight. Additionally, although the facility may be the result in part at least of increasing engine design know-how and improvements in fuel rather than inherent in the glow plug itself, most modern glow-plug engines appear easier for a novice to start and keep running than did ignition engines. Certainly there are far less parts to adjust and keep in good order, and the amount of fuel fed and the precise mixture of fuel and air do not seem to be as critical for fairly efficient running as in a spark ignition engine when the glow-plug engine is used for ordinary sport flying. In competition flying, where the comparative engine performance is of paramount importance, glow-plug engine adjustment must, of course, be as knowingly precise as with any other type of engine. However, by the time a model aviation hobbyist goes in for activities of this type it may safely be assumed that he has mastered the finer points of engine regulation that can come only through experience.

All that is necessary in a model airplane powered by a glow-plug engine is the engine itself and the fuel tank. With a spark ignition engine there must also be carried a timing device built into the engine, an ignition coil to produce a sufficiently "hot" spark, a condenser to reduce excessive sparking and resulting wear of the timing points, a battery or batteries, a starting switch, and the requisite wiring to connect these electrical components. A matter of perhaps only a few ounces to be sure, but an important weight factor in a small model airplane and, indeed, in any model airplane.

In a glow-plug engine, on the other hand, the firing element of the glow plug initially is heated sufficiently to explode the compressed fuel mixture by means of a starting battery located outside the model airplane itself. This ignition battery, which is disconnected once the engine starts running, is the only battery that enters into the scheme of things. The battery must have sufficient power to make the firing element of the glow plug hot enough to fire the initial charge of fuel; proper dry cell ignition batteries are available at any hobby shop. In starting, a wire is run from one terminal of the battery to the insulated post on top of the glow plug, and the other wire from the other terminal of the battery to the uninsulated portion of the plug or to the cylinder head. The most convenient method is to employ a special glow-plug starting clip to which the battery wires are permanently attached. The clip is slipped onto position on the glow plug and readily pulled off once the engine has started. Using a starting clip of this type leaves both hands free. Once the engine starts to run, the glow-plug element is kept sufficiently hot by the explosions of the fuel—thousands of explosions every minute—so that there is a continuous action of the glow plug exploding the fuel and being kept sufficiently hot by the heat of the explosion to fire the next charge of fuel as it is fed up and compressed by the compression stroke of the engine. (Spark ignition engines also require an outside starting, or booster, battery that is disconnected once the engine has started and can rely on the smaller batteries carried in the plane itself for further power.)

Despite the fact that the glow-plug unit itself to a large extent physically resembles a spark plug, the glow-plug engine is in fact more closely analogous to the semidiesel, or hot-bulb or hot-wire diesel engine long used in various commercial installations than it is to the spark ignition engine. The hot-wire ignition idea was used in a number of the early internal-combustion reciprocating engines in pioneer airplanes, including those of Langley, Whitehead, and the Wrights, and also was applied to a number of model engines operated in the early years of the century. Semidiesels, hot-bulb diesels, and hot-wire diesels are not true diesel engines in any sense, despite the popular name, but work in a manner quite akin to glow-plug engines. As a matter of fact, in the late 1940's and early 1950's, glow-plug model airplane engines were at times accurately classified and referred to as semidiesel engines.

DIESEL ENGINES

In a true diesel engine there is no separate means of igniting the fuel mixture, even for the initial firing. The fuel used is such that it can be made sufficiently volatile so as to explode itself when sufficiently compressed by the upward movement of the piston in the cylinder. Once the engine is started by turning over the propeller, it keeps running by repeating the cycle of compression to the point of self-explosion, the explosion creating the power stroke downward and then the next compression stroke to the point where the new fuel charge fires itself. There is nothing very complicated or awesome about the working of a diesel

Fig. 99. Accessories for glow-plug engine operation. Shown here are a special engine wrench (which should always be used to remove and insert glow plugs and glow heads), control-line snaps, a filler hose and filter cap for fuel cans, and a special clip used for attaching the starting battery to the engine.

L. M. Cox Mfg. Co., Inc.

engine, despite the strange degree of awe and prejudice that has to a considerable extent attached itself to this type of miniature aircraft engine in the United States. Although some diesel engines for model airplanes are made with a fixed compression ratio (as are all spark ignition and glow-plug engines) and can be recognized by their plain, unadorned cylinder heads, most diesel engines are provided with a variable compression, and sport an adjustable compression screw emerging in the form of a little handle or lever where the plug would be located on a spark-plug or glow-plug engine. This handle is used to raise or lower a compression plate or contra piston at the top of the cylinder. When the compression plate is lowered, the compression ratio of the engine is increased; when the plate is raised, the compression ratio is decreased. That is, there is respectively less or more room between the top of the piston and the working head of the cylinder. Diesel engines customarily are built with much higher compression ratios than are spark ignition or glow-plug engines. In model diesel operation it is usual to start the engine at a higher compression ratio, and then, once the engine is running smoothly, to reduce the compression ratio slightly in order to obtain the best ratio for continued running on a given adjustment of fuel and air, and to preclude premature combustion as a result of the engine itself heating up.

The fact that the operation of a glow-plug engine calls only for the adjustment of the fuel and air mixture, by means of a needle valve, while most diesel engines require a rather coordinated adjustment of both the needle valve and the compression screw, might be considered a disadvantage and one cause of the seemingly widespread belief among modelers in the United States that diesel engines are quite difficult to start. Over and over again, when questioned as to why they have abandoned diesel engines, American modelers who have had experience with this type will reply that they found them hard to start. This statement amazes British modelers, who, as a general rule, feel they have no trouble whatsoever starting diesel engines

Fig. 100. In these photographs the ignition battery, which is used to start a glow-plug engine and disconnected once the engine is running, has been attached to the glow plug (the engine in the photograph at right is installed in an inverted position), and the hobbyists are about to spin their propellers in a counterclockwise direction to start their engines.

Rich's Hobbytowne, Inc.
Hobby Industry of America, Inc.

and who, in the main, appear to prefer them to glow-plug engines. There are, as a matter of fact, a great many American model airplane hobbyists who are diesel-engine enthusiasts, who use them regularly, and who evidently find them quite manipulatable. However, for the most part, these American diesel-engine fans are flying with imported, mainly British, engines. At the time of this writing there is no such thing as an American-made model airplane diesel engine on the market!

A number of valiant attempts have been made to manufacture model airplane diesel engines in the United States, and a number of excellent engines reached the market as a result of these efforts; all have been discontinued for lack of popular support and enthusiasm. The question must naturally arise as to why British model airplane hobbyists so enthusiastically accepted the diesel engine after the Second World War, while their counterparts in the United States have reacted so adversely to this type. No entirely satisfactory answer can be found. In attempting to investigate this point, some of the suggested reasons bordered on the facetious; the replies to queries seldom attempted to go beyond the already mentioned popular American conception that diesels are difficult to start. One point did develop that may throw some light on the matter, although it accounts mainly for the initial popularity of diesels in Great Britain without fully explaining their continuing favor there and the parallel lack of popularity in the United States. Had the same conditions as to the relative ease of securing fuels existed in the United States immediately after the war as they did in Great Britain, it is possible that the model diesel engine would have attained as much popularity in the United States. It appears that for some time after the end of the war gasoline fuel for conventional spark ignition engines and alcohol-based fuels for glow-plug engines continued in extremely

short supply in Great Britain. Kerosene was more readily obtainable by model fans, and hence the kerosene-burning diesel engines captured a position of popularity that they have maintained ever since in that country. Kerosene was of course plentiful in the United States, but so were gasoline and menthanol. Accordingly, many hobbyists never were compelled to explore the possibilities of the diesel engine and to master such specialized techniques as this type may require.

To be absolutely accurate from the technical standpoint, the model airplane engines known as diesels are not true diesel engines either, although they explode the fuel charge spontaneously under compression, as do true diesels, and therefore much more closely approach the true diesel engines in their functioning than do the semidiesels. However, true diesel engines receive their charges of air and fuel separately in the cylinder, whereas the so-called model diesel engines mix the air and fuel before they reach the cylinder. The best name for the model diesels that those seeking an apt description appear to have been able to come up with so far is that of compression ignition engines, although this term obviously is broad enough to cover true diesel engines as well.

ENGINE TERMINOLOGY

The beginner frequently finds engines described not only by their capacity or displacement —explained in Chapter 1—but also by initials that mainly are confusing to novices simply because no one evidently ever has felt it necessary to provide a concise explanation. The most frequently met designation is that of the letters RC, which may be rendered in that form, or as R.C. or R/C. In modelmaking as a whole, the initials RC have long indicated remote control. In model airplane engines they generally are understood to stand instead for "radio control," which often causes some confusion, although more in the precise translation of the initials than in any physical difference among model airplane engines themselves. The control function provided on engines of this design is always that of speed regulation. As we have seen, it is possible to regulate the speed of a model airplane engine by means of an additional line on control-line models as well as by means of signals transmitted to a radio receiver carried in a model airplane. Therefore it actually makes little difference if a hobbyist understands RC to stand for "remote control" or "radio control" as far as model airplane engines are concerned, although "remote control" would be in truth a more accurate and broadly based interpretation than "radio control." Originally the change of engine speed usually was effected either by opening or closing a choke on the air intake or on the exhaust, or by the use of two needle valves adjusted to different settings and using the radio-control apparatus to regulate the flow of fuel through one or the other at will, thereby deriving two different engines speeds by variations in the fuel and air mixture. Such engines frequently were designated as two-speed engines rather than RC engines. Today the usual practice is to provide for speed changes by manipulating the spray bar, which then serves as a throttle valve itself, around a single needle valve setting, usually at the same time opening and closing the exhaust a complementary degree by means of mechanical linkage connected to the throttle. Some engine designers still regard two needle valves as desirable in combination with the throttle valve and exhaust valve linkage combination. In such engines one needle valve is set so as to provide a fuel mixture sufficient only to allow the engine to idle. When the throttle is completely closed, this idling needle valve jet comes into play.

In any case, any engine today designated as an RC, R.C., or R/C engine will have some form of operating throttle control. An alternate designation for the same thing that is sometimes found is TV, standing for throttle valve.

The initials RV or RR have nothing to do with radio or remote control, but rather refer to the valve type and placement. RV indicates rotary valve (although the initials could as truly abbreviate reed valve, but they are never used in this meaning). RR stands for rear rotary, meaning the engine has a rotary valve and intake located at the rear of the crankcase rather than at the front. BB or BR show that an engine is equipped with ball bearings, BR standing for ball race. A ball race is merely the housing or container within which the balls that form a ball bearing rotate;

Fig. 101. Model internal-combustion reciprocating two-stroke cycle diesel engines with integral tanks, and accessories. The engines have 1 and 1.49 cubic-centimeter displacement. The larger engine is fitted with a radio-control throttle and mufflers or silencers. The lower photograph shows the mufflers separately.

Marown Engineering Ltd.

Fig. 102. An adjustable muffler for certain types of engines that permits control of the sound level to whatever pitch may be desired. Mufflers of this type are available as accessory units for engines already in use; also, complete muffler-equipped engines are now manufactured.

L. M. Cox Mfg. Co., Inc.

Fig. 103. An adjustable test stand for internal-combustion reciprocating model airplane engines, used in bench testing or, when required, running in of an engine. No engine should ever be clamped directly in a vise for running; lack of freedom for expansion of the heated metal can result in severe damage to the engine.

Polk's Model Craft Hobbies, Inc.

the term does not necessarily indicate that the engine in question is a specialized engine for model airplanes designed for racing, although a ball-bearing engine may very well be intended for this purpose. Whether or not ball bearings were a worthy addition to a model airplane engine was itself once a subject of considerable debate, some hobbyists and engine designers feeling that they were needed in a model engine only when it was intended for use in a model boat or racing car where the balls helped carry the weight of the fly-wheel. This argument is now rather academic, since the great majority of model airplane engines do not have ball bearings and are excellent engines. At the same time, if ball bearings can be incorporated into the design of an engine without materially increasing the weight, they obviously are a desirable feature for any engine intended for high-speed running, specifically for racing engines. Naturally their inclusion adds to the cost of an engine.

Beginners may also be confused by references to radial or beam mounting, indicating the position of the fixtures for securing an engine in a model airplane and, accordingly, the mode of mounting. A beam-mounted engine has its mounting lugs located on the sides of the crankcase. A radial-mounted engine has its mounting lugs radiating from the rear of the engine; sometimes, in the case of small engines, from the rear of the fuel tank, which is an integral part of the engine. In short, a radial-mounted engine is bolted to the fire-wall, usually a plywood bulkhead, with bolts running parallel to the center line of crankshaft; that is to say, with horizontal bolts. A beam-mounted engine is bolted with vertical bolts to beams extending forward from the firewall, or otherwise built into the model airplane, with the bolts running at right angles to the center line of the crank-shaft. Generally speaking, smaller engines are mounted radially while larger engines are mounted on beams, but this cannot be considered a hard-

and-fast rule. Some engines are provided with lugs for optional beam or radial mounting. It is also possible to obtain special cast aluminum engine mounts that permit a beam-mount engine to be mounted radially. Sometimes these mounts incorporate a fuel tank or landing gear within the mount.

BREAKING IN OF ENGINES

The average hobbyist, especially the newcomer to model aviation, is, of course, less concerned with the intricacies of model engine design and manipulation than with gaining the basic knowledge essential to his understanding and intelligent selection of an engine or engines and their use. While many hobbyists own a considerable variety of engines, it is one of the nice things about model airplane engines that an enthusiast does not have to have a separate engine for each model plane he builds and wishes to fly. A great many hobbyists use a single engine that they transfer from one plane to another and that serves them faithfully for a considerable period of time. In order to use any engine efficiently and make it last as long as possible, it is necessary to understand the basic principles of engine performance and care.

First, it is important that the hobbyist read, understand, and follow the instructions that come with his particular engine. Much grief would be avoided if enthusiasts realized that not every engine is by any means identical in its requirements as to fuel, breaking in, handling, and so on. There are engine experts, to be sure, who over some years have acquired sufficient knowledge and experience that they can readily turn from using one particular engine to another and obtain a similarly high performance from each. Most of today's engines are reasonably well made and efficient. (In the old days perfectly good engines often were discarded simply because hobbyists who were familiar with one type could not or would not familiarize themselves with a different make or model. So do rely fully on the manufacturer's instructions. Take the oft-debated matter of whether a model airplane engine needs to be run in or broken in before flying. The answer is quite simple: with today's engines it depends entirely on the engine. Some engines require a running-in period while bench-mounted before they are flown; others literally are ready-to-run when purchased and require no breaking in. If the instructions tell you that a particular engine does not require running in, you can accept this. The manufacturer has nothing to gain by steering you wrong on this. By the same

Fig. 104. An adjustable-pitch propeller, shown here with a safety propeller nut. The pitch of this propeller may be changed in a few seconds, allowing the propeller to be perfectly matched for optimum performance to any given model airplane and engine combination.

Tatone Products

token, if the instructions advise breaking in for a certain period of time with a certain size propeller, follow this advice to the letter.

It should also be noted that if such breaking in is advocated, no sort of grinding compound, no matter how mild, should ever be used as an accompaniment of breaking in, in a misguided effort to shorten the time required for this process or with the idea in mind that it helps set up the engine better. There is a diehard myth current among some modelers that using jewelers' rouge or silver polish or some similar material is a trade secret that will help free up a new engine. This is quite untrue, and the use of any sort of abrasive will simply ruin an engine.

Whenever an engine is bench run, whether for purposes of testing or breaking in, it should be securely mounted in a special wooden engine test stand, or screwed to a block of wood that, in turn, is held fast in a vise. Under no circumstances should any part of an engine ever be held fast directly in a vise. This leaves no room for expansion of the metal as the engine develops heat, and assuredly will result in a badly damaged, if not completely ruined engine. This applies whether the crankcase, cylinder, mounting lugs, or any other part is placed between the jaws of the vise.

Model airplane engine cylinders, being air-cooled, customarily are made with fins so as to expose a greater overall surface of metal to the air and dissipate the heat better. (Model boat engines usually are water-cooled and have a smooth-surfaced jacket around the cylinder through which water is circulated; except for this difference many models are identical with model airplane engines of the same make.) The point often arises, what with the obvious attention to cooling indicated by the presence of the fins, as to whether model airplane engines may not run too hot, especially when they are enclosed in a cowling, as on many scale models, for the sake of realism, and on many speed models, in the interests of streamlining. It is possible of course for an engine under certain circumstances to run so hot as to destroy the lubricating quality of the oil and thereby suffer serious damage, but in actual practice this seldom happens. As a matter

Fig. 105. Special engine mounts for converting beam-type mount engines to radial mounting. The mount at the left is made with an integral fuel tank for smaller-size engines. The amount at the right is designed for engines using separate fuel tanks. It permits down- and side-thrust adjustments to be made with ease.

L. M. Cox Mfg. Co.
Tatone Products

of fact, cooling is hardly a serious problem with model airplane engines today, so long as provision is made for a little flow of air over and around the cylinder. Difficulties sometimes arise when model airplane designers provide a point of entry for cooling air at the front of a cowling but neglect to provide the necessary corresponding opening for the egress of air at the rear of the cowling. Model glow-plug and diesel engines both require a certain amount of heat in the upper cylinder to obtain satisfactory combustion. If anything, the head of the cylinder of a diesel engine will become hotter during operation than the head of a glow-plug engine, and the diesel engine head may require correspondingly better cooling.

CARBURETION

The successful running of any model internal-combustion reciprocating engine depends on obtaining the proper mixture of fuel and air. In a real airplane or automobile this is accomplished by means of a fairly complicated carburetor. Similar carburetors of the float type have been successfully tried on model engines, as have wick-type carburetors and other designs. At present, however, model aircraft engine carburetion, which simply means the combining of air with vaporized fuel in the proper proportions to produce the desired gaseous mixture that is sucked into the crankcase, has more or less settled upon an extremely efficient and simple means involving the use of a combination of a simple fuel tube and a needle valve. The pointed, or needle, end of the valve can be adjusted in relation to the fuel tube to permit a varying amount of fuel to be atomized into the intake of air that, continuing past the orifice of the fuel supply lines, carries the combined mixture of air and vaporized fuel into the crankcase of a two-stroke cycle engine.

The air first enters through the air intake, which may be placed either at the front or the back of the engine. The intake of air is sufficient in either position, for the air does not merely flow into an open tube facing toward the direction of travel of the model airplane, as some believe, but is pulled into the intake by a combination of the suction developed in the crankcase as the piston rises and the suction created by the venturi conformation of the inside of the air intake itself. The air intake pipe sometimes is incorrectly referred to as the venturi. Venturi actually refers to the internal shape of this pipe, narrowing as it approaches the point at which the fuel intake is located and widening again past this point. The fuel line enters the side of the intake at a right angle and usually continues across it, with an opening in the center. The needle valve enters this tube, or spray bar as it is known, from the other side, with its point over the opening. By adjusting the regulating screw or the external handle of the needle valve, the point may be moved further into the spray bar, or withdrawn a ways, as desired. By making this adjustment of the needle valve, the relative richness or leanness of the final vaporized fuel mixture is regulated. A rich mixture is one in which there is a high ratio of fuel proper to air; a lean mixture is one in which there is a low ratio of fuel proper to air. The term fuel itself may refer to either of two things: the liquid fuel proper as placed in the fuel tank, or the final vaporized mixture of fuel and air that goes into the crankcase and eventually into the cylinder to be exploded. The more the needle bar is withdrawn, the richer the mixture; the more it is advanced, the leaner the mixture. Of course there is at best a relatively short range of possible movement for the needle valve to deliver a fuel mixture that will satisfactorily operate a given engine. The needle-valve setting therefore is critical, both in the sense that it must be adjusted fairly delicately to provide a satisfactory mixture at all and that it is the means by which an engine can be brought to its state of highest possible efficiency and operating speed on a given fuel under any specific set of atmospheric conditions. On a model diesel engine with variable compression, both the needle valve and the compression screw must be adjusted; on a glow-plug or spark-plug ignition engine the needle valve is the sole adjustment.

The delicacy of the operation of properly setting the needle valve is further complicated by the fact that all fuel mixtures tend to become leaner, or to "lean out," as it usually is expressed, once the model airplane leaves the ground. It is not enough, therefore, merely to set the needle valve to produce the fuel mixture that best operates the engine while the plane is on the ground. For best results it is necessary to ascertain this point of adjustment and then withdraw the needle slightly to make the mixture a little richer to compensate for the fact that the fuel will lean out of its own accord once the plane is airborne.

Different needle-valve settings would be required on the same engine depending on whether it was being used in a control-line or free-flight model. With a control line, a model plane may be headed up or down or kept on a level course during powered flight, as the operator desires. A free-flight model airplane, however, is normally always heading upward while under power. It should climb until the fuel supply is exhausted or is shut off; when it starts down it should be in a

powerless glide. The normal operating position for a free-flight plane while in the air therefore is with the nose somewhat elevated—a different position from that of the plane on the ground at the time the engine is started and adjusted. It is not that the position of the engine itself is important between that on the ground and that in the air, but rather the relative positions of the engine and fuel tank. The farther away from the engine the fuel tank is located, when the plane noses up in flight, the relatively lower is the fuel tank in relation to the engine. Bear in mind that the fuel is not fed into the engine merely by gravity; it is to a large extent literally pulled into the engine by the suction developed. The farther away from the engine, or the lower in relation to the engine is the fuel tank, the harder the engine must pull to maintain an adequate flow of fuel. It is a vicious cycle, for the engine must operate at a high speed to create adequate suction to draw fuel, and it must draw fuel in sufficient volume in order to continue to operate at the necessary speed. This is one reason why for free-flight planes, engines with integral tanks or with tanks mounted immediately behind the engine are desirable. However, it usually is necessary to bring the fuel through a timer on its way from the tank to the engine so that the timer will operate to cut off the flow of fuel at the proper moment and limit the duration of the flight. Nose up, tank down, and the fuel mixture leans out automatically even more than it customarily does when a control-line plane becomes airborne. Accordingly, when starting the engine before takeoff, the needle valve must be adjusted to compensate for the difference between the ground and the in-flight relationships of the engine and fuel tank. Once the engine is started, the plane should be held in the same attitude that it will take in flight and the needle valve be set for even a little richer mixture than is required to satisfactorily pull the fuel into the engine to compensate for the normal leaning out of any engine when airborne.

FUELS

As already noted, the basic fuel for glow-plug engines is a combination of menthanol and castor oil; for diesel engines it is a mixture of ether, kerosene, and castor oil. In spark ignition engines the usual fuel was white gasoline mixed with automotive oil, usually a heavy oil like SAE (Society of Automotive Engineers) No. 70, although sometimes lighter oils were used in cold weather. This is not to say that in the closing days of the great period of spark ignition engine popularity, when engines with higher compression ratios were coming into favor, especially for racing, white gasoline was not in many cases found inadequate. Consequently there was a trend toward high-test, or so-called "special" or "extra," gasoline and even, finally, to fuels blended of alcohols and castor oil similar to those now commonly used for glow-plug engines.

Inasmuch as castor oil is common as the lubricant to both glow-plug and diesel fuels, it is appropriate to examine it first. Castor oil is necessary as the lubricant for an alcohol-based fuel because ordinary automotive or petroleum oils will not mix completely with alcohol. However, castor oil is available only in one thickness or viscosity, and therefore the relative amount of lubrication must be determined by the ratio of oil mixed with the fuel proper. The higher the oil content of a fuel mixture, the less zip to the engine, but also the less wear on the engine. The lower the oil content, the better will be the performance of the engine and also the greater the wear. (We are speaking now of outright mixtures of basic fuel and oil, without taking into consideration the factor of power additives that go into the makeup of most fuels.) Consequently the fuels designed for racing engines usually are compounded with less castor oil in proportion than are fuels intended for everyday flying. Under these conditions, of course, racing engines do not have as long a potential useful life as do the engines employed in sport flying. The more castor oil in a fuel mixture, the better the lubrication and the longer the useful life of an engine. Indeed, the compression of an old and worn engine often can be held by using a fuel with a high castor oil content, which forms a thick film around the piston, while the same engine would fail to operate at all with a fuel with low castor oil content.

Apropos of the fact that petroleum oils will not blend with alcohol-based fuels, necessitating the substitution of castor oil, castor oil will not by itself mix with kerosene when the latter is used alone. Consequently ether is added to model airplane diesel fuel, as its presence acts to allow all three components to blend successfully. Ether itself is, of course, a fuel and acts as such in a compression ignition engine. Some authorities regard it as a comparatively poor fuel as such, whose main usefulness is through the comparatively low temperature at which it ignites, which serves as a substantial aid in getting a diesel engine started.

From time to time the hobbyist may hear much concerning gum in castor oil and the necessity for using degummed oil. There are those who maintain that there is no such thing as gum in castor oil and that what is usually referred to as gum or varnish actually is castor oil that has become oxidized because of high temperature or exposure to air and that the so-called gum can readily be washed away by the oil itself. Be this point as it may, what is vitally important in the handling of all fuels and what is universally recognized as a great potential source of serious engine damage are the impurities, dust, dirt, and other minute particles, that may be picked up by any fuel during processing and handling. Not only can these particles build up so as to perceptibly clog fuel lines and the spray-bar orifice, but even more deadly, once they get into the crankcase or cylinder they can act as a grinding compound that could even ruin an engine. The fuel for any engine should therefore always be filtered between the can in which it comes and its entry into the tank. Fuel is either poured from the can by means of a filler hose directly into the tank, or the filler hose is attached to a small hand-operated pumping device that draws it from the can. In either case, a filter or strainer of very fine wire mesh should be used. It is possible to secure special filler caps that replace the ordinary can cap during the filling operation and include built-in filters. Some hobbyists

place another small filter in the fuel line between the tank and engine in the model airplane itself. Many fans who engage regularly in contest flying insist on filtering all their fuel through a piece of chamois or silk before it goes into their tanks. This naturally provides an even finer strainer than does a metal screen type of filter, although the latter should prove adequate for the flying done by the average model airplane enthusiast.

Glow-plug engine fuels need no third component added to the menthanol and castor oil to act as a blending agent, as does the ether in diesel fuel. However, additives in varying amounts cusstomarily are placed in all commercial fuels, partially to help provide easier starting, but primarily to produce a "hotter" fuel that will deliver greater speed. The most commonly used additives are the so-called "nitro" group, and include nitromethane (the most widely used), nitroethane, and nitropropane. In sports-type fuels a very small proportion of nitromethane or similar additive is used, the proportion increasing in the specialized high-speed or racing fuels, until the point may be reached where a formula may contain as much as 50 percent nitro! Such fuels should be used only by experienced hobbyists, for it is literally possible to burn out an engine by employing unduly hot fuels for prolonged running. The average sports flyer will probably find that all his fuel needs will be taken care of—and best taken care of—by using one of the standard brands of sports flying fuels. If the engine manufacturer also produces his own blends of fuel, it is logical and wise to use his fuel. In all cases, and particularly with the small engines of the type customarily supplied in ready-to-fly model airplanes, follow the fuel recommendations of the manufacturer of the engine.

At times the weather conditions may have some effect on the choice of a fuel for a particular day. On cooler days it may be best to use a slightly hotter fuel than is satisfactory on warm summer

Fig. 107. Clockwork timers for limiting the duration of a model airplane's free flight. The two models at the left cut off the fuel supply at the desired time, while the model at the upper right releases fuel into the venturi to stop the engine. The model at the lower right releases pop-up tails or similar flight-spoiler devices.

Tatone Products

days. The milder glow-plug fuels usually contain a higher proportion of castor oil and are therefore especially adapted to older engines, or to any engines that require a considerable amount of lubrication. As the nitro content goes up, the proportion of castor oil generally goes down, and in any event an engine runs hotter, so that even if the amount of oil in a given quantity of fuel remained the same, it would not provide as much lubrication. The higher the compression ratio of an engine, the more it will favor higher nitro-content fuels.

Diesel engine fuels generally run to fairly large or almost equal proportions of the three basic ingredients: castor oil, kerosene, and ether. A sports fuel for diesel engines might run about one part castor oil, one part of kerosene, and one and a half parts of ether. A hotter fuel would contain proportionately more kerosene, such as a mixture of one part each of castor oil, kerosene, and ether, with an additive of 2 percent amyl nitrite. When a small amount of nitrite or nitrate is added to diesel fuel, its purpose is to hasten ignition and provide smoother running and greater power. Speaking broadly, increasing the proportion of kerosene in a diesel fuel provides added power; increasing the proportion of ether will make for easier starting. For the same reason, the ether proportion may be increased slightly in cold weather. Ether evaporates very quickly; it has even been asserted that once some fuel is drawn from a can the ether in the fuel remaining will partially evaporate within the can and that more ether should be added to the can before additional fuel is drawn from it, in a sort of rough-and-ready effort to restore the balance of the ingredients.

The hobbyist who can obtain ready-mixed fuels certainly should make use of them and not attempt to mix his own, although American hobbyists may experience some difficulties in obtaining ready-mixed fuels for diesel engines at the present time. Some fans have reported employing substitute model diesel fuels based on mixtures of actual diesel truck fuel and ether. A substantial number of fans do mix their own fuels, either because they cannot get prepared fuels, for real or imagined reasons of economy, or for experimental purposes in an effort to obtain a better formula than that of a commercial fuel. It should be obvious that the home handling, mixing, and storage of these highly volatile fluids is hardly the most desirable procedure under any circumstances. As far as practicing it in an effort to obtain a hotter fuel, it is quite true that different engines perform differently under different weather conditions and even when used for different types of flying. The commercial fuels

Fig. 108. Another type of timer for free-flight internal-combustion-reciprocating-engine-powered model airplanes. The fuel line is run through the two connections, and the timer automatically breaks the flow of fuel to the engine when the time span for which the timer has been set has elapsed.

Austin-Craft Co.

must be somewhat in the nature of compromises to enable the average engine to perform well under average conditions. If technicians working in a fully equipped laboratory knew in advance what the air temperature and humidity were to be on a given day, and what engine was to be used in what type of flying, they might be able to compound a special fuel for the occasion that would produce better performance than one of the standard commercial fuels. As this obviously is impossible, it is best for model flyers to stick to one of the commercial blends. Another thing about home brewing: many such experiments result in a fuel that actually decreases the power of an engine. This is not always evident because the mixture does make the engine run smoother. The experimenter therefore is under the erroneous impression that he has increased the speed of his engine. The rpm of any engine can accurately be ascertained only by using a special measuring instrument, and comparatively inexpensive versions suitable for hobbyists are available. Anyone who is going in for home fuel blending should first provide himself with one of these indicators if his efforts to produce a superior fuel are to be worth anything. Furthermore it should be noted in connection with home fuel blending and experimentation that some of the usual ingredients involved are difficult to obtain, and certain of them are of the prescription drug variety. In general it is sound advice to avoid trying to prepare fuels for internal-combustion reciprocating model airplane engines at home and to stick with the excellent and more than adequate commercial fuels sold in hobby shops.

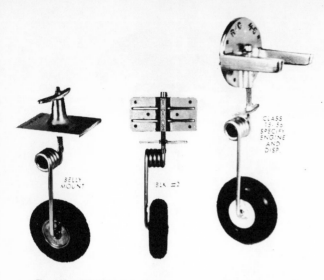

Fig. 109. Steerable nose landing-gear assemblies for multichannel radio-controlled model airplanes. The model at the left is designed to mount on the underbelly of a plane, that in the center to mount to a special bulkhead, and the one on the right is combined with an engine mount.

Tatone Products

ENGINE MISCELLANY

Special engine wrenches are available at hobby dealers or from manufacturers of engines. They provide openings of the exact fit for removing glow plugs and cylinder heads. A tool of this type should always be used, rather than attempting to employ pliers or ordinary wrenches. There are many parts involved in model engine design that, if overtightened, will be damaged or ruined. Too much torque should never be applied to any model engine part; nothing should ever be forced. Engines should always be allowed to cool before any work is undertaken except where it may be necessary to remove a glow plug or glow head from an engine and replace it with a new one during the course of flying activity. Here, too, nothing should be forced. A little fuel should be poured over the glow plug or glow head (do not run it over the cylinder on a glow-head engine, and try to get as little as possible on the cylinder head of an engine with a separate glow plug). This should cool the glow plug or glow head sufficiently to permit it to be removed without difficulty.

When not in use, the engine should be wrapped in cloth to protect it from dirt and dust. If any dirt gets into the engine, as for example when a plane crashes, it should be dismantled and thoroughly cleaned. Sometimes dirt just builds up through continued use alone. This is particularly true in the case of engines that are mounted in the model airplane in an inverted position, for the air intake is then facing downward and can suck up dirt and dust directly from the ground. Some engine instruction sheets tell you to wash out a dirty

engine. This is quite correct, but it does not mean to wash them out with water! If an engine is not too dirty, it can be washed out with its own fuel, but the best procedure is to wash out an engine with kerosene until every particle of dirt has been removed. Even a small particle of dirt or grit of any kind left in an engine can ruin the engine when it is run under power again.

Complete replacement parts customarily are available for any engine of current manufacture. Importers of engines generally maintain fully adequate stocks of parts for their products, so little problem exists with the standard brands of foreign engines. In many instances when either a cylinder or a piston requires replacement, it is necessary to purchase a complete replacement of both cylinder and piston. The reason is that these parts are matched to each other for the exact fit, and must accordingly be replaced with a new factory-matched combination if an engine is to function properly or at all. Most internal-combustion reciprocating engines for model airplanes employ lapped pistons where the surface of the piston makes a precisely fitted direct contact with the walls of the cylinder, unlike the pistons used in automobile engines that are fitted with rings that make the actual contact with the cylinder wall. However, some model airplane engines do have pistons with rings.

There is no question that an internal-combustion reciprocating model airplane engine does make noise while being operated. This can be quite annoying to neighbors, and has led to an increasing trend to restrict the use of engine-powered model planes in areas of high population density, especially if the engines are not equipped with mufflers. There has always been considerable resistance to the use of mufflers, or silencers as they are called in Great Britain, on the part of a great many model airplane enthusiasts because it has been felt that they reduce the power and speed of engines that are equipped with them. Debates as to just how materially mufflers may impair the relative efficiency of an engine continue; many feel that the reduction is usually slight. Actually, we still know comparatively little in the way of hard facts as to the workings of mufflers and concerning the overall noise problem of model airplane engines. Considerable experimentation is now being undertaken in regard to this problem. There are indications that a substantial part of the noise of model engines is caused by the functioning of the intake of these two-stroke cycle engines as well as by the exhaust. While these experiments continue, so does much agitation to bar the flying of engine-powered model aircraft in various areas. Any evidence of an intractable attitude on the part of hobbyists can serve little or no useful purpose. It may well come down to the fact that if much flying is to be done at locations convenient for enthusiasts, it will have to be done using mufflers or there will be no flying at all. A number of manufacturers now produce mufflers to fit their engines and sell them as an extra. Regardless of what is eventually found to be the facts regarding the supposed necessity of an unmuffled engine for optimum performance, the fact is that the average sports flyer is not likely to find any pertinent difference in the amount of fun he derives whether he flies with or without a muffler on his exhaust. As suggested, whether a hobbyist is ready to accept it or not, the handwriting is quite obviously on the wall as far as the flying of unmuffled engines in most communities goes. It may not seem particularly valorous to many, but it would appear prudent and in the interests of the long-term endurance and continuing popularity of this type of model airplane flying if hobbyists willingly cooperated in these noise-abatement campaigns.

ENGINE TUNING

Some British engine manufacturers offer an engine-tuning service and will tune their own engines if they are sent back to the works, or accept orders for tuned engines. Usually the same basic fee is charged whether the engine is sent back for tuning after some use or whether a new engine is tuned before delivery. The manufacturers prefer, however, to tune engines when they are new. It is emphasized that tuning adds to the horsepower and peaking speed of an engine but does not necessarily make it more economical on fuel. In the United States tuning customarily is done by specialists in this art rather than by the engine manufacturers themselves. (There also are such specialists in Great Britain.) A highly tuned engine is primarily of advantage in speed events. However, enthusiasts of team-racing and rat-racing, events

that include fuel stops, should keep in mind the aforenoted fact that tuning an engine does not automatically result in running farther on a given amount of fuel; tuning may, in fact, have the opposite effect.

Engine tuning is an art that is definitely not for the amateur. It sometimes involves merely bringing moving parts to a state of a very high polish in an effort to reduce friction and drag. From this point it may extend to such a complete rebuilding of an engine—changing piston baffle contours, chromium-plating various parts, replacing parts with those of other materials, and so on —that the original manufacturer of the engine can scarcely recognize his own product. Some superbly performing engines are turned out by expert practitioners of this craft. On the other hand, there undoubtedly exists a certain element of mythology attendant on the topic of engine tuning that results in things being done that are quite unnecessary or that risk destroying the usefulness of an engine in an effort to gain just a few more rpm. Certainly the average model airplane enthusiast is likely to do his engine more harm than good in any attempt to tune it. It should be emphasized that this is strictly a task for someone experienced in what truly amounts to an art, although presumably there must exist somewhere a continuing class of engine-tuning apprentices who are learning how to do it properly.

To the beginner, who hears of engine tuning, the idea often has considerable appeal, suggesting as it does the attainment of a sort of extremely elevated position on the part of those who can tune an engine or even possess a tuned engine. Actually, the ordinary flyer-for-fun in unlikely in any event ever to have occasion to benefit by an engine modified in this way. Of course, if the thought of possessing or flying with a professionally tuned engine seems to exert an almost uncontrollable appeal to any hobbyist, there is no reason why he should not arrange to provide himself with such a gem if he is willing to invest the necessary price.

CHAPTER 6

Other Realms of Model Aeronautics

So far specific discussion has been confined largely to more or less conventional types of heavier-than-air model aircraft and, in the case of flying models, to the by far most popular forms of power, rubber and internal-combustion reciprocating engines. This is not the whole story by any means, for working model aircraft may include less well-known prototypes, other forms of power and, of course, lighter-than-air as well as heavier-than-air machines. The topic of model rockets is in itself somewhat broader than may appear at first glance, and embraces certain categories other than what appears, at the time of writing at least, to be the mainstream of this subject, the solid-fuel rockets described in detail in the following chapter. Thus while this chapter must serve somewhat as a repository for a collection of somewhat varied material that must be assembled somewhere in order that the present book may live up to its title, it serves also somewhat as a bridge between airplanes and rockets.

This is not to imply that many of the in some cases relatively unrelated topics covered in this chapter are of a purely minor key, save insofar as certain of them may have, for any one of a number of reasons, a somewhat limited number of active enthusiasts at the moment. Take, for example, the autogyro, the helicopter (not the simple "flying top" of this name, but models of the actual aircraft of this type), and the ornithopter. All are extremely interesting models to build and fly, and

all are provided for under the competition rules of most of the contest governing bodies. Each has, indeed, an enthusiastic following both in the United States and in Great Britain, although possibly there is somewhat more activity in these fields in the latter than in the former at the present time. The ornithopter stands somewhat apart from the others, representing man's ages-old natural conception of the means by which he could obtain flight, yet never fully realized in prototype machines. (Experiments continue to this day, although some may question their practicability.) The position held by the ornithopter in the world of models is somewhat paradoxical, for it is not at all difficult to build a successful flying model of this type that functions in miniature exactly as would a man-carrying machine if the latter existed. Yet there is no such thing as a prototype ornithopter; therefore the hobbyist who produces one has a working model in the sense that he has built a functional miniature but not in the sense that "model" implies a small reproduction of a larger object.

ORNITHOPTERS, AUTOGIROS, AND HELICOPTERS

Many model ornithopters have been and continue to be built and flown. In many cases, rubber power is employed, usually attached to a light-

weight crankshaft that imparts the movement to the wings. Internal-combustion reciprocating engines often also are employed. In fact, some quite large successful model ornithopters have been built, proving the practicability of the type in the eyes of its aficionados. Around 1935–1936 Harry D. Graulich, an alumnus of the pioneer New York Model Aero Club, pioneer pilot, and a lifelong worker in and about aviation who has been associated with a number of leading aircraft companies, built and successfully flew in tethered flight a "half-size" ornithopter powered with a four-cylinder air-cooled engine at Walden, New York. "Half-size" refers of course to the size of the model in relation to that of the man-carrying ornithopter that it was proposed eventually to build along the same lines; the model had about a 16-foot wingspan. Experiments with and enthusiasm for ornithopters continue unabated. Perhaps the leading enthusiast for model ornithopters at the present time is P. H. Spencer, another pioneer pilot and longtime airplane designer whose work includes the design for the Republic Seabee Amphibean. Mr. Spencer has been developing and building model ornithopters, both rubber- and engine-powered, since 1930, ranging from about 18-inch to 8-foot wingspan. The Whamo Bird, a rubber-powered ornithopter of which hundreds of thousands were sold around 1960, was his creation. He has since developed and currently is anticipating commercialization of free flight and control line ornithopters using internal-combustion reciprocating engines as small as .020 cubic inches. It is obvious that there exists an enduring fascination connected with the building and flying of model ornithopters—they invariably arouse much spectator interest—both because of the unusual mechanical design itself and also because of the fact that every man evidently carries within himself a subconscious primitive urge to be able to fly by beating wings as birds do.

The model autogiro (from the trade name Autogiro), which in prototype practice combines a somewhat conventional wing and propeller power with nonpowered vanes that rotate in the airstream, is not too difficult to build and fly. Such a model, whether powered with rubber or with an internal-combustion reciprocating engine, flies much as does any model airplane, with the addition that the vanes turn in the airstream and possibly produce some additional serviceable lift in the process.

The helicopter is the most difficult of all models to get any real results from. It is quite easy to build a model helicopter, again usually rubber-powered but not necessarily so, that will

Fig. 111. A rubber-powered flying model autogiro constructed by Howard G. McEntee, a noted designer and builder of flying model airplanes of all types. Autogiros combine conventional propeller and wing design with rotors operating in a horizontal plane.

Howard G. McEntee—"Model Airplane News"

rise beautifully to a considerable height. What is being done, however, is simply the attachment of a glorified version of the old helicopter toy or "flying top" to a model airplane structure that more or less conforms in appearance to that of a real helicopter. Helicopters are readily built with both rubber and internal-combustion reciprocating engine power. Another form mounts small pellet-fuel rocket engines directly on the rotor assembly so that the effect is, in a horizontal plane of operation, precisely akin to that obtained on a vertical plane when pinwheel fireworks are set off. Only in the largest-sized models, with suitable radio-control equipment and control, does it seem there is much practical opportunity for constructing

model helicopters that actually will function as do the real flying machines—moving forward or hovering.

Rubber-powered model ornithopters, autogiros, and helicopters are not required by competition rules to have landing gear, and the method of launching them is left to the option of the contestant. Often they are hand-launched, although ROG models can and have been constructed. While autogiros may be tested by gliding them, as are regulation model airplanes, this is not possible in the case of ornithopters and helicopters; these types must be working under power to test their performance in the air and to secure the information required to make any adjustments necessary for their more successful flight.

LIGHTER-THAN-AIR CRAFT

Lighter-than-air craft, ranging from the balloon to the dirigible, continue to exert a powerful attraction on such segments of the public who are fortunate enough to have the opportunity to witness the prototypes in flight; on serious designers and developers who foresee a continuing future for this type of equipment for commercial, scientific, and military purposes, and on a substantial number of model builders. The latter group, although at the moment quite small in comparison with the total number of model aircraft enthusiasts, embraces those who are lighter-than-air advo-

Fig. 112. Working model helicopters provide an interesting field for experimentaion. At the top a hobbyist compares his model with the real thing. The helicopter at the lower left is powered by means of small opposed pellet-fuel jet engines mounted at the ends of two of the blades. At the lower right is shown an unusual ducted model helicopter powered with an .049 cubic-inch internal-combustion reciprocating engine.

Academy of Model Aeronautics

Fig. 113. The vee balloon is a new development in lighter-than-air craft. Employed for logging operations, it consists of two cigar-shaped balloons connected at the nose and joined by a horizontal fin at the tail, and is tethered and controlled by cables attached to winches on the ground.

Goodyear Aerospace Corp.

cates themselves; builders of models of all types of aircraft from a historical standpoint, and hobbyists who, from time to time, simply like to change pace and turn their hands to the building or flying of something different from the more usual styles of model aircraft.

The lighter-than-air machine has, of course, a history of practical use in the cavalcade of human flight going back much farther than heavier-than-air craft. Men were ascending in balloons both in the United States and in Europe during the last years of the eighteenth century, and balloons were used for military observation purposes as early as 1794 at the Battle of Fleurus and were extensively employed in the Civil War (where the Prussian military observer Count Ferdinand von Zeppelin, whose name came to be applied to a type of airship, first encountered and studied them) and in the Franco-Prussian War. It may be difficult for many younger readers to realize that until the early 1930's, most people tended to regard the airship rather than the airplane as possessing the greatest potential for the large-scale transport of passengers and cargo by air; the airplane was looked upon largely as suitable for short hauls, the carrying of mail, and as a military weapon. Unfortunately, several notable tragedies to large lighter-than-air craft, the reasons for which space does not permit the proper examination of in detail here, in combination with limitations of funds due

to then prevailing economic conditions, acted to damp further substantial development in certain areas. Many persons, including even many comparatively well versed in aviation history, are unaware of the considerable role that continued to be played by lighter-than-air craft, particularly in defense, although the balloon barrages of beleaguered London occupy their niche in the history of those times. Far less well known, however, is the fact that during World War II the United States Navy had 168 airships in operation and they were extensively and most successfully used as aerial escorts for coastal convoys. While 532 vessels were sunk by enemy submarines in these waters during the war, the navy airships escorted a total of 89,000 ships in this period, without a single vessel being lost while under escort by an airship. Airships were again used in the Korean conflict, and later as part of the United States' early-warning defense network. However, the United States Navy finally phased out its lighter-than-air program in 1962.

Yet this step did not by any means mark the end of lighter-than-air craft use and development in the United States. Aside from the fact that privately owned blimps travel from coast to coast and often appear at important events, the long years of experimentation continue and have resulted in some exciting new developments. Curious as it may seem to some at first glance, the space program has itself given a certain further impetus to continuing airship development. An airship could, for example, move enormous missile components from the Pacific Coast to Cape Kennedy, Florida, in three to five days, as compared with the eighteen days it requires the National Aeronautics and Space Administration to transport these parts by sea.

BALLOONS AND AIRSHIPS OF TODAY

Before considering the possibilities of model lighter-than-air craft, hobbyists might be interested in the latest developments in lighter-than-air craft

Fig. 114. The **Aereon III** is a new dirigible with three parallell hulls. It is actually derived from similar airships built in 1863 and 1866 by Dr. Solomon Andrews. The drawing at the left shows Dr. Andrews's **Aereon I** of 1863; at the right is a drawing of the new **Aereon III**.

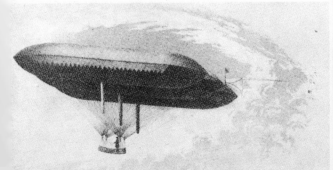

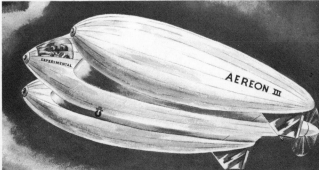

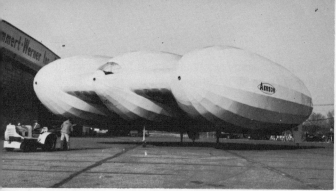

Fig. 115. Two views of the new dirigible **Aereon III**. The left photograph is taken from the front and shows the triple-hull construction, joined by flat, gas-filled lifting surfaces. The right photograph is taken from the rear and shows the propeller, elevons, and one of the rudders.

Aereon Corp.

in the United States today. They appear to take two major forms: the unmanned vee-balloon and the manned Aereon dirigible. Both of these types represent major departures from familiar forms, although the Aereon is admittedly uniquely akin to lighter-than-air craft developed and flown over a hundred years ago. Unlike most previous lighter-than-air craft, both the vee-balloon and the Aereon dirigible employ more than a single bag or hull in conjunction with a substantial gas-filled horizontal lifting area in order to provide maximum aerodynamic lift from the movement of the craft through the air as well as increased stability. Both are ideal subjects for display or flying models, although still so new that as yet little has been done in this direction.

The vee-balloon was developed by the Goodyear Aerospace Corporation of Akron, Ohio, and has already been proved in use in logging operations in the Pacific Northwest. Unmanned and unpowered, the vee-balloon is tethered and controlled by cables attached to winches on the ground. The great advantages of the vee-balloon in logging operations are that they permit lifting out the logs in rough, inaccessible areas while reducing the

amount of costly logging roads that have to be built and reducing soil erosion as well. The first vee-balloon, built and successfully tried in 1964, had a capacity of 75,000 cubic feet of helium, and was 110 feet long. The "second generation" is represented by a 175,000-cubic-foot balloon, 142 feet long, built in 1965. Essentially a vee-balloon consists of two cigar-shaped balloons joined at the nose in a V formation, while a large horizontal fin connects the two sections at the rear. There also are vertical tail fins as aids to greater stability. Not only the two main bags but the horizontal and vertical tail fins are gas-filled members. In order to retain the relatively flat conformation of the large horizontal fin under the pressure of gas that would normally force it into a rounded shape, internal ribs are built across the width of the fin section. In a sense, part of the vee-balloon may be said therefore to embody certain of the principles or features of a dirigible. The vee-balloon originally was designed for use in carrying instruments aloft to great heights for long periods of time in conjunction with the space program. It was not until later that its possibilities for logging operations were perceived and experiments undertaken in this

Fig. 116. At the left, a plastic display model of a blimp. A limited number of the kits for building these models were sold only through tire dealers and automotive stores, and it is uncertain when or if additional supplies may be available. At the right is pictured a 17-inch-long model of the famed British dirigible R-100, readily available in kit form from hobby dealers.

Goodyear Tire & Rubber Co.
Lines Bros., Inc.

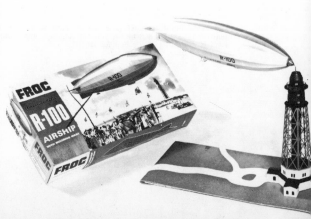

Fig. 117. Two beautiful scale display models of U.S. Navy blimps extensively used for convoy duty during World War II. Both models are fabricated entirely of mahogany including the bags, and are 1/65th the size of the originals. The model of the K type (left) is 46¼ inches long and the M-type model is 57¼ inches in length.

Goodyear Aerospace Corp.

direction. When used for logging the vee-balloons seldom are required to ascend to a height of more than 500 feet.

THE AEREONS

Interesting as indeed the vee-balloon is, at the present time it is conceived of and used only as a nonpowered, unmanned device tethered to and controlled from the ground. The *Aereon III,* on the other hand, built at Lakehurst, New Jersey, by the Aereon Corporation, is a small powered and manned dirigible. It is intended, if it proves successful, as the forerunner of a much larger vessel to be used as a cargo ship. If plans go according to schedule, *Aereon III* should have become airborne by the time this book appears. *Aereon III* consists of three parallel envelopes or hulls, connected for almost their entire length by flat, gas-filled, lifting surfaces, the entire structure being composed of a rigid frame covered with a smooth skin. The name and general concept of the three parallel hulls derive from *Aereon I* and *Aereon II,* airships built and flown during the 1860's by Dr. Solomon Andrews of Perth Amboy, New Jersey. The *Aereon I* was offered by Dr. Andrews to the United States Government during the Civil War, and a model built by him was placed in the basement of the Capitol for examination by a commission appointed by Secretary of War Stanton after An-

drews had seen President Lincoln and addressed a petition to Congress in an effort to overcome the original lack of interest expressed by the war minister. The commission reported favorably, but the craft was never taken into government service.

In fact, *Aereon I* appears to have been built by Dr. Andrews largely to convince Stanton of the utility of the craft. *Aereon I* was flown in 1863 and *Aereon II* in 1866, including flights over the Amboys, Staten Island, and parts of Manhattan Island. The relative potential of Dr. Andrews's airships at that time can be judged by the fact that more than a decade earlier the Frenchman Henry Giffard (1825-1882) had built and flown a 145-foot-long, steam-powered airship. However, with government interest fading at the conclusion of the war, and lacking other backing, Dr. Andrews was forced to bring his experiments to a halt, and died before he was able to obtain means to continue his efforts.*

Aereon III makes other important departures from *Aereon I* and *Aereon II* and, in fact, from all previous airship design. It incorporates a built-in adjustable mooring mast in the center hull that enables the pilot to control the angle of attack to the wind. Thus, by raising the craft on the mooring

---

*Dr. Andrews related his experiments in great detail in his book *The Art of Flying.* The specifications of his patent (No. 43,449, issued July 5, 1864) give a very complete description of *Aereon I* and its performance in flight.

Fig. 118. An animated but nonflying scale model of the U.S. Navy's dirigible **Macon**, measuring 10 feet, 6 inches in length, built by Mercle C. Gillette. The model includes 8 electric motors that drive the propellers, and is illuminated by 60 miniature bulbs.

Merle C. Gillette

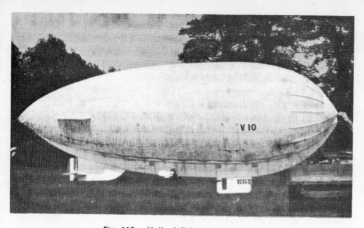

Fig. 119. At the left is a 10-foot-long scale flying model of the French V-10 semirigid airship, powered by two diesel engines, flown on a single control line. At the right is shown a 17-foot, 8-inch-long scale flying model of the air-inflated Goodyear blimp **Resolute**, in the course of its construction by Raymond Morse, who also built the 10-foot model.

Wingfoot Lighter-Than-Air Society

mast, it can be put into a positive angle for takeoff; by lowering it on the mast, it can be placed into a position of negative attack so that it will more or less hug the ground in a wind. Another feature is that, unlike other airships, the control and crew quarters and the engine are entirely streamlined within the hull rather than hanging from it. By thus placing the power plant along the center axis of the craft it is expected that all or most of the pitching movements caused by the usual off-center positioning of the engine or engines will be eliminated. Control is effected by rudders at the rear of the two outboard hulls and by means of combination ailerons and elevators (known as elevons) at the rear of the flat lifting surfaces. *Aereon III* is 85 feet long, 53 feet wide, and 18 feet high, is inflated with 40,000 cubic feet of helium in 18 plastic cells (6 in each hull), and is designed for a two-man crew of pilot and copilot. It is, in fact, conceived as an experimental craft of the smallest possible size successfully to demonstrate the potential of the design and to permit tests to be made looking forward to the creation of much larger airships for use as economical cargo and passenger carriers, as well as in space and defense applications.

Aereon III is powered by an 80-horsepower Solar Titan gas turbine engine weighing 50 pounds, on loan from the United States Government. The propeller powered by this engine actually is an 18-foot-long helicopter rotor blade mounted in a vertical plane, as would be a standard pusher-type propeller, and the pitch of the blade can be varied and the direction of the pitch completely transposed so as to provide an optional reverse thrust when desired, as well as the normal forward thrust. Furthermore, the angle at which the rotor is mounted can be varied as much as 24 degrees to provide horizontal- and vertical-thrust components. The projected speed for *Aereon III* is 100 to 150 miles per hour. Such speed is regarded as well within the service requirements of commercial cargo shippers in the United States. *Aereon III* embraces a number of other new or refined technical features, in addition to those mentioned here. It may be that a new era of revitalized lighter-than-air craft is in the offing.

MODELS OF LIGHTER-THAN-AIR CRAFT

The hobbyist who is interested in building models of lighter-than-air craft has, strictly speaking, the same two main paths open to him as are

Fig. 120. One of the finest working lighter-than-air models ever built was this 17-foot-long scale model of the U.S. Navy blimp K-72, constructed in the shops of the Naval Air Station at Lakehurst, New Jersey, in 1952. It weighed only 7½ lbs, held 103 cubic feet of helium, was powered by two glow-plug engines, and was completely radio controlled. It was later replaced by an even larger model, 22 feet in length, which is still in existence.

Max E. Ripken

Fig. 121. A model hot-air balloon contest is held each year at Akron, Ohio, at the annual picnic of the Wingfoot Lighter-Than-Air Society. At the left a winning balloon built by Joe Rochford is being filled. It set a new record by staying aloft for 5 minutes and 20 seconds. At the right is pictured in flight a balloon built by Rosemarie Foord.

Wingfoot Lighter-Than-Air Society

available to the builders of models of regular airplanes: nonoperating display models and actual flying models. Actually, either of these two paths presents the lighter-than-air model builder with comparatively greater difficulties than do the parallel paths in the realm of heavier-than-air model construction. The big problem is the lack of availability of commercial kits, which simply means that the hobbyist is thrown almost entirely on his own resources as to securing suitable materials and in collecting and organizing working data, prototype photographs, and drawings. To many this is all to the good since it compels the model builder to create and build, rather than merely to assemble prepared components. Very occasionally kits are available for the construction of model airships, but the lighter-than-air model fan cannot count on securing such kits at any given time. The most recent venture of this type in the United States that comes to mind was produced as a promotion by a manufacturer of airships and was not distributed through regular hobby merchandise channels. A limited quantity of kits was released to the public through the company's own dealers and automotive service stores.

In any event, the man who wants to construct nonoperating display models of lighter-than-air craft can build them, provided he possesses sufficient ingenuity and skill. Consider, however, the almost insurmountable barriers that confront the hobbyist who desires to construct an actual flying model of an airship, even assuming he is capable of constructing an airtight bag or hull: The usual principles embodied in flying model airplane design to assure the return to earth of the model, once the fuel is exhausted or cut off, are of no use in a flying lighter-than-air ship. An airplane is heavier than

the air it displaces. Its lift and flying ability are sustained only by its powered movement through the air. Once there is no longer any power, the model airplane automatically is attracted back to earth by the pull of gravity. If the model airplane is properly designed and adjusted, it returns to earth in a gentle circular glide. If this is not the case, it glides down at some distance from the operator, or it crashes. One way or another, it comes down within what usually is practical recovery distance.

This would not be the case with a successful lighter-than-air model. Even with a completely radio-controlled model, it would not be desirable to ever let it fly until the fuel was exhausted. The natural buoyancy of the craft might prevent it being landed successfully by radio control of the elevators and rudders, and it might well float far out of sight. It would come down eventually, of course, but chances for its recovery would be slim. This would apply as well to a far smaller and simpler model that had been launched without radio-control equipment. Perhaps the finest flying models of lighter-than-air craft were 17-foot-long and 22-foot-long replicas of a United States Navy blimp which were constructed at the Navy's lighter-than-air base at Lakehurst, New Jersey, in 1952 and subsequently displayed at a number of model airplane meets and on other occasions both as an example of modelmaking and as an aid to recruiting. These models were completely radio controlled within a radius of about 1,000 feet, the radio signals operating the rudder for direction and the elevators for height. The 17-foot model was filled with 103 cubic feet of helium and flew at a speed of 15 miles per hour under the power of two ½A glow-plug engines, which the navy, incidentally, classified as semidiesels. These models

Fig. 122. Carbon dioxide for model aeronautical purposes is now available in the form of cartridges of ihe type pictured here. The gas from the cartridges can be used to drive a reciprocating engine, but the usual application today is to mount a cartridge on a model airplane as a means of jet propulsion.

Kidde Mfg. Co., Inc.

caused a lot of excitement and enthusiasm wherever flown. Naturally, it would be extremely difficult, although not impossible, for a private model builder to build (and transport) a model airship of such size. In any event, the danger of losing such a model, or any commendable flying model of a lighter-than-air prototype, would make free-flight attempts very hazardous.

That would limit the prospects chiefly to control-line or tethered models. A control-line airship would prove interesting, and would present enough problems in construction to make the finished model a praiseworthy accomplishment. Or an airship model could be operated on a tether. Gradually, by progressive steps of limiting the relative need for control, we approach by this thinking the conception of a model simply flying on a rod around a pylon or central post, perhaps in this case modeled in the form of an airship moving mast. When and if this point is reached, the question naturally would arise as to the necessity or desirability of making such a model as an actual gas-filled, lighter-than-air craft. Thus by a series of stages of detraction we arrive at the idea of an airship model made of wood or other materials both supported and powered by the rod that guides it around a central point of mounting.

GAS FOR MODEL AIRSHIPS

However, if the latter conception does not appeal and a model aircraft hobbyist desires to build any form of lighter-than-air craft that performs in a manner substantially like the real thing, he must prepare a gas-tight bag, envelope, or hull —call it what you will—and fill it with a suitable lifting gas. The simplest gas that can be used is hot air, which, being lighter than the surrounding air, will cause the light envelope of a small balloon or airship to rise at an increasingly slower rate as the

hot air becomes cooler and more closely approaches the temperature of the surrounding air. Small model balloons and airships can successfully be launched using hot air if the envelope or hull is sufficiently light. This usually means using paper for the construction of the bag. A fair-sized hot-air airship might even have sufficient buoyancy to support a small motor stick, rubber strand, and propeller that would impart a forward motion in combination with the lifting motion, and fly successfully indoors. Larger model hot-air balloons and airships can be flown out of doors. These are fairly easy to make and there is quite a little experimental background material available on powering such airships with rubber.

An opening must, of course, be left in the bottom of a hot-air balloon or airship to receive the heated air. This opening should be surrounded by a hoop of wire of as light a weight as will retain the desired shape. The best procedure for filling an outdoor hot-air balloon is with a length of stovepipe held about a foot and a half above the ground, with the fire lighted under it. The pipe may be propped with rocks or mounted on metal legs or held with a pair of tongs. The balloon should have a loop of cord or paper pasted at the top through which a long stick can be passed so that the hobbyist can stand to one side and hold the balloon in position over the stovepipe while it is being filled with hot air. When the balloon starts moving upward and pressing against the stick and swaying from side to side, it should be released. It will then start to ascend. The filling with hot air from the fire is, frankly, as far as a prudent individual will go in preparing a hot-air balloon for launching. The old-time practice, frequently advocated and employed by model balloon fanciers from the beginnings of model ballooning even into the 1930's, of putting a "fireball" of lighted alcohol-soaked sponge or waste on crosswires mounted on the

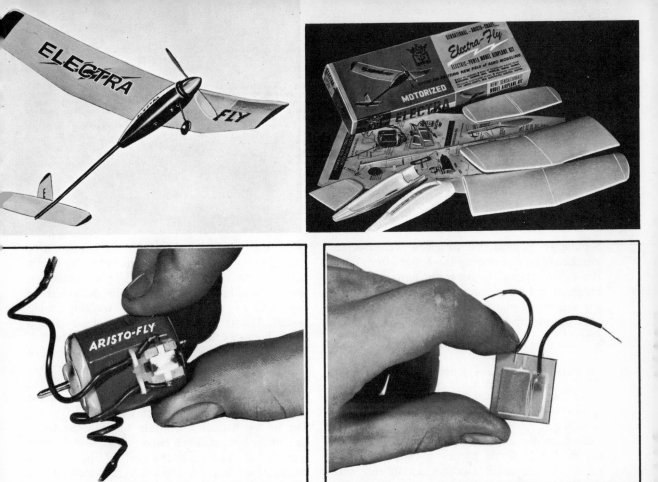

Fig. 123. Electrically propelled free-flight model airplanes are now available in kit form. Shown here are a finished model, the kit with Styrofoam components, the electric motor, and the tiny wet cell that makes these models practical. The cell is activated immediately before flight by placing salt water in the bag. Two cells are used to power the model pictured.

Aristo-Craft Distinctive Miniatures

hoop just before the balloon was released amounts to sheer idiocy from the standpoint of safety. It is quite true that such a balloon will rise more swiftly and sustain itself in the air longer than one merely provided with hot air from a fire on the ground. However, the idea of sending aloft any model aircraft, much less a free-flying one, containing a lighted fire is obviously too dangerous to consider.

A hot-air balloon, although it can be satisfactorily built to quite large size (up to several feet in diameter), is not the most satisfactory type of model airship. For better results and far easier launching, the modeler must turn to a gas similar to those used in real airships. Hydrogen is the lightest of gases, and was usually used for real balloons and airships in the absence of helium. Hydrogen is extremely inflammable, and highly explosive when combined with air. Neither its preparation nor its use should be attempted by model aircraft fans, and it would be utter madness to attempt to fly an internal-combustion-reciprocating-engine-powered model airship using hydrogen. In

fact, it should be taken as a strict injunction that the model builder who wishes to construct and fly working models of lighter-than-air craft either content himself with the admittedly limited possibilities of hot air or use helium.

Helium is the lightest gas known next to hydrogen and is approximately one-seventh the weight of air. Unlike hydrogen, helium is not inflammable. It is found only in the United States, and at one time was quite rare and expensive and its use largely limited to the airships of the United States Army and Navy. In fact, in the early 1920's the available supply of helium was so limited that following the delivery of the dirigible *Los Angeles** in 1924 there was not enough to keep both this airship and the *Shenandoah* operating at the same time, and until the loss of the *Shenandoah* on

---

*There exists a persistent and seemingly undying rumor among enthusiasts of lighter-than-air models, inspired no doubt by wishful thinking, that the *Los Angeles* is still in existence and presumably needs only to be filled with helium to take to the air again. This is not correct. The *Los Angeles* was stricken from the United States Navy list on October 24, 1939, and subsequently dismantled and sold for scrap.

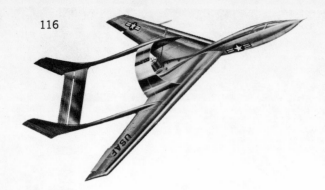

Fig. 124. Variously described as a fan/jet or a ducted-fan model, this ready-to-fly internal-combustion reciprocating engine control-line model airplane presents a unique type of flying model. A pusher-type propeller or fan is located at the rear of a completely rounded duct, the lower half of which is not visible in the photograph.

AMF Wen-Mac Division

September 3, 1925, the dirigibles were operated alternately by transferring the helium from one to the other. Today, however, helium is relatively common and inexpensive. It is used by vendors of toy balloons at playgrounds and fairs, and is available for use by hobbyists, at least in the United States.

BALLOON AND AIRSHIP ENVELOPES

The great essential for a successful flying model balloon or airship is, of course, a light, air-tight bag or envelope. Suitable material itself is not difficult to obtain. That usually employed in hot-air models is tissue paper or brown wrapping paper. For helium-filled models, a more substantial covering must be used. Almost any sort of light fabric can be employed (synthetic fabrics generally are favored today) if it can successfully be rubberized or coated with neoprene to make it airtight. The great difficulty in fabricating the envelope for a model balloon or airship is in properly and accurately laying out and cutting the sections, or gores, that go to make up the assembled envelope, and in gluing them together. Owing to the conformation of the finished craft, these gores generally take an irregular shape resembling that of the side view of an old-fashioned cigar. Each gore is widest in the center and tapers to a point at each end. In making a hot-air balloon, the shape is pointed at one end to form the top of the balloon, but is cut off square across the pattern at the other end, where the opening and hoop are to be located. Each gore must be a little wider than its exposed area on the finished airship to allow the gores to overlap each other slightly when one is glued to the next one. Some sort of inlet and valve must be provided in one gore, usually the bottom one, to allow for filling with helium. The best procedure is to make a cardboard pattern of the proper conformation and cut each individual gore from the cloth in accord with this pattern.

Making a model airship by this method is admittedly a delicate job. The hobbyist who undertakes it should be prepared for the likelihood of having to lay out several patterns before he finally achieves the correct shape. While a number of good models have been built by this method, there is another way to construct a small working airship model. This is to employ several ordinary round toy balloons as the actual gas containers. The balloons are placed within a sketchy framework of thin balsa wood, and a covering of model airplane tissue applied over the balsa wood to conceal the balloons and give the outer conformation of the airship in the form of a dummy envelope. The inlets to the balloons protrude through the tissue skin at the bottom. Each balloon is separately filled with helium and its intake tied off. In a typical model of a blimp constructed by this method, not all the balloons can be inflated to the same size: those placed in the tapering nose and tail of the dummy envelope receiving less helium than those placed in the central section of the envelope or hull. This method of construction, although it involves considerable delicacy in the building process, can be quite successful, and a rubber-powered propeller can be mounted in a car suspended below the envelope.

The drawbacks to this form of construction are that the balloons must be inflated very carefully; an overinflated balloon will very likely break the delicate balsa and tissue envelope before the balloon itself bursts. If, on the other hand, one of the balloons breaks or develops a leak, it is necessary to remove a portion of the tissue covering in order to extract the damaged balloon and replace it with a new one. Nevertheless, this method of construction has much to recommend it as against the complexities of cutting and assembling gores to form an airtight envelope. It is probable that the dummy envelope and separate balloon model airship will require a little balancing, usually by adding a small weight at the nose. It is essential that the balsa frame be as light as possible consistent with containing the balloons, for the balloon construction substantially reduces the cubic capacity of a model airship of any given size in

Fig. 125. Model aeronautics and rocketry combined with model railroading. These HO-gauge (British OO-gauge) cars offer a variety of action effects: launching rockets, a satellite (lower left) and a helicopter and airplane, all from the tracks of an indoor model railroad.

Lines Bros., Inc.

relation to the capacity of a model of similar size but with an airtight envelope.

OTHER TYPES OF
LIGHTER-THAN-AIR MODELS

In building a control-line airship, it is essential that the bell crank and the cable running from the bell crank to the elevator horn be kept *outside* the envelope. The bell crank can be mounted in or to the car, and the cable must be arranged to run back in an exposed position from the bell crank to the elevator horn. As far as is known, all experiments attempting to place the bell crank or at least the elevator cable in a position where they must run through the envelope have resulted in failure. It does not seem possible to construct entry ports and valves so as to permit the cable to operate within the envelope and still keep the envelope airtight. Conceivably some ingenious hobbyist may someday do this successfully. One suggestion, which does not depend on tiny valves, involves the construction of a slanting tube within the envelope, opening over the car at one end and near the elevator horn at the other, similar to the single firetube sometimes used in model locomotive boilers. Such a tube, which would have to be constructed of the same airtight material as the envelope itself, might be a practical solution to this problem, but it would be rather difficult to construct, and would certainly add materially to the already considerable effort required to assemble a satisfactory envelope.

Fig. 126. Display models of military rockets, launchers, and transport vehicles also come within the ken of overall model rocketry. These are models, built from kits of plastic parts of the Hawk rockets, together with launcher and mobile radar unit (left), and the Mace missile together with its "Teracruzer" carrier.

Renwal Products, Inc.

It is not necessary to say much specifically concerning the building of nonoperating display models of lighter-than-air craft. The most usual method of construction is to carve the envelope from a solid piece of wood, either balsa wood or in some instances comparatively hard woods such as mahogany. If the model builder becomes involved in the use of a fabric covering, instead of painting the wood to resemble fabric, construction becomes somewhat more complicated but not unduly so. The fabric covering can either be laid over a solid wood base or it can be mounted over a skeleton frame. In either case the hobbyist is, of course, confronted with substantially the same problem of preparing a pattern and gores as is the builder of a flying model, except that the gores may be glued to a frame—a somewhat easier task than assembling them only to one another—and there is no necessity for attaining an airtight construction. Most lighter-than-air models must be displayed either suspended by a cord or wire or, in the case of airships, moored to a miniature mooring mast of the same scale (or at least the upper segment of a mooring mast must be modeled and included in

Fig. 127. Catapult- or slingshot-launched rocket plastic rocket with space capsule and a larger space capsule alone. These models are shot into the air by means of the launching device pictured to the left of each model, and return safely by means of attached parachutes.

Gladen Enterprises, Inc.

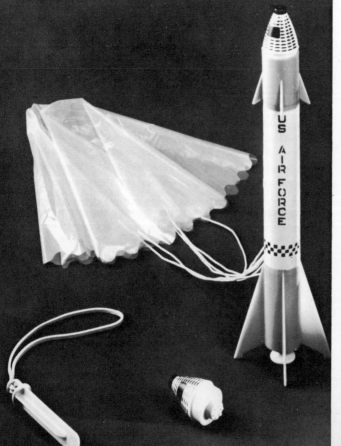

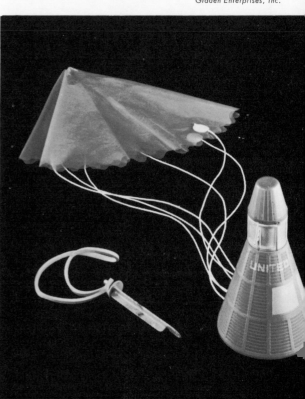

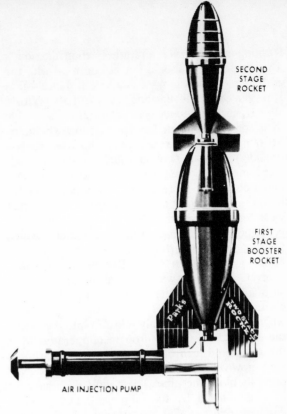

SECOND STAGE ROCKET

FIRST STAGE BOOSTER ROCKET

AIR INJECTION PUMP

Fig. 128. Miniature plastic rockets launched by means of the compression of water using a special pump. At the left is a 15-inch rocket that travels upward for about 150 feet and then releases a space capsule that is parachuted back to earth. At the right is a two-stage rocket that releases the second stage at a height of about 100 feet.

Park Plastics Co.

the display for this purpose) or resting on a special cradle.

Fascinating as assuredly are models of lighter-than-air craft, present interest in these types constitutes a comparatively small facet of the model aircraft hobby today. Perhaps a resurgence of airships in full-size practice would alter this picture. In any event, in order to carry out an adequate overall survey of the hobby it is necessary now to return to models of heavier-than-air machines.

OTHER TYPES OF MODEL AIRCRAFT POWER

The most widespread type of power used in model aircraft of today, following rubber and internal-combustion reciprocating engines in relative popularity, is jet or rocket power. Before going into this field at length it is appropriate to examine the present and possible future usage of other types of power that have made or are making their mark in the flying of model airplanes. These alternate forms of power are steam, compressed air, carbon dioxide (CO_2), and electricity. Of the first two, steam and compressed air, it is fairly evi-

dent that time and new technical developments have made them obsolete. Both were first used to power model airplanes in the nineteenth century, steam as early as 1848. Interest on the part of hobbyists in applying steam power to model flight appears to have faded completely in the 1920's. Compressed-air engines remained a force in model aviation somewhat longer, well into the 1930's before finally giving way before the increasing availability of internal-combustion reciprocating engines.

Carbon dioxide power, introduced to model aviation later than steam or compressed air, attained a certain measure of popularity in the 1920's and 1930's (compressed air and CO_2 engines usually could be operated by means of either form of power). This form of power has a tendency to reappear again and again at intervals in a limited measure of popularity for use in reciprocating engines. More important in the overall picture, CO_2 is a very definite and established force in the miniature jet power picture, and its ready availability in cartridge form with that purpose primarily in view also lends weight to the possibility of the further use of this gas as a source of power in small reciprocating-engine-driven aircraft. Carbon dioxide is a nontoxic gas; it should not be confused with the carbon monoxide gas—a deadly substance—that is produced by gasoline engines. Until after World War II, carbon dioxide was not generally available in a convenient form for use by model builders. Most model airplane hobbyists who used carbon dioxide for power (not as a fuel, for the gas itself was simply employed directly to move the piston of an engine by force alone; it was not exploded in an internal-combustion reciprocating engine) were forced to generate their own gas in a special generator or, as some termed it, "boiler," which they loaded with carbide, dry ice (known as carbonic acid snow in Great Britain), and water. Conversely, if CO_2 was obtained under high pressure in steel cylinders, as a few model airplane enthusiasts did obtain it, there was a danger that when the gas was suddenly released into the model there would be such a drop in temperature that the gas would turn back into dry ice or carbonic acid snow within the engine intake pipe and at least partially block the pipe! These difficulties have all been eliminated by the aforementioned present-day availability of CO_2 in cartridges. In the main, however, its continued application to model aircraft seems likely to be primarily in the field of jet models, although it is by no means farfetched to suggest that carbon dioxide engines may not from time to time again attain a measure of popularity for small models.

Carbon dioxide cannot be used as a fuel or for direct power in an internal-combustion reciprocating engine. It will operate a special CO_2 engine or a compressed air engine or, if admitted under sufficient pressure, a miniature steam engine. In any case, in its passage through an engine it acts as does steam—it is not, as noted, a fuel in itself, merely a form of power when released under pressure.

ELECTRICALLY POWERED MODEL AIRPLANES

Of the four powers noted above, electricity is the most recent to become successfully harnessed to the free flight of propeller-driven model aircraft. At the present time, of the four, it appears to give the greatest promise of continuing future development. Experimenters have long sought to employ electricity for free flight; this form of power has long been used in tethered models. The drawback to the use of electricity in free-flight model airplanes has always been the matter of weight: more particularly the weight of the batteries that had to be carried in a model air-

plane to operate a very small motor capable of driving a propeller at sufficient speed to enable the craft to fly—in short, the power/weight ratio.

Although individual hobbyists achieved some measure of success from time to time, it is only recently that the electrically powered model airplane has become a reality and kits have been made available. This has been due primarily to developments in battery design, although advancing small electric motor technology also has played its part. It should be emphasized that electrically powered free flight is still only in its earliest stages. Such model airplanes are rather limited in size and weight, as is the duration of the flights that generally are achieved with present equipment. There is no doubt, however, that this will prove a field of continuing progress and considerable interest. While complete kits are available, the small motors and batteries included in them also are readily obtainable separately for those who wish to experiment further on their own. The most interesting component is the tiny "postage stamp size" wet cell, weighing only fifteen grams, with a voltage of 1.1 per cell. The cell itself is a small plastic bag and can be stored indefinitely. It is activated only immediately before flight by placing a few drops of salt water into the bag. Two cells usually are used together to form the battery required to power the motor. The most interesting thing about these tiny cells is that they can be used only once —to power a single flight. They must then be discarded and a fresh set placed in the model. All costs are naturally comparative and depend on one's individual viewpoint. The present batteries are comparatively inexpensive and have made electrically powered model airplane flight available to a substantial number of enthusiasts. Obviously, the ready availability of reuseable batteries suitable for this type of flying would be a very important step in furthering the use and popularity of electric model airplanes.

The first electrically powered model airplane kit introduced on the American market provided molded styrofoam parts to build a 19-inch wingspan monoplane weighing one ounce without motor or batteries. The addition of the motor and two batteries adds approximately an additional two ounces to the model.

JETS, ROCKETS, AND DUCTED-FAN MODELS

Many hobbyists tend to use the terms "jet" and "rocket" more or less interchangeably, or else express their awareness of a difference between the two but confess an inability to define it properly.

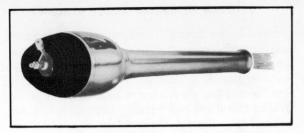

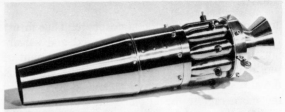

Fig. 129. Two powerful miniature jet engines suitable for large model aircraft. The model on the left measures 21½ inches in length. The model on the right is a complete working model of a turbojet engine with 8 cylindrical combustion chambers (at the right), each with its own glow plug for ignition. It is 12 inches long and 2¾ inches in diameter, a most formidable power plant for the advanced model airplane builder and experimenter.

Curtis Dyna-Products Corp.
Turbocraft

In terms of a form of power, both jets and rockets operate by means of propulsive thrust rather than by torque or turning power as with propellers. There is, in fact, much confusion of terminology and definition in the area of jets and rockets. The best basic differentation is that in a rocket the fuel includes its own supply of oxygen; the functioning of a rocket is therefore self-contained, whether it uses a solid fuel or a liquid fuel wherein the fuel proper and the oxygen necessary for combustion are both carried on the rocket and separately injected into the combustion chamber and exploded. A true rocket, therefore, does not have to "breathe"; it is not dependent on oxygen in the air for any part of its functioning, and consequently can operate at high altitudes where there is no oxyyen. Accordingly the rocket must be used for space flights.

While some classification systems list solid-fuel rockets and liquid-fuel rockets along with the various types of jet engines under a single heading of rocket types, there is actually the aforementioned basic distinction between rockets and jets. Jets, or, more properly, jet engines, are open at both ends, and suck in air at the front to receive the oxygen necessary to the combustion of the fuel. Accordingly jets cannot operate at high altitudes where there is no oxygen. There are three main types of jet engines used in actual aircraft practice: the pulse jet, the ramjet, and the turbojet. The usual form of pulse jet employs a resonating reed valve toward the front. Air enters the combustion chamber by forcing this valve open. The air mixes with fuel in the combustion chamber and is exploded. The pressure of the explosion forces the reed valve to close; and inasmuch as once this is done the only opening for the escape of the gas is at the exhaust, the gases rush out at the rear in the powerful thrusting motion that causes the reaction that makes the jet move forward. In a ramjet engine the force of air rushing in at the front takes the place of the valve of the pulse jet. The intake force must be sufficient in itself to build up a wall of pressure that resists the explosion of the mixed air and fuel charge and

causes the gases to exhaust at the rear. Because of this necessity for the intake air to build up its own wall of resistance, ramjet engines will function only when operating at high speed; they cannot be launched directly from a standstill but must attain an air speed of about 200 miles per hour before they will function. Consequently ramjet-equipped aircraft must also incorporate some other form of power plant to enable them to become airborne and to bring them to sufficient speed for the ramjets to operate and take over. In actual practice, the inrushing air in a ramjet goes through a compressor to build up the airwall to sufficient strength to withstand the force of combustion and to direct the resulting gas out at the rear. The most highly developed type of jet engine at the present time is the turbojet, which, as its name implies, includes a turbine. The turbojet engine is started by means of an outside power source and, upon reaching sufficient speed, sucks air in at the front by means of vanes that serve as a compressor. The compressed air then is diffused into the combustion chambers where, mixed with fuel, the explosion take place. The expanding exhaust gases pass through jet nozzles that play upon the turbine wheel, thereby turning the shaft that runs forward to operate the compressor vanes located ahead of the combustion chambers (which are arranged around the shaft). As the gases leave the turbine, they eject at the rear of the engine and provide the thrust of propulsion.

In some real turbojet engines what is known as an afterburner is fitted. This injects additional fuel into the hot exhaust gases behind the turbine to provide additional thrust before the gases finally are exhausted. In prop-jet airplanes, the power of the turbine is also employed to operate a regular propeller as well as the compressor.

Essentially, jet propulsion in a real or model airplane may be described as a means of securing motive power wherein an aircraft is carried through air by means of gas ejected to the rear in jet form, thereby creating a thrust of propulsion. This thrust can exist only when the jet velocity in relation to the airplane exceeds the velocity of the airplane in relation to the atmosphere. Thus thrust increases as jet velocity is increased and as air-mass flow is increased. The greater the amount of fuel that is burned in a given time, the greater is the thrust of the exhaust gas and, consequently, the more rapidly the airplane moves through the air. Working miniatures of both pulse-jet and turbojet engines are available for use in model airplanes of larger sizes. The characteristics of the ramjet engine that require it to move through the air at a high rate of speed before it can function preclude its use in working model airplanes. Generally speaking, model pulse-jet engines and turbojet engines are not for the beginner; they are truly powerful mechanisms and must be treated with respect. In actual practice most model jet-powered airplane flying is done either using carbon dioxide cartridges mounted on the model and punctured so as to release their pressurized contents directly into the atmosphere to the rear to provide a propulsive jet, or with pellet-fuel rocket engines. Both usages provide a jet power that performs in the same manner as the jet released by an actual jet engine, and model airplane flying accomplished in this manner may truly be considered jet propulsion, even though a working model of a prototype jet engine is not actually employed. The pellet-fuel engines actually are a form of the small solid-fuel rocket engine, distinguished chiefly by size and power and the form of the fuel charge from the larger solid-fuel rocket engines discussed in the following chapter, although one of the leading brands of fuel and engines of the pellet-fuel type incorporates the word "jet" in its trade name.

The model airplane hobbyist may encounter a type of model airplane known as the ducted-fan type. These models were developed in an effort to achieve jet propulsion using regular internal-combustion reciprocating-type engines. Instead of a propeller, a multibladed fan, or impeller, is attached to the engine, which is entirely hidden within the fuselage of the plane behind an opening in the nose that serves as an air intake. The fan draws air in through this opening and forces it back through a passage or duct built into the fuselage and extending to the rear of the model where the air is ejected with sufficient force to provide the propulsion thrust required to fly the model. The ducted-fan construction is especially suited to flying scale models of modern jet-powered prototypes whose realism would be spoiled by the presence of a propeller. It should be borne in mind that a ducted-fan method of propulsion is never so efficient as a conventional propeller in a model of a given size and weight. Consequently, with a given engine, a ducted-fan model should preferably be lighter (consistent with necessary strength of construction) or smaller than a propeller-driven model of the same plane using the same engine. It is difficult to construct a control-line ducted-fan model for substantially the same reason that it appears virtually impossible to carry control lines through the envelope of a model airship. For any sort of efficiency, the duct must be kept airtight from the point of air intake to exhaust, and a control cable cannot be carried through the duct itself. Consequently, most ducted-fan models are of the free-flight type, although it is possible with some planning and work to devise a control-line model.

OTHER TYPES OF ROCKETS

Heretofore in this chapter rockets have been spoken of in the context of working rocket engines themselves, with the implication that such engines would be used in model rockets that would take to the air through the thrust of the exhaust gases in precisely the same manner as do real rockets. This type of model rocketry forms a major part of operating model development, as does the use of similar rocket engines on jet-propelled model airplanes. The subject of model rockets, of course, also embraces a vast field of nonoperating display models and of models that operate by means entirely different from those used in prototype rockets. Furthermore, rockets and the modeling of rockets and related equipment embrace a considerably greater area than the type of rockets used in the exploration of space, although this is the application that naturally most readily comes to mind today. However, there are also purely military rockets, and by extension this brings many rocket-model hobbyists into the field of rocket carriers and launchers and even to rocket-carrying naval vessels. This, in turn, often means an overlapping between the model rocket hobby and the hobbies of building or collecting model automobiles, military vehicles, and ships. Furthermore, there are the modeling and operation of trains that carry rockets or rocket-launching devices, or varied types of aircraft and spacecraft. The combination of the two hobbies of model aircraft, spacecraft, and rockets and of model railroading presents a number of interesting possibilities that have attracted the attention of quite a few enthusiasts. The model railroader will find available a number of cars, or even complete trains connected with aircraft, spacecraft, and rockets, in both HO (British OO) gauge and O gauge. These include cars from which helicopters and airplanes can be launched, cars that carry or launch rockets and

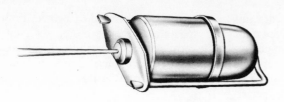

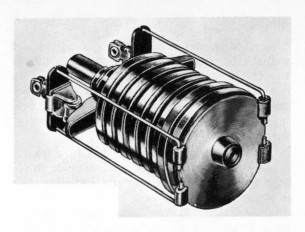

Fig. 130. Two pellet-fuel jet engines. The propulsive thrust of these engines is developed by the gases resulting from the combustion of the fuel pellets that are loaded into the engine cases and ignited by means of a special wick. Engines of this type may be used for lightweight model airplanes, rockets, or helicopters.

Aristo-Craft Distinctive Miniatures

missiles, and other types that relate to space and defense operations.

Most of the model railroad launching devices are spring-operated. There also are a number of model rockets available that are given flight impetus by similar spring-actuated devices. In addition, there are further types of toy and model rockets and related craft available involving other types of propulsion of which mention should be made at this point so as to cover the subject thoroughly, even though some of these devices, either in their mode of operation or in their external design, may well not be embraced in the general pattern of interests and endeavors of some more advanced model rocket fans. For one thing, for example, there are on the market catapult-operated miniature rockets, space capsules, and satellites that can be launched to a considerable height and that may include parachutes for their safe return to earth. Another type of rocket involves the compression of water by means of a special pump to provide the force required to hurl model rockets into the air for a considerable distance. Models of this type include two-stage rockets, with the second stage automatically released for further travel upward from a height of about a hundred feet, and rockets with space capsules that are released high in the air and are returned to earth by parachute. In models of this latter category the pumped water serves to compress the existing air within the rocket body. Upon release the water is ejected first, and then the jet of compressed air that provides the main propulsion thrust. Such models are, accordingly, actual jet-operated devices.

MODEL PULSE-JET AND TURBOJET ENGINES

As noted, working models of both pulse-jet and turbojet engines available for use in larger model aircraft. Such models should always be operated by means of control lines tested to sufficient strength to assure absolute safety and as a further precaution secured to the operator's hand by means of a safety thong. Such devices are capable of pulling the handle from the hobbyist's hand if great care is not exercised. Every possible precaution must be taken to prevent this. The free flight of such powerful, hot, and explosive devices is completely unthinkable. The operation of such formidable devices should be carried out only by experts. The noise alone made by such engines in flight is enough to confuse and distract an amateur handler. There is a special AMA competition class for control-line speed flying of such models. Some idea of the potential of such models may be gathered from the fact that the regulations for this event specify that only steel or other metal lines may be used and that if a single line is employed it must have a minimum diameter of .028 inches (more than ¼th inch). Or if two lines are used, each must have a minimum diameter of .016 inches (more than ⅛th inch). A protecting wire screen generally is used around the flying circle for such events, and obviously is highly desirable. If there is no such screen spectators must be kept at least seventy-five feet from the outer edge of the flying circle. Jet-engine models with no more than 1.25 square-inch cross-sectional area of the tail pipe at its point of minimum cross section may also be flown in some other control-line events. Obviously planes with engines of this type are never flown indoors.

Miniature pulse-jet types of engines will run satisfactorily on plain gasoline. It is not necessary to include a lubricant in the fuel as it is with internal-combustion reciprocating engines. Model turbojet engines are quite formidable affairs, marvelously designed and crafted and as appropriate for university instructional demonstrations and actual aircraft research and design work—for all of which they are primarily intended, in fact—as for hobby flying. They are about a foot long and are literally complete modern turbojet engines in miniature. They are also rather expensive, although parts, drawings, and specifications are available for modelmakers who wish to construct the unit themselves rather than purchase it in completed form. A fairly well-equipped workshop and a comparatively high degree of skill are requisites for the construction of a model of this type from a kit.

Miniature turbojet engines may be run on a number of types of fuels. In one group are petroleum types of liquid hydrocarbons, including aviation gasoline, butane, and propane. A second group of liquid hydrocarbons generate greater static thrust than the petroluem group but also have the disadvantage of generating excessive heat in the engine, although this can be somewhat reduced by the addition of chemical coolants to the fuel. This second group of fuels comprises nitromethane, methanol, and acetone. The fuel system is pressurized, and fuel must be delivered into the injector-valve port of these engines under a pressure of from 80 to 100 pounds per square inch. Futhermore, an afterburner system can be attached to these engines. In fact the manufacturers note that dynamic model airplane performance during takeoff can be realized only with the use of an afterburner system. However, the AMA rules prohibit the use of afterburners. The model has eight combustion chambers, each with its own glow plug. An auxiliary electric motor is used for starting, and is detached from the turbojet shaft after starting and before takeoff.

No working-model jet engine of any type should ever be bench operated for more than brief intermittant periods of a minute or so, and should always be allowed a substantial time for cooling between such runs. Adequate ventilation should always be provided, regardless of the type of fuel used, preferably by connecting a stovepipe directly from the engine exhaust to the outside of the building. Again, let is be remembered at all times that all working models of pulse-jet and turbojet engines are formidable machines and that great care must constantly be exercised to protect both operator and spectators. Furthermore, such engines are quite prone to damage through misuse, particularly during bench running. One would prefer to see them operated only in the hands of true experts.

PELLET-FUEL ENGINES

Fortunately for the average flying model hobbyist, relatively inexpensive and safe jet propulsion is available for smaller models in the form of carbon dioxide cartridges and pellet-fuel rocket engines. Little additional need be said concerning the CO_2 cartridges. They are mounted directly on the model and the gas is released by punching the center of the neck with a special tool. The pellet-fuel engines are in far more widespread use today, and the system is somewhat more intricate in its ramifications and handling procedures. A number of model airplane kits are available, especially ln Great Britain, for building model airplanes for this type of power, including kits for rockets; a few ready-to-fly models also are to be had in Great Britain. In the United States some model airplane kits, although designed chiefly with internal-combustion reciprocating engines in mind, are also indicated by their manufacturers as especially suitable for pellet-fuel engines. Many other kits are adaptable with a little extra work, or the hobbyist can build his own models. Model rockets can also be built and powered with these engines, although many of the more sophisticated model rocket enthusiasts feel that the power even of the largest model pellet-fuel engines is insufficient for this purpose, and use the type of solid rocket fuels described in the next chapter.

The pellet-fuel may be described as a gas-producing fuel with a controlled rate of burning. It is not an explosive. The fuel is supplied in the form of solid pellets of varied sizes to fit the different model engines. Each pellet has a gas-producing

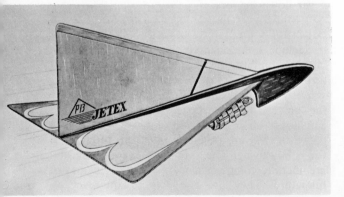

Fig. 131. A lightweight balsa-wood glider converted into an efficient jet-powered working model airplane by the installation of a pellet-fuel jet engine similar to those shown in Fig. 130. The engine, held in place by a spring clip, is easily removed for refueling and cleaning.

Aristo-Craft Distinctive Miniatures

duration, when ignited, of anywhere from four to nine seconds, usually about seven to eight seconds in most models. A special rocket engine and fuel produce a comparatively higher thrust but for a shorter period of about four to five seconds. It is possible to put two or even three fuel pellets into an engine for a single charge. This increases the duration of the power thrust, although in practice it does not multiply in precise relation to the number of pellets to the time derived from a single pellet. The best time that can be had from three pellets of the longest gas-producing duration might be slightly over twenty seconds. This may seem like a rather short period of time to many readers. It will not appear quite so short when it is considered that most free-flight internal-combustion-reciprocating-engine-powered flights are timed to cut off the fuel supply after fifteen or twenty seconds of powered flight. It does mean, however, that pellet-fuel engines are almost universally looked upon as unsuited to control line flying, although model airplanes so powered present no physical problem in regard to mounting the bell crank and carrying the cables as do airships and ducted-fan airplanes. AMA regulations have established a special competition event for pellet-fuel models, designated as the free-flight rocket-powered class.

Essentially the pellet-fuel engines consist of a steel case (earlier models had aluminum cases and should not be used with the present-day fuel pellets which are somewhat more powerful) mounted on a clip that is secured to the model airplane. The case is removed from the airplane and opened for loading with one to three fuel pellets. The pellets should be scraped with a knife blade to clear away the protective varnish coating; they may also be scored or dimpled as an aid to ignition. The pellet or pellets are inserted in the case and a coil of special igniter wick (plastic over a very thin metal core) laid over the surface of the last pellet and held in place by a gauze disc, one end of the coiled ignited wick extending toward the end of the case. The fuel pellets and gauze disk are then held in place by closing the case and securing the removable end in place with the locking spring. This locking spring also serves as a safety valve. If for any reason the normal exhaust port should clog, the pressure of the gas would permit it to escape via the spring-loaded end cap of the case. The engine is then remounted on the clip on the model airplane and a short length of the igniter wick slipped through the jet opening so that one end comes in contact with the coiled internal wick, while the other end extends about a quarter inch outside the engine. When ready for launching,

this exposed wick is ignited, preferably with a piece of punk, a special igniter stick, or a cigarette, to avoid the necessity of holding a lighted match near the structure of a model airplane. The fuel charge will start to burn shortly thereafter. The first indication that the charge has fired should be the blowing of the ignited wick core out of the nozzle. If it sticks it should immediately be plucked free. It is a wise preparation to wet the thumb and forefinger immediately before lighting the external wick so as to be ready to pull out the wick core if necessary. Two or three seconds after the wick core is blown, a steady hissing sound should be heard, indicating that propulsive thrust has been developed and that the model airplane can be launched. Most hobbyists prefer to employ hand-launching. This is not because a pellet-fuel-engine-powered plane will not take off from the ground by itself if provided with a free-running landing gear but because the power used for take-off, plus that required to compensate for the weight and drag of the landing gear during flight, will reduce the time of the flight itself.

It is also possible to fire the fuel charge by means of an electric spark, as is commonly employed in solid-fuel rockets as described in the next chapter, However, in practice this usually leads to complications in manipulating the wires and so on. This procedure really is not required for safety or other reasons with engines of the pellet-fuel type, although it is a necessity with larger rockets and fuel charges.

It is absolutely essential that both the fuel pellets and the igniter wick be kept absolutely dry and protected from any dampness. This is the purpose of the varnish coating that is scraped from the fuel pellets immediately before loading. The wick should always be kept stored in the airtight metal container in which it comes. Failure to fire is due almost invariably to either or both the fuel or wick having been exposed to dampness. It is possible to increase the thrusting power of engines of this type (at the expense of the duration of flight on a given fuel charge) either by mounting an extension to the jet outlet, known as an augmenter tube, or by scoring the surface of the pellets or by drilling a hole through their center, or by both. Another method is to cut a groove across the top and bottom of the length of the fuel pellet and to wrap a long length of igniter wick twice around the groove before coiling the end of the wick under the piece of gauze. All these methods of increasing thrust that involve cutting into the fuel pellets operate by thereby exposing a greater area of fuel-pellet surface to early ignition than with the unmarred pellet. These methods should be approached slowly, and the results of each such alteration studied separately. Increasing the amount of fuel exposed to ignition also greatly increases the amount of heat to which the case is subjected. No attempt should be made to soup up the fuel charges in this manner if the earlier type of aluminum cases is used. Such procedures sometimes were advised for the older engines, but it should be remembered that at the time these suggestions were made the earlier fuel formula that was more compatible with the aluminum cases was also in use. In fact, considering the low cost of these engines, anyone still using one of the earlier models would be well advised to replace it with the latest type of steel-case engine, which is much more suitable for the improved fuel that now is universally supplied.

The use of an augmenter tube increases the thrust of a pellet-fuel engine by about 25 percent and also permits the enclosure of the engine in a scale model. The augmenter tube can itself be used as an actual structural part of the model airplane fuselage, with bulkheads slid over the tube and the longitudinal stringers of the fuselage mounted on them. When the engine is thus enclosed it is necessary to provide for a trapdoor or removable section of the fuselage over the engine so that it can be removed for cleaning and loading. The augmenter tube is wider at the point where it surrounds the engine exhaust than at its own exhaust point. Air is drawn into the larger end, and gains velocity as it is forced down the narrower throat where it combines with and accelerates the exhaust gas of the engine, thereby increasing the propulsive thrust at the point of final exhaust. The presence of an augmenter tube makes it somewhat more difficult to fire the fuel charge, as the external wick extends from the engine nozzle only a short distance into the augmenter tube. It is therefore necessary to use a special wire holder in which an igniter stick can be mounted, and insert the holder down the augmenter tube to ignite the external wick. The holder is formed with a wire loop the diameter of the inside of the augmenter tube so as to guide the igniter stick directly to the wick in the engine nozzle. When the augmenter tube is used, an air intake opening must be provided in the nose of the plane of at least as great a diameter as the opening in the larger end of the augmenter tube. Or the air may be taken in through two intakes, one on each side of the model, provided their total area is at least equal to the large end of the augmenter tube. When the augmenter tube is thus used enclosed in a scale model, it is unwise to attempt to increase the thrust further by scoring or cutting into the fuel, as this may result in the engine becoming so hot as to damage the model airplane structure itself.

Pellet-fuel propulsion engines may also be used to power model helicopters. Two engines of equal size are mounted in opposed positions on one of the rotor blades, and the fuel charges are ignited at as near the same instant as possible. It is possible to fly pellet-fuel-engine model airplanes indoors as long as adequate ventilation is provided in the room. Usually when flown indoors such models are tethered to a center post. Indoor free flight with engines of this type also is possible in a sufficiently large hall and under proper conditions of supervision and ventilation.

Pellet-fuel engines require frequent cleaning of the nozzle and internal surfaces to remove accumulated ash and soot from burnt fuel charges. The cap sealing washers also will become soft, and require replacement after a number of charges have been fired.

CHAPTER 7

Solid-Fuel Rockets

The serious hobby of model rocketry has been growing by leaps and bounds ever since man started successfully questing in space in the late 1950's. Today this hobby is closely allied to the established model aircraft hobby, yet in many ways independent of it, with its own governing body, the National Association of Rocketry (see Appendix I), and its own problems and techniques. To what eventual state of development model rocketry may attain, or what its relationship to conventional model airplane building and flying might become, is admittedly uncertain. That it must always remain closely connected, if not actually allied, to the model airplane hobby becomes clearer if an examination is made as to precisely what model rocketry is and, even more important, what it is not, and what each group, the model aircraft enthusiasts and the model rocket enthusiasts, seem to feel lies in the future.

The National Association of Rocketry and, as far as can be seen, all the manufacturers of model rocket equipment, kits and supplies, and virtually every articulate individual concerned with the hobby strive to make clear a very definite distinction and unbridgeable gap between what they define respectively as *model rocketry* and as *amateur rocketry*. The definitions and boundaries that have been laid down between model rocketry and amateur rocketry may be summed up as enlightened self-interest on the part of model rocket enthusiasts. These hobbyists want to see the creation,

maintenance, and growth of a sound, safe model rocket hobby—both as a hobby in itself and, of course, as a path toward interesting the young men and women of today in careers in aerospace, just as model airplane building always has played an important part in leading to careers in aviation, and always will continue to so lead. For obvious reasons, just as the Armed Forces have long been interested in promoting the hobby of model aviation, so too are they today, together with the National Aeronautics and Space Administration, interested in the promotion of safe and sane model rocketry. So, too, are the counterpart organizations in Allied countries.

INTELLIGENT MODEL ROCKETRY

Every effort on the part of those who are interested in promoting the hobby of model rocketry is directed to channeling this hobby into a set program of optimum safety: safety in the selection of materials and fuels, in the design and building of model rockets and in their use. Model rocket hobbyists do not handle or mix their own fuels. With the execption of the pellet-fuel engines described in the preceding chapter (which in fact are generally regarded as lacking sufficient thrusting power and duration for most model rocket work), the engines employed in model rocketry are not reusable. No attempt is ever made to reload them. Rocket engines are factory built and loaded, as-

Fig. 132. Blast off! A solid-fuel model rocket rests on its launching pad, in this case rather elaborately modeled as a scale model with ramp, in the photograph at the left. At the right is seen the same model rocket ascending, a moment after ignition.

Estes Industries, Inc.

suring that each engine of a given type has an identical load and will provide exactly the same characteristics when fired. Model rockets themselves are light in weight, recoverable and reflyable. They are built from light materials such as cardboard, balsa wood, and plastics. They are fired by means of electrical ignition under careful control. Model rocket hobbyists follow a rigid safety code as set forth by the National Association of Rocketry. The result has been a safety record that is most enviable. The serious model rocket hobby in the United States now claims that over a million model rockets have successfully been launched without any rocket-caused injuries.

Obviously, these are laurels that never can be rested upon. Safety in model rocketry requires an ever-continuing vigil. The utmost care must be observed in each individual new rocket that is built, and in the firing of each successive rocket. At stake is both the personal well-being of the hobbyist and the future growth and standing of the entire hobby.

Stories frequently appear in the press of persons injured during the preparation or launching of homemade rockets, sometimes quite seriously. It is the contention of the model rocket hobby—and the facts appear to bear them out—that these mishaps occur to the so-called "basement bomber" type of amateur rocket fans, individuals who experiment in rocketry outside the approved safety standards of the NAR, or who lack sufficient knowledge or equipment. Such individuals may range from young boys who have read some details of real rockets, including material relating to engines and fuels, and have tried to transfer professional rocketry techniques to the home workshop, to adults who should know better! These amateur rocketeers often mix or attempt to mix (explosions often interrupt their activities at this point) their own solid fuels or experiment with liquid fuels, or attempt to build and launch large rockets embodying substantial metal components. They would be better off keeping a live royal Bengal tiger as a house pet, or attempting to extract rattlesnake venom at home. The activities of these "basement bomber" types of amateur rocketeers are well summed up in the often-heard expression that they glibly attempt things that would send a professional rocket engineer into a nervous break-

Fig. 133. A typical firing range at an organized model rocket event. The rocket-launching rods are mounted on a sawhorse in the foreground, while behind it is the command table with control box and communications with trackers. The model rocket has just received ignition but has not yet started to move upward.

National Aeronautics and Space Administration

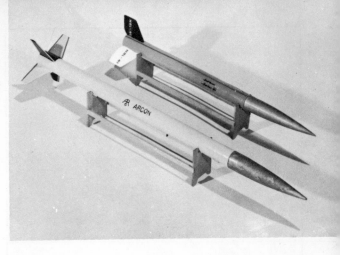

Fig. 134. Two typical solid-fuel model rockets, shown on horizontal display stands. They are 14 inches and 18 inches long respectively and scale models of actual rockets. After reaching peak height, they eject parachutes that bring them safely back to earth.

Model Missiles, Inc.

down, or at least sprinting to the nearest bomb-proof shelter. It is more than just advice, then—it is imperative that anyone interested in this model hobby become a model rocketeer and *not* an amateur rocketeer.

MODEL ROCKETS ARE NOT FIREWORKS

Furthermore, it should be made abundantly clear that model rockets are not fireworks. Many who have previously been familiar with the rocket in the form of the noisemaker and sky-burst spectacular of lights often associate model rockets with these devices used to attract night visitors to fairs and amusement parks or to mark the Fourth of July or Guy Fawkes Day. However, the model rocket is a scientific device that presents a thrilling

sight when it is fired and becomes airborne, and finally ejects a parachute, allowing it to float safely back to earth. Its purpose is not to create either an audible or a visual effect the way an ordinary fireworks rocket or, indeed, any form of pyrotechnic display does. As a matter of fact, most model rockets produce a comparatively limited amount of noise during their launching, less noise probably than the average conventional flying model airplane with an unmuffled internal-combustion reciprocating engine. The noise of a model rocket is, like that of a real rocket used for a launching at Cape Kennedy, more a sustained hissing sound during the period of ignition and powered thrust than that of an ear-clapping explosion.

The model rocket hobby and industry sometimes appear to newcomers to the hobby to be somewhat overconcerned with the supposed con-

Fig. 135. An assortment of solid-fuel model rockets and rocket gliders representing some of the types for which easily assembled commercial kits are available, and a miniature Mercury space capsule. In the foreground is an altiscope, an instrument used to determine the height to which a model rocket ascends (see also Fig. 153.).

Estes Industries, Inc.

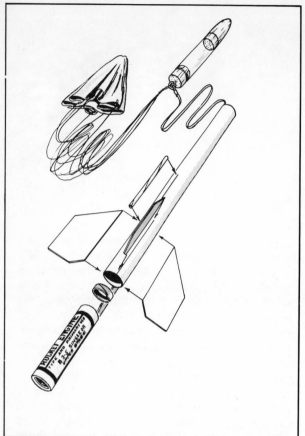

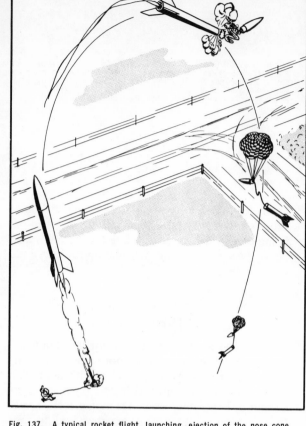

Fig. 136. The components of a typical solid-fuel model rocket, including engine, the rocket body itself, and the detachable nose cone and parachute that are released in flight.

Estes Industries, Inc.

Fig. 137. A typical rocket flight, launching, ejection of the nose cone and parachute, and safe recovery by parachute.

Estes Industries, Inc.

nection between model rockets and fireworks rockets than might seem called for, and to engage in an unwarranted degree of attempting to distinguish between the two forms. There is a valid reason for this. Many states and localities in the United States have laws designed to prohibit or regulate the transport, sale, or discharge of fireworks, including rockets. Standing laws, although written with fireworks rockets in mind, in many cases also apply to model rockets, although model rocketry was in most instances completely unknown at the time these laws were drafted. It is therefore important to model rocketry that the distinction between ordinary fireworks rockets and model rockets be made clear in order that efforts can be furthered to have existing laws modified to permit the use of proper model rockets. As of now, the situation in the United States in regard to the legal use of model rockets is somewhat spotty. In some areas there never were any regulations to militate against their use. In other places, changes have already been effected in existing fireworks regulations to permit the pursuit of the hobby of model

rocketry. In some communities model rocketry is still illegal under the present regulations governing fireworks, or a special license must be obtained to permit an individual to discharge a model rocket. Hobbyists must find out what the situation is in their community. There are cases where model rockets are illegal in one state but legal in an adjoining state, so that hobbyists living in the one must cross to the other to launch their model rockets.

Obviously, what is needed in order to effect changes in existing regulations is to make clear the true distinction between fireworks rockets and model rockets. Also, because of bad publicity that inevitably occurs following an amateur rocket accident, a similar distinction must be made between model rocketry and amateur rocketry. In some localities, where model rockets were previously permitted, accidents to "basement bombers" have caused considerable agitation for legislation barring all sorts or rocket activity, including model rockets.

An idea of the important status of model

Fig. 138. A demonstration rocket tube assembly in a transparent housing with a special cutaway dummy engine to show the interior detail of a typical single-stage solid-fuel rocket. The engine is at the bottom, and above it a considerable length of the tube is occupied by the carefully folded recovery parachute wrapped in its lines.

Estes Industries, Inc.

Fig. 139. The contents of a kit for building an elaborate model rocket, in this case the 25-inch-long three-stage model with payload capsule shown in assembled form in the center. The checkered material is for making the parachute. At the right are shown various typical components: tube sections, an adapter or reduction fitting, and a nose cone.

Estes Industries, Inc.

rocketry today is contained in a recent circular issued by one of the manufacturers of model rocket equipment:

"Model rocketry has been recognized by the Academy of Aeronautics, the National Aeronautics Association, the Fédération Aéronautique Internationale, the United States Air Force, and other organizations as an aero-modeling sport. The Air Force has, in fact, banned all other forms of non-professional rocketry while endorsing and recommending model rocketry for its personnel and their dependents. The fourth annual national model rocketry championship contest was held with Air Force sanction at the Air Force Academy, and the fifth annual championships will be held at the Air Force's Hanscomb Field in Massachusetts. The Boy Scouts of America do not consider model rockets as fireworks and are considering their application for a possible merit badge. It is certain that these outstanding organizations carefully considered all of the various aspects of model rocketry, and had they regarded model rockets as fireworks they certainly would not have approved them for use by their members."*

---

*Estes Industries, Inc. Most model rocket manufacturers supply helpful technical information in their catalogs or as supplements to them. The writer has found the Estes *Technical Reports* particularly elaborate and helpful and has made considerable use of them in preparing this chapter. Estes also publishes a booklet, *Model Rocketry*, 1964, Penrose, Colorado. Another publication of value to those who wish to delve more deeply into the ramifications of the subject is the *Handbook of Model Rocketry* by G. Harry Stine, 1965, Chicago, Illinois, the NAR Official Handbook.

Model rocketry is not merely the building and flying of miniature rockets up to the point where the highest possible altitude is reached by constructing a rocket powered by the most powerful of the existing engines. (It is obviously rather pointless to build a model rocket that will reach so high an altitude that it will fly out of sight; even the largest models will start to pass from sight between 2,000 and 2,500 feet. Many model rockets, including most of the smaller ones that are the most popular and widely flown types on the average ascend to heights of about 400 to 600 feet.) No, model rocketry is not just a matter of attaining height; it is a scientific hobby intended to provide a wide range of activities in most cases closely paralleling those of real rocketry: the construction and flight of single- and multistage rockets, the carrying aloft and safe return of a payload (a raw egg is considered the ideal standard for a model rocket flight), recovery devices, ignition and launching methods, stability and other factors of design, tracking systems, and instrumentation, including aerial photography and the inclusion of radio devices. Radio as applied to model rocketry is completely different from its application to model airplanes. In the radio control of a model airplane, the transmitter is on the ground and signals to the receiver in the plane to direct its movement. In model rocketry, it is the radio transmitter that is sent up in the model, to send signals relaying a variety of information to the receiver

Fig. 140. A rocket-firing range at a National Association of Rocketry meet. The ignition wires run from the control box in the background to the base of individual launching rods. Most solid-fuel model rockets are launched from rods of this type. The more elaborate towers on the sawhorse at the right are employed only for very large models.

National Aeronautics and Space Administration

on the ground in the same manner, although naturally somewhat simplified, that radios in actual satellites and rockets relay pertinent information back to earth.

Even ignoring such fascinating advanced specialties, there are endless possibilities for the model rocket experimenter to engage in meaningful studies and developments in model rocket design. Suppose a simple rocket with a given diameter and length of body tube is selected and experimentation confined to a single model rocket engine. Suppose there is available a choice of only ten shapes of fins, all of approximately the same size, and a

choice of only five fin cross sections or airfoils. That means fifty different possible combinations. Then build the same fifty fin shape and airfoil combinations, using both three and four fins on the same basic rocket body tube and engine. That gives a hundred combinations. Turn to the other end of the tube, the nose end, and assume a choice is available of only ten different nose-cone shapes and sizes. If the hobbyist builds a model rocket with each of the hundred different fin arrangements with each of the ten nose cones, he will have constructed a total of one thousand model rockets! The object? Intelligent and purposeful experi-

Fig. 141. Two typical single-stage solid-fuel model rockets built from kits. Both models weigh the same, .65 ounces. Note the variations in the construction at the base and the shape of the fins and nose cone. The model at the right is a scale replica of the WAC Corporal rocket. These models are 12 inches and 11¾ inches high respectively.

Estes Industries, Inc.

mentation to ascertain which design will not only fly the highest (remember, all are using the same engine) but also present the greatest stability in flight.

The figures of a thousand model rockets, each differing slightly, may seem enormous. Remember, however, that there are more than ten possible fin shapes; each shape may be made in almost any number of sizes; there are more than five possible airfoils; there are more than ten sizes and shapes of nose cones; the rocket body may be varied with different lengths of body tubes, while still retaining the same diameter; there are various model rocket engines, each of which may be tried with different combinations of the other components; there are different types of recovery systems—in fact, the actual number of possible experimental combinations is virtually endless! A hobbyist could literally spend years in design and experimental work simply seeking to achieve the greatest stability and highest altitude of a single basic small rocket!

Of course, the average model rocket fan will not build a thousand variations or even a hundred, and as he becomes more and more familiar with rocket design and flight he probably will gradually acquire an innate knowledge of the performance of various design factors and the comparative merits of different shapes of fins and airfoils and nose cones. Nevertheless, the foregoing will demonstrate just how much an experimental hobby model rocketry can be and the almost literally unlimited possibilities for serious and continuing study and research.

MODEL ROCKET SAFETY CODES

Reference already has been made to the Safety Code of the National Association of Rocketry. This is a good guide for everyone interested in model rockets, whether a member of the NAR or not. It is an indispensable prelude to model rocket design and construction and launching techniques, and should be studied now, before specific aspects of the subject are explored in greater detail. The NAR Safety Code comprises the following fifteen articles:

"1. I will obey the laws regarding rockets.

"2. I will not mix my own rocket propellants or delay trains, etc.

"3. I will not make my own rocket engines. I will use pre-loaded, factory-made commercial model rocket engines that do not require mixing the propellant.

"4. I will treat all rocket engines with care, keeping them from heat and not dropping them.

"5. My model rockets will contain no substantial metal parts.

"6. My model rockets will contain a recovery device to return them safely to the ground so that they may be flown again.

"7. My model rockets will not contain explosive warheads.

"8. I will fly model rockets with adult supervision in open areas away from houses, buildings, trees and power lines.

"9. I will use a remotely-operated electrical firing system to ignite model rocket engines, and I will not install the electrical ignition element in a rocket engine until shortly before launching.

"10. I will always use a launching device that is pointed within 30 degrees of the vertical.

"11. I will not fly model rockets against targets in the air or on the ground.

"12. I will not fly model rockets in windy weather or in conditions of low visibility.

"13. I will not fly model rockets where they may endanger aircraft in flight.

"14. I will always act in a mature manner, with safety uppermost in mind.

"15. I will not engage in any operation that may endanger myself or others.

The NAR Safety Code is the most widely publicized; and, of course, application for membership requires agreement to abide by the NAR Safety Code. There is another code, lesser known but containing considerable additional and extremely valuable, well-thought-out and informative regulations. In some instances it specifies and spells out safety procedures and limitations to a greater degree than the NAR Safety Code. This is the Astron Rocket Society Safety Code.* It does not in any way conflict with the NAR Safety Code, so it would be wise to follow the combined restrictions and specifications of *both* codes. The Astron Rocket Society Safety Code consists of ten articles, as follows:

"As a model rocketeer I will act in a mature manner with safety foremost in my mind in all my model rocket activities and will obey this safety code at all times.

"1. I will not attempt to compound propellants or other combustible chemicals or tamper with pre-manufactured rocket engines. I will inspect each rocket engine before use and never use an engine which shows signs of physical damage, remembering that any rocket propellant can be explosive under certain conditions.

"2. I will not smoke near rocket engines,

---

*Courtesy Estes Industries, Inc.

launch my rockets in the presence of highly combustible materials, or engage in any activity which would present a fire hazard.

"3. I will never use any metallic rocket engines, will not construct my model rockets with substantial metal parts in the area of the engine, and will not launch any rocket over 16 ounces in weight or containing more than 4 ounces of propellant in compliance with Federal regulations.

"4. My model rockets will be electrically ignited, using a launch system with either a switch protector or a safety interlock to prevent accidental ignition of the rocket engine, and I will remain at least 10 feet away from any rocket which is being launched.

"5. I will launch my model rockets using a launching rail or other suitable guide means aimed within 25 degrees of the vertical to assure a safe and predictable flight path, and will launch only rockets whose stability characteristics have been predetermined.

"6. I will not fly model rockets in high winds, conditions of low visibility, in the vicinity of low-flying aircraft, near tall buildings, near people not aware of the launching, or under any conditions which might endanger property or persons.

"7. I will not launch rockets so that their ballistic trajectories will carry them against targets on the ground and will never use an explosive warhead in a rocket.

"8. My model rockets will contain recovery devices which will deploy at an altitude of at least 50 feet to return the rocket safely and undamaged.

"9. To prevent accidental eye injury I will always either place the launcher so the end of the rod is above eye level or cap the end of the rod with my hand when approaching it.

"10. I will launch my model rockets with adult supervision and will remember that the safety of myself and others depends on my own actions."

The only substantial point of difference between the specifications of the two codes is that the NAR code precludes launching at an angle of more than 30 degrees from the vertical, while the Astron code limits the allowable angle to not more than 25 degrees from the vertical. In actual practice the way to launch a rocket is in a perfectly vertical position, or as near that as possible. Not only is this the normal position of launching a prototype rocket (except for military rockets) and the position from which most model rockets achieve the greatest stability in flight and the highest possible flight, but a vertically launched rocket will come down fairly near the launching site, and consequently a much smaller field area is required for model rocket activities when this method is followed.

The reference to avoiding launching model rockets in the presence of real aircraft is not a facetious one. Some of the more powerful standard model rocket engines will thrust a model rocket into the air so that it will be traveling at a speed of some 400 miles per hour within 70 feet of leaving the launching pad! The limitations cited as to no more than 16 ounces gross weight for the entire rocket and 4 ounces of propellant tie in here too, as does the reference to Federal regulations in Article 3 of the Astron code. Model rocket flight in the United States is under the control of the Federal Aviation Agency. If a hobbyist wanted to fly anything larger than a 16-ounce nonmetallic model or with more than 4 ounces of propellant, it would be necessary to secure specific Federal

Fig. 142. A 7-inch-high rocket, weighing .28 ounces, built from a kit designed especially for beginners in model rocketry. Unlike most of the other model rockets shown, this model does not eject a parachute, but is balanced so as to tumble gently back to earth after its powered flight.

Estes Industries, Inc.

Fig. 143. An extremely interesting sequence of photographs showing a lineup of rockets of different designs being fired. In the first picture, No. 2 is ascending (the tower at left counts as launch pad No. 1), and 3, 4, 5, and 6 await their turn. The second picture was taken after No. 3 was fired, and No. 4 is just taking off. The third picture shows No. 5 almost at the top of its guide rod, while No. 6 still waits.

Estes Industries, Inc.

Aviation Agency clearance for the flight. Within the 16-ounce rocket, 4-ounce propellant, nonmetallic construction limits, no clearance is necessary to launch a rocket. In short, in the eyes of the FAA, a nonmetallic rocket weighing less than 16 ounces and with less than 4 ounces of propellant is a model; anything over this in weight specifications—or under it if of metal construction—is an actual aircraft, and accordingly each flight requires FAA clearance! In point of fact, most model rockets carry far less than 4 ounces of propellant; the majority probably using something like a quarter of an ounce of propellant for each flight. A large model rocket carrying 4 ounces of propellant would be a large and husky beast indeed!

WHAT KIND OF HOBBY IS IT?

That model rocketry is a highly educational hobby no one would attempt to deny. In many instances it presents teachers with an easy and attractive path to teaching in various areas, particularly science and trigonometry; any modern science course must of necessity embrace information on space flights and rocketry. In view of this, coupled with the generally acknowledged need to enhance interest in continued studies in science and engineering, it is not surprising to find that model rocketry is becoming a part of many junior and senior high school courses, or that supplementary school rocket clubs are being established in many educational facilities, usually under the guidance of the science teacher. None of this means,

however, that model rocketry is by any means essentially or primarily a hobby for the young, although there are many instances where comparatively young model rocketeers have rapidly achieved an understanding and mastery of the subject that many an elder hobbyist can have just cause to envy. Model rocket activity and clubs in schools today play a role similar to that of the numerous school model airplane clubs that flourished from early in the century up to the end of the 1930's or thereabouts. As observed a little earlier, from the standpoint of an experimental hobby, model rocketry today occupies a position similar to that once held by model airplane building back in the days when most hobbyists designed and built their own model airplanes, instead of relying mainly on highly prefabricated kits of already tested and proved designs. In short, model rocketry today is an accepted serious hobby for enthusiasts of almost all ages.

BASIC MODEL ROCKETS

In its simplest form, a basic model rocket consists of a cardboard body tube to which are attached fins at its lower end, and an eyelet (usually a section of ordinary sodawater straw) mounted on one side to ride upon the verticle guide wire used in launching. A model rocket engine is mounted, usually by a simple press fit, in the lower end of the tube. The upper end of the tube is fitted with a nose cone, usually of balsa wood and also mounted with a press fit. The nose cone is

Fig. 144. Five different solid-fuel model rockets. Note the numerous variations in proportions, design, and construction, especially the different shapes employed for fins and nose cones. It is possible for the hobbyist to experiment almost limitlessly with any one given basic model rocket design in an effort to attain the most efficient unit.

Estes Industries, Inc.

attached to the main rocket body tube by means of a cord or piece of rubber hidden inside the tube during flight. The rocket engine is fired by electrically igniting the engine, and thrusts the rocket upward into flight. After the main propulsive thrust of the engine is exhausted, there is a pause, and then a small second charge of propellant ignites at the head, or upper, end of the machine. This charge is known as the ejection charge and is directed to thrust upward so as to blow the nose cone out of the rocket body tube. Bear in mind that the cone is attached to the tube by means of the cord or rubber that holds it tied to the tube after the cone is blown. Blowing the nose cone destroys the aerodynamic balance of the model rocket and causes it to fall slowly back to earth, tumbling over itself as it descends. This method of bringing back the rocket is known as "tumble recovery." In more complicated or larger model rockets, blowing the nose cone is accompanied by the release of a paper or cloth streamer, which serves to slow the descent of the rocket, or by the release of a complete miniature parachute that opens and deploys and brings the rocket body and nose cone back to earth.

The foregoing describes the essential working of all model rockets, whether they are free-lance designs or scale models of an actual prototype rocket. If more than one rocket engine is used, as is the case with multistage model rockets, the ejection charge of one rocket engine is employed to ignite the main propulsive thrust charge of an adjoining rocket engine.

Readers will probably be curious as to the actual size of model rockets. The body tubes generally range from about ¾-inch diameter to less than 2½-inch diameter. A small rocket may have a ¾-inch body-tube diameter and an overall length of only 6 or 7 inches, possibly even less. The largest commercial rockets tend to run about 3 feet in length. There is not necessarily a fixed relationship between the length of the rocket and the diameter of the body tube, although naturally many longer rockets use larger-diameter body tubes. However, many relatively long rockets make use of a ¾-inch diameter tube, and some small rockets are built with comparatively large-diameter body tubes. All depends on the particular design and what the model rocket designer is seeking to achieve in performance. In the case of scale model rockets, the relationship of the body-tube diameter to overall length is, of course, dependent on the dimensions of the prototype. Nor need a model rocket necessarily have a body tube of the same diameter throughout. Often, larger rockets are built with a lower body tube smaller in diameter than the upper body section, the two tubes of different diameter being joined by what is termed an "adapter" or "reduction fitting." Likewise, in some cases, model rockets are built with the lower body-tube section of larger diameter than the upper section.

A model rocket with one portion of the body tube of a larger diameter than another section is not necessarily a two- or three-stage rocket, although many multistage rockets are built with

Fig. 145. Two small model rockets with three standard-size solid-fuel engines. Although the engines are built for the most part to the same dimensions, they are available in a wide variety of types, each type specifically designed to provide a certain performance and for certain uses.

Estes Industries, Inc.

this form of construction. Many multistage model rockets are built with the body tube the same diameter throughout. Similarly, single-stage rockets may at times have tubes of more than one diameter. A lower body tube of larger diameter than the upper tube section often indicates that a cluster of rocket engines is being used for the main propulsive thrust rather than a single engine. The outer formation of the body tube, however, is never in itself a certain indication as to the precise type and performance capabilities of a given model rocket.

MODEL ROCKET PARTS

While a great many model rockets are built from kits that furnish easily assembled parts to produce a rocket of standard design, an enormous amount of construction is done using separately purchased or homemade components. The catalogs of many of the model rocket manufacturers include extensive and extremely interesting listings of individual parts and materials. Arrayed in these catalog listings are great varieties of rocket body tubes, nose cones, payload capsules, couplers, bulkheads, engine mounts, adapters or reduction fittings, and so on. Indeed, so great is the fascination of these listings that merely to study them at length almost invariably stirs a desire to design and build a model rocket.

In tubular construction of any kind, both the inside and the outside diameters are important; in the case of model rockets the inside diameter is particularly critical. The standard inside diameters used in model rocket construction are .710 inch, .725 inch (¾ inch), .765 inch, .950 inch to 1 inch, 1.3 inch, 1.595 to 1.6 inch, although, as has been noted, larger diameters sometimes are used. Most model rocket engines have an outside diameter of .690 inch, and accordingly make a good press fit in a .710-inch inside diameter tube. If

there is any slight looseness in the engine mounting, this can be taken up by wrapping masking tape or a rubber band around the engine. A few of the largest engines have an outside diameter of 1.062 inch and press fit into a 1-inch inside diameter tube. When a rocket engine is used in a tube of larger inside diameter than the usual .690-inch outside diameter of the engine, a special engine mount is used to hold and center the engine in the larger tube.

Some model rocket supply manufacturers give the inside and outside diameters of body tubes; others specify the inside diameter and the tube wall thickness that, when combined with the inside diameter, of course gives the outside diameter of the tube. On the tubes themselves and on many of the fittings, such as nose cones, the inside diameter is the crucial measurement. Even on parts on which the outside diameter is important, such as nose blocks and engine blocks, it is the inside diameter of the body tube that is to be used with the part that regulates the necessary outside diameter of the component. Nose cones are available in a great variety of shapes, usually machined of balsa wood, sometimes constructed of plastic, rubber, or hardwood. Hardwood cones usually are hollow bored to reduce their weight. It is sometimes desirable to use a hardwood nose cone to achieve proper rocket balance and stability. As a matter of fact, nose cones must sometimes be weighted with special weights for the same reason. The cord or rubber—called the shock cord—that ties the nose cone to the body tube is usually attached to the nose cone by means of a screw eye. If any weights are used on the nose cone, they usually are held in position by this screw eye. Nose cones are designed to match the standard-diameter rocket tubes, the lower end of the nose cone intended to fit within the tube being relieved to an outside diameter to match the inside diameter of a given body tube. For example, a nose cone intended to fit a .710-inch inside-diameter body tube would have an outside diameter on the relieved portion of .710 inch; a cone for a .950-inch inside-diameter tube would have an outside diameter on the relieved portion of .950 inch.

Similarly, units intended for use inside the body tube, such as nose blocks or solid bulkheads, as they sometimes are called, or engine blocks, hollow bulkheads used to position the engine and prevent it moving upward in the body tube but at the same time allowing gases to pass upward to eject the nose cone, must have an outside diameter that permits them to make a precision fit within the body tube. Thus, a nose block or engine block intended for use in a .710-inch inside-diameter tube should be precision turned to an outside diameter of .710 inch. Another interesting part is the tubing coupler or stage coupler, which usually consists of a short length of tubing with an outside diameter that matches the inside diameter of the two sections of tube that are to be joined, and sometimes also serve as engine mounts in multi-stage rockets. When permanently secured to both adjacent sections of tubing, this part serves as a tubing coupler. When permanently secured to one section of tubing and making only a press fit with

the other section so that a second-stage rocket can separate itself from the first (or a third stage can separate from the second), the same part acts as a stage coupling.

Perhaps one of the most interesting of standard model rocket parts is the adapter or reduction fitting, usually of precision-machined balsa wood but sometimes of paper, that can be used either permanently or temporarily to connect a body-tube section of one diameter to a tube section of a larger or smaller diameter. For example, adapters are available to connect a .710-inch body tube to a 1.00-inch tube or to a 1.30- or 1.60-inch tube, or to connect a 1.00-inch tube to a 1.30- or 1.60-inch tube, or to connect a 1.30-inch tube to a 1.60-inch tube. In practice this means that virtually all possible connections are available, except for the comparatively little-used .765-inch inside-diameter tube. It also means that three different diameter tubes can be used on the same rocket if desired, such as a 1.60-inch section, a 1.30-inch section, and a .710-inch section. In fact, rocket bodies of four different diameter tubes are possible, although there appears seldom if ever to be need for such a combination.

Fig. 146. These diagrams show the internal combustion of the two major series of standard solid-fuel rocket engines, together with time/thrust curves of an example of each series. Series I engines burn their fuel slowly, and the thrust is extended over a greater period of time than with Series II engines, which put virtually all their power into the initial thrust.

Estes Industries, Inc.

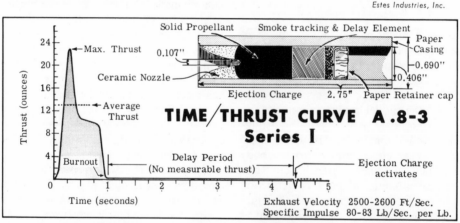

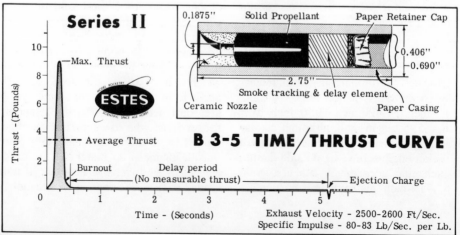

Fig. 147. Preparing for launching. The hobbyist at the left is inserting the launching rod into the guide sleeve built along the edge of his rocket tube. This rocket will then be lowered to the bottom of the rod, as are the model rockets to the right, and the ignition wires will be connected to their engines.

National Aeronautics and Space Administration

Fig. 148. The electrical ignition wires are shown here being connected to the actual ignition wires or fuses leading to the engines. The central firing-control panel is kept locked during this operation so that accidental ignition cannot take place while adjustments are being made. The model at the extreme right is a front-engine boost rocket glider; hence its ignition wires lead almost to the top of the model instead of to its base.

National Aeronautics and Space Administration

Another interesting rocket part is the payload capsule or payload section, which is used to send aloft instruments or specimens such as an egg, or simply weights to test the capacity of a given rocket. Payload capsules, which include a nose cone, may be of the same diameter as the rocket body tube or of a larger diameter, and the actual payload section may be made of regular tubing or of clear transparent plastic. The body-diameter ends are, of course, machined to fit standard-tube inside diameters. It is also possible to obtain plastic payload capsules that are actually hollow models of a Mercury space capsule.

Stabilizer·fins for model rockets usually are cut and shaped by the individual builder according to his own ideas, using high-quality balsa wood sheet stock, usually of 1/32-inch to ¼-inch thickness. For the greatest strength, the fins should be carved so that the grain of the wood follows the leading edge of the fin. Silk is sometimes used to strengthen the glued joint between the fins and the body tube. It is also possible to purchase balsa sheets imprinted with the outlines of proved fin designs for model rockets, or, in a few cases, molded plastic fins. Fins are usually set parallel to the body tube. When they are set at an angle the result is to make the model rocket spin as it ascends.

A variety of model rocket recovery parts, including material for streamers and parachutes, and complete miniature parachutes also is available.

The adhesive usually recommended for model rocket assembly work is white glue. It sets quickly and makes a strong joint with cardboard, balsa wood, cloth, and the other materials commonly used in model rocket construction.

A great number of other parts, some of major importance such as engines, which are discussed below, many of a small and secondary (but often extremely helpful) nature, also are available from model rocket manufacturers. There also are to be had a number of finishing materials, such as paints, dope, masking tape, and decorative decalcomanias, for the ideal model rocket is usually beautified before being launched. The use of these finishing materials on model rockets is substantially the same as their application to model airplanes, as already described in an earlier chapter.

Some model rocket manufacturers also offer packaged parts assortments, made up of a balanced quantity of body tubes, nose cones, recovery devices, fin material and other major and minor parts that provide the material for a hobbyist—or a group of hobbyists —to design and build a number of different rockets. Such an assortment may well provide an ideal starting point for the enthusiast who is just getting started, especially as they allow rockets to be planned by using the actual parts that will be employed in the model, rather than requiring that each rocket be completely designed in advance of ordering the specific individual parts that are to be used in its construction.

MODEL ROCKET ENGINES

Solid-fuel engines for model rockets are factory manufactured and contained in cylindrical paper casings, which have been standardized to three sizes. The paper casing provides an ideal heat-insulating material to protect the body tubes of the model rockets, and is surprisingly strong. Inasmuch as the purpose of a model rocket engine is to provide a propulsive thrust from the nozzle at one end (and, in many cases, a secondary thrust for a nose cone and recovery device ejection from the other end), there is no virtually complete enclosure of the charge that would result in an explosion in the usual sense upon the engine being ignited. No one should attempt to engage in model rocketry unless he is prepared to confine himself to standard factory-manufactured engines. Under absolutely no circumstances should anyone attempt to reload the casing of a factory-made engine that has been used.

The National Association of Rocketry has set up a code of model rocket engine identification. This code designation appears on every model rocket engine. Broadly following model airplane engine classification practice, the basic or total-impulse classification of a model rocket engine is given as a letter. However, there are more categories in model rocket engines than in internal-combustion reciprocating model airplane engines. Except for the general method of adopting letters, even fractional letters, with the least powerful engines assigned letters nearest the front of the alphabet, there is absolutely no parallel between the classifications for model rocket engines and for internal-combustion reciprocating engines. The letter classifications for model rocket engines indicate the total impulse or total power produced by a given engine as measured in pound-seconds. There are now eight engine classifications, as follows:

Letter Code	Total Impulse
¼ A	0– .175 lb.-sec.
½ A	.176– .350 lb.-sec.
A	.351– .700 lb.-sec.
B	.701– 1.20 lb.-sec.
C	1.21 – 2.00 lb.-sec.
D	2.01 – 4.00 lb.-sec.
E	4.01 – 8.00 lb.-sec.
F	8.01 –16.00 lb.-sec.

The second designation on a model rocket engine identification is a number representing the engine's average thrust in pounds or decimal fractions of a pound. In actual practice, eliminating the very smallest ¼ A and ½ A engines and the very largest D, E, and F engines, the majority of engines used today in model rocketry are rated at either .8 pound's or 3.0 pounds' average thrust. The third designation refers to the delay time in seconds between the burnout of the main propulsive thrust charge and the firing of the nose cone and recovery-device ejection charge. Upon the exhaustion of the main thrusting charge, a delay charge located between the main charge and the ejection charge is ignited. This is a slow-burning charge, and is sometimes referred to as the smoke-tracking and delay charge. This charge produces virtually no thrust, but during its burning the rocket is, so to speak, coasting upward toward its peak altitude on the continuing momentum gained by the original propulsive thrust charge. A certain amount of smoke is emitted by the burning of the delay charge that aids in keeping the ascending rocket in sight. When the delay charge is about burned out, it ignites the third or upper charge in the rocket engine, which thrusts so as to eject the nose cone and recovery mechanism. Delay charge times are in most cases approximate, and may vary within a half a second; a rocket given a delay-time rating of 2, for example, may blow the nose cone in 2 to 2½ seconds after the cessation of the main propulsive thrust. A rocket engine with a delay time rating of 4 may take 4 to 4½ seconds before the nose cone is ejected.

Thus, a rocket engine designated as a ½ A .8–2 would possess a total impulse of .176 to .350 pound-second; an average thrust of .8 pound, of the main propulsive charge and the activation and a delay time of 2 seconds between the burnout of the main propulsive charge and the activation of the ejection charge. An engine rated as a B .8–4 would have a total impulse of .701 to 1.20 pound-second, an average thrust of .8 pound, and a delay time of 4 seconds. In actual practice, most model rocket engines tend to have the highest or almost the highest, total impulse permitted within the given class of each unit. Thus the ½ A .8–2 engine has a total impulse of .35 pound-second, although

Fig. 149. A control box operating a number of different launching pads. The actual firing and consequent launching of a model rocket is accomplished by closing the individual switch wired to its pad. On a properly constructed model rocket range, a number of key and other interlock devices prevent accidental firing of any model rocket.

National Aeronautics and Space Administration

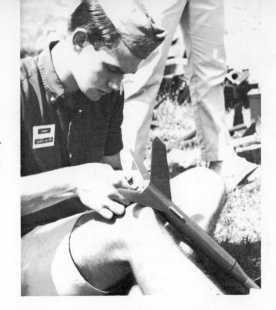

Fig. 150. This solid-fuel model rocket is powered by a cluster of three engines, all of which must be ignited simultaneously for a perfect takeoff and for optimum flight power. Note the guidance sleeve on the side of the rocket for slipping over the launching rod.

National Aeronautics and Space Administration

the classification system rates an engine as a ½ A if it has a total impulse of .176 to .350 pound-second. The B .8–4 engine has a total impulse of 1.15 pound-second, although the B range is from .701 to 1.20 pound-second.

Sometimes rocket engine designations end with an O, instead of a figure indicating the delay time in seconds, such as an A .8–O engine. When the engine code ends in an O instead of a number, it indicates that the engine contains no delay charge and no ejection charge. Such engines are often referred to as booster engines, and are generally used in multistage model rockets as the engine or engines in the lower stage or stages. As they burn out, they burn through the forward, or upper, wall of their combustion chamber and immediately ignite—there being no delay or ejection charge—the next engine higher in the model rocket. The final or highest engine in a multistage model rocket always is of the type with a delay-and-ejection charge, and blows the nose cone and recovery system in the same manner as is done in single-stage model rockets. Model rocket engines without delay-and-ejection charges are also sometimes used as ignition engines, being located under a cluster of engines that provide the actual propulsive thrust, the ignition engine being ignited and then simultaneously firing all the engines in the main engine cluster when the charge of the ignition engine burns through its upper end. Usually only very small engines, such as ¼ A .8–0 engines, are used in this manner as ignition engines.

MORE ABOUT ENGINES

When one model rocket engine is used to ignite another by means of hot gases and burning particles from the first engine pushing into the combustion chamber of the second engine (or engines, if a cluster of engines is involved), it is desirable that the second engine have a rather large exposed propellant ignition area in order to assure greater reliability of ignition. This brings us to a second factor in standard model rocket engine design, the existence of three separate series of rocket engines in the smaller sizes, designated as Series I engines, Series II engines, and Series III engines. As was seen in the discussion of pellet-fuel rocket engines in the preceding chapter, exposing a greater amount of the surface of a solid fuel to ignition—by scoring the surface or boring a hole through the pellet in the case of the pellet-fuel engines—results in a greater thrust level but a shorter duration of thrust. Standardized solid-fuel model rocket engines are divided into two classes on the basis of this principle.

Series I engines might be described as essentially end-burning engines. The fuel charge is packed solid except for a comparatively slight indentation at the point of ignition immediately adjacent to the nozzle. This indentation exposes a sufficient area of fuel to almost immediate ignition, providing the high initial thrust needed to stabilize the rocket in flight. From this point on, the fuel charge burns down much as does a lighted cigarette; burns in what is termed an end-burning grain. The thrust level drops but is sustained at an intermediate level for the duration of the burning of the propellant charge. If a time/thrust curve made showing the performance of such an engine were to be examined, it would be found that there was a high initial thrust for about half a second, then dropping to a sustained thrust of less than half this force for another half second or so.

Series II engines are center, or core, burners. Their fuel charge is burned in much the same manner as is the fuel for a pellet-fuel engine when it has had a hole drilled through it. Series II engines

Fig. 151. The ignition wires have already been connected to the base of this rocket. The hobbyist is making a final check of the packing of the parachute and lines that will be ejected in flight when the nose cone, which he holds in his left hand, is blown out of the model rocket by a delayed-ejection charge from the engine.

National Aeronautics and Space Administration

are made with an open core, or hole, through much of the length of the entire fuel charge, running from immediately behind the nozzle. This means that a considerably greater area of fuel is quickly ignited, with a resultant terrific kickoff of thrust, rising to its peak in a fraction of a second. A time/thrust curve showing the performance of a Series II engine would reveal that virtually all the power of the fuel charge goes into this enormous initial thrust, with the power of the engine dropping almost to nil immediately thereafter.

It should be observed that the designations Series I and Series II refer entirely to the basic arrangement of the propellant charge: end-burning or core-burning, and that both Series I and Series II engines include models with a delay-and-ejection charge and models built without a delay-and-ejection charge (the latter's code designation ending in O). It is at this point that much of the beginners' confusion concerning model rocket engines arises. They usually tend to confuse the difference in the main fuel-charge arrangement and burning method with the difference between engines with delay-and-ejection charges and those without. Perhaps the best way to readily distinguish a Series I engine from a Series II among the usual smaller engines, up to and including Class C, is by

the middle portion of the identification code. Series I engines in this range have an average thrust of .8 pounds, while Series II engines in the same categories have an average thrust of 3.0 pounds.

Within these sizes, Series I and Series II engines have a standardized size 2.75 inches in length and .690 inch in diameter. Then, adding further confusion for most novices, there are the Series III engines. Series III engines are end-burning engines; they are in fact simply miniaturized versions of Series I engines of the same identification code and are of the same .690-inch diameter, but they are only 1.75 inch long. Series III engines, in addition to their visual difference, are identified by a terminal S in their coding; for example, a ½ A .8–4S is a short Series III engine corresponding to a ½ A .8–4 Series I engine. The only other difference is that the shorter Series III engines have a lower initial weight and a lower weight when burned out than have the matching Series I engines. Series III engines are favored in small rockets where weight or size is especially critical. One or two of the very lightest and least powerful engines are made only as Series III engines. Other engines are available only as Series I units, while still others are manufactured in both series. At the present time, however, only ¼ A and ½ A engines are produced in Series III.

The very largest and most powerful engines, such as E and F classes, are made in a larger size: 5.0 inches long and 1.062-inch diameter. They are available as both Series I and Series II engines and with and without delay-and-ejection charges. These extremely powerful engines are used only in very large model rockets. Only the comparatively well advanced and experienced model rocketeer should work with them. In fact the initial weight of some of the F Class engines exceeds the 4-ounce limit prescribed by the Astron Safety Code, thus necessitating Federal Aviation Agency clearance for each flight.

Most model rockets are powered with ¼ A, ½ A, A or B Class engines, or combinations or multiples of these. It should not be supposed that because there can be an extremely large number of different types of rocket engines that every possible type of engine is manufactured. This is not the case. Although an ideally suited engine for almost every imaginable purpose is available, engine manufacturers have found that a range of less than 24 models in Series I, II, and III will take care of all requirements in the ¼ A, ½ A, A and B classes. As a matter of fact, only two of these are Series II engines, the B 3–0 and B 3–5. There appears to be only one Class C engine manufactured at the present time, the C .8–0, and no Class D engine in production at all. Some manufacturers also color code the labels of their rocket engines for easy identification as to their class, the code being: Class ¼ A, green; Class ½ A, blue; Class A, purple; Class B, red; and Class C, black.

Still another matter often adds to the beginner's confusion about model rocket engines; this is their frequent division in chart or tabular form into three classes based on use: single-stage engines, upper-stage engines (also suitable as single-stage engines in extremely light models), and booster engines (the latter with codes all ending in O). Naturally, many perusing model rocket literature for the first time tend to think there is some definite relationship between these three groups and the three series of engines. This is not the case. (Occasionally a fourth group, that of special-purpose engines, is included on these charts.) These charts can be rather confusing at first glance, particularly as to why certain engines are included in the group designated as single-stage engines while others that seem to differ but slightly in their specifications are put into the group of upper-stage engines. The main difference is that the upper-stage engines have a slightly longer delay time than similar engines in the single-stage group, and consequently a very slightly higher weight.

Those who study these charts carefully may find data that apparently contradict the remarks made previously as to the desirability of using Series II engines as upper-stage engines or as the engines clustered for simultaneous engine ignition by means of a single lower engine. There are only two core burners or Series II engines, the B 3–0 and the B 3–5, the latter being the only Series II engine with a delay-and-ejection charge. The fact is that a core burner does ignite much more reliably from a lower-stage engine than does an end burner. Experiments have shown that in ordinary multistage model rocket construction there was only about 40 percent ignition reliability on the part of the upper engine when the lower engine fired into an end-burner engine, as contrasted to about 80 percent efficiency when a core-burning engine was fired into by the lower engine. Obviously, it was not always practical to use Class B engines in every multistage model rocket; in fact, the Series II engines are not classified on the charts as upper-stage engines (the B 3–5 engine is regarded primarily as a single-stage engine, and the B 3–0 as a booster engine). On the other hand, several Series I and Series III engines, ranging from Class ¼ A to Class B, are the engines usually specified as upper-stage engines, and there are many, many multistage rockets in which these types must be used. In the usual arrangement of

multi-stage engines, one engine usually was simply placed next to the other, so that they could separate readily. This too easy separation is not desirable. It was found that this arrangement was quite insufficient, and the main cause of failure to ignite the upper-stage engines. The gas from the booster engine would often simply push the upper-stage engine away instead of igniting it. It was found that for successful multistage ignition the two (or more) engines had to be taped together with cellophane tape in an absolutely straight line; not merely coupled mechanically. At the proper time the gases build up sufficiently to break the tape and allow the burned-out lower stage section to drop away, but before this point is reached—it all takes place in less than a second—the tape-sealed joint between the two engines will assure the upper-stage engine igniting in almost every case. It is therefore possible to attain almost 100 percent reliability in firing the Series I and Series III engines listed in the usual engine charts as upper-stage engines if this taping procedure is followed. If it is not, however, the chances for ignition of a Series I or Series III upper-stage engine are less than fifty-fifty.

In arranging engines for multistaging it is important that they be in perfect alignment, and care must always be exercised to make certain that the engines are placed in the proper order. Quite often a simple mistake results in the upper-stage engine with its delay-and-ejection charge being put below instead of above the booster engine. The same care for alignment and proper positioning of the engines must, of course, be observed when a rocket of more than two stages is being armed. Three-stage model rockets are not uncommon, and even four-stage units have been built and

Fig. 152. Most solid-fuel model rockets are recovered by means of parachutes carried in the rocket itself. Here a young rocket hobbyist rushes forward to catch his rocket as it descends at the end of flight. The dark object on the cord between the rocket body and the parachute is the ejected nose cone of the model rocket.

National Aeronautics and Space Administration

Fig. 153. Being able to measure how high a model rocket ascends adds much to the interest of the hobby, and at organized competitions elaborate instruments often are employed. Shown here is a simple and inexpensive device known as an "altiscope," by means of which the average hobbyist can determine the altitude reached by his rocket.

Estes Industries, Inc.

launched. It is, however, desirable for the hobbyist first to acquire a fair amount of experience in building and flying two-stage rockets before going on to three- and four-stage units.

While a simple press fit in the tube often is sufficient in itself by way of installing an engine in a model rocket, mounting methods may differ with various model rockets. A safe rule is that the engine be installed in such a way that a force of ten pounds will not move it forward in the model rocket body tube. A securely mounted hollow bulkhead in advance of the engine often helps to assure this. Often it is desirable to wrap the rocket engine with several layers of masking tape, or to loop a rubber band around the engine several times. Some model rockets are built with spring engine holders made of very light wire or strip metal, which are cemented to the outside of the body tube by overlaying with gauze and gluing the entire assembly to the tube. This method may also be used for clustered rocket engines; or alternately, for clustered engines, the engine holders may be glued inside the body tube. Whenever engine holders are used, it is important to see that they do not interfere with the fins of the rocket. Clustered rocket engines may also be mounted by wrapping the group in sufficient layers of masking tape to make a tight fit, or by first gluing the engines to one another and then putting tape around the entire group. When a cluster of engines is used, it is necessary to fill the spaces around and between the engines with facial tissue or similar material to seal the rear of the body tube. A single-engine model rocket provides its own seal to control and direct the gases. While theoretically any number of model rocket engines might be clustered in a single model rocket, in practice only three engines usually are used, and generally prove sufficient. For one thing, it is very difficult to ignite more than three engines simultaneously, whether by means of direct electrical

ignition or by mounting a single ignition engine below the cluster.

IGNITION AND LAUNCHING

In the continuing stress on safety precaution, here are a number of points taken from a model rocket engine instruction sheet. Two or three of them may already have been mentioned or included in one of the two model rocket safety codes presented earlier in this chapter:

1. These engines should be used only on devices which are specifically designed to perform properly with the type of engine being used.

2. All engine mounts and materials surrounding the engine must be constructed of nonmetallic materials, such as paper, plastic, wood, etc.

3. Never fire a rocket that does not have incorporated within it some type of recovery system that will break the aerodynamic stability for return flight.

4. Never stand closer than 12 feet away from any rocket engine when it is being operated.

5. Always fire rockets in a vertical direction only, using a suitable launching system that will maintain a vertical flight direction until the rocket has reached sufficient speed to stabilize itself.

6. Do not launch model rockets in the vicinity of buildings.

7. Always store engines in a cool, dry place.

8. Never subject a rocket engine to heat greater than 150 degrees F.

9. Do not in any way tamper with or attempt to alter the engine casing, propellant, nozzle, and so on.

10. Never attempt to reload an expended engine casing.

11. Care should be taken when hooking up ignition to keep the fingers and body away from the nozzle.

12. Under *no* circumstances should the nozzle be aimed toward the face.

13. Do not smoke near rocket engines, and do not store near highly combustible materials.

14. Never attempt to ignite a rocket engine by other than electrical means.

The last point means that many of the types of ignition used on occasion with the pellet-fuel engines of the type described in the previous chapter—lighted cigarettes, punk, igniter sticks, and so on—are absolutely taboo with regular solid-fuel model rocket engines. As a matter of fact, electrical ignition would be desirable when using the pellet-fuel engines. With the solid-fuel model

Fig. 154. Three examples of rocket boost gliders are pictured here. The upper two models are individually designed and built rear-engine boost gliders. The lower photograph shows a front-engine boost glider built from a kit. It has a wingspan of 10 inches, is 12 inches long, and weighs .40 ounces.

Estes Industries, Inc.

rocket engines that come with the fuel load already packed within the one-time-use engine, electrical ignition is an absolute necessity.

The discussion of electrical ignition may be logically divided into two parts: the mechanics of actual ignition and the safety precautions that are desirable, especially when more than one launching pad is used at the same scene of model rocket activity.

The usual method of igniting a model rocket engine is with a short length of nichrome resistance wire, the same wire that is used in electric toasters and similar appliances. This wire heats to a red-hot glow when it is electrified. A short length of nichrome wire is cut—usually about 2 inches, and doubled back on itself after forming a double loop in the center by wrapping it around a nail or a small rod. This loop is then pushed up into the nozzle of the engine in the model rocket as far as it will go, usually about ½ inch. A small piece of cotton or facial tissue is then tamped in behind the wire to hold it in place. The electrical system is attached to the two protruding ends of the nichrome wire just before firing. In fact, the ignited wire itself should not be inserted in the rocket engine until as close to the time of firing as possible.

The electrical system in its simplest form consists of a battery, two wire leads from the battery, one of them broken by an open switch, and two very small clips, one at the end of each wire. One clip is placed on each of the two leads of nichrome wire. Special miniature clips about an inch long are available for this purpose. Some model rocketeers simply use ordinary paper clips to which the wires from the battery are secured, and slide one on each nichrome wire lead. A good 6-volt ignition battery usually is sufficient to fire almost any model rocket. For heavy-duty work a 12-volt battery may be used instead. In any case it is important that the battery be in good condition and capable of putting out sufficient amperage at the moment of ignition. If a wet-cell automobile battery is used, as sometimes is the case, it must be kept charged between model rocket events. No. 32 nichrome wire is generally used for the igniters when dry batteries are used, and the heavier No. 30 wire employed with automobile batteries. If the nichrome igniter wire is too long, or if the battery clips are placed too far down the wire from the engine, ignition may be very slow or in some cases it may not take place. It is important to see that the battery clips on the nichrome ignition wire do not touch each other, or they will of course short-circuit when the current is applied, resulting in no ignition and possible serious drain on the battery. When the usual countdown from 10 to 0 that usually is employed with model rocket firings, just as with real ones, is completed and the switch closed, the electrical circuit will be completed, and the nichrome wire will glow sufficiently hot inside the rocket engine to ignite the propellant charge. Once the propellant is ignited, it continues burning and igniting itself. As soon as sufficient ignition has taken place to produce enough thrust for the take-off, the model rocket will start to zoom upward.

A typical model rocket launching countdown will run as follows:

10. Install the engine in the model rocket.
9. Install the igniter wire in the engine.
8. Place the rocket on the launcher.

7. Attach the battery clips to the nichrome wire leads.

6. Clear the area, check for low-flying aircraft, and alert the recovery crew and trackers.

5. Arm the launch control panel (this refers to closing any safety circuit such as key-operated switch or a mechanical interlock).

4.

3.

2.

1.

LAUNCH! Press the master switch button controlling the electrical launching circuit.

This method is satisfactory when a single model rocket launching pad is used. When, as is usually the case at rocket competitions or meets of model rocket clubs, a number of launchers are set up, usually in a row, it may be necessary to arm a number of rockets and set them on the launchers ready for firing before any one rocket is launched. In such cases the countdown may vary somewhat, and chiefly be involved with making sure the area is clear, alerting the recovery and tracking crew, and manipulating the safety key and interlock. In such cases a single launching control panel with individual switches for ten, twelve, or more launching pads is used. Usually there are two officials in final charge of the operation. One, who is in charge of the launching device, carries the safety-lock key. The other, who is in charge of the range, carries the safety interlock and removes it and takes it with him whenever it is necessary for him to go upon the range. It is impossible to fire any rocket unless both the keylock switch has been closed and the interlock put in place on the control panel. Panels of this type often are quite elaborate, and use rotary switches to select the launcher that is to be used next, so that only one of the number of switches for individual launchers is ever actually completely armed. Thus it is impossible for two or more switches to be fired at once.

The simplest type of firing switch for use with the electrical system of a single launching device as used by individual hobbyists is an ordinary doorbell switch. Such switches are sometimes pressed accidentally before the proper moment or they may stick in a closed position, which results in firing prematurely at the moment the second clip is attached to the nichrome ignition wire leads. For this reason a better device is an open spring switch that can be covered with a piece of rocket body-tube material that is removed just before firing. However, the tendency now is to buy or build a special small launching panel, usually consisting of a push-button switch for the actual final firing, a key-lock safety switch to prevent accidental launchings, and a pilot light that lights only when the keylock switch is closed and the battery is connected and the clips to the nichrome wire are making contact. In such a system the pilot light makes use of the battery current and prevents sufficient current from reaching the igniter, even though it is in the circuit, to heat the nichrome wire. The nichrome wire simply acts as a segment of ordinary wire in the circuit to the pilot light. (If the pilot-light bulb burns out, the circuit to the igniter wire automatically is broken and is not completed until the firing push button is depressed.) When the firing push button is depressed, the current passes through this closed switch instead of through the pilot light, and the full force of the current goes through the nichrome igniter wire, causing it to become hot and the engine to ignite.

It is also possible to use the igniter wick supplied for the pellet-fuel engines described in the preceding chapter as an igniter for solid-fuel rocket engines, and some hobbyists prefer to employ this wick in place of nichrome wire. This wick consists of a thin metal wire core covered with plastic. The plastic covering, which acts to insulate the wire electrically, must be scraped from exposed ends of the igniter wick when used in an electric firing system and the power clips attached to the exposed ends of wire.

The pellet-fuel engine igniter wick often is used to fire a cluster of model rocket engines when a separate lower igniter engine is not employed. Separate wicks of equal length are placed in each

Fig. 155. To be able to launch a rocket containing a raw egg and to bring the egg back safely and unbroken is usually considered the standard of achievement in the art of lofting a model rocket with a payload. Here a hobbyist proudly displays the unharmed egg from his recovered rocket before the judges at a model rocket contest.

Estes Industries, Inc.

of the engines in the cluster; then the external portions of the wicks are twisted together into a single cable and a piece of nichrome wire is fastened to the cable and the battery clips are attached to the ends of the nichrome wire. It is also possible to obtain direct electrical ignition of all the engines in a cluster by using nichrome wire igniters in each engine and attaching battery clips to each wire so that the three igniters are wired in parallel. With a three-engine cluster, each of the two battery lead wires would have to be divided near the end into three separate leads, each with its own clip. This is a rather delicate method of firing, and great care must be exercised in arranging the wires so that none of the clips short-circuit against a clip from the opposite battery lead. Also, it requires a considerable amount of current, as there are three separate nichrome wire elements to be brought to ignition heat. A well-charged 12-volt automobile battery usually is needed for this method of clustered-engine ignition.

In any clustered-engine model rocket there always is a danger that one or possibly more than one of the engines will not ignite, or will at least not ignite simultaneously. The rocket may have sufficient thrust to take off, but will veer off course in flight. Particular efforts should be made to design highly stable model rockets when using clustered engines for propulsion. The usual number of engines in a cluster is three. It is, however, possible to build and fly a rocket with a cluster of only two engines, although this leaves a substantial proportionate area of empty space in the bottom of the body tube that has to be plugged up. Sometimes a cluster of four rocket engines is used satisfactorily, but three is the most common number and is generally regarded as the most satisfactory. The engines used in a cluster should always be of the same type as far as the class (total impulse) and average thrust are concerned. Occasionally a model rocket is constructed wherein one of the clustered engines is of the delay-and-ejection-charge type, and is used to launch a separate parachute for the recovery of the lower stage after it breaks away from the upper stage, although this involves rather complicated model-rocket-construction techniques and, although spectacular in operation, is not to be recommended to the beginner.

Beginners should be careful to distinguish between clustered-engine usage (engines side by side) and multistage construction (engines in line), as quite a bit of confusion seems to exist on this point. When a separate engine is used as an ignition engine below a cluster, it has nothing to do with multistaging in itself; the lower engine is

Fig. 156. Another achievement in model rocketry, and one that is gaining a most enthusiastic following, is to send a camera aloft in a model rocket, automatically snap an aerial photograph, and then bring the camera down again in a safe recovery. The rocket shown here is especially designed for that purpose and carries a special yet inexpensive camera in its head.

Estes Industries, Inc.

simply used to ignite the engines in the cluster simultaneously. A very small engine, usually a ¼ A Class, is always used as an ignition engine. Its slight thrust is insufficient in itself to start a rocket of the size and weight usually used with clustered engines. When the main engines in the cluster fire, the ignition engine and its mounting bulkhead are immediately blown out of the rocket by the great thrust of the clustered engines. Only then does the gas of the clustered engines exert thrust outside the rocket body tube to permit takeoff. In a multistage rocket the lower-stage engine or engines are always termed booster engines. It might be noted that it would therefore be possible to divide engines into another sort of grouping of three types, according to their use: ignition engines, booster engines, and delay-and-ejection-charge engines.

It may be that certain types of model engines will be provided with operating and ignition instructions somewhat different from the methods and procedures outlined here, or that new types of engines will be developed and marketed in the future for which other procedures are recommended in the manufacturers' instructions. In any such cases, naturally, such alternate instructions take precedence over anything appearing in these pages and should be followed implicitly.

LAUNCHING DEVICES

It is quite difficult to launch a model rocket without the use of some sort of special launching device to hold it in a steady course until it gathers sufficient speed to assure stability and a true vertical takeoff. It is almost impossible and potentially dangerous to attempt to launch a model rocket without a launcher. Its use constitutes another cardinal safety rule of model rocketry. The rocket-launching device should be firmly secured to the ground so that it cannot be blown over by the wind. This is both to prevent a model rocket taking off at an angular or horizontal course, and also to protect the model from damage by striking the ground. There is, in fact, no necessity for a model rocket launcher being located directly on the ground. Mounting the launching device on a table or sawhorse or similar elevation will not only permit it to be easily secured in an upright position but will also carry the top of launching rods above eye level, a highly desirable safety measure (refer to the Astron Rocket Society Safety Code on page 133, Article 9.

There is no hard-and-fast rule as to the necessary height of the launcher; it will vary depending on the length of a particular model rocket. A 36-inch-long rod seems to be favored as a more or less standard length for simple launching devices, consisting primarily of a vertical steel rod 1/8 inch or 3/16 inch in diameter set in a suitable base. The 1/8-inch-diameter rod is the size generally used for small model rockets. It would be possible to make a launching rod longer than three feet. However, if the rod were made much longer, problems of the flexibility of the rod material itself would be encountered; it is difficult to maintain a 1/8-inch-diameter rod in a steady vertical position if it is much longer than three feet. Therefore when a large or heavy rocket is to be launched, it is usual to substitute a special launching tower for the simpler rod launcher. At most model rocket meets a number of launchers are provided, including both rod and tower types.

There is no definite formula as to the relative height of a launcher required to the length of a rocket itself. The power of the rocket itself has much to do with this. In general, the greater the takeoff thrust of the model rocket itself, the shorter need be the launcher in order to assure the rocket's trueness of course. Thus, a rather small rocket with comparatively little thrust might well require a launch-rod travel of two or three times its own length for successful launching, while a larger rocket with a much greater power thrust might satisfactorily take off from a launcher not much higher than the model itself. In any event, while some small and light rockets might take off from a shorter launcher, the 36-inch rod seems to be pretty well standardized. It is safe to say that the longer the launching device the better will any model

rocket take off. Tower launchers are not necessarily much longer than rod launchers; some towers have the same 36-inch height as most rod launchers, and towers higher than 48 inches seldom are encountered. What the tower launcher adds is not so much greater launcher height, but the firmness of construction desirable for the launching of larger and heavier model rockets.

Anyone can build a simple rod type of launcher by inserting a 1/8-inch-diameter steel rod in a suitable wooden base in a verical position. One other element should be included, a steel or asbestos jet deflector at the base of the rod. The purpose of the deflector is not only to protect the wooden base from the initial takeoff blast of the rocket engines but also, with many types of model rockets, to deflect these gases away from the lower segments of the fins of the model rocket itself. It is possible to buy two-piece launcher rods so that a model rocket launcher can be dismantled for easy portability. It is, in fact, also possible to buy sectional rod so that a rod type of launcher can be extended to a greater height than 36 inches, in 18-inch units. Thus, on occasion, rod-type launchers are built to 54-inch or even 72-inch height for use with heavier model rockets or those of somewhat questionable stability, but in truth, such models should properly be launched from a tower and not from a rod. Whenever a rod launch is used, it is necessary to equip the model rocket with a launching lug, usually a length of ordinary sodawater straw glued to the body tube, that slips over the rod. It is vital that such launching lugs be mounted absolutely parallel to the main rocket body tube.

It is possible to purchase inexpensive kits for building a rod type of launcher, sometimes with an electrical lead-in assembly built into the base. Sometimes such launchers are provided with adjustable tripod legs so that they can be set up on virtually any terrain, no matter how uneven, and also so the launching rod can be adjusted to any desired angle. Here we arrive at a matter that may well have puzzled readers who have noted the insistence that a model rocket be launched in a vertical position and found a seeming contradiction in the injunctions in the safety codes that a model rocket be launched at no greater angle than that of 25 or 30 degrees from the vertical. The only reason a model rocket ever is launched at any angle is in an attempt to compensate for wind direction and speed. However, judging when this is necessary and just how much of an angle should be employed—and only a very slight angle ever should be used—is a rather delicate matter and one that should be entered into only after a hob-

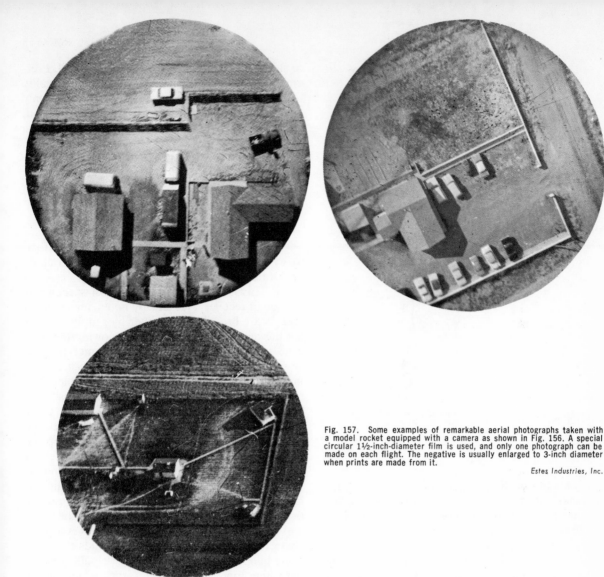

Fig. 157. Some examples of remarkable aerial photographs taken with a model rocket equipped with a camera as shown in Fig. 156. A special circular 1½-inch-diameter film is used, and only one photograph can be made on each flight. The negative is usually enlarged to 3-inch diameter when prints are made from it.

Estes Industries, Inc.

byist has become comparatively well experienced as a model rocketeer. The safest rule for the beginner to follow is always to launch vertically and not to attempt to launch at all if the weather is not perfect and there is a perceptible breeze.

The launching tower is an impressive-looking piece of equipment, usually built up with an external frame of steel arranged in a latticework pattern. The purpose of this framework is to provide support for the actual launching guides, usually three in number, which are arranged around the model rocket. These are usually adjustable, like the jaws of a three-jaw chuck, to accommodate model rockets of varying body diameters, although sometimes towers are built with fixed guides capable of fitting only one model body diameter. It is also possible to build simple towers of wood. A great many of the metal towers that have been constructed so far have been poorly finished, with little attention paid to smoothing rough or sharp

metal surfaces. Hobbyists should exercise care in handling and using steel towers. It is possible to build model rocket-launching towers without these imperfections, if enough care and time are devoted to their construction, and such towers have been built. Unfortunately the poor workmanship, sharp edges and burrs left unremoved on some of these towers, particularly on some of the hastily constructed early ones, have tended to give them a bad name among many hobbyists. There are a number of standard parts available as used in metal construction sets that might gainfully be employed in the easy construction of model rocket-launching towers, and their superior finish should commend them to this work. When this is suggested, the point sometimes is raised that such parts customarily are assembled with screws and nuts and that such construction usually loosens under the kind of use given to model rocket-launching towers and therefore is unsatisfactory.

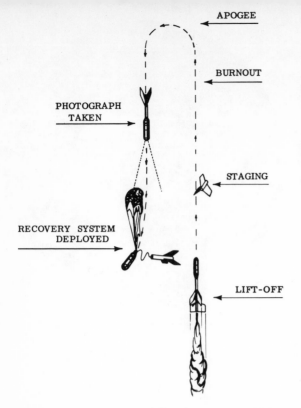

APOGEE

BURNOUT

PHOTOGRAPH TAKEN →

STAGING ←

RECOVERY SYSTEM DEPLOYED →

LIFT-OFF ←

Fig. 158. This diagram shows the working of the camera pictured in Fig. 156. The camera is lofted in a two-stage rocket, and the picture is taken automatically as the rocket-bearing camera descends, before the parachute is ejected and deployed. The camera may be adjusted for either oblique or directly vertical photographs, and weighs less than one ounce.

Estes Industries, Inc.

The solution to this is first to assemble the components with the usual fastening devices and then to take the tower to an automobile shop and have all the joints spot-welded.

Most model rocket-launching devices are designed and built for service only, and make little effort to reproduce actual rocket-launching facilities in miniature. A number of model rocket hobbyists have, however, endeavored to build launchers that will combine the necessary launching rod with some measure of simulation of an actual rocket launch pad with its attendant towers, cranes, fueling, and other facilities reproduced more or less to scale. It is, of course, seldom possible to achieve anything approaching complete scale fidelity, other than to a predetermined scale for the rocket base equipment, because the model rockets actually launched from these miniature bases most likely will differ considerably in actual scale, if they are scale models of specific prototype rockets, or in relative scale, if free-lance model rocket designs. However, some very commendable models of this type have been seen, combining conventional model-building realism with the functionalism of a model rocket-launching device.

Whenever a rod type of launcher is employed, a safety cap should be prepared and used to shield the upper end of the launching rod. Preferably painted bright red, and large enough readily to be seen, this safety cap should be removed only when the model rocket is to be put on the rod, and should be replaced until just before launching if the model is not to be launched immediately. After firing, the safety cap should immediately be replaced on the rod before the model rocketeer leaves the launching site to recover the model.

RECOVERY AND TRACKING

There is hardly a more fascinating sight than to witness a model rocket ascend, break out its miniature parachute, and float gently back to earth. This is both the best and most spectacular method of recovery. As already noted, many model rockets are brought back either by simply disturbing the aerodynamic balance by blowing the nose cone or by means of a paper streamer to slow down their descent. The parachutes usually are made out of very light plastic material colored in bright patterns to provide optimum visibility. Streamers usually are made of plastic or crepe paper. Whenever streamers or parachutes are used in a model rocket, a wadding of special flameproof material should be packed in the model rocket between the top of the ejection-charge engine and the parachute or streamer. This material, which is known as recovery wadding or parachute-protection wadding, is obtainable from manufacturers and dealers in model rocket supplies, as is a parachute lubricating powder that both aids the parachute in opening and creates a dust cloud when the parachute opens that may serve as an aid in tracking.

Basically, tracking means keeping the model rocket in sight both as it ascends, in an endeavor to see how high it will go, and as it descends so that it can readily be recovered upon landing. However, to most model rocketeers tracking usually implies a process whereby the height to which the model rocket ascended is mathematically determined, sometimes known as altitude tracking. Although such tracking is always a part of model rocket meets, and an absolute necessity at such competitions, in all candor it must be admitted that if altitude tracking was an absolute necessity to the practice and enjoyment of model rocketry, and each individual launching had to be tracked and the height accurately computed, the vast majority of those who now enjoy the hobby probably would seek some other avocation.

Tracking is based on the principle of trigonometry that all of the sides and angles of any triangle can be found if three of these six parts, including the length of one side, are known. In model rocket tracking the length of this side of the angle is known by measuring the distance from the point of launching to the point of observation, the tracking station. The launching is assumed to be vertical, so there is a 90-degree angle at the intersection of the line between the tracking station and the launching device at the point of launching. A second angle is ascertained by the tracker who follows the model rocket in flight with a theodolite, an optical instrument that measures angles. Actually, many model rocket trackers do not employ a regulation theodolite equipped with a telescope, but use a simpler and often homemade device where the flight of the rocket is followed simply by sighting along a board, which is connected to a protractor. Such a device, known as an altiscope, also is available in ready-to-use form. In any event, the ascent of the rocket is followed by the tracker, and he locks his observation instrument in position when the model rocket reaches its highest altitude. The scale is then read, which gives the angle of the theodolite or other tracking instrument. This provides the second angle of the two needed, in conjunction with the length of one side of the triangle to determine the third angle and the length of the remaining two sides of the triangle. The important length to the model rocketeer is, of course, that between the 90-degree angle formed by the line between the tracking station and launcher and the still unknown angle. This length, when determined, provides the measure of the altitude attained by the model rocket in flight.

The next step is to determine the tangent of this angle, for which use a table of tangents for right-angle triangles is consulted. The tangent is multiplied by the distance from the tracking station to the launcher, and the result is the altitude achieved by the model rocket. This method of tracking is admittedly a rough-and-ready one, at least in the eyes of those to whom mathematics is a pure delight, and calculations as to altitude are usually rounded off to the nearest ten feet. A much more complicated system of altitude tracking, involving two tracking stations instead of one, provides much more accurate altitude computation, although with much greater accompanying mathematical procedures. This highly professional method is used at organized model rocket meets, although it is of course practical for any group of hobbyists to employ provided they have two instruments, one for each of the tracking stations. For accuracy it is essential that both trackers lock their instruments in position at exactly the same time. To achieve this it usually is necessary that

Fig. 159. The two-stage solid-fuel model rocket equipped with camera is on a launching pad and ready for takeoff. This photograph also shows the type of individual launching pad used by most individual rocket hobbyists when not flying on fully equipped ranges with multiple launching pads. The circle under the rocket is a deflector that protects the wooden base from the rocket blast.

Estes Industries, Inc.

a telephone system be installed between the two tracking stations, so that one of the trackers or a third observer can call the signal for the immediate locking of both theodolites. There is no point in going into the particulars of the advanced mathematics involved in two-station tracking here. For those interested, precise data will be found in the publications mentioned in the footnote on page 131.

ROCKET GLIDERS

Rocket gliders or rocket-boost gliders, as they sometimes are called, provide a distinct group of rocket-powered models and of model rocket activity. The essential difference between a solid-fuel-engine rocket-boost glider and any other kind of model glider, including light gliders launched with the thrust power of a pellet-fuel engine of the type described in the preceding chapter, is that a rocket-boost glider must rise perfectly vertically in the same manner as does a regular model rocket, and without relying on any lifting surfaces. Upon reaching its peak altitude under rocket propulsive thrust, the rocket glider then, in effect, ceases to be a rocket and becomes a heavier-than-air aircraft. It returns to earth in a gentle, circular glide, although it is possible in the case of certain models that thermic air currents may catch it up and it may rise or travel a considerable way before finally setting down. Rocket gliders are now an established segment of the overall model rocket picture, with a considerable and enthusiastic following of their own, and a number of assembly kits are available. Many hobbyists, of course, take equal delight in flying both regular model rockets and model rocket gliders.

Many interesting and sometimes entirely new problems arise in the design of rocket gliders, owing to the necessity of their first performing strictly as rockets. Even in their second, or glider, phase they usually must be constructed on different principles than ordinary model gliders are, although in many cases successful model rocket gliders have been designed and flown that to a considerable extent outwardly resemble actual aircraft. Furthermore, two interesting returns to popular early-model airplane designs may be detected in many successful model rocket gliders, although not by any means necessarily combined in the same model rocket glider. One such return is the adaption of the canard principle in a number of models, involving the placing of the lateral stabilizing surface ahead of, rather than behind, the primary lifting surface (wing). The second is the positioning of the vertical fin or rudder below rather than above the horizontal stabilizer. This is a direct return to a popular model airplane practice of the earliest period of model airplane construction, as described in the historical chapter. Both of these developments, or rather reversions, are highly interesting both from a purely historical and from the technical standpoint. It is as yet too early to assess just how far-reaching an effect the very thorough studies in model rocket glider design, which have resulted in their at least partial adaptation, may have on the future of glider and flying model airplane design in general.

Model rocket-boost gliders divide themselves into two main groups: rear-engine boost gliders and front-engine boost gliders. Essentially they are ordinary model rocket body tubes fitted with lifting and stabilizing surfaces. The front-engine boost glider in some ways resembles a regulation model glider or airplane, and has the rocket engine mounted in a short tube or pod carried on a pylon at the front of the model. Some model rocket gliders are cleverly arranged to make use of the force of the ejection of the engine at the expiration of rocket-powered lift to actuate movable surfaces, usually elevons, so as to change the trim of the craft and transfer it from the basic rocket lift vehicle into a more efficient and stable glider.

The great problem in all model rocket design, whether ordinary model rockets or rocket gliders, is that stability during rocket-powered flight is achieved by placing the center of pressure *behind* the center of gravity. This is one reason it is de-

sirable to build a model rocket with the fins as far to the rear as possible. As a demonstration example, it is possible to build two similar rockets except for the placing of the fins. When the fins are placed as far back as possible on one of the two rockets, it will prove quite a satisfactory flyer. If, however, the fins are mounted on the other rocket about a third of the way up toward the nose from the bottom of the tube, the rocket will not fly satisfactorily until a one-ounce weight is placed in the payload compartment just behind the nose. This will of course add one ounce to the total weight of the rocket, but it will at the same time once again move the center of gravity ahead of the center of pressure and make the model capable of stable flight. This problem is, if anything, exaggerated in model rocket-boost glider design. For the model to function satisfactorily as a rocket as it ascends, the wings and stabilizers must be designed and located so that the center of gravity remains ahead of the center of pressure. This is the reason so many home-designed model rocket gliders, including those that appear to perform extremely well as gliders in test glides, fail when sent aloft as rockets in vertical flight. Instead of demonstrating the requisite stability, they start to wobble and rotate and then fall head over heels back to earth.

In short, for the reasons described, the creation of a model rocket glider is for the most part entirely different from the designing of any other sort of glider, just as, in fact, basic model rocket design of all kinds is quite different from the designing of other types of model aircraft. This holds true despite the fact that much of the equipment that can be used in designing and testing model rockets, such as the wind tunnel, is similar or identical to units employed in similar experimental and development work with model aircraft. It cannot be too often reiterated that model rocketry at the present time is a truly experimental hobby. This is not to infer that perfectly developed model rockets are not available, either as commercial kits, models built from published plans, or in many cases individual free-lance designs. What it does mean is that there is a tremendous area open wherein the individual who revels in experimentation and study and the proving or disproving of theories can enjoy a tremendous field day and one very likely to prove profitable both to himself and to countless other model rocketeers.

A great many model rocket fans take a great deal of interest in this experimental work, with its accompanying tests and the preparation of graphs and reports. There are even now available on the market comparatively inexpensive static test stands to test and automatically chart time thrust curves of model rocket engines, and a special type of static test engine is manufactured equipped with a safety plug to prevent blow-through for use in this type of experimentation.

PAYLOADS

In real or model rocketry, "payload" refers to any equipment or instrumentation carried above and beyond the actual necessary components of the rocket itself. When model rocketry first became popular, all sorts of odd payloads were experimented with, often just to see what could be done. Today payloads in the eyes of most serious fans consist of weight alone, to see just what a model rocket is capable of lifting, raw eggs as a test of model rocket stability in flight and the ability safely and gently to land a delicate load, and what might be called actual instrumentation. The latter category covers the sending up and actuating of cameras to take actual aerial photographs, or of radio transmitters to send signals back to the ground.

The egg trick probably will long remain the standard test of model rocket launching and safe payload capsule descent and landing. The lofting, operation, and safe return of a camera appears at the moment to present the most interesting and exciting phase of model rocketry available to the average enthusiast. Radio transmission from a model rocket, as discussed in the following chapter, is still a rather complex and advanced phase of somewhat limited interest and of unpredictable potential. Everyone who sees pictures taken from a model rocket, however, appears quite excited at the prospect, and the entire mechanism for successfully taking such pictures now has been made available in kit form. Of course, a number of model rocket hobbyists have and no doubt will continue to build their own camera rockets for the making of still photographs, and there even are instances where model rocketeers have successfully sent up 8 mm. motion-picture cameras and obtained satisfactory lengths of film covering both the ascent and descent of the camera. In any event, still photography from a model rocket, which is now readily within the capabilities of every model rocket fan, appears to be creating as much enthusiasm and excitement as did photography from kites in the 1890's, when the first aerial pictures were made. In some ways, in fact, model rocket still-photography equipment parallels that used at that time; it involves a return to film packs, each holding a single circular cut film, which must be loaded in a darkroom or else purchased in the form of already loaded film packs. Only one picture can be taken on each model rocket flight using the standard equipment presently available.

The streamlined camera, which takes the place of a nose cone or payload capsule when used, is mounted on the head of the rocket with its lens pointing upward and, of course, loaded with a single film holder. The entire camera and film assembly actually weighs less than one ounce and can be used on a number of lightweight model rockets, either single or multistage. When the camera is ejected it falls into a lens-down position and the shutter is operated by a special line attached to the rocket body, and the picture is made. The camera nose cone and the rocket body then descend safely by means of a parachute. Variations in the adjustment of the shutter cord can provide varying oblique photographs, sometimes showing the land for a considerable distance, or directly vertical photographs, showing the scene directly under the camera lens. The film and original negatives are 1 1/2 inches in diameter, and the film usually is enlarged to produce a 3-inch-diameter finished print.

CHAPTER 8

Radio Control

Many hobbyists believe that radio control of model aircraft is extremely complex, that to enjoy it one needs to possess the mind of a Marconi, and that the equipment is terribly expensive. In fact when one reads of model airplane radio-control outfits costing hundreds of dollars or pounds, the natural reaction is first to question the wisdom of even considering risking sending such valuable equipment aloft in a model airplane.

Radio-control equipment can, it is true, be extremely complex and costly. However, it is important that three basic things be kept in mind. One is that the great majority of radio-control model airplane enthusiasts make use of equipment that is relatively simple and inexpensive. Second, that such equipment is virtually mandatory for the beginner in radio control. Third, it is possible to attain a remarkable degree of radio control over a model airplane with just such simple and comparatively inexpensive equipment. This is not to say that the more elaborate and expensive equipment is not worth the added cost in terms of what it achieves and the way in which additional functions are added and controlled. However, an amazing amount of radio control can be attained over a model airplane that is equipped with the simplest type of control over the rudder function only. In radio control, rudder control (right or left) is the basic control function, just as in control-line model flying the elevator control (up or down) is the basic control. Invariably, a hobbyist

who is not familiar with radio-control flying is amazed at what a relatively skilled flyer can accomplish in the way of precision control, including acrobatics, with a radio-controlled model airplane that is equipped with rudder control only. The best proof of what rudder-only control is capable of achieving lies in the contest results that have been attained. As noted in Chapter 1, the AMA Radio Control Pattern Event Regulations divide the competitions into three classes, of which the first and simplest class is for planes controlled about the yaw axis, that is to say, rudder control only. The second class is for model airplanes with radio control of both the yaw and pitch axes (rudder and elevator), and the third class for planes with radio control of the yaw, pitch, and roll axes (rudder, elevator, and ailerons). Yet, at the hobbyist's option, a Class I plane with rudder control only may be entered in competition in Class II or Class III (similarly, Class II planes may be entered in Class III contests). As has been proved again and again (and the rules, of course, would not allow for this if it were not possible), Class I planes with rudder-only control have won in Class II and Class III events, flying against planes with far more sophisticated control functions. Participation in competitive events of any of these classes involves putting the radio-controlled model airplane through a complicated series of standardized maneuvers: flying in a complex precision pattern, loops, rolls, figure eights, and so on. The fact that

Fig. 160. Many hobbyists feel that radio control is the closest possible approach to actually piloting a model airplane. At the left a model taxis for a takeoff at a meet at a U.S. Air Force base. Right: an enthusiast exercises complete control over his model airplane in the air by means of a 12-channel transmitter.

Ace R/C, Inc.
Derritron Ltd.

rudder-only models can compete in such events among themselves, much less in competition with models with additional controls, is ample testimony to the enormous flying possibilities of rudder-only radio control. It might be noted that auxiliary controls, including engine control, is permissible in any or all of these classes, and some form of engine speed control usually is used by such contest fliers. This point does not, however, detract from the major proportion of the evidence presented by the performance of rudder-only models in these events as to the enormous amount of controlled flying practical with only this one of the three major control functions operative.

In any case, virtually every radio-control model airplane enthusiast starts with a rudder-only controlled model. Mastering competent flying by manipulating only the rudder is complicated enough for the beginner without attempting to complicate the acquisition of practical skills by attempting to include elevator- and aileron-control functions. There are those who claim that, once the manipulation of the control or controls on the transmitter is mastered, it is easier to fly and control a radio-controlled model on which the elevator and ailerons can be manipulated as well as the rudder. Yet in spite of this, it is safe to assert that the vast majority of radio-controlled model airplane enthusiasts, regardless of the type of equipment they eventually employ, begin with a rudder-only model. It is equally true that the majority of radio-control model airplane hobbyists fly with rudder only as far as the prime three control functions are concerned (yaw, pitch, and roll) regardless of how long they have continued active in this branch of model aviation.

The question must naturally arise as to how a model can artfully be flown, much less put through loops and rolls and other precision acrobatic stunts, when the only operative control function is that of moving the rudder to the right or to the left, or returning it to a control or neutral position. Actually, it almost is easier to perform these maneuvers than it is clearly to explain the principles involved. Part of the answer lies in the fact that a properly designed radio-control model airplane, and especially one for rudder-only control, is a specialty in itself. Satisfactory radio-controlled flying seldom is attained simply by putting the radio receiver and accompanying control devices into a free-flight model picked at random. Normally, in a model airplane especially designed and trimmed for radio control, the plane will climb when the rudder is in the normal centralized or neutral position. When the rudder is shifted to its right- or left-hand position, the plane banks and turns, more or less at the same level at which it was flying when the turn was begun. However, as the model is designed and trimmed to climb on neutral rudder, turning it in either direction long enough will tend to make it descend in a circular course, right- or left-hand depending on the position in which the rudder is held. Restoring the rudder to neutral will then cause the plane to climb again in a straight line. Thus, by judicious manipulation of the radio-controlled rudder, it is possible for an experienced hobbyist to make a rudder-only radio-controlled model airplane perform almost any conceivable aerial maneuver!

In short, apart from all other considerations of design and balance, a free-flight model airplane is designed to climb in a circular course by offsetting the rudder before flight. In contrast, a radio-controlled model airplane is designed to climb with the rudder in a centralized position. Obviously, there must also be variations in the adjustment of the engine and fuel tank between models used in free flight and in radio control if optimum results are to be attained. A free-flight model is always climbing while power is on; consequently, as noted earlier, it is desirable that the engine be adjusted to give the best performance

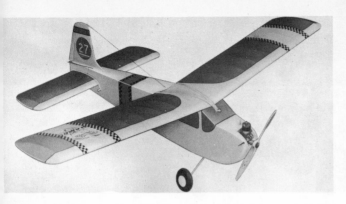

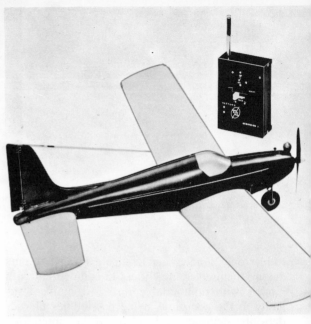

Fig. 161. A model airplane especially designed for use as a training ship by beginners in single-channel (rudder-only) radio control. This model is furnished as a construction kit and has a 48-inch wingspan. It uses .09 to .19 cubic-inch engines.

Sterling Models

Fig. 162. A complete ready-to-fly radio-control outfit. The 44-inch-wingspan molded plastic monoplane with Styrofoam wings is supplied with the receiver and other internal apparatus already installed and connected to the rudder and .049-cubic-inch engine, and with a matching transmitter.

Testor Corp.

in a slightly nose-up position of the model airplane, and the fuel supply arranged with this powered flying position in mind. In a radio-controlled model, the engine should preferably be tuned so as to perform as nearly as possible equally well in a level position, in a nose-up position, and in a nose-down position. The fuel tank must also be designed and positioned so as to allow fuel to be drawn to the engine equally well regardless of the position of the model airplane. For this reason, pressurized fuel tanks that deliver fuel under equal pressure to the engine while the model is in any position frequently are used on radio-controlled model airplanes, especially on the larger models.

It is possible to achieve, with comparatively elaborate (and correspondingly expensive) radio-control equipment, a perfect external simulation of real aircraft performance. A radio-controlled model airplane can be set down on a runway, the engine started in the conventional manner, and the

human operator can then back away and not touch his model again by hand. From this point on radio control can take over. The engine can be set to idling speed. It can be revved up to taxi speed. Working brakes on the wheels can be loosened by radio. The model taxis down the runway, turned as desired and placed in position for takeoff. The engine speed can be increased still more, and the model taxis again, faster and faster and finally becomes airborne. The landing gear is retracted; the wheels are pulled up into the fuselage and the doors closed, again by radio control. While in the air the model can be flown immediately overhead or at a considerable distance, and can be put through almost every imaginable maneuver that could be carried out by a real airplane. Flying time over, it can be brought into a landing pattern similar to that of a full-sized airplane. By radio control, the doors are opened and the landing gear lowered and locked into position. The model plane

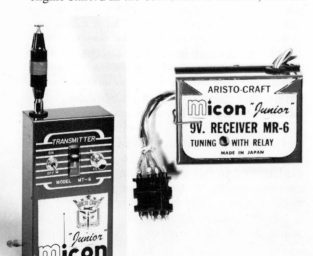

Fig. 163. A wide selection of makes and models of comparatively inexpensive radio receivers and matching transmitters is available to the radio-control enthusiast. The receiver at the right measures 1-9/16 by 2-1/16 by 15/16 inches and weighs less than two ounces. It is of course considerably smaller than the matching transmitter (right).

Aristo-Craft Distinctive Miniatures

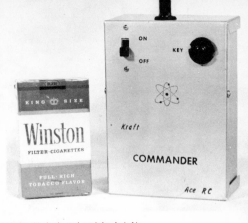

Fig. 164. The relayless super-regen receiver at the left measures only 1¾ by 1⅛ by ½ inch and weighs but ½ ounce. It is shown with a British threepence piece, a coin slightly smaller than a nickel. The uncased superhet receiver in the center is 1⅞ by 1-7/16 by ¾ inch and weighs only one ounce. Not being airborne in model airplanes transmitters do not require the same great efforts toward miniaturization as do receivers, but often are built quite small for convenience, as in the case of the model shown at the right.

Modelectric
Citizen-Ship Radio Corp.
Ace R/C, Inc.

is brought in, makes a perfect landing, taxis to the feet of the operator, the motor put into idling speed again or cut off completely, and the wheel brakes set—all by radio control!

Thrills galore and all the flying fun that anyone could wish for? Indeed yes!

THE COST OF RADIO CONTROL

The foregoing example typifies the ultimate in radio-control model airplane operation. Attainment of the measure of control described above is by no means an inexpensive thing, however, at least in the financial frame of reference of most hobbyists. As already noted, it is not necessary to have such elaborate equipment, either at the beginning or even at any later point, to thoroughly enjoy radio-control flying. What the average hobbyist is primarily interested in is just how inexpensively he can get into practical radio-control flying. This of course means radio control in its simplest and most basic form, single-channel rudder-only flying with no auxiliary controls whatsoever.

Radio-controlled model airplane flying actually is a great deal less costly than many imagine who approach it for the first time.

A survey made just before this volume went to press indicated that a hobbyist could enter radio-controlled model aviation with rudder-only control at a total cost of about fifty to fifty-five dollars in the United States. This would be about eighteen to twenty pounds in British currency.

These estimates include everything necesssary to become airborne and radio-controlled: a matched transmitter and receiver (the largest items by far on the budget), an escapement for operating the rudder, batteries, and battery holder, a ½ A Class glow-plug internal combustion reciprocating engine, fuel and a kit for building a model airplane

especially designed for radio control with about a 30-inch wingspan. The package might even be brought in for under fifty dollars. Most radio transmitters and receivers are sold in assembled, ready-to-use form, obviously the ideal for anyone who is not himself already a radio expert. However, a few transmitters and receivers also are available in kit form, and if the hobbyist felt competent to assemble this apparatus himself, instead of securing it readymade, a further saving could be effected. Note that the type of engine included in these calculations is not an especially designed and designated radio-control engine, that is, an engine with a variable-speed control, as described in Chapter 5, but rather a small, standard engine of the least expensive type. This is all the engine that is required in a basic rudder-only small radio-controlled model airplane. The somewhat more costly variable-speed engine is not required unless an additional control function to manipulate the speed of the engine is added to the simple rudder-only control. In short, one of the special R/C engines is not required in every radio-controlled model airplane.

Even for a rudder-only radio-controlled model airplane, the initial costs could of course be pushed up considerably over the estimate given here by selecting more sophisticated radio equipment, a larger model airplane, a larger or more refined engine, and so on. Most radio-controlled model airplanes are assembled from kits containing components and involving assembly techniques exactly like those for free-flight and control-line models. (Despite what has been said concerning the essential differences in design between free-flight and radio-control models, some hobbyists have successfully assembled free-flight kits, equipped the resulting models with radio control, and successfully flown them as rudder-only radio-controlled models.) Radio-controlled airplanes

can vary greatly in size. All may be rudder-only controlled if desired, but usually somewhat larger models are used when there are many additional control functions employed, because of the added weight of the equipment. Again, however, this is not a hard-and-fast rule, particularly as radio equipment is in a constant state of development, tending usually to smaller and lighter components. For model airplanes of about 30-inch wingspan, as included in our estimate of costs, a little .020 engine (.327 cubic centimeters) usually will prove adequate as a power plant. Bear in mind that the prices cited here are estimates and may vary in either direction in the future. Mass-production economies conceivably may result in some lower costs. On the other hand, technical advances, including further miniaturization or other factors, may result in higher prices.

Incidentally, radio-control models have been built and successfully flown with engines as small as the .010 (.163 cubic centimeter) size, although in most cases the engines involved were comparatively "hot" .010's. Model airplanes with as little as 20-inch wingspan, or even a little less, have been reported successfully flown as rudder-only radio-controlled models. Probably no phase of model aircraft is subject to greater continual technical development than is radio control. Almost every year finds a number of new and improved transmitters, receivers, and associated equipment being made available, or new and improved modes of using existing components to attain ever more sophisticated control being publicized.

A recent innovation in radio control, possibly signifying a landmark in its development and certainly indicative of the enormous interest it holds, has been the placing on the market of a completely assembled and ready-to-fly radio-controlled model airplane complete in one package with matching transmitter. The availability of such models should prove a boon to those who are anxious to get to actual radio-controlled flying as rapidly as possible or who wish to avoid as much as possible of the work of installing and adjusting the radio equipment within a model airplane.

Fig. 165. Four 30-inch-wingspan model airplanes designed for single-channel (rudder-only) radio-control operation, and constructed from kits. The first two models are replicas respectively of the Cessna 180 and of the Piper Cub. Engines of .020 to .024 cubic-inch displacement are recommended for use in these models.

Scientific Model Airplane Co.

THE FACTS ABOUT LICENSING

Whenever a hobbyist operates a radio transmitter to direct the movements of a model airplane or other model, he is in fact legally operating a radio station, and in so doing is subject to government control and licensing. In the United States this control is vested in the Federal Communications Commission (FCC), in Canada in the Air Services of the Department of Transport, and in

Fig. 166. Examples of the interior layout of present-day model airplane radio-control receivers. Both are super-regen types. The model at the left is equipped with a relay, which may be seen at the left of the base. The model at the right is a relayless receiver.

C & S Electronics

Great Britain in the Radio Services Department of the General Post Office (see Appendix II for addresses). The regulations that cover the radio control of models have been subject to many changes over the years, usually in the direction of liberalizing the regulations in favor of the hobbyist. Naturally, the regulations differ among the various countries, and any hobbyist entering the field should check to ascertain the regulations governing radio-controlled models in the country of which he is a citizen or resides, and to make certain that he fully understands the regulations and the necessary modes of complying fully with them. Failure to comply with radio licensing regulations can result in the imposition of penalties.

Up to 1950, the use of any radio-controlled model in the United States required that the operator hold a regular amateur radio license, such a license being issued only after an examination, the passing of which required that the applicant show a substantial knowledge of radio and the operation of an amateur radio station. In short, the licensing requirements for the transmitter (all licensing pertains to the transmitter equipment, not to the receivers) and its operator were such that in effect it was just as difficult for a hobbyist to obtain permission to operate a radio-controlled model airplane as to obtain authorization to set up and operate an amateur radio station with which he could carry on communications with other amateur radio enthusiasts. In 1950, Vernon Macnabb, a model airplane enthusiast and manufacturer of equipment for radio control, secured permission from the Federal Communications Commission to produce radio-control equipment, operating on a frequency of 465 megacycles, that could be used as examination-free (but not license-free) equipment. This step enabled model airplanes to be radio-control operated in the United States by the average hobbyist, without having to obtain a regular amateur radio license.

It was not until 1952 that what had become known as the Citizens Radio Service was fully activated by the FCC, with bands of 465 megacycles and 27.255 megacycles assigned for general examination-free use of transmitters of limited power (up to five watts input). Many model hobbyists somewhat overenthusiastically and quite erroneously have the impression that the citizens' bands were set up in the United States and other countries that provide similar bands entirely at the request of and for the benefit of radio-control model fans! Actually, although the modelers did play a role in this liberalization of regulations, the Citizens Radio Service and its counterparts elsewhere* came into being because of the great number of low-power radio units that were coming into widespread use for a number of commercial and private applications, such as dispatching taxicabs and other vehicles, in-plant paging and communications systems, opening garage doors, and so on. Model radio control was but a facet of this overall picture. It was not so much model radio control that made the Citizens Radio Service necessary as it was the creation of the Citizens Radio Service that made model radio control practical on a widespread basis. Once the citizens' bands had been set up, it was easy for a vast multitude of model airplane and other model enthusiasts to engage in the radio control of models with comparatively inexpensive commercial equipment and without the need of taking and passing a difficult examination.

---

*It appears that Great Britain preceded the United States in this direction with the Wireless Telegraphy Act of 1949, permitting the use of the low-power transmitters on frequencies of 26.96 to 27.28 and 458.5 to 459.5 megacycles.

Fig. 167. At the top, radio-control hobbyists display their models with the captain and executive officer of the USS **Lexington** prior to flying their models from the flight deck of the aircraft during a model meet. Below, radio-control model airplanes waiting their turn at a contest.

Ambroid Co.
Ace R/C, Inc.

Fig. 168. A "family" of radio-control model airplanes built from kits. All are substantially the same design, built to 37-inch wingspan for .049 to .074 engines and single-channel control; 56-inch wingspan for .09 to .19 engines and single- to six-channel control; and 69-inch wingspan for .35 to .45 engines and ten-channel or proportional control.

Carl Goldberg Models, Inc.

In the United States the citizens bands were subsequently expanded to include 26.995, 27.045, 27.095, 27.145, 27.195, and 27.255 megacycles. These are the frequencies in which commercial radio-control equipment for models are available today. The 465 megacycle frequency is little used any more and evidently is rapidly completely passing out of the picture. These are the examination-free frequencies obtaining in the United States and Canada today. Of course, if anyone for any reason wishes to build and use a transmitter operating on some other frequency for model radio control, or a transmitter more powerful than specified in the Citizens Radio Service requirements or for any other reason not complying with their regulations, it automatically falls into the regular amateur-radio category and is subject to all the rules governing the operation of such equipment. The availability of six close frequencies in the 26.295- to 27.255-megacycle range means that as many as six radio-controlled model airplanes can be kept in the air and independently controlled from the same flying field if desired. It also means that highly selective (and more costly) superheterodyne receivers must be used in place of the superregenerative receivers found in the less-expensive equipment but which will provide adequate service under many conditions where only one radio-controlled model airplane is flown at a time. However, the fact that there is an ever greater amount of other radio equipment in operation on similar or adjacent frequencies in many localities makes it appear increasingly desirable that model radio-control receivers be as selective as circumstances will permit.

As it stands now, no examination is required for any citizens' band radio operation in the United States, but a license is required for any transmitter of higher than 100-milliwatt input. This license (FCC Form 505; a copy of the form usually is included in the box with a model radio transmitter) can be obtained by mail from the Federal Communications Commission, filled out, notarized, and returned to the FCC, which will thereupon issue the license. No transmitter should ever be put into service before the license is received. It is also necessary, prior to filling in the license, that the applicant obtain and study a current copy of the FCC rules pertaining to the Citizens Radio Service. This is known as Part 19 and is obtainable from the Superintendent of Documents, Government Printing Office, Washington, D.C., 20025. Licenses will be issued to those twelve years of age or older. There is also now one class of model radio-control equipment that is not only examination-free but literally license-free. If a transmitter has an input of up to 100 milliwatts, it may be operated without a license in the United States. There are model radio-control transmitters on the market today that have such an input and accordingly may legally be operated without a license.

The licensing requirements for any transmitter should be checked very carefully, however. Under no circumstances allow yourself to be fluffed off or influenced by an overeager salesclerk who may inform you that you do not have to worry about licensing procedures, as no one is likely to bother you. The Federal Communications Commission and Her Majesty's Ministries have corps of field inspectors who make an alarming habit of popping up to see that the laws are observed. At times they are alerted by complaints from someone that they are experiencing a peculiar interference with their own radio or television sets. On the other hand, it is the duty and pleasure of these officials to assist properly licensed radio-control model airplane hobbyists in overcoming any difficulties that they may be experiencing because of interference from other sources.

Owing to the possibilities of creating interference with other radio (or wireless, as it is known in Great Britain) activity, it is essential that the transmitters employed for model airplane radio control employ a satisfactory means of frequency stabilization. Furthermore, it is highly desirable

Fig. 169. A group of large radio-control model airplanes. The third model down has radio-controlled retractable landing gear. The first three models are standard designs built from kits. The fourth model is a demonstration mock-up showing the mounting of the radio control equipment, including a bank of four servos operating rudder, elevator, ailerons, and engine speed.

deBolt Model Engineering Co.

that the frequency of the transmitter be checked and verified from time to time by the use of suitable and accurate measuring apparatus to make certain that the transmitter emissions are within the duly licensed bands. This is one reason why so much attention is paid to testing and measuring instruments among more advanced model airplane radio-control enthusiasts. A good combination test meter, such as is sold as an accessory for radio-control enthusiasts, may well prove a worthwhile investment for anyone who contemplates doing considerable radio-controlled flying. From a purely utilitarian standpoint of radio-control operation and flying safety, it is also important to keep a check on the condition of the batteries used in the transmitter and in the model plane itself for the receiver and other equipment. Battery failure during flight means loss of radio control. Batteries should always be tested under a load for a true reading.

A number of types of batteries are used in radio-control flying. Ordinary dry cells, including pencells for use in the plane itself, are favored by many, especially beginners, and are probably the most readily obtainable and least expensive in terms of original investment. Weight is of course not of too great importance in the transmitter batteries (although the lighter the entire unit, the easier it is to hold in the hand), but of course of extreme importance for the batteries carried in the model airplane itself. Nickel-cadmium cells have recently come into considerable favor among radio-control enthusiasts, as they are easy to recharge and keep up to full charge at all times. A battery charger is another item of accessory equipment associated with considerable activity in radio-controlled flying, and such a unit often is owned by enthusiasts.

Battery holders or battery boxes are standardized devices for holding various required combinations of batteries in position within a radio-controlled model airplane and permit easy removal and replacement of batteries. They also perform the function of assuring that the batteries are making good electrical contact with the contacts that lead to the takeoff wires, regardless of the vibration to which the batteries are subjected. Battery holders and battery boxes, but particularly the open-type holders, are available in an enormous variety of sizes and types, and it should not be difficult to find a suitable model for any particular application. All the apparatus carried in a radio-controlled model airplane is subject to considerable vibration inevitably caused by the action of a (usually) single-cylinder internal-combustion reciprocating engine, and is also subject to shocks received in landings. As noted, the batteries should

Fig. 170. Radio-control actuating devices. The first two units are selective escapements that provide right or left rudder at will. The third device is a tiny 1½-ounce electric-motor-driven servo that can be used by itself or to selectively actuate a secondary control unit, such as a standard escapement, as well.

Citizen-Ship Radio Corp.
Modelectric

be mounted so as to protect them from working loose or becoming disarranged. It is also important to protect the radio receiver itself from vibration or shock insofar as this is possible. Usually the receiver is protected by mounting it in a surrounding of cushioning foam rubber or suspending it by means of rubber bands. The former is by far the preferable method.

Bear in mind apropos of battery failure that radio control not only serves to guide the model airplane while in powered flight but also functions while the plane is in a powerless glide. In a free-flight model airplane, failure of the engine during flight, or deliberately cutting off the engine by limiting the fuel supply, results in a properly designed and trimmed model going into a glide that should

Fig. 171. Three detail views of one of the radio-control model airplanes pictured in Fig. 54, showing the installation of an escapement controlling both rudder and elevator. Torque rods extend rearward from the escapement to the operating rods moving the control surfaces as shown in the photograph to the right.

C & S Electronics

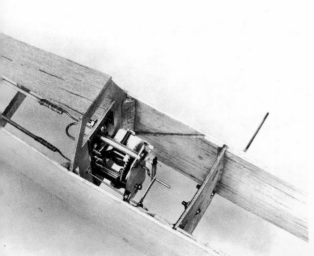

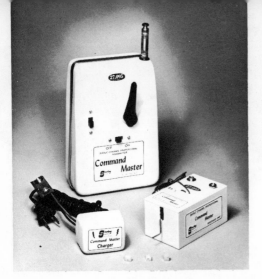

Fig. 172. A complete radio-control outfit providing proportional rudder and engine speed control. (The special throttle escapement is an additional unit, not pictured here.) This set includes transmitter, battery charger, and a receiving unit with permanently installed rechargeable batteries. The rudder actuator unit is also built into the receiver housing.

Sterling Models

can go wrong and cause the loss of radio control while a model is in flight; some faults or mishaps cannot be prevented no matter how carefully all the equipment has been checked before flight, but battery failure is perhaps the most common and certainly the most easy to prevent by simply exercising a little care before flight.

Some of the more elaborately equipped radio-controlled model airplanes are now fitted with a "fail safe" device to protect the model in the event of loss of control through battery failure, interference from other transmitters, or any sort of failure of equipment other than batteries. In such an event the "fail safe" system automatically operates, usually to put the engine into a low-speed throttle setting and to put the control surfaces into a neutral position, save for a slight upward setting of the elevator. When this occurs, assuming that the model is properly trimmed, it goes into a gentle downward movement, not precisely a glide as such, for the propeller is still operating under low power. Usually the model lands without suffering substantial damage. Should the engine itself shut off, the action of the "fail safe" would be the same, except that the plane would then come down in a true, powerless glide. If a spark ignition engine were employed, the "fail safe" action could easily incorporate means to stop the engine, by breaking the electrical flow to the ignition system, so the model would descend without power. When using a glow-plug or diesel engine, however, the best that can be done with the usual adjustable throttle and exhaust system is to put it to the lowest possible normal speed setting, so that the plane comes down under a certain measure of power. This does not seem the most satisfactory method, for a harsher landing is almost inevitable under these conditions than would be the case with a powerless glide. It would not appear too difficult to advance the basic idea one step further and provide a "fail safe" function that would completely cut off any type of engine by stopping the flow of air or fuel—although there might be some difficulty experienced

bring it safely back to earth. Failure or cutting off of the engine of a radio-controlled model still leaves the radio control of the control surface or surfaces functioning, and these can be used in gliding the model in to a controlled landing. On the other hand, failure of the radio-control system, due usually to battery failure through neglecting to check the batteries before flight and assuring that they are sufficiently charged, results in loss of control of a model airplane and at times loss of the model itself. With most simple radio-control systems the rudder goes into its centralized or neutral position, providing straight-line flight, and the plane merrily flies away, climbing as it does. It is amazing how far a small plane can fly in only a few seconds, even if it is not assisted by the wind. When the engine finally cuts out for lack of fuel, the model glides down, frequently out of sight. Obviously it is of the gravest importance that no radio-controlled model airplane be launched without first making sure that both the transmitter and receiver batteries are sufficiently charged to prevent loss of control over the model through battery failure. Of course, there are other things that

Fig. 173. Radio-control biplanes. Biplanes are ideal radio-control stunt models with their low wing loading permitting quick maneuvering. The picture at the left shows 66-inch-wingspan multi-channel stunt models for .25 to .66 cubic-inch engines. In the photograph at the right is a 25-inch-wingspan model suitable for single-channel radio-control or freeflight flying.

deBolt Model Engineering Co.
Flyline Models

in designing a system that would do this quickly
enough to be of real value in slowing down the
descent of the model. Also, the "fail safe" system
as described assumes that the model airplane will
not have retractable landing gear and that the
landing gear will be in position to take up at least
some of the shock of landing. (Of course, this assumes the model is properly trimmed for its descent and does not hit the earth in an outright nose
dive, but this factor of trim is assumed in the basic
idea of setting up the "fail safe" system.) Or, the
"fail safe" might conceivably be arranged so that
on a model with retractable landing gear the landing gear is lowered as part of the process of going
into "fail safe."

Admittedly, this is getting a little ahead of
the story, for a "fail safe" system is practicable
only on a quite advanced type of radio-control
system, incorporating, usually, radio control of
rudder, elevator, ailerons, engine speed, and other
functions, involving what is known as a proportional-control system. The working of such a system will be explained a little later. However, having logically approached the "fail safe" idea
through a discussion of the results of engine or
radio failure in simpler radio-controlled models,
the discussion of the subject might well be completed here with reference to the difference of
opinion that exists among some radio-control
modelers as to the relative merits and desirability
of incorporating a "fail safe" system into a somewhat advanced radio-controlled model airplane. Not
all proportional-control systems include a "fail safe"
by any means. The argument customarily raised in
opposition to including a "fail safe" is that if the
model airplane is trimmed so that it will go into a
good glide when the "fail safe" functions, it cannot
be trimmed so that it can be flown as a Class III
precision acrobatic model. Often the assertion is
heard that, in effect, flying a model with "fail safe"
is comparable to merely flying a free-flight model
airplane that has been equipped with radio control. This concept would appear to be entirely in
error, for with a properly contrived model, the
"fail safe" trim has no effect on or relationship
with the normal flying trim. For regular flying, including all types of competitive stunting and precision maneuvers, the model plane is trimmed so as
to perform in the same manner as any elaborate

Fig. 174. A transistorized servo for multichannel radio control with
its cover removed, showing the amplifier with which this particular
model is equipped. Center, a bank of four servos of this type, ready
for mounting in a model airplane. At the bottom is shown the
interior of another type of servo, not transistorized, and designed
to be operated by means of a relay.

C & L Developments, Ltd.

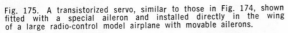

Fig. 175. A transistorized servo, similar to those in Fig. 174, shown
fitted with a special aileron and installed directly in the wing
of a large radio-control model airplane with movable ailerons.

C & L Developments, Ltd.

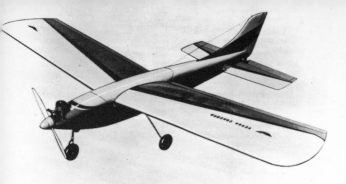

Fig. 176. A 66-inch-wingspan monoplane designed for 4- to 10-channel radio control and built from a kit. Four-channel usage would provide either rudder and engine speed control, or rudder and elevator control. The use of additional channels would further increase the control potentials. The model may also be used with other forms of multiradio.

Model Aircraft (Bournemouth) Ltd.

radio-controlled model with a number of control functions. The "fail safe" trim is adjusted entirely independent of the normal trim, and functions only when for one reason or another proper radio control is lost over the model and "fail safe" is called upon automatically to take over.

THE BASICS OF RADIO CONTROL

Without attempting to go into the technical intricacies of radio as such, let us try to see exactly how radio control of a model airplane functions. The transmitter sends out a radio wave to the frequency of which the matching receiver has been carefully tuned. The receiver picks up this wave or signal essentially as any radio receiver detects and responds to a radio signal transmitted on the particular frequency to which the receiver is tuned at the moment. In model radio-control work the re-

quirement is for the receiver to pick up only one wavelength, and tuning is of course done prior to flight. Properly tuned, the receiver picks up the signal from its matching transmitter. It is usual to divide the transmitters and receivers made for model airplane radio-control work into two types: carrier wave (CW) and tone or tone-modulated. This implies to many that two entirely different types of radio waves are respectively involved, which is not the case at all. In both cases the radio wave is exactly the same thing: a carrier wave that transmits a signal between the point of emission at the transmitter, through the transmitter antenna or aerial that radiates the radio wave into space, through the antenna on the airplane itself and into the radio receiver. The difference between a plain carrier wave and a tone-modulated wave is this: The carrier wave is transmitted only when it is desired to actuate the control function on the

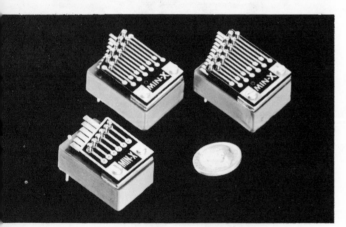

Fig. 177. Multichannel model airplane radio receivers and equipment. At the upper left are shown three examples of the tiny reed banks used in equipment of this type (6-, 10- and 12-channel models) along with a dime for size comparison. Below are shown two complete receivers of 10 and 12 channels respectively.

Min-X Radio, Inc.
Derritron, Ltd.

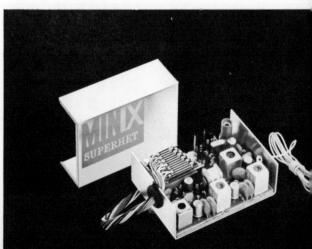

model airplane. There is no continuous wave between transmitter and receiver. Press the button on the transmitter, and a wave of energy goes out to be picked up by the receiver. The wave flows and is received only as long as the button is pressed, or keyed. Carrier-wave transmitters and receivers are the simplest and least expensive form of radio-control apparatus. Tone-modulated transmitters and receivers are coming into more and more frequent use for all types of radio control, even the simplest, and are necessary when more complicated systems are used.

In a tone-modulated system, sometimes termed an audio-modulated system, a basic carrier wave is transmitted continuously between the transmitter and receiver as soon as the transmitter switch is turned on. The receiver picks up this signal but does not respond to it. Then, when the radio-control operator desires to command the performance of some control function, he manipulates a button or key on the transmitter that imposes a tone on the carrier wave. When the receiver in the model airplane detects this changed signal, it responds, with the result that a large current increase is present in the final stage of the receiver. For the moment we shall consider trans-

mitters and receivers that operate only with a single fixed tone; later it will be seen how variations in this tone are employed in more complicated and sophisticated radio-control systems. For the moment, in discussing the simplest form of model airplane radio control, we shall group carrier-wave and simple tone transmitters and receivers together. Both provide an increase in electrical current at the final stage of the receiver when the button or key on the transmitter is worked, and the problem is to take this increase in current at this point and employ it to perform useful work in the control of the model airplane. That is, to translate the increased but still relatively weak electrical energy derived from the receiver into electrical or mechanical energy, or a combination of both, sufficiently strong to move a control surface. In the case of such simple radio-control devices, the control surface that is moved is, of course, the rudder of the model airplane.

In the earlier receivers, using a tube or tubes, there was never sufficient higher current in the final receiver stage directly to operate in itself the device that performed the actual control function. The best that could be done was to employ the receiver current to operate a very sensitive relay

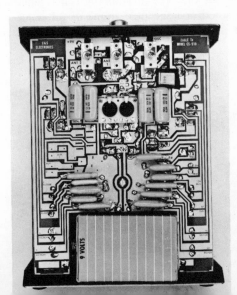

Fig. 178. Multichannel transmitters. On the model at the left the channel-control switches are numbered for identification; on the model in the center, shown with matching receiver, the switches are designated according to their control functions. The third photograph shows the interior of the latter transmitter, with its printed circuitry.

Derritron, Ltd.
C & S Electronics

Fig. 179. Today it is possible to accomplish many multiple-control functions with single-channel radio control that previously were limited to multichannel equipment. This shows a special single-channel servo giving both rudder and elevator control, and a special coding box controller to operate it.

Aristo-Craft Distinctive Miniatures

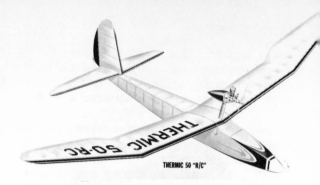

Fig. 180. Gliders also may be radio controlled, as in the case of this 47-inch-wingspan model built from a kit, and equipped with an auxilliary .010-cubic-inch engine. A model of this type can be kept soaring in the air for hours at a time by means of radio control of the rudder.

C. A. Zaic Co., Inc.

(electrically operated switch) that would then bring additional batteries into the circuit that operated the control device, generally known as the "actuator." Today, with most receivers designed to make use of transistors in place of tubes, it is often possible to obtain sufficiently high current in the final receiver stage to operate the actuator directly from the receiver. Such receivers are designated as relayless receivers, in contrast to relay receivers that require the use of a separate relay to put sufficient current into the circuit to trigger the actuator. The tendency of today's developments is certainly toward the eventual use entirely of relayless receivers, except possibly with certain very specialized control functions.

ACTUATORS

Whatever the precise methods and design of the components employed, in the final stage of providing any radio-control-directed movement, the action must be a mechanical one. The terminology regarding actuators is by no means standardized, and there is admittedly much confusion in this area, the natural result perhaps of so many differing types of units. Broadly speaking, however, if only for the sake of attaining some generally understood and accepted frame of reference, actuators may be divided into two groups: escapements

and motor-driven servos. The use of servos is virtually mandatory in more complicated forms of radio control. These are operated by small direct-current permanent-magnet motors, usually geared down considerably to provide usable power at a comparatively slow rate of speed, and are reversible by reversing the polarity of the leads to the brushes from the batteries that power them. Servos usually are encased in a box designed to protect the mechanisms and to permit easy mounting to the airframe, with exposed linkage or cams to which the actual control rods are attached. Escapements are almost invariably used in the simpler forms of radio control, including the basic single-channel rudder-only control systems. However, more complicated escapements or combinations of escapements often are used to achieve more than one control function with a simple single-channel radio-control system.

Oddly enough, experience has shown that the escapement, although the standard control actuating device of the simplest systems and actually itself the simplest in operation, usually is far more difficult for the beginner in radio control to understand than the considerably more complicated motor-driven servos employed in more advanced devices. This is probably because the servos are basically made up of units with whose working the average hobbyist already is familiar—motors,

Fig. 181. A special radio-control pulser for single-channel rudder-only control. It is in effect an electronic key for attaining proportional control of a model airplane rudder, and is used in conjunction with a transmitter.

Ace R/C, Inc.

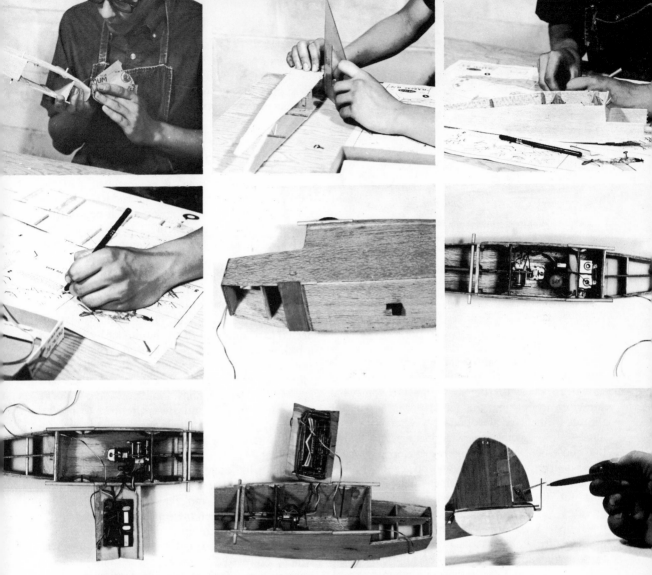

Fig. 182. Steps in the assembly of a radio-control model airplane. The fifth picture shows the receiver on-off switch mounted in the bottom of the fuselage. Next are shown the escapement, receiver, and battery box in position, with the rubber strand whose power is released by the escapement. The seventh and eighth photographs show the removable mount that holds the receiver on one side and the battery box on the other. The final picture shows the adjustable rudder linkage that permits the throw of the rudder to be varied.

Ace R/C, Inc.

gears, and levers—while the principle of the escapement is usually unknown to most hobbyists, and even the name in this application is regarded by many as a misnomer, or at least ill chosen from the standpoint of clarity. Escapement is, in fact, a clockmakers' and watchmakers' term. The escapement is the mechanical device present in every normal spring or weight-wound clock that regulates the gradual use or escape of the power stored up in a wound spring or a raised weight so that it is released gradually and at a continuously even rate of speed regardless of whether a clock or watch is fully wound up or almost run down. The escapement ticks off an even second of time and power; stops and locks, is released, and ticks off another second.

Like the escapement in a clock, the device designated an escapement in radio-control work does release and tick off a measured beat of power, releasing mechanical energy—in this case most frequently to move the rudder to right or left. However, the power is not released in a continuing flow as in a clock but, rather, only when the radio transmitter is keyed so as to let the escapement move one beat. The escapement itself is released by means of an electromagnet, which responds to the impulse of current fed to it momentarily or held in it over a period of time, depending on how long the transmitter key is held in a closed position. The electromagnet merely releases a device that holds and locks the escapement; the electromagnet does not power the escapement; it does not

Fig. 183. Two versions of a radio-control model airplane. Some kits, such as the one these models are built from, may be assembled into either single- or twin-engine versions of the same plane. This model has a wingspan of 56 inches, may be flown on one to ten channels, and takes .09 to .19 cubic-inch engines.

Carl Goldberg Models, Inc.

provide the force that turns the escapement in its beat. Most hobbyists approaching radio-controlled model airplanes for the first time are somewhat surprised to find that the actual power source for the escapement is a wound-up rubber strand! It almost always seems somewhat incongruous that in the midst of a mass of highly developed modern radio-control components the power of rubber should continue to play such a vital part, and a part not dissimilar to that which it plays in an ordinary rubber-powered model airplane, where the rubber is wound up and released to drive the propeller for as long as its stored-up power lasts. In its application to the radio-control escapement, the rubber acts in exactly the same manner except that its power is released only in momentary impulses; that is, only long enough to provide the force to turn the escapement star wheel a half or quarter turn (depending on the type of escapement), before the star wheel is caught and held fast until the releasing electromagnet is again energized. This means that the power stored in the wound-up rubber, instead of running down quickly as it would if driving a propeller, is sufficient to power hundreds of movements of the escapement. Remember that the current taken from the last stage of the radio receiver is at best a comparatively weak one and is actually much weaker in terms of energy than the energy stored up in the rubber strand. Consequently the electrical current serves only to release the mechanical energy in the rubber. This energy, coming in short pulses controlled by the movement of the escapement is sufficient not only to move the escapement arm or star wheel but also to move the rudder of the model airplane itself from side to side. Some larger

model airplane escapements have been built and used provided with actual clockwork mechanisms to supply the power, but the rubber-powered escapement is the type almost universally employed today.

MORE ABOUT ESCAPEMENTS

The simplest type of escapement, and the only kind that is necessary when rudder-only control is used, is what is known as self-neutralizing or self-centering escapement. The star wheel has only two claws; it is, in fact, more of a straight arm that rotates in a circle than any form of wheel. The arm is arranged with an ingenious pin-and-yoke arrangement so that it will move an upright torsion arm slightly to the right or left at alternate positions of the star wheel. The upright arm is connected to a control horn on the rudder by means of a rod, usually known as a pushrod. When the torsion arm moves to one side or the other, it also moves the rudder from one side to the other. The star wheel actually has four positions, neutral, right, neutral, left, and always returns to neutral when the current is withdrawn from the electromagnet, hence the name given to this type of escapement.

With the escapement in either of its neutral positions the torsion arm is centered; the rudder is also centered, and the model airplane flies straight ahead. When the transmitter key is closed, or "pulsed," as it often is expressed, the electromagnet is energized and releases the star wheel, which, powered by the rubber strand, makes a quarter turn. This moves the torsion arm into whichever direction is coming up next. As long as the transmitter button is held closed, the torsion arm and rudder will be held in this position. As soon as the transmitter button or key is released, the electromagnet in the escapement is deenergized and the escapement makes a quarter turn and goes into a neutral position again. The rudder returns to center. Key the transmitter again and the escapement makes another quarter turn, and the rudder turns in the opposite direction and is held in that position until the escapement is directed, by releasing the transmitter key, to go into neutral again. Suppose the hobbyist wants to make a right turn and the next position coming up on the escapement is the left turn position? This is no problem. The radio-control flier keys his transmitter button twice in succession, once just long enough to put the rudder in the left-turn position momentarily, long enough to snap the escapement and rudder over but not long enough for the model plane to substantially respond to the rudder. The second time the hobbyist keys the control he gets the rudder into position for the right turn that is wanted and holds the button or key in this position long enough for the model airplane to respond and turn as desired. In between the two key-on positions (carrier-wave transmitted in a carrier-wave system; tone-superimposed on the wave in a tone-modulated system), the escapement has of course dropped into a neutral position with the rudder centralized for straight flight, but this position too has been passed through so rapidly as to preclude the model responding materially. The effect for all practical purposes, and, as seen from the ground, is for the model airplane to go from straight flight into the desired right turn.

However, as we have seen, a radio-controlled model airplane has a tendency to start to descend when it is put into a turn. If a hobbyist tried to make a long turn, much less a complete circle by holding the rudder continuously in a right- or left-hand position, the model would start to spiral downward, with possible loss of control or at least the performance of some unanticipated and undesired acrobatic maneuver. Therefore, a radio-controlled model airplane is put through any considerable turn by a series of control movements, first rudder to the position of the turn, then quick neutral, then the opposite turn position quickly—not long enough for the model fully to respond—then neutral again, and finally back to the turn position desired. For a long turn or complete circle this sequence may have to be gone through several times. Its execution calls for considerable skill in pulsing the control. It is because of the difficulty of thus pulsing the transmitter for this maneuver,

as well as in more complicated control systems, that various types of pulsing-control devices have been made available whereby pulsing is carried out automatically.

A self-neutralizing model airplane radio-control escapement is then, essentially, a sequence switch, a designation that usually is much more understandable to many modelers. If it is thought of in this way, its design and working will probably be much more readily understandable, particularly to those who are familiar with other branches of modelmaking. A majority of hobbyists probably prefers the self-neutralizing escapement, and it certainly is to be recommended to the beginner, with the rudder always automatically self-centering. Another type of escapement is the four-arm type, with a star wheel with four arms or claws. This type is not self-neutralizing, as an impulse is required to move it to each of its four positions, although the usual sequence of operations is the same: neutral, right, neutral, left. To go from right to left requires that two pulses be transmitted: to neutral and then to left, instead of only one pulse as in the case of the two-arm or self-neutralizing escapement. On the other hand, it is not necessary to keep the transmitter sending in order to hold a turn position. It is only necessary to pulse the escapement into the correct position and then not to pulse again until it is desired to go to neutral (centralized rudder) or the opposite turn position. With a two-arm escapement a turn position can be held only as long as the transmitter is sending a signal. With a four-arm escapement it is possible to have half- as well as full-turn positions in the sequence. Thus, the following sequence can be employed:

Fig. 184. A transmitter for single-channel pulse proportional control with a built-in control stick whose movements correspond to those of the control stick of a real airplane. Beside it is shown a dummy model airplane with receiver and other equipment. At the right is shown the construction of the control-stick mechanism. The smaller levers are used to adjust the width and rate of the pulses.

Min-X Radio, Inc.

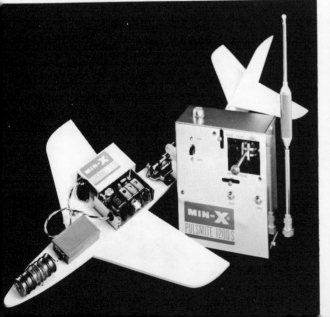

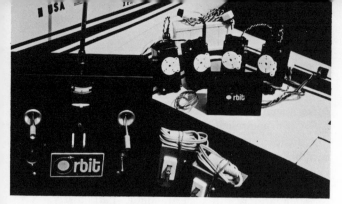

Fig. 185. The equipment for a complete digital proportional radio-control system is shown here, transmitter on the left; with receiver, four servos, and battery box on the right, and battery chargers in the center foreground. This system provides for four primary and three supplemental control functions.

Orbit Electronics

neutral, half right, full right, half right, neutral, half left, full left, half left, and then through the sequence again. Pulsing is somewhat more difficult and confusing, of course.

The most advanced type of escapement in general use is the compound escapement. The compound escapement does not go through a sequence of movements; there is only one neutral, and the escapement automatically returns to this position when current is withdrawn from its electromagnet. A single pulse always turns the escapement to right rudder; two pulses always turn it to left rudder. There is also a third operating position, attained by transmitting three pulses. This third position can be the key to a great number of additional and more complicated control actions, for when the escapement is in this third position the rudder is neutral, but a set of electrical contacts is held closed. It is possible to use these contacts

to energize additional control devices, such as another escapement employed for engine-speed control or for elevator control. It is, in fact, possible to "cascade" or "pyramid" three or even more escapements to obtain various additional control functions. There is virtually no end to the ramifications that an ingenious radio-control hobbyist can build into his equipment, all controlled by variations in pulsing on a single-channel receiver.

MULTICHANNEL RADIO CONTROL

Before examining further the possibilities of advanced single-channel control systems it is advisable to speak of multicontrol radio control. At one time multichannel appeared to be the ultimate in radio control for model airplanes. Developments in expanded single-channel systems have enabled many hobbyists who once aspired to multichannel operation to feel that other systems serve their purpose equally well; this is, of course, a matter of personal preference, and multichannel radio control does continue to play a major role in model airplane radio control. In multichannel control the radio equipment must be tone-modulated, for it is by making precise changes in the tone as transmitted that independent and precise direct control is obtained over the various separate control functions of the model aircraft. Multichannel is also sometimes referred to as tuned-reed radio control, because the essence of the system lies in a bank of delicately tuned reeds carried in the model airplane that, in effect, sort out and respond to the variantly tone-modulated signals transmitted, picked up by the receiver, and thence fed to the reeds.

Original experiments with multichannel equipment resulted in the working of only a few channels. Today developments have progressed to the point where the minimum number of channels employed usually is six, while ten- twelve-, and even fourteen-channel equipment is available. Six channels are regarded as necessary for ordinary Class III stunt flying, providing control over rudder, elevator, and ailerons. Two channels are required for each control function; one channel, for example, giving right rudder, and a second channel, left rudder; one channel gives up elevator and another channel provides down elevator. No escapements are used; there is no sequence pulsing in-

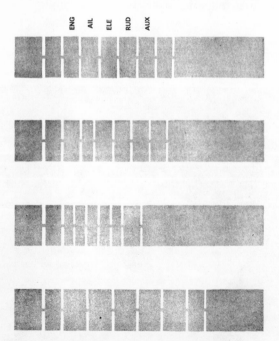

Fig. 186. These drawings explain the basis of the mark/space system of pulse proportional control, in this case of five functions: engine speed, ailerons, elevator, rudder, and an auxiliary control. In the second band the aileron control is being moved to the left, shortening the duration of this pulse while the others remain the same. The third band shows all pulses being shortened at once, while the fourth band shows the reverse condition with all pulses simultaneously being lengthened.

F & M Electronics, Inc.

volving a neutral position. Commands are transmitted to each function directly through key switches, usually one key being provided on the transmitter for each function, that is, for each pair of channels. One key will control the rudder. When put into one position it will transmit the proper tone to the reed that controls right rudder; when the key is put in the opposite position it will transmit the proper tone to the reed that controls left rudder, and similarly with elevator, ailerons, motor speed, landing-gear retraction, and other functions. The actual movement of the controls is carried out by means of motor-driven servos. These motors, of course, have to be capable of being reversed so that they will operate in either direction. On the rudder-control servo, for instance, one direction of movement of the motor gives right rudder; reversing the motor will take it to a neutral position wherein the rudder is centralized, and carrying it past this neutral position in the opposite direction will start to move the rudder to left-rudder position. In most applications of multichannel control there is therefore one servo for each pair of channels and matching pair of reeds. Obviously, this is a very complex and delicate system, although a very nicely acting and highly desirable one.

The heart of the system lies in the reed bank. The transmitter sends out the proper tone or audio-modulated signal on command. There is an actual audio output at the final stage of the receiver that is fed to the reed bank. Each reed is precisely tuned to respond to a particular audio frequency, and each reed will vibrate only upon receipt of its own resonating frequency. As a given reed vibrates, it touches an adjacent contact and closes the circuit to an extremely sensitive relay that in turn closes and feeds current to a particular servomotor with the current polarity arranged to cause the servomotor to move in the proper direction. As long as the transmitter sends out a given modulated tone, the receiver will issue this audio tone to the reeds; the reed of the correct length will pick it up and vibrate, keeping the sensitive relay (which has a delayed action to compensate for the oscillating current provided by the vibrating reed) closed and the servomotor moving in the proper direction. Furthermore, in modern multichannel equipment, it is possible to transmit and receive more than one different tone at the same time. Therefore it is possible, for example, to change the rudder setting and the speed of the engine simultaneously!

A reed bank for a radio-controlled model airplane is a marvel of delicate miniaturization. So, indeed, is virtually all the equipment now on the market intended for use in the model itself, both in terms of physical size and of weight. This applies to equipment intended for simple single-channel rudder-only control, as well as to that relating to the more complex forms of control. Receivers are measured in inches or fractions of inches and weighed in ounces and fractions of ounces. It is possible, for example, to purchase a receiver measuring an inch or less in each of its three dimensions and weighing but half an ounce without its requisite two pencell batteries. This is a receiver for basic single-channel control. However, even the most elaborate and complex receivers are very small and light. For example, a typical receiver for ten-channel multichannel control, including its reed bank, measures 2⅛ by 3¼ by 1 1/16 inches and weighs but 4 ounces. Naturally, the great need for miniaturization and light weight is felt in the equipment that goes into the airplane itself. Many present-day transmitters are, however, fairly small and light and can be conveniently held in the hand. Many hobbyists use a shoulderstrap arrangement for convenience in carrying heavier transmitters. Simple and very small transmitters can be obtained for single channel weighing less than a pound with batteries; sometimes substantially less. On the other hand, more elaborate transmitters may well weigh several pounds with their batteries. Incidentally, although most transmitters require batteries providing no more than 67½ volts, this current is stepped up to considerably higher voltage within the transmitter when it is in operation.

ADVANCED SINGLE-CHANNEL RADIO CONTROL

As mentioned earlier, all sorts of complicated control circuits may be used with single-channel radio control. From the starting point of a simple model with a self-neutralizing escapement and rudder control only, it is possible to achieve an amazing variety and delicacy of control functions while still operating with a single-channel transmitter and receiver. Not only is it possible to control many different independent functions, both escapement- and servo-actuated, or by using escapements and servos together, but it is also possible in many instances to attain a proportional or positional control over these functions, much in the same way that a multichannel system provides controlled proportional movements of its motor-driven servos to set rudder, elevators, ailerons, engine throttles, or other functions in exactly the position desired. It is not practical to attempt to go into all or even a representative selection of these systems here without endeavoring to make this present volume into an almost limit-less treatise on radio control, and there are many others who are better qualified than the present writer to undertake such a task and who have already undertaken it. Also, in a seemingly end-less welter of control systems, it would be quite difficult to select those which most fans would agree were typical or representative.

However, as many of these systems operate by making use of what is known as mark/space ratio pulsing, it is important that this be explained here so that those approaching radio control for the first time will understand what this means. In speaking of simple rudder-only control with es-capements, reference was made at times to the act of keying the transmitter or operating the button in sequence as pulsing. It is a very simple form of pulsing, indeed, and usually can easily be done by the hobbyist manually without the need of any special pulsing device, whether mechanical or elec-tronic, although such pulsers are available and are sometimes used as a convenience even in elemen-tary radio-control flying. With any pulsing action there is possible a definite pulse rate, even though it may be a quite haphazard one with simple man-ual pulsing to pull an escapement through one or more positions. A little consideration of pulsing will reveal that it can be reduced to a set pattern and that the pulse rate can vary both in terms of the time between each pulse and the duration or width of the transmitted pulse itself. The ratio between the timing between pulses and the dura-tion of each pulse is termed the mark/space ratio. If a mechanical of electronic device is used to pulse transmitted signal—in which case what we have is a pulse-modulated signal—the mark/space ratio can be very accurately transmitted and varied. By making use of variations in this mark/space ratio it is possible to set up a number of in-genious control systems. Suppose, for example, the rudder is to be controlled by pulse. Normally a very fast pulse is continuously transmitted. This rapidly pulls the rudder first to one side and then to the other; the movement actually is so fast that the rudder literally oscillates. The effect of such rapid movement from right rudder to left rudder to right rudder to left rudder, and so on, actually is in practice equivalent to neutral or centralized rudder, and the model airplane flies in a straight course. However, if the mark/space pulse ratio is slowed down, so is the corresponding movement of the rudder-operating servo. If the pulse rate is slowed sufficiently (by means of a key or lever on the pulser, which may be built directly into the transmitter), the rudder remains in one position long enough to turn the model airplane in the di-rection desired.

At the present time a very considerable in-terest exists in a more complicated system of pulse control that provides results somewhat akin to those obtained with a multichannel radio-control system. Instead of using different tones audibly to modulate the radio signal and operate reeds, as with multichannel, this system in effect modulates the mark/space ratio so as to operate selectively different control servos as desired. It involves gen-erating a pulse within each servo on the model airplane itself. In effect—and the workings of this system are almost human in their intelligence—the servo reads the pulse rate sent out by the trans-mitter! If the transmitted pulse rate is the same as the servo's own pulse rate, the servo does nothing. However, if the transmitted pulse rate differs from that of the servo, the servo responds with a suit-able movement, and continues until its pulse rate matches that of the transmitted signal. In the meantime, the servo is also in effect "feeding back" information concerning its own pulse rate, with the result that it will always position its control exactly as directed by the control at the transmit-ter. This would suffice to work one servo, but systems are now available that will work up to five servos independently by this method. This is ac-complished by varying the width of the pulses in different combinations in order to convey differ-ent control orders to the model in flight. Within the radio receiver a decoder actually sorts out all these pulses and directs them to the individual servos. As already explained, a given servo reacts if the signal it receives differs from its own pulse rate, and stops as soon as it has performed the desired command.

Fig. 186 should serve to explain the general idea behind this system, and to make it much clearer than any written explanation might. It will be seen that although this system performs five functions, there actually are seven pulse widths in each group. The two extra periods are provided actually to give the receiver time to make sure that each pulse transmitted is sent to the proper servo! The working of radio-control systems of this type is truly almost incredible. The pulses vary in terms of ten-thousandths of a second. The basis of systems of this type is very similar to that used in actual aerospace work to transmit infor-mation to and receive information from satellites and rockets, and when applied to models this sys-tem may truly be considered space-age radio control.

RADIO CONTROL AND MODEL ROCKETS

Although the common term "radio control" often is applied to the use of radio in model rocketry, the application is not that of control of the rockets in the manner in which model airplanes are radio controlled, but rather in the use of radio to send back signals from a model rocket in flight. The positions of the transmitter and the receiver are reversed in model rocketry; the transmitter is lofted in the rocket, and the receiver is located on the ground. It is of course quite difficult to send up sufficient apparatus in the payload compartment of even a fairly large model rocket to detect and transmit much information. Such a system also usually requires rather elaborate and expensive decoding equipment on the ground to make any sort of a meaningful interpretation of the information transmitted back from the model rocket in flight. About all the average hobbyist can hope to do, at least at the present stage of things, is to demonstrate that he actually is receiving a radio signal of some kind being transmitted from the rocket.

A few advanced model rocket and radio enthusiasts have worked out schemes actually to receive and decode information pertaining to such things as light and heat, transmitted from a model rocket in flight, but it is not known if these experiments actually have been carried out or how successful they may prove. It can probably be said that for some time to come most efforts in the direction of combining radio and model rocketry will be confined to sending up a transmitter, receiving a signal from the rocket in flight, and finally landing and safely recovering the radio transmitter.

CHAPTER 9

The Story of the Model Airplane

The story of the model airplane is actually the story of the real airplane itself, a unique situation that obtains with no other species of models. It is apparent that man has always dreamed of flying, either through the power of his own body or in some sort of machine. There is no need to enumerate and burnish the many early legends here; we are concerned with actual historical attempts at working miniature heavier-than-air flying machines. As a matter of fact, both the boomerang and the kite are in effect heavier-than-air flying machines of sorts. It remains a prime puzzle to anthropology as to how one of the most primitive cultures in the world, that of the Australian aborigines, instinctively perfected such a perfect instrument as the boomerang (if you cut a piece from a boomerang you will find an almost ideal airplane wing cross section or airfoil). Some of the early American Indian tribes also employed boomerangs. The kite, of course, was well known and brought to a high state of perfection in the Far East long before it was introduced into Europe. While elements of both the boomerang and the kite may be said to have played a role in the eventual development of the airplane, neither may perhaps properly be considered a direct forebear.

While it is generally accepted that the Greek savant, Archytas of Tarantium (Taranto). who lived from 428 to 347 B.C. successfully flew some sort of heavier-than-air model in the shape of a dove or pigeon, the secret of its working remains hidden within the mists of almost twenty-five centuries. It is possible it was a true ornithopter, or beating wing machine, powered by steam or compressed air; it is also possible that it was merely a kite in the shape of a bird, or even a roughly pigeon-shaped hot air balloon.

In any event, the major ancestor of the airplane, real or model, is the helicopter, not the complete flying machine with fuselage that is known by that name today, but the simple device that lofts either itself or simply a propeller vertically into the air, known through the years by many different names: helicopter, hélicoptère, hélice, hélice aérienne (all deriving from helios, the Greek word for screw), aerial top, flying top, Chinese flying top (indicative of a belief held by some that it originated in the Orient), screw spinning top, flying propeller, and so on. When it is observed that forms of the helicopter were being mass produced and hawked by toy peddlers in the streets of Paris at least as early as the fifteenth century, much of the seeming mystery—and, regretably, much of the glamor—that has usually surrounded most of the seemingly inexplicable accounts of miniature flying machines from the days of Friar Roger Bacon down to the dawn of the nineteenth century vanishes. The "little birds" that Gianello Torriani or Turrianus built and flew for the Holy Roman Emperor, Charles V (1500 to 1558) become quite credible in this light; so too does the famous "brass fly" of Nuremberg

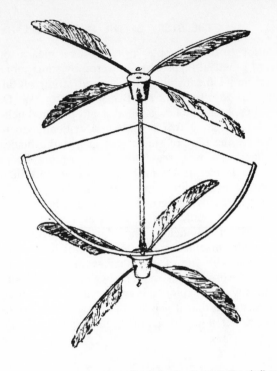

Fig. 187. Sir George Gayley's 1809 helicopter drawing. The shaft was wound with string which was kept under tension by means of the bent whalebone bow. Cayley had experimented with similar models more than a decade before, and the basic design was of even earlier origin.

New York Public Library

flying top. Sir George Cayley (1773 to 1857) was throughout his entire life a devoted student and advocate of aeronautics, operating on both a theoretical and a practical level, first building and flying a model glider as early as 1804 (and possibly as early as 1799) and attempting a boy-carrying glider flight in 1849. By the end of 1807 Cayley had built the first miniature internal combustion reciprocating engine intended specifically for use in experimental model aircraft. This engine, designed for a model ornithopter, used gunpowder for fuel but was never actually tried in a model aircraft as Cayley quickly appreciated that the engine was far too heavy in relation to its power output to have become airborne by wings of any such size as it was capable of driving. In 1849 or 1850 Cayley constructed another and more efficient gunpowder engine but evidently without any intention of using it in a flying model and employed it to test experimental flappers or ornithopter wings.

The common form of commercial helicopter of much of the nineteenth century, widely sold as a toy and philosophical device, had a wooden handle to which was fitted a movable spindle around which a cord was tightly wrapped, fitted with a two-, three- or four-bladed propeller of feathers, stamped metal, or other material. When the cord was pulled away suddenly, the spindle spun rapidly, in turn imparting the necessary spinning force to the propeller to lift it off the spindle and send it twisting upwards into the air. Many early aeronautical experimenters paid serious at-

and elsewhere that continually crops up with various attributions in writings on aeronautical development, where it always is assumed that this literally was a model of the insect of that name. Much immediately becomes clear when it is understood that the vane type of regulator in the earliest clocks was known as the "fly" (or *fliege* in German) or the "fan fly." Twisted so as to provide lift, the "fly" or *fliege* vane readily became a helicopter in the hands of an ingenious craftsman and a "brass fly" as contrasted to the feather propellers of the cheap toy helicopters or the cloth-covered vanes of somewhat more prepossessing models.

Until the beginning of the nineteenth century, the common helicopter was evidently a device similar to that pictured in Fig. 187, making use of a cord twisted under the tension of a whalebone bow as the motivating force. The drawing in Fig. 187 was published by Sir George Cayley who observed that this was the first experiment he had ever undertaken on the subject of mechanical flight. Cayley did not invent the helicopter as often is stated nor, to do him justice, did he ever claim to have done so. As has been seen, the helicopter was known long before Cayley; it was in fact known long before Leonardo da Vinci, who is also sometimes credited with its invention. It is interesting to note that in describing the helicopter in 1809 Cayley referred to the propellers as "flyers"; some years later he called the helicopter a Chinese

Fig. 188. A more or less standard design of helicopter or aerial top as commercialized during a large part of the nineteenth century. This particular illustration, which shows the mode of operation, is reproduced from an 1862 British catalog.

G. William Holland

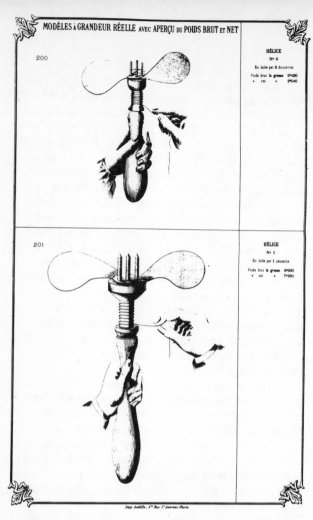

Fig. 189. A page from a French toy manufacturer's catalog of the 1880's offering two sizes of string-wound helicopters or hélices. Models of this general design were manufactured well into the early years of the twentieth century.

Mark Haber

Fig. 190. A helicopter, or flying top, as pictured in a British book of 1853, but which may be of considerably earlier origin. An elaborate hollow device with internal shaft and a base, it was not as suitable for mass-production manufacture as the types shown in Figs. 188 and 189.

G. William Holland

tention to the helicopter principle as a means toward practical flight when powered by some more substantial means than the wound string of the popular toy. In 1842 the British inventor, W. D. Phillips, built and flew a metal steam-powered helicopter weighing two pounds and evidently operated by the play of steam jets against the blades rather than by a regulation reciprocating steam engine. In fact, it was probably nothing more than a boiler fitted with propellers. The helicopter is reported as flying across "two fields" but unfortunately no indication is given as to the actual breadth of the fields. The blades were missing when the machine was recovered which, in conjunction with the other rather scanty data available concerning this model, suggests that the device may have exploded in midair and been carried the distance that it was by the force of the explotion rather than the action of its propellers.

HENSON AND STRINGFELLOW

In the late 1830's and early 1840's the airplane was developed and proclaimed by William Samuel Henson of England in substantially its modern form. In fact, because of Henson and his associate, John Stringfellow, the airplane was in practical reach of the world in the 1840's and failed of fruition only because of disbelief and the resultant lack of support. Even this might have been overcome if Henson had proceeded, as Stringfellow later induced him to, after the harm had been done, first with models and then with the promotion of the real thing, instead of in the reverse order. Aeronautical experts may argue eternally as to the origin or derivation of this or that feature of Henson's plane—from Cayley, from Henson's own observations and creativity, or from other sources. The basic fact is that Henson brought together in a single unit the necessary and practical elements for a successful airplane: the cambered fixed wing, the wheeled landing gear, engine-driven propellers, and devices for achieving stability and control. As one authority has noted, if England were to revive his basic patent of 1843 for a single year, the license fees would serve to erect for Henson the greatest monument on the face of the earth.* Yet it is hardly surprising to find that outside the ranks of aeronautical historians his name and that of Stringfellow are largely unknown and do not even command entries in most encyclopedias or in the British *Dictionary of National Biography*.

*A. F. Zahm, *Early Powerplane Fathers*.

Fig. 191. William Samuel Henson conceived the airplane in substantially its modern form in the late 1830's and 1840's. Between 1845 and 1847 he and John Stringfellow built a steam-powered 20-foot-wingspan model of Henson's design, pictured here, but were unable to attain more than tentative flight from it.

The Smithsonian Institution

Henson who, like Stringfellow, resided in Chard, England, at the time of the inception of the great project, already had marked himself as inventive. Stringfellow, who was engaged in the making of special machinery for lace manufacturing, was to prove himself remarkably adept in designing and making small steam engines and boilers with a power-to-weight ratio that surpassed anything that had previously been thought possible. It is not certain how closely the two men were associated in the initial stages of the development of the airplane, for the basic patent was in Henson's name alone. The two men are known to have been actively collaborating somewhat

earlier, leading some authorities to believe that the whole affair originated with their joint interests and that Stringfellow was involved from the start. What is certain is that by 1840 at the latest Henson was experimenting with model gliders at Chard and preparing certain parts at least, including a light steam engine, although whether for a model or for a full-size airplane is not certain. At a slightly later date, Henson is known to have built at least two models, the first powered by a spring and the second by a steam engine, the engine then being replaced by a spring drive in this model as well. Henson claimed to have achieved flight with these models, after launching them down a ramp

Fig. 192. Like a giant bat, John Stringfellow's original 10-foot-wingspan, steam-powered model airplane of 1848, the first successful free-flying model, its fabric-covered propellers already somewhat ravaged, was posed in a Victorian photographer's studio before a nondescript assortment of props and painted backgrounds.

The Science Museum, London

Fig. 193. Another view of Stringfellow's 1848 model airplane. This photograph and that in Fig. 192 were taken in 1866, and probably represent the first photographs ever made of model airplanes. There is evidence that Stringfellow actually may have achieved flight with this or similar models as early as 1846; there is no doubt that this model flew successfully in 1848.

The Science Museum, London

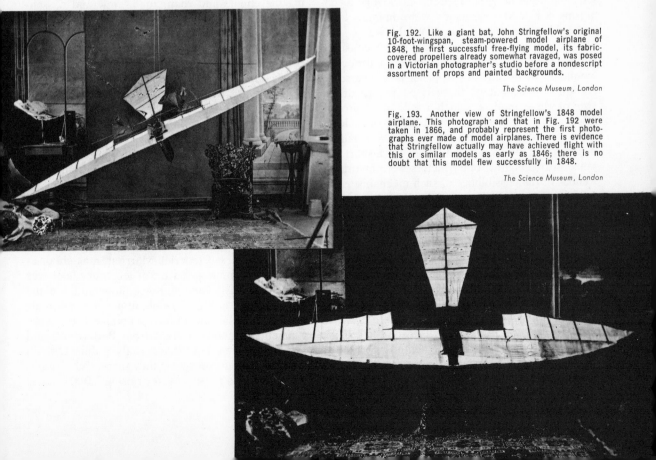

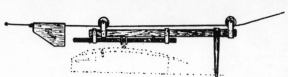

Fig. 194. Stringfellow's method of launching all his model airplanes was to start them suspended from a wire by means of a special launching carriage as shown here. At a point where it was calculated sufficient speed had been reached, a block placed on the wire pushed back the release bar, and the model was released and continued in free flight.

Fig. 195. John Stringfellow (1799–1883), the designer and builder of the first successful flying model airplane.

to help build up momentum for the takeoff, the same method he envisioned for his full-size planes. But he never regarded the results as wholly satisfactory. Especially in the light of this, there is no particular reason to doubt his claims, but as there appear to have been no witnesses to these events, aeronautical historians have not accorded them much importance.

Flight powered by a spring does not necessarily imply a clockwork mechanism as such, although most of those who have discussed these models have assumed that this was the case. It may have been, for clockwork-powered models were later built and flown and special clockwork mechanisms for model airplanes were manufactured and sold in the years prior to World War I. It is also possible that Henson's spring drives consisted simply of a long coil spring for each propeller, wound up by turning the propeller in a reverse direction. Unfortunately, there is no record of the size of these models, which would date around 1841 and 1842. Either a coiled spring or a clockwork would be capable of driving a small or medium-size model through the air for a short distance in free flight if other factors were favorable. Echoes of the possibilities of such mechanisms are found as late as the early 1930's. What is referred to here is, of course, the use of springs or clockworks in free-flying model airplanes, not the application of such devices to tethered models or toys, or to toys in the form of an airplane that merely ran on the floor by powering the wheels in the same manner as many clockwork toy automobiles, both of these being applications that were frequently employed by toy manufacturers down to the present day. In any event, Henson himself did not consider the results attained with these models satisfactory, and his interest in the models at this time appears to have been purely experimental and

with no clear-cut intention of publicly demonstrating a successful model as evidence of the practicability of his invention. In fact Henson seems to have felt that the difficulties he met with in the models could readily be overcome in a full-size man-carrying airplane.

It was for this goal and nothing less that he was aiming. His projected airplane was no small affair merely to demonstrate that a man could become airborne in a power plane, but a 140-foot-wingspan monoplane, powered with two 20-foot pusher propellers. It was to be in effect a transport plane, with a cabin slung below the wing containing the engine and room for a crew and passengers or cargo. Henson thought of it as capable of carrying passengers, troops, government dispatches, and mail to the farthest reaches of the British Empire. In fact, except for the cabin and its large size (a wing area of 4,500 square feet plus 1,500 square feet of additional lifting surface in the tail), Henson's projected airplane was quite similar to some of the first successful airplanes of the early 1900's. Henson clearly understood such things as the need for bracing the wing so it would be properly supported both on the ground and while airborne, and the value of streamlining to reduce air resistance.

In the enterprise of the Aerial Steam Carriage, the first of which was to be named the *Ariel,* Henson and Stringfellow associated themselves with two others: Frederick Marriott, a neighbor at Chard who about a quarter of a century later was to build and fly a combination balloon and airplane in California, and D. E. Columbine, a London attorney. The plan was to form a company, to secure a patent, to obtain a grant from Parliament, and to promote the sale of shares to the public. Only in the first two purposes were they successful. Columbine drew up a prospectus for raising 2,000 pounds

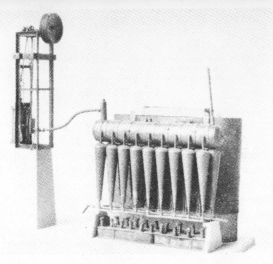

Fig. 196. A Stringfellow model airplane steam engine and boiler. This particular model is the prizewinning engine of 1868, which developed a little over one horsepower and was subsequently purchased by Professor Langley. The general design is, however, similar to most of Stringfellow's model airplane power plants.

The Smithsonian Institution

Fig. 197. The steam-powered helicopter built in 1863 by the Vicount de Ponton d'Amecourt and repeatedly successfully flown in France. The boiler and frame were of aluminum.

Warshaw Collection of Business Americana

in 100-pound shares,* but inasmuch as the patent had not yet been granted, nowhere in this blissful solicitation was anything said as to the nature of the invention in which people were being asked to invest other than that they had been confided to Columbine and it was truly a "Great Plan" that should shortly return 300 pounds for each 100 pounds put in. A greater pig in a poke there could be none; it is not surprising that no one responded to this proposal; the only matter for wonder is that Columbine could have expected a response. The only possible explanation is that Columbine himself must have been carried away by his own sincere enthusiasm for the project; the prospectus throbs with an enthusiasm for the possibilities of what is to be undertaken that seems genuine. Parliament readily granted a charter to the Aerial Transit Company in 1843 and as readily declined to grant any funds. Henson's patent was provisionally issued in 1842 and finally sealed on March 29, 1843. The news of the chartering of the company and of the patent created a worldwide sensation, partially enthusiastic, partially ridiculing. Henson became a world figure (he was named as one of the passengers in Edgar Allen Poe's famous transatlantic airship hoax in 1844), but no support was forthcoming.

It was at this point, in November, 1843, that the more practical Stringfellow wrote to Henson proposing that the best way to further the project would be for them to construct a working model capable of proving the practicality of the idea. Henson agreed, broaching the idea they should buy out Marriott and Columbine and continue entirely on their own. Both had undoubtedly proved

somewhat weak reeds: Marriott, who supposedly had friends in Parliament who would assist in obtaining funds from the government, and Columbine, whose premature solicitation appeared to have done more harm than good. These gentlemen were agreeable and probably emerged from the affair as the only ones to make money in any form out of the Aerial Steam Carriage, other perhaps than lithographers and caricaturists who had enjoyed a brief field day in 1843. From this point the story enters strictly into the realm of models, steps that led finally to the successful realization of the airplane.

THE MODEL AIRPLANES OF 1843-1847

Stringfellow's son, F. J. Stringfellow, who later endeavored to continue his father's work, was in close touch with the experiments at Chard from 1843 to 1847 and provided a fairly good record in a pamphlet he published in 1892,† although it should quickly be noted that this is by no means the sole record of the experiments. What principally involved the attention of Henson and Stringfellow from the end of 1843 to 1847 was the construction and proving of a large or 1/7th-size model of the *Ariel*. As the original full-size Aerial Steam Carriage had been projected as having a wingspan of 140 feet, the 1/7th-size model worked out to a 20-foot span. At first secondary or supplementary to this, but eventually to take on far more importance, was the construction of a smaller model or models. The first of these, or the first form of this model that it took in the new series of experiments, was a spring drive. This may have

---

*This interesting document is reprinted in full in *Henson and Stringfellow*, by M. J. B. Davy, a most fascinating volume for the student of aeronautical history.

†It is somewhat modestly if cumbersomely entitled *A Few Remarks on What Has Been Done with Screw-Propelled Aeroplane Machines from 1809 to 1892.*

Fig. 198. A front view of the steam-powered model built in Great Britain in 1867 by J. N. Kaufmann. It combined fixed wings for lift with beating wings for propulsion, and is not known to have flown.

Warshaw Collection of Business Americana

been an attempt to modify or rebuild one of the earlier models, or it may have been an entirely new construction. The records pertaining to the smaller model or models at this period are rather vague; they may pertain to modifications on one model or to several successive models. In any event the final smaller model had a wingspan of 10 feet; it was half the size of the larger model, or 1/14th the size of the actual proposed *Ariel*. Unlike the 20-foot wingspan model, it cannot be considered as a model of the *Ariel* as such, although it retained many of the features of that machine. By the time Stringfellow was done with it in 1848, it was a somewhat different machine, both in appearance and in performance.

The 20-foot wingspan model and the smaller model or models usually are referred to respectively as the Henson model and the Stringfellow model. This is far too neat an arbitrary distinction. The large model was Henson's in the sense that it was in effect a scale model of his proposed prototype and, also, in that its eventual failure evidently served to take much of the heart out of him as far as aircraft development was concerned. While all the engines for both models were almost entirely the work of Stringfellow, both men evidently worked equally on both the large and small models, with the main effort being directed toward the larger one in this period. Much work was done on the engines and drive—at one point compressed air was tried instead of steam, but this probably involved the customary modelmaker's method of

testing a steam engine by means of compressed air rather than that any plan was considered to attempt to fly the model with it carrying a tank of compressed air. Between 1845, when the large model was put in more or less finished form and tried, and 1847, many refinements were introduced, but all attempts to obtain satisfactory flight failed. The model was repeatedly launched down its ramp, became airborne briefly, and then gradually descended. According to calculations—which have not been essentially disputed by subsequent students of aeronautics—the model should have flown and indeed probably would have flown if there had been room to try it indoors. This was not possible; the model usually was stored at night in a tent put up on Bala Down, two miles from Chard, and experiments conducted in the damp of early morning when the dew and moisture played havoc with the wings and bracing. It is also evident that the location was unsuited because of strong ground currents of air. Stringfellow was of the opinion that it would be impossible to get the wings rigid enough and that a smaller model would prove far more practical and manageable, as indeed it did. In any event the 20-foot wingspan model was admittedly not a success in the eyes of its creators, although aeronautical experts who have studied the model have failed to find any one deficiency that might render it incapable of flight. In short, under better circumstances, possibly with a different mode of launching, the model should fly. It seems extremely unlikely that any at-

Fig. 199. John Stringfellow's steam-driven model triplane of 1868, built for the first Aeronautical Exhibition in London that year. The span of the upper wing was about 10 feet. Though it was the great attraction of the exhibit, from the standpoint of performance it cannot be considered an improvement over the model of 1848.

The Science Museum, London

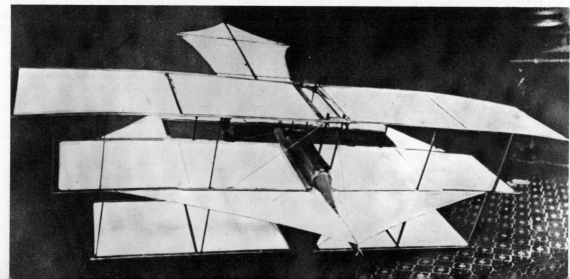

Fig. 200. The world's first Aeronautical Exhibition, held at the Crystal Palace, London, in 1868. The figure to the left foreground wearing a cap is John Stringfellow. Near the ceiling is his triplane model. The Kaufman model rests on a table in the center. At the lower right is a Henson-Stringfellow type of car and engine, and in the center foreground a boy in kilts holds a helicopter.

Fig. 201. In 1886, John Stringfellow's son, F. J. Stringfellow, built this 10-foot-wingspan, steam-driven tractor biplane, with wing shape deriving from his father's 1848 model. The capability of this model in free flight was never ascertained because of a lack of suitable indoor or enclosed flying space.

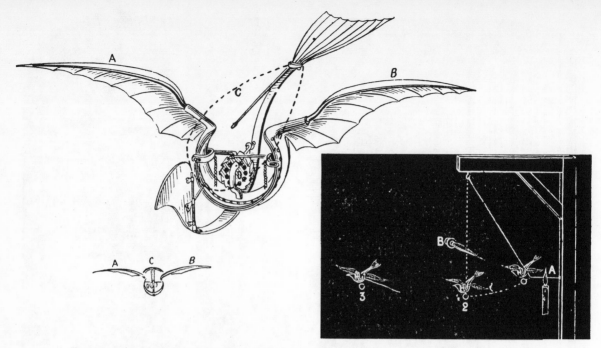

Fig. 202. Gustav Trouvé of Paris successfully flew this bird-shaped ornithopter, powered by the explosion of a series of cartridges, in 1870. The method of launching is also pictured, the bird being released by a candle at A and going into free flight when the gas jet flame at B burned through the passing suspending cord.

tempt ever will be made to test the restored model in flight and in any event the original boiler has been lost. The general verdict is that the model would fly under ideal circumstances but would in all events be extremely unstable.

It does not seem possible from this late point in time to pin down and precisely weigh all the factors that induced Henson seemingly to terminate his aeronautical activities after the failures on Bala Down in 1847. He evidently did not participate in Stringfellow's continuing experimenting that led to eventual success in 1848, although he did not leave England until 1849, settling in the eastern United States. He appears to have removed from Chard in the early part of 1848 and to have married shortly thereafter. There is no doubt that Henson was discouraged, although others have labored for far longer periods of time at similar projects without losing hope or interest, and had suffered financially through his experimentation. It seems likely that his forthcoming marriage was a determining factor in his turning everything over to Stringfellow. William Samuel Henson, the "Father of the Airplane," died in Newark, New Jersey, on March 22, 1888, almost thirty-five years to the day after his historic patent had been sealed.

THE FIRST FLIGHTS

Stringfellow, however, was far from being discouraged or downcast upon finding himself in sole proprietorship, as it were, of the Aerial Steam Carriage. Rather, he felt that he and Henson had worked through until they stood almost on the very threshold of success and that just a little more effort would bring the efforts of years to fruition. He had no illusions that financial returns would crown his endeavors or that man-carrying heavier-than-air craft would immediately come into being. He was evidently motivated primarily by a desire to prove that he had been on the right track all along and that he could build a successful steam-powered model airplane, a true free-flying model. As a matter of fact, there is some reason to believe that as early as 1846 he had achieved a substantial measure of success with the 10-foot wingspan model or one of its predecessors. It is certain that between 1846 (or an even earlier date) and 1848 Stringfellow built at least three twin-pusher-type monoplane models, each with a differing wing conformation but possibly all with the same engine.

Stringfellow's 1848 model was successfully flown, both at Chard and in London, in that year. Stringfellow had devised a much more satisfactory method of launching than the downhill run on a ramp employed with the experiments with the Henson model; in fact, Stringfellow's models were not equipped with wheels or any sort of takeoff or landing undercarriage. The models were launched from a wire, being fitted to an apparatus that rolled along the wire on grooved wheels until the model airplane had achieved sufficient speed and momentum entirely from the power of its own engine and propellers to become airborne in free flight. A block was affixed to the wire at the point where it was judged that that speed would be reached. The block pushed back a release bar on the carriage or trolley that in turn automatically freed the model airplane, which then continued in free flight. This launching device will be found pictured in Figs. 194 and 200. The distance of wire-supported travel necessary successfully to launch the 1848 model was found to be about 22 feet. The important point was whether upon the release of the model into free flight it would then climb under power—that is, truly to fly—or if it would merely continue in a more or less straight or gradually descending course, either of which might still, at this date and under the circumstances, be considered a notable achievement. The model did rise and fly, rising at times as much as one in seven (one foot of height for each seven feet of forward travel)! In fact, it flew so well in the initial demonstrations at Chard, in a room about 66 feet long and 10 or 12 feet high, in a lace factory, that the starting wire had to be placed quite low in order to allow height for the model to ascend after its release. In all cases, both at Chard and in longer flights later in London, the flight of the model was halted by means of a piece of canvas placed across its path to stop it. This method was always employed to terminate the flights. The model was essentially an indoor model, and no attempt seems ever to have been made to try it in the open to see just how far and how high it would fly before its power was exhausted and whether it would then glide back to earth.

Marriott, who was then a journalist in London and with whom Stringfellow had remained in touch, was invited to Chard to witness some of the flights, and brought with him Lieutenant George Gale of the Royal Navy, who had made many notable balloon flights, including ascents from Cremorne Gardens, an amusement park or pleasure gardens in London. A Mr. Partridge, and Mr. Ellis, the lessee of Cremorne Gardens offered to build a covered way of considerably greater size than the room available at Chard for continued tests and, evidently, public demonstrations. Upon arriving at the Gardens, Stringfellow was somewhat disappointed in what had been provided, apparently a walled-in area only about 150 feet long, and uncovered.* However, trials were undertaken, and the model airplane flew 120 feet

until it reached the canvas barrier. Among other things, this proved beyond question the essential stability of the model in flight under at least partially open-air conditions, and there is no question that it was capable of flying longer distances if space had been available for tests.

At the same time the flights of the model seem to have attracted little public interest and enthusiasm. This was due partially no doubt to the fact that the general public then, as for many years thereafter, appreciated little distinction between a heavier-than-air and a lighter-than-air flying machine. A 10-foot model flying 120 feet seemed as nothing compared to witnessing a man going up in a balloon. Lieutenant Gale, who had crossed the English Channel in his balloon (actually a main balloon assisted by two smaller balloons), fell to his death in 1850, cutting off any possibility of his enthusiasm furthering Stringfellow's efforts, if, indeed, such expectation played any part in Stringfellow's thinking. Stringfellow regarded his experiments as purely scientific, and the amusement-park aspects of the London tests had little appeal for him. He had demonstrated the ability of his model to fly and to fly well, and, in the words of his son, he "rested for a long time, satisfied with what he had effected," although still interested in the subject and contemplating an eventual "renewal of his experiments."

What actually is the measure of Stringfellow's accomplishments of 1848? The flight indoors, or in a semienclosed area, of a steam-powered 10-foot-wingspan model airplane weighing some 9 pounds or less and with a total supporting area of just about 18 square feet may not appear a particularly spectacular accomplishment by modern standards. Nevertheless, Stringfellow had shown that a powered airplane was possible. To those who were willing and able to receive the lesson, it was from that point onward obvious that the successful realization of the airplane depended only on achieving the most desirable form and area of lifting surfaces and the correct power-to-weight ratio of the power plant required to make them airborne. It is interesting to observe that although Stringfellow himself and many other early experimenters with both models and real airplanes would transfer their activities to multiple planes, the monoplane of Stringfellow's model of 1848 is the form in which the present-day airplane has eventually evolved. Stringfellow never referred to his models as airplanes. The term "aero-plane" or "aeroplane" was originally not applied to the entire plane but explicitly and only to the lifting surfaces or wings. Although for years others interested in heavier-than-air machines would devote themselves to

---

*Davy quotes an unidentified newspaper announcement of demonstrations of steam-powered "Models" unassisted by gas (that is, the lifting power of gas enclosed in a balloon). Is the use of the plural form of any significance? Did Stringfellow bring more than one model to London?

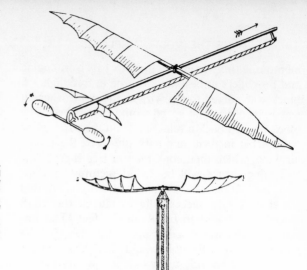

Fig. 203. The Pénaud "planophore" of 1871 was a realized rubber-powered pusher type model airplane. Pénaud attained a substantial measure of inherent stability in this model. This is the most contemporary illustration that can be found and pictures a model without a vertical fin.

Warshaw Collection of Business Americana

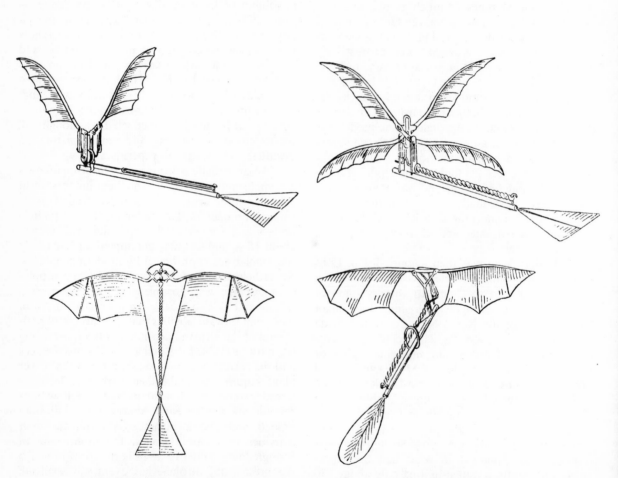

Fig. 204. Four rubber-powered French model ornithopters of the early 1870's. The first two models are by Jobert (1871 and 1872). Below are ornithopters built in 1872 by Dr. Hureau de Villeneuve and Pénaud respectively.

Warshaw Collection of Business Americana

Fig. 205. M. and Mme. Pichancourt proudly posed for this photograph in the late 1870's or 1880's, holding one of the rubber-powered model ornithopters that Pichancourt manufactured. The drawing indicates the details of the working of these models but shows a much heavier skein of rubber than the photograph indicates.

The Smithsonian Institution
Warshaw Collection of Business Americana

experiments with helicopters (which are now, of course, a commonplace form of heavier-than-air machine) and ornithopters (which have never met with material success), Stringfellow clearly marked out the main path along which the actual airplane was eventually to be brought to success. As to the length of his flights in 1848, they were, as has been seen, limited to his best record of 120 feet by the space available rather than by any deficiency in the model itself. Clément Ader in France flew only 164 feet with his full-sized steam-driven airplane in his first flight in 1890, and the very first flight of the Wright brothers at Kitty Hawk, North Carolina, on December 17, 1903, was by a striking coincidence exactly the same distance traveled by Stringfellow's model in 1848, 120 feet, although before the day was out the plane made a flight of 852 feet. Such comparisons are of course somewhat pointless except insofar as they help to put Stringfellow's achievement into perspective.

It might well be noted here that the authenticity of claimed accomplishments for early flights, both real and model, do not necessarily rest solely on the statements of witnesses, sometimes made long after the event. The science of aeronautics has long since advanced to a point where, given the design and size of a particular aircraft, together with information on the power plant and airscrew size and design, aeronautical experts can quite readily determine whether a given unit was capable of flight at all and whether capable of the flights claimed for it. It should also be noted that if arbitrary standards are set up as to what constitutes actual flight, it is possible, using such standards as a basis, to come to a number of different conclusions and determinations as to what craft did or did not fly. For example, if Professor Langley, whose steam-powered models, not much larger than Stringfellow's, flew over half a mile in 1896, proposed a recognition that true flight of such a model must consist of being airborne for over a thousand feet, then by this standard Stringfellow's model did not fly at all! Of course, Professor Langley (who owed much to Stringfellow and purchased one of his later engines) set up no such arbitrary standards, although they have been advocated from time to time. In fact, a standard of a thousand feet for any flight, real or model, would mean that none of the Wright flights of 1903 would qualify either. This is not the place for an extended discussion of these points. If many people found it difficult to distinguish between lighter-than-air craft and airplanes in the nineteenth century and even in the first years of the twentieth century, this is not the case today. The average modern man

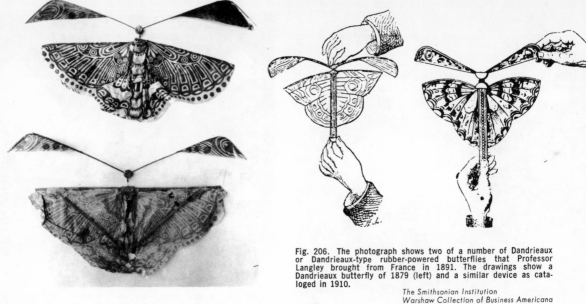

Fig. 206. The photograph shows two of a number of Dandrieaux or Dandrieaux-type rubber-powered butterflies that Professor Langley brought from France in 1891. The drawings show a Dandrieaux butterfly of 1879 (left) and a similar device as cataloged in 1910.

knowns exactly what an airplane is, and is well equipped to form his own opinions of heavier-than-air flight achievements.

Stringfellow himself subsequently modified the ¾-inch bore, 2-inch-stroke steam engine used in his 1848 model. Although he retained the airplane itself and other relics, he passed the engine and boiler on to the proprietor of a lacemaking concern in Tivorton, England, where it was used for many years to drive a small piece of machinery. Possibly he felt the engine was of little importance, or was already contemplating the making of a better one. It seems more probable, however, that he received a sudden call for a small engine in the course of his regular business of making lacemaking machinery and, finding the airplane engine suitable, decided to make use of it. The engine supposedly was transferred to the works of John Heathcote & Co. in the 1850's and it was used by them for many years. It is now on display, along with the other remains of the model of 1848, at the Science Museum at South Kensington, London.

TWENTY YEARS OF PROGRESS

The twenty years that elapsed between String-fellow's triumph of 1848 and the holding of the first Aeronautical Exhibition in London in 1868 were far from devoid of aeronautical model interest, experimentation, and progress, especially in France and Great Britain. Unfortunately, most of these events now appear as if seen through a mist, dimly and occasionally. This does not mean that enthusiasm had slackened—merely that recording and reporting were far less adequate than we would wish them to have been. Details are in many cases

sadly absent, and the account of these years must perforce be somewhat brief and episodic. There also is evidence that model aeronautical activity in the United States during these two decades was somewhat greater than has generally been believed, but again we are at a loss for many details.

France, 1845. One Monsieur Cossus experimented with helicopters and built a steam-powered model composed of three propellers on parallel shafts, a large center propeller with slightly smaller and lower propellers on each side.

Great Britain, 1849. Sir George Cayley built and experimented with a model glider, 14½ feet long and weighing 16 pounds, that was equipped with a vertical fin rudder mounted above the elevator, possibly the first model with this now standard arrangement of elevator and rudder. By 1853 he had refined this to an even more sophisticated design.

France, 1857. Félix du Temple built a steam-powered single-propeller tractor monoplane model, possibly the first of several. The interest in this model, of which we would gladly know more, is quickened by the fact that, fifteen years later, du Temple sent a full-size version of this machine, piloted by a sailor, down a ramp in the first recorded attempt at launching a full-size powered airplane. The craft left the ground, but with results too negligible to be rated by most historians as an actual flight.

The United States, 1857. James Henry Beard, an artist and the father of Daniel Carter Beard, the founder of the Boy Scouts of America, built a large model airplane in his studio. Unfortunately, Dan Beard, despite his later considerable interest and involvement in kites and model airplanes,

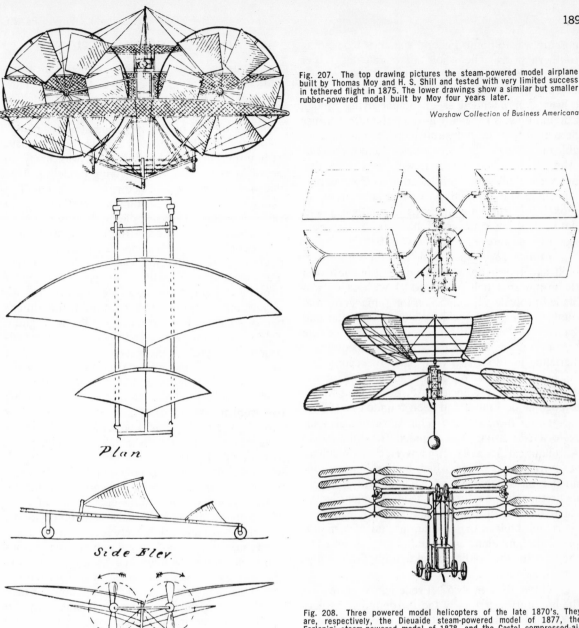

Fig. 207. The top drawing pictures the steam-powered model airplane built by Thomas Moy and H. S. Shill and tested with very limited success in tethered flight in 1875. The lower drawings show a similar but smaller rubber-powered model built by Moy four years later.

Warshaw Collection of Business Americana

Plan

Side Elev.

End Elev.

Fig. 208. Three powered model helicopters of the late 1870's. They are, respectively, the Dieuaide steam-powered model of 1877, the Forlanini steam-powered model of 1878, and the Castel compressed-air model of 1878.

Warshaw Collection of Business Americana

never seems to have gone into further detail, except that his failure to enumerate special features implies that the model was rubber powered and not unlike those with which he was familiar in the 1920's. Dan Beard left no doubt that this was a heavier-than-air flying machine, not an airship. This model remains a tantalizing question mark.

France, 1858. Pierre Jullien built and successfully flew a rubber-powered twin-propeller model airplane. This is the earliest rubber-powered model actually known. The rubber was stretched around a cone, similar to the fuse of a clock, in an posed by Cayley in 1853. The early use of rubber

for model airplane power seems largely to derive its practice from clock design, the rubber being used, as it were, as a substitute for the steel spring of a clockwork, either wound around a drum or around a cone, similar to the fusee of a clock, in an effort to achieve even power and speed throughout its unwinding.

The United States, 1862. Captain William C. Powers of the Confederate Service built a steam-powered model helicopter with two continuous vertical screws instead of conventional propellers, plus two long horizontal screws of similar design for forward or reverse propulsion. Its purpose supposedly was to bomb Federal warships blockading southern ports. The whole affair remains rather obscure, and it is not known if any attempt was ever made to test the model in flight or if, indeed, it was ever intended as an actual flying model. Captain Powers reputedly gave up the idea because he feared that the industrial North would be capable of turning them out in greater quantities if one ever fell into their hands. It will be recalled that no such inhibitions precluded the Confederacy launching and attempting to use a submarine, although it is true, of course, that a bombing plane, unlike a submarine, could have been employed against land forces as well as vessels.

France, 1863. Vicount de Ponton d'Amecourt built and repeatedly flew a remarkably successful steam-powered helicopter model with twin two-bladed propellers mounted on the same shaft, and supposedly equipped with an aluminum boiler and frame. De Ponton d'Amecourt was one of the organizers of the Société d'Auto-locomotion Aérienne in 1862, two years later to become the Société d'Aviation, reputedly the first use of the word aviation. (A Société Aérostatique et Meteorologique de France had been founded in 1852.)

Great Britain, 1866. The Aeronautical Society of Great Britain was founded (now the Royal Aeronautical Society). Francis Herbert Wenham read his famous paper, which had an immense influence on Stringfellow's further activities, before its first meeting on June 27, 1866. Wenham advocated the use of several superimposed wings, in short, the biplane or triplane, instead of a monoplane design. Plans were laid this year or early the next for the holding of an aeronautical exhibition in London.

Great Britain, 1867. Frederick W. Brearey, the honorary secretary of the Aeronautical Society of Great Britain traveled to Chard in an endeavor to induce Stringfellow, whose fame had not flagged in aeronautical circles even if his name was comparatively unknown to the public, to build a model airplane for the forthcoming exhibition. Stringfellow was already aware of plans for the exhibition, and his old interest and enthusiasm had been aroused. He responded to Brearey's visit with the results described shortly.

Great Britain, 1867. J. M. Kaufman built a steam-powered model airplane with both fixed wings for lift and flapping wings for propulsion and fitted with wheels for traveling on the ground, evidently also with display at the pending exhibition in mind. There is no evidence that this model ever successfully flew.

THE GREAT EXHIBITION

Thus the real and model aeronautical world had been brought by progressive stages to a definite landmark in aviation history, and Stringfellow had been brought back to activity, a most vital point, for there is no doubt that he literally "made" the exposition. Brearey was correct in his evident assumption that only Stringfellow was likely to prove capable of building a flying model airplane that would perform satisfactorily at the event. The exhibition was held at the famous Crystal Palace in London in June, 1868—it did not by any means of course occupy the entire structure. Apart from a considerable display of balloons and other lighter-than-air craft, kites, and various other material, there were displayed fifteen engines, a prize of £100 being offered for the engine that would prove to have the best power-to-weight ratio, and a number of heavier-than-air models. Of the engines, eight were steam-powered and seven were internal-combustion types, using guncotton, gas, or oil as fuel. One of the engines, and destined to win the prize, was Stringfellow's. Of the heavier-than-air models that were placed on display at the opening two were fixed-wing airplanes, Stringfellow's new triplane and the combination fixed- and flapping-wing model of Kaufmann's; two were helicopters, including de Ponton d'Amecourt's notable model, which was not, however, operated during the exhibition; the remainder were ornithopters. The descriptions both of some of the engines and of some of the flying machine models were quite vague, and the Aeronautical Society complained afterward that some of the internal-combustion engines had been entered without their action and method of working even being explained by their inventors!

This was not true of Stringfellow's prize-winning masterpiece, of course. It was found to be probably the most efficient steam engine ever constructed up to that date, weighing 13 pounds and developing better than one horsepower. This may not sound very sensational today, but it assuredly was in 1868. The total weight of the engine, boiler, water and fuel, car and propellers was 16¼ pounds. It is interesting to note, however, that there was a much smaller steam engine for model aeronautical use displayed and operated at the exhibition, one built by Camille Vert and weighing less than 2 pounds. This approaches the weight of many modern model airplane internal-combustion reciprocating engines and is less than the weight of many engines used in twentieth-century model airplanes. It is not impossible this engine might have proved to have a superior pow-

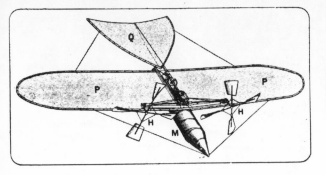

Fig. 209. One of the best known of the early powered model airplanes is this twin-tractor compressed-air model with about 4-foot wingspan, built by Victor Tatin in 1879. Contrary to popular impression, the Tatin model never flew in free flight, but performed only as a tethered model.

Warshaw Collection of Business Americana

er-to-weight ratio to Stringfellow's; but, curiously, it was never tested by the prize committee on the grounds that it was too small for any accurate evaluation of its power. This explanation sounds implausible, although the judges seem to have been unequipped to deal with fractional horsepower, as evidenced by their assessment of Stringfellow's engine merely as "rather more" than one horsepower, although their own figures indicate that they could have pinned it down to almost exactly 1 1/11th horsepower.* As the purpose of the competition was to bring forth the lightest engines possible in relation to their power, it would seem that the judges should have provided themselves for any contingencies that would arise if extremely small engines were entered. The shops of London were filled with beautiful British-made model steam engines; a treatise on model steam engines had been published; and there must have been a number of men available in the London area who could have accurately calculated the output of the Vert engine, which was hopefully set in motion but remained untested on what seems today at least rather specious grounds. The inventor's reactions are not recorded, as far as is known.

On the basis of the facts as they appear today, it is difficult to escape the conclusion that

*They took 33,000 foot pounds as equaling one horsepower, and calculated that Stringfellow's engine delivered 36,000 foot pounds per minute.

seeing there was only one other engine in possible competition with Stringfellow's, the judges gladly availed themselves of the excuse noted above to avoid testing it. This is not to detract from Stringfellow's achievement, but it does suggest that Camille Vert also had produced a rather remarkable example of modelmaking. If, as his name suggests, Vert may have been a Frenchman, this factor may also unconsciously have entered into the thinking.

There is some confusion as to precisely what Stringfellow entered in the exhibition, some later accounts referring to two engines, others to two model airplanes. There was only one airplane, the triplane that was flown on a wire stretched across a transept of the building. This plane of course contained an engine built by Stringfellow, which should not be confused with the prizewinning engine that formed a separate exhibit. This makes two engines, counting the one in the model triplane. Stringfellow also entered a third exhibit, rather unsatisfactorily described as a one-horsepower "copper boiler and fire-place" weighing about 40 pounds. As Stringfellow obviously knew the difference between a steam engine and boiler with firebox and a boiler and firebox alone, it must be assumed that the latter components were all that formed this third exhibit, but it remains rather mysterious and obscure, and is no doubt responsible for a large measure of the confusion that arose in later years concerning Stringfellow's exhibits.

Fig. 210. The compressed-air-powered model ornithopter—or, more properly, semiornithopter, for the large supporting surfaces were fixed, and only the small segments beat up and down for propulsive force—built by Lawrence Hargrave and presented by him to the Smithsonian Institution during his visit to the United States in 1893.

The Smithsonian Institution

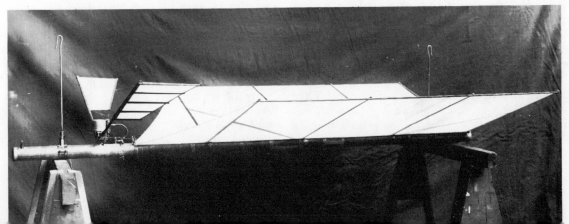

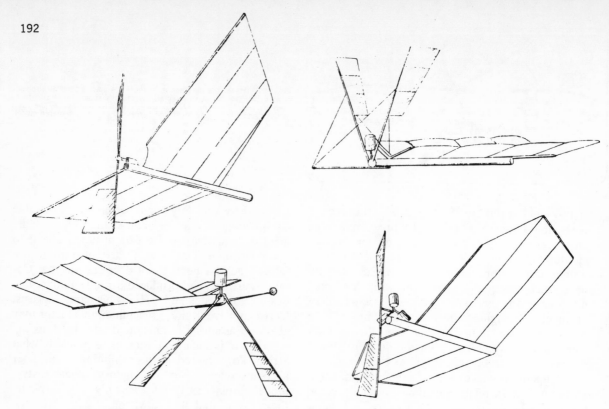

Fig. 211. Four flying models built by Lawrence Hargrave. The first is a rubber-powered model airplane (1889); the second and third are compressed-air-powered semiornithopters (1890); and the fourth is a compressed-air-powered model airplane (1891).

THE MODEL TRIPLANE OF 1868

While from a technical standpoint Stringfellow's prizewinning engine was a more than outstanding achievement, it was of course his working-model triplane that was the center of attention for everyone who visited the exhibition, including the Prince and Princess of Wales. The Prince was so entranced by the model that he had Stringfellow brought to him to explain it and aeronautical navigation in general. (Did the Prince, later King Edward VII, recall the day when, a shade over forty years later in March, 1909 he journeyed from Biarritz to Pau, France, to witness two flights by Wilbur Wright?) In truth, Stringfellow is reported to have been in a state of euphoria throughout the exhibition, which represented the high point of his life. "Uncle John was in his element," wrote his niece. He was almost sixty-nine, and the builder of the first successful powered model airplane had at last achieved the recognition that was his due. His name alone was singled out for mention in newspaper accounts, and when the artist for the *Illustrated Times* sketched the exhibit he portrayed him in the foreground, energetically expounding some article of aeronautical lore. Yet the artist was a somewhat better delineator of people than of models. In his drawing (Fig. 200) may be seen

Stringfellow's model triplane suspended from its wire in a place of honor, as well as the canvas that caught it at the end of each trip along the wire, but the proportions are quite wrong and there is no sign of the large elevator (unless it was removed during the exhibition because of its tendency to force the model upward against its supporting wire).

On a table in the center is an ornithopter, or at least an engine fitted with ornithopter wings, while a little farther to the right, Kaufmann's model rests on another table. In the lower right is a Stringfellow-Henson type of car or cabin, the steam coming from the smokestack toward the front indicating its engine is running. It has been suggested that this is the prizewinning engine, which is known to have been displayed in a car and fitted with propellers, but the car seems rather large for an apparatus of this size, and if the propellers shown adjacent to it are attached to it, at least one is shown facing the wrong way and both are of the four-bladed type that Henson and Stringfellow had long since seemingly abandoned. It may be that this car (which the artist portrays as a miniature of a two-story cabin) actually is the 40-pound boiler and firebox that formed Stringfellow's third exhibit. No doubt the artist made rough sketches at the Crystal Palace and finished his

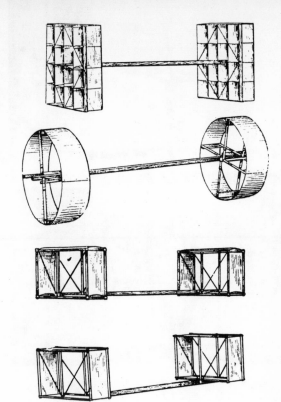

Fig. 212. Box kites built by Lawrence Hargrave in 1893. After this date, Hargrave turned his attention primarily to kites as the solution of the problem of heavier-than-air flight. Some of the first successful airplanes of the early 1900's were in effect powered combinations of Hargrave kites.

Warshaw Collection of Business Americana

Fig. 213. In 1893 Horatio Phillips built this steam-powered multiplane, with its many narrow wings resembling a venetian blind, and flew it in tethered flight in Great Britain. More than a decade later he constructed and flew with limited success full-size airplanes on this principle.

Warshaw Collection of Business Americana

drawing in leisure, which would possibly account for some seeming discrepancies in size and detail. Fittingly, in the very center foreground, a boy is placed holding the ubiquitous helicopter toy.

The 1868 triplane model was somewhat heavier than the 1848 model, its total weight being reported as just a little less than 12 pounds. The propellers were 21 inches in diameter, and the steam engine about 1/3 horsepower, driving the propellers at about 600 rpm. There were three rectangular wings, one above the other, each of different length, with the longest wing on top, giving a substantially greater total wing area than the 1848 model, but with approximately the same wingspan on the longest wing. The tail, which again was entirely an elevator, no rudder being provided, was quite similar to that of 1848, additional triangular supporting surfaces being added fore and aft to the center wing. The car was considerably modernized and less ornate than in the earlier model, a circumstance that has led the present writer to theorize that the older form, with its decorations representing a double-decked affair, shown in the lower right of the *Illustrated Times* drawing, may actually have been the original car of the 1844–1847 Henson model, regardless of what changes might have been made in its contents. It has been suggested that Stringfellow may have employed the rectangular wings because a time factor was involved in getting the exhibits ready for the Crystal Palace and they were easier to build than the tapered wings of 1848. This is somewhat confirmed by the fact that his son later reverted to wings of the earlier type in the models he built after his father's death. It may be noted at this point that the 1868 triplane does not seem to have been any great improvement on the 1848 model and in certain features appears definitely to have been inferior, possibly because of lack of time for certain desirable tests and refinements. The three wings appear to have provided added drag that was not seemingly compensated for by the greater overall lifting surface. In the main, therefore, it does not seem that the triplane can be considered a real improvement over the monoplane of 1868. Much has often been said in a complimentary way of Stringfellow's readiness to incorporate Wenham's theory of superimposed planes in the 1868 model; in truth Stringfellow might very well have produced a better model if he had not so readily adopted the superimposed-plane idea but instead had merely endeavored to refine his 1848 monoplane design. Withal, it can only be said that if Stringfellow had never built and flown his 1848 model, the triplane of 1868 would in itself constitute an achievement of primary importance in both real and model airplane history. However, it must be observed that in the main neither of the Stringfellows ever surpassed the results of 1848.

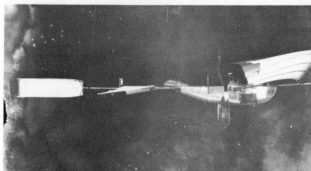

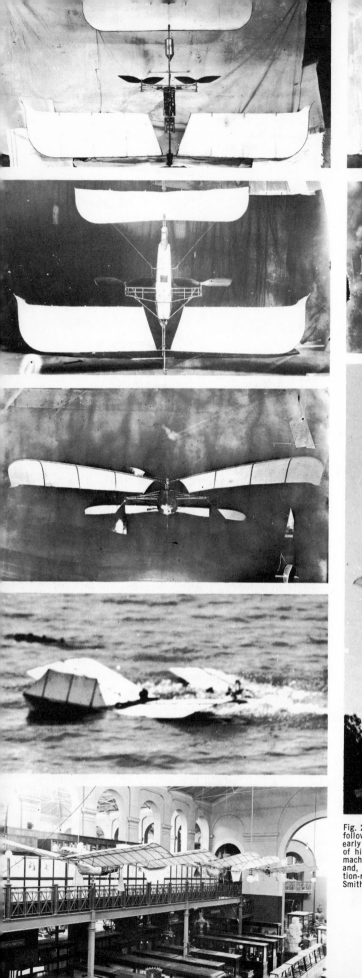

Fig. 214. The work of Professor Samuel P. Langley. The first two and the following three photographs respectively show views of two of Langley's early steam-powered models. The sixth picture shows the actual launching of his successful Aerodrome No. 5 on May 6, 1896. Next is shown the machine landing in the Potomac River after one of its successful flights and, finally, two of the steam-powered models and the internal-combustion-reciprocating-engine-powered model of 1901 on display at the Smithsonian Institution.

Fig. 215. Charles M. Manly (left) and Professor Samuel P. Langley on board the boat from which the Langley aerodromes were launched. Manly was largely responsible for the design and construction of the internal-combustion reciprocating engines used in the later model and in the full-size aerodrome.

The Smithsonian Institution

Fig. 216. The Langley internal-combustion reciprocating engine model aerodrome of 1901. This model, with a wingspan of a little over 12 feet, was designed as a ¼-size reduction of the full-size aerodrome. The model repeatedly flew successfully in 1901, both as a tandem monoplane, as pictured here, and as a tandem biplane.

The Smithsonian Institution

The manager of the Crystal Palace, no doubt with good and sufficient reasons where such an uncertain device as an aerial steam carriage (as Stringfellow still designated his model) with an alcohol lamp was concerned, declined to permit the model to be demonstrated in free flight during the exhibition. As a result the triplane was shown in movement only when suspended from its launching carriage during the show and was evidently demonstrated in this manner many times a day, so often in fact that the engine afterward required repairs. On these flights the model was observed to lift after it had gathered sufficient speed and at times raised the supporting wire itself for several feet. While this showed the model was capable of flight, such performance was not desirable under the circumstances, and this tendency evidently was controlled when desired, either by allowing the model to start along the wire before the propellers had reached full speed or, as suggested earlier in this account, perhaps by removing the elevator.

At the close of the exhibition, the model was taken into the basement of the Crystal Palace and an attempt made to test it in free flight, but the results were not satisfactory—no record seems to have been made of the length of flight or the length of run on the wire before the model triplane was released. The impression left by Frederick W. Brearey, who assisted in the experiment, is that there was not sufficient space available for a proper test or that the engine had become so worn by use during the exhibition as to impair its efficiency materially, or both. Somewhat later an attempt was made to fly the model outdoors at Chard, but each time it was started down the launching wire the passage of air blew out the flames on the wicks of the alcohol lamp so that nothing could be accomplished.

Stringfellow continued his aeronautical experiments almost up to his death on December 13, 1883. He used his prize of £100 to erect a special building more than 70 feet long for this purpose at Chard, but there is no report of his ever attempting to fly the model triplane, which was of course designed for use indoors, in this building. He does seem to have undertaken to rework the triplane engine and increase its power, but with not altogether satisfactory results. Toward the end of his life he was laying plans to build a full-size man-carrying airplane, but died before these plans could be carried very far along. The engine and boiler of the 1868 triplane model have been preserved, but the plane itself seems to have vanished. It is not at the Smithsonian Institution, as is sometimes reported, no doubt because the Smithsonian possesses a replica—seemingly not accurate in all details—of this model, which incorporates a few of Stringfellow's parts that were obtained from his son. What is at the Smithsonian is the original prizewinning engine and boiler of 1868. This was purchased for £25 from Stringfellow's son by Professor Samuel Pierpont Langley, the Secretary of the Smithsonian Institution, in 1889. It was bought by Langley at the time, not as a historic relic or exhibit for the Smithsonian, but for use in his own experiments in aeronautics, which he was about that time starting to press fervently. He found the engine unsuited for his purposes and built his own engines for his famous steam-powered model airplanes of the 1890's. However, as a result of this purchase, Stringfellow's award-winning engine now is one of the prize aeronautical displays at the Smithsonian Institution.

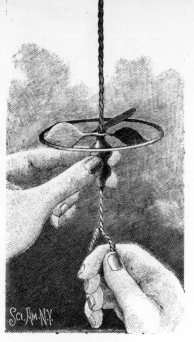

Fig. 217. A helicopter, or aerial top, of 1893, manufactured in the United States. The rimmed propeller, or "wheel," may or may not have been an American origination, but the use of the square twisted rod as a launching device does appear to have originated in the United States. This design gained little general acceptance, however.

The Scientific American

Fig. 218. Ladis Lewkowicz was one of the first real airplane pilots and also one of the first manufacturers of flying tops in the United States, producing, in 1908 and 1909, the Ladis Flying Cupid and the Ladis Flying Airship pictured here.

G. William Holland
"Playthings"

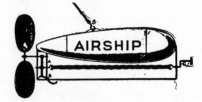

Stringfellow's son, F. J. Stringfellow, shared his father's interest and enthusiasm, and tried to carry on his work whenever time was available to him. He built several engines and two steam-powered model airplanes. The first and most important model was a biplane constructed in 1886. This had two tapered wings, similar in design to those of the 1848 model, the upper wing having a 10-foot span; the lower wing was 14 inches shorter, and the model was equipped with what might be called a typical Stringfellow tail. Unlike the 1848 and 1868 models, the 1886 machine was a tractor type, with the two propellers carried ahead of the wings on a special uncovered framework. Aside from this, the model is of historical importance as probably being the first biplane model, and the use of the two tapered wings likely represented to a certain extent at least the last best thinking of the senior Stringfellow on the subject of real and model airplane design. Unfortunately, the model was never tested in free flight owing to lack of suitable indoor space. Subsequently F. J. Stringfellow also built a monoplane model similar to the 1848 model, or perhaps it is more correct to say he rebuilt the 1848 model with a more powerful engine

and larger boiler, for he used the same wings. Little is known concerning the results achieved with this model, and it seems likely that lack of suitable space for testing indoors in free flight inhibited this as it had the biplane. Presumably the building that his father had erected specifically for flying tests no longer was available to him. It is evident that he was greatly hindered in his work by lack of time and funds, but he lived until August 25, 1905, long enough to witness the birth of the modern air age and to be called upon to send much of his father's surviving material, which by then had assumed tremendous historical importance, back to London for exhibition, along with his own biplane.

AFTER THE STRINGFELLOWS

It is with reluctance that one leaves the Stringfellows to record some highlights of model aeronautical development that followed the Exhibition of 1868, for it is impossible to escape the conclusion that John Stringfellow was the towering giant of early model airplane development and that not until Hargrave and Langley, and particularly the

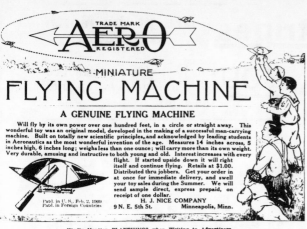
Fig. 219. One of the first flying model airplanes manufactured in the United States was the rubber-powered Aero Miniature Flying Machine, introduced in 1909 by the H. J. Nice Company. It remained a popular seller for some years thereafter.
"Playthings"

Fig. 220. The Lee Toy Aeroplane, a rubber-powered model more closely resembling our conception of an airplane than the model shown in Fig. 219, also reached the market in 1909 but appears to have been manufactured only for two or three years. It was made in the home town of the Wright brothers, Dayton, Ohio.
"Playthings"

latter, does anyone of even comparable import arise. Yet it must be admitted that some portion of this feeling is due to the care and detail with which Stringfellow's work has been recorded by Brearey, F. J. Stringfellow, Davy, and others. However, if any extenuation of enthusiasm for Stringfellow seems called for, it need only be pointed out that his work proceeded on the major lines along which the real airplane did develop, whereas many of the others in the years that followed continued to devote themselves to the helicopter or ornithopter, to some extent at least because these gave the greatest success in the creation of small flying models.

Aeronautical interest had always been strong in France, and it increased greatly following the London Exhibition of 1868 and particularly after the Franco-Prussian War, wherein the balloon played so stirring and important a role in bringing men and messages out of besieged Paris from September, 1870, to January, 1871. French enthusiasm for aviation in the ensuing years was based to a large extent on the belief that the balloon had saved the honor of France by carrying Premier Léon Gambetta from Paris to where he could set up a free government and raise new armies. Prior to the war, largely through the personal interest of Napoleon III, the French had perfected the mitrailleuse, one of the first practical machine guns, but it was regarded as so secret a weapon that many of the French gunners themselves were not properly instructed in its use, although the Prussians, as it proved, were well informed of it by their spies. When the use of the mitrailleuse became widely known (the mitrailleuse was not, of course, by any means the first conception of the machine gun), inventors tried to adapt the idea to flying-machine propulsion. Even while the war was being waged, Gustave Trouvé

successfully flew a model ornithopter about two hundred feet, powered by means of exploding a series of cartridges in rotation.

The name of Alphonse Pénaud figures importantly in even the most sketchy accounts of model aeronautical progress in this period, and anyone who attempts to investigate anew is of necessity startled by the mass of conflicting and even often contradictory dates and claims reported and the relative paucity of hard facts. Pénaud evidently was born in 1850 and died in 1880 and, during the 1870's, experimented with, built, and flew a number of rubber-powered model heavier-than-air flying machines, including airplanes, helicopters, and ornithopters. What appears to be the most reliable information is that in 1871 he built and flew his model airplane, or his first model airplane, a single pusher-propeller monoplane type, which he called a "planophore"; that in 1872 he produced and flew a model ornithopter; that between 1870 and 1874 he built and flew various model helicopters, one of which hovered for a startlingly long twenty-six seconds. Pénaud often is held up to view as a sort of boy model builder who constructed the first rubber-powered model airplane. Actually, he was twenty-one at the time he built his planophore, and he was far from the first to use rubber for powering a model airplane, or even the first to use it stretched in a straight line between the propeller and a retaining hook as in modern practice. In the same year that Pénaud constructed his planophore, another Frenchman, Jobert, also was building models involving a similar use of rubber, and it would appear evident that the idea was by then a fairly well-known one whose origins are presently lost somewhere in the mists of aviation history.

Accounts vary as to the length of flight and

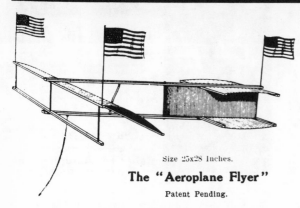
Fig. 221. The Aeroplane Flyer also appeared on the market in 1909. It was not a powered model airplane, however, but a flag-bedecked glider with 25-inch wingspan, and evidently intended to be flown on a line.

"Playthings"

the speed attained by Pénaud with his planophore. The best performance recorded is 60 meters, or approximately 200 feet, in 13 seconds; other accounts say its best flight was about two-thirds that distance. Pictorial representations of the model (models?) or replicas also differ as to whether or not the planophore was equipped with a vertical fin on the tail. The earliest illustrations indicate no fin on the tail either of the planophore or Pénaud's ornithopter, which would seem decisive. What Pénaud did achieve—and this and not the supposed first use of rubber is his real contribution—was a measure of inherent stability, attained by means of dihedral wings and by separating the two main surfaces, wing and tail, by a substantial distance.

This principle was not understood by many early designers and experimenters, including Henson and Stringfellow, and may in fact not have been understood by Pénaud himself, for when he came to attempt to design a steam-powered full-size airplane with Gauchot in 1876 they reverted to an almost Stringfellow-type tapered wing with a tiny elevator placed immediately behind the wing, but with a rudder. Within Pénaud's lifetime, by 1879 at the latest, his countryman, Pichancourt, had begun the manufacture of very creditable toy or model rubber-powered ornithopters in Paris, thus inaugurating the model airplane business as distinguished from the long-established fabrication of helicopters. Instead of being hailed as the pioneer

Fig. 222. In 1911 the Goff Aeroplane Company of Chicago advertised themselves as the largest and oldest manufacturers in the United States, and offered a 28-inch-wingspan rubber-powered Blériot model for $5.00. They were also agents for Nomie engines, which could be operated on compressed air, carbonic acid gas, or steam.

New York Public Library

Fig. 223. Rubber-powered flying model airplanes, available both as kits and in built-up form, from the 1912 catalog of the White Aeroplane Company. The models are, respectively, the Langley aerodrome, Blériot monoplane, Curtiss hydroaeroplane, Antoinette monoplane, two views of the Wright biplane, and two views of the Nieuport monoplane.

Howard G. McEntee; G. William Holland photographs

Fig. 224. A 1911 advertisement of the White Aeroplane Company, using the then popular designation "Knocked Down" to indicate a model supplied in the form of a kit.

New York Public Library

Fig. 225. Early model airplane catalogs. Shown here are a White catalog of 1912; Ideal, 1919; Ritchie-Wertz, 1919 and 1920; Wading River, 1922; and U.S. Model Aircraft Corporation, 1929. The last two were, in turn, successors to White.

Howard G. McEntee and Charles Hampson Grant;
G. William Holland photograph

of what was to become a great industry, Pichancourt has at times, not unpredictably, been criticized by model airplane enthusiasts for being interested only in the commercial, rather than scientific or hobby, aspects of models. Early French manufacturers of helicopters whose names have been preserved are Rabiot and Journet, the latter seemingly having invented or reinvented the helicopter in the form of butterflies which he called the *spiralifères,* and which were later known in English as "paper highflyers" or, simply, as "flying butterflies." They were still found in American toy dealers' catalogs in the years immediately preceding World War I and in British model aircraft catalogs as late as 1928. Journet brought an action against Rabiot and other French toymakers who he claimed were infringing on his patent, and was sustained by the Civil Tribunal.* However, the toy or close variations of it were evidently continued in production by others, or else Journet assigned his rights, for in the 1880's a leading manufacturer of these flying toys was Dandrieaux, who was also keenly interested in full-sized aeronautics. Professor Langley brought back quite a quantity of Dandrieaux's "flying butterflies" from Europe. They are powered by strands of rubber; it is not certain if Journet's original models were of this type or were similar to the conventional cord-operated helicopter toys.

MODELS ON BOTH SIDES OF THE ATLANTIC

In 1875 Thomas Moy and R. E. Shill attempted to demonstrate a rather large steam-powered model airplane—its weight is given as from 120 to 150 pounds—in London. The model was tethered to a center post and ran on a board track, from which it succeeded in lifting itself for a few inches, despite the fact that it obviously was grossly underpowered with only a three-horsepower engine. Moy was a considerable student of flight, but placed himself in a somewhat ludicrous light by claiming that his experiment had been the first successful demonstration of the ability to fly by means of steam power, although most would consider the relative success of his machine, despite its far greater weight, far inferior to what Stringfellow had accomplished in 1848. Four years after his steam model, Moy built a similar but smaller rubber-powered model.

The helicopter still attracted the attention of

many inventors. In 1876, in the United States, W. J. Lewis was trying to promote the building of a full-size machine that in many ways curiously resembled a modern helicopter. It combined a fuselage with twin upright propellers at each end, a cabin, supporting wings, and additional propellers at the rear for forward propulsion. Lewis stated that he had previously successfully flown a model of this design, and it appears probable that he had indeed flown some kind of steam-powered model; not surprisingly, nothing ever came of his plans for a full-size machine that he claimed would be capable of flying as far as from New York to Philadelphia and attaining a speed of 100 miles per hour. Little known during his lifetime and now largely forgotten, Lewis appears to have been not without merit as an aeronautical engineer.

In 1877 E. Dieuaide, a French patent attorney, chronicler of aviation history. active in French aeronautical circles, and a great admirer of Thomas A. Edison, made a model steam helicopter. Sometime around this period occurred the somewhat dubious story of Edison's involvement with heavier-than-air flying machines. According to a story Edison supposedly related some years later, James Gordon Bennett the younger, the publisher of the *New York Herald,* gave Edison a thousand dollars to devote to experiments in heavier-than-air flight, and Edison built a model helicopter operated by an internal-combustion reciprocating engine using stock ticker paper impregnated with guncotton and carried through the cylinder of the engine in order to obtain successive explosions. Edison supposedly finally gave Bennett the world-shaking information that when an engine could be developed with sufficient power-to-weight ratio, the helicopter would be a success. The story does not stand up on several grounds. Bennett indisputably was interested in aviation and later gave prizes for balloon and airplane races. He financed Stanley's expedition to Africa to try to find Livingstone, and the De Long polar expedition. For his part he must have been aware that a thousand dollars would not begin to buy the perfection of heavier-than-air flight, and he was well able, if he were interested in such a project, to expend many, many thousands. Edison, for his part, had just worked out the phonograph and was deeply absorbed in developing his electric light at this time; it is hardly creditable that he would have been induced to turn his attention to aeronautics for the sake of a thousand dollars. (Sir Hiram Maxim was to spend over $200,000 on his similar quest in the 1890's.) At best Edison may have agreed to attempt to build a working model for this price for some inventor in whom Bennett had

---

*The information concerning this matter is found in an undated clipping from an English newspaper that at some time was attached to Cayley's 1855 drawing of the helicopter in the British Patent Office Library and as a result is reproduced, quite incidentally, in C. H. Gibbs-Smith's *Sir George Cayley's Aernonautics 1796-1855.*

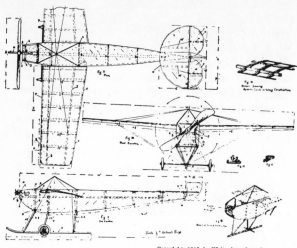

Fig. 226. An example of an early commercial plan sheet for constructing a model airplane, in this case the plans of the White Aeroplane Company for their model Nieuport monoplane.

Howard G. McEntee; G. William Holland photograph

Copyright, 1912, by White Aeroplane Co.

Fig. 227. Making real and model airplanes frequently sometimes went hand in hand in the early days of the hobby. In 1911, H. G. Carter, a pioneer British pilot, and his son offered to sell a kit for building a rubber-powered Blériot model for $2 or a full-size Blériot for $500 without engine or propeller.

"Toys and Novelties"

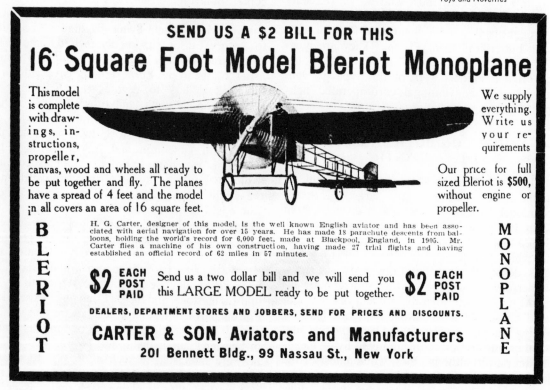
taken an interest. More likely, at the time Lewis received publicity on his endeavors there was considerable interest aroused in flying machines and much loose talk to the effect that Edison would build or was actually building such a machine, and Edison may even have let drop something to this effect himself. Either Dieuaide or Dr. Hureau de Villeneuve, whose archives Dieuaide credited as the source of his pictorial material, designed and drew up out of his own head a giant transport plane that forms the final figure on an illustrated historical table of aviation that Dieuaide published in Paris in 1880, captioning it as Edison's great projected flying ship and, by implication, the realized airplane. The craft reveals no means of propulsion unless it was intended to be a huge six-

Fig. 228. As the achievements of the real airplanes made headlines, there arose a demand for anything that would fly. The Empire helicopter of 1909 (left) and a number of similar products were not dissimilar to the helicopters of the nineteenth century. At the right, boxed, is shown another variety, the Hi-Flyer with a formed wire handle to pull the cord.

"Playthings"

winged ornithopter. In later years Edison evidently tacitly accepted responsibility for the design, or at least fluffed off direct questions with statements to the effect that he had not undertaken the actual construction of an airplane. The important point is not that Dieuaide's dream has at times found a serious place in aviation history as Edison's airplane but that Dieuaide is a major source for much other aeronautical model lore, including information on Pénaud's models. Taking into consideration the part he played in the Edison matter, any of his material must be regarded with considerable care before it is accepted.

Dr. Hureau de Villeneuve was himself an indefatigable builder of model ornithopters, building in all some 300 models over a period of about a quarter of a century, evidently starting in the early 1870's; his attic was said to resemble a veritable aviary of mechanical birds. One of his first models, if not his first, was a rubber-powered ornithopter he built in 1872, the same year as Pénaud. From such models he finally worked up to a man-carrying steam-driven ornithopter of 50-foot wingspan. By means of a flexible hose, he connected its engine to a boiler located on the ground, and bravely took off in it, whereupon it flew so successfully that he became afraid he would fly beyond the reach of the hose and shut off the steam, causing the ornithopter to fall. In the mid-1890's he was still hopefully awaiting the perfection of a light enough power plant to be carried entirely in his craft, so that he could safely fly it. A somewhat different means of escaping from the necessity of carrying a boiler in an aircraft was employed in a steam-powered model helicopter built by an Italian, Professor Forlanini, in 1878. The boiler was built in the form of a globe hanging from the machine, and steam was generated by heating the

water-filled globe over a fire on the ground. With this apparatus, which weighed 77 pounds, Forlanini was able to attain flights of up to 20 seconds duration and heights of up to 42 feet. In the same year Castel, a Frenchman, built a compressed air-powered model helicopter with no less than eight propellers. It appears that this model also was powered, via a flexibe hose, from a source outside the aircraft itself.

A few other experimenters deserve mention. In 1879 Victor Tatin constructed a twin-tractor model monoplane with about a 4-foot wingspan powered by compressed air stored under pressure in a cylinder that formed the fuselage. This French model frequently has been heralded in historical sketches of model aviation as the first compressed-air-powered model, as indeed it may have been in terms of a model carrying its own tank of air, as somewhat later became a not uncommon means of powering model airplanes. The implication usually is that the Tatin model, like its successors in the early 1900's (and even into the 1930's), was a free-flight machine, but actually it was flown only when tethered to a center post, under which conditions it rose 5 or 6 feet and flew for 50 or 60 feet until the supply of compressed air was exhausted. The Tatin craft had a Stringfellow-type tail and evidently no rudder, nor did it, of course, require one under the conditions of tethered flight. In 1893 Horatio Phillips of England built a single-pusher-propeller model of great size with what are best described as Venetian-blind wings—there were 20 narrow, curved slat-like rings—which also was flown tethered and lifted itself a few feet in the air. In the early 1900's, both Tatin and Phillips attempted to build and fly full-sized airplanes, but with unsatisfactory results.

In 1893, after considerable experimentation

Fig. 229. The hand-propelled helicopter was probably known much earlier, but attained tremendous popularity around 1907–1912. At the left are pictured "Skidoo Butterflies," manufactured by E. B. Estes and Sons. At the right is a brand of hand-propelled helicopter unabashedly designated the "Air-O-Plane."

"Playthings"

with models, Sir Hiram Maxim built a giant 3½-ton airplane that would carry a crew of three and was powered by two steam engines developing a total of 350 horsepower. However, actual flight controls were never developed. The airplane flew in its first test, but no one dared try to take the plane up any substantial distance because of the lack of control, and owing to the same lack of control it was soon blown over on its side. Sir Hiram then constructed a special railroad track for testing, with guardrails that would allow the plane to lift a little but not to climb more than a short distance above the ground. On the second test, in 1894, the tremendously powerful machine exerted so much force in attempting to climb free that it broke the guardrails and started to go up; but, aware of the plane's lack of suitable controls for free flight, Maxim killed the engines.

Nineteenth-century interest in the development of the airplane was worldwide. An indefatigable experimenter was Lawrence Hargrave of Sydney, Australia. Beginning in the 1870's, Hargrave built numerous successful flying model airplanes—monoplanes, biplanes, triplanes, and multiplanes—powered mostly by rubber but sometimes with compressed-air engines. Hargrave demonstrated his models in public and scientifically reported the results of his experiments to the Royal Society of New South Wales, although he once remarked that "the people of Sydney who can speak of my work without a smile are very scarce." Nevertheless, as early as the winter of 1888–1889, when W. Edmunds Spon,* later one of the founders of *The Modelmaker,* visited Sydney, he found a number of cases filled with Hargrave's models proudly displayed in the local museum. About this same time

Hargrave appears to have turned his attention to ornithopters, and is reported to have built and flown no less than seventeen such beating-wing models. In 1893 he attended and read a paper at the First American Conference of Aerial Navigation at Chicago. It was during this visit to the United States that he presented the Smithsonian Institution with the specimen of one of his compressed-air-driven ornithopter models that is still preserved there. Upon his return to Australia he perfected what was known as the Hargrave box kite, destined to be widely used for weather observations—in the later 1890's the United States Weather Bureau maintained sixteen stations throughout the country where regular meteorological observations were made by sending aloft instruments in Hargrave kites—and in larger versions of which Hargrave himself and subsequently others made actual ascensions. By the close of the 1890's Hargrave appears to have become convinced, through the great feats attained with his kites, that the kite rather than the airplane would prove the eventual solution to the problem of aerial navigation. In 1906, in France, Alberto Santos-Dumont, the Brazilian who had already achieved international fame through his airship flights, put a 50-horsepower engine into what was essentially a construction of Hargrave box kites, and flew it as what many consider the first substantially successful airplane in Europe, although his best flight was only about 700 feet.†

---

*W. Edmunds Spon was related to the family of London publishers, E. and F. N. Spon, Ltd., and, with William Chamberlain, later founded the house of Spon and Chamberlain, New York. Spon and Chamberlain were, accordingly, the American publishers of V. E. Johnson's 1910 classic on model airplanes. They also published plans for the prizewinning model airplane the Percy Pierce Flyer, and other plans suitable for model airplane builders. They also produced construction kits for the Pierce plane, as well as at least two other models around the years 1911—1914. The Pierce kit contained plans, but the other two were furnished without drawings!

†Ader flew 50 meters in 1890, made flights of up to 100 meters in 1891, and there are those who believe an excellent case can be made for his having been airborne for 300 meters in 1897. T. Vuia made the first airplane flight in France, if the machines of Clément Ader are excepted from consideration, flying 24 meters (about 80 feet) on August 19, 1906, using carbonic acid fuel. On November 12, 1906, Santos-Dumont made his memorable flight of 220 meters (about 700 feet) in 21½ seconds. By comparison, the Wright brothers had made flights of over 20 miles and of over a half-hour duration by this time. Those interested in early European airplane flights also are directed to the flights or hops made by Karl Jatho in Germany in 1903, and to the tethered flights made in Denmark in 1906 by J. C. H. Ellehammer, followed by free flights in 1907. Before attempting free flights, Ellehammer adapted model airplane practice to his full-sized airplane. He had evidently previously done considerable experimentation with tethered model airplanes, but unfortunately little information is available.

Fig. 230. The big city Buffalo Pitts Company of Buffalo, New York, pictured their Hi-Flyer (see Fig. 228) helicopter zooming over New York's famous Flatiron Building, while in the same year of 1911, the Hampden Toy Company portrayed their Aeroflyer helicopter as flying over the steeple of a rural New England church.

"Playthings"

Another interesting path of investigation as to the effect models had on manned flight may be found in the glider experiments of Octave Chanute and his assistant, Augustus M. Herring, in the United States in the 1890's. Chanute's work is particularly important in connection with models for several reasons; he was a patron of the Wright brothers, and his preliminary work with models may well have rendered such experimenting with miniatures unnecessary on their part; the Chanute models and the resulting full-size Chanute gliders led to what may have been the first manned power-airplane flight in the United States, on the part of Herring; and Herring, who will reappear in this chronicle later, when model airplane engines are discussed, built one of the first working model internal-combustion reciprocating model airplane engines. Chanute was a civil engineer, noted for his achievements in bridge building, and made use of his knowledge of bridge trusses in the bracing and staying of multiple-wing gliders, mostly biplanes. His work to some extent was also indebted to the Hargrave box kite. Chanute first built and flew a number of model gliders and then built remarkably successful full-size gliders that, mainly piloted by his assistants, including Herring, made some 2,000 flights, starting in 1896. In 1898 Herring felt that the glider was ready to be flown as a power plane

with an engine—some feel that it was at this point and on this issue that Chanute and Herring came to a parting of the ways—and built a biplane with a powerful compressed-air engine. This adaptation from model airplane practice was, of course, never intended to be capable of flights of more than a few seconds (in fact many airplane flights of the early 1900's were measured in terms of only a few seconds), and Herring did claim to have flown the machine for a short distance. If true, this claim would make Herring the first man to have made a flight in a powered airplane in the United States, and of course the claim has been hotly disputed by proponents of the Wrights. In 1909, when Herring entered into partnership with Glenn H. Curtiss in the manufacture of airplanes, the craft was named the Herring-Curtiss Aeroplane, and it was advertised that Herring had "the distinction of being the first human being to navigate in the air in a self-propelled heavier-than-air machine."

Two points might well be made here. The first is that, though it may seem strange today, by the end of the nineteenth century it was very widely felt that the problem of heavier-than-air flight had been successfully solved at last through the efforts and experiments of Hargrave, Maxim, and Langley, particularly the latter. The second is that, although we generally mark the beginning of the

Fig. 231. The Carter Manufacturing Company of St. Louis, Missouri, evidently had no connection with the firm of Carter and Son of New York (see Fig. 227), but their lower-priced models, introduced in 1910, despite a certain inaccuracy in nomenclature, sold in large quantities. The Aeroplane Model Co. suggested (1911) that any boy or man buying and studying their Bleriot Monoplane Flier might become a wealthy airplane inventor.

"Playthings"

airplane age from 1903, when Langley tried his full-size machine and the Wrights made their first flights, the public at large had little more knowledge or consciousness of the airplane until around 1907 to 1909 than they had had in 1899. An appreciation of these two facts will help to make clear much that otherwise may today appear inexplicable in connection both with real and model airplane history.

LANGLEY'S TRIUMPH

Starting before 1887, when he was a professor of physics at the Western University of Pennsylvania and director of the Allegheny Observatory, Samuel Pierpont Langley—whom many thoughtful people credit as the chief inventor of the airplane—deliberately set out in a scientific way to solve the problem of heavier-than-air flight and eventually to build a man-carrying airplane. Langley, as others had before him, built a test rig for airplanes—that is to say, for lifting surfaces, in the terminology of that day. He soon proved to his own satisfaction that much of the existing and accepted scientific dicta on the amount of energy required for heavier-than-air flight was erroneous and that if an airfoil were moved through the air rapidly enough it was possible to sustain it with

a fraction of the power that hitherto had been accepted as necessary for a given weight. Coming to the Smithsonian Institution as secretary in 1887, Langley continued his aeronautical experiments in Washington. He set before himself the task of first building models, and did build over 300 flying model airplanes—a prime example of how in aviation modelmaking preceded the real thing—some using rubber power and others compressed-air engines. From the start Langley believed that Henson and Stringfellow had been on the right track, and concentrated his endeavors on propeller-driven machines with fixed wings, not on helicopters or ornithopters. From these experiments with small models he evolved what was to be substantially the form of his airplanes, or aerodromes (air runners) as he called them, tandem monoplanes, each with two wings placed one behind the other. Starting in 1891, he began the construction of a series of models with a wingspan of slightly less than 14 feet, which he envisaged as quarter-size models of the machine that would subsequently carry a human pilot.

For the powering of these model aerodromes Langley turned to steam power, and of course encountered all the problems of building a satisfactory light steam engine and boiler that had confronted Stringfellow and others. It has already

Fig. 232. Edward Imeson Horsman (left) first brushed shoulders with the model airplane when Gustave Whitehead (right) worked for him in the 1890's. Horsman played a leading, if not the leading role, in popularizing first kites, and then, in the period around 1908–1912, model airplanes and other flying devices to the trade. At the lower left is pictured one of Whitehead's experimental model airplanes of the 1890's.

G. William Holland
New York Public Library

Fig. 233. Presumably this painting portrays a French boy, a French beach, and a French model airplane. E. I. Horsman used the picture in 1910 to promote the sale of a complete line of French-made rubber-powered model airplanes for which he was the American distributor.

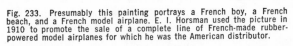

"Playthings"

been related how Langley purchased Stringfellow's prizewinning engine and boiler of 1868 from the latter's son but found it unsuitable for his purposes. The design of the aerodrome itself already had been perfected with the aid of smaller models; what remained was the need for a proper engine. At times Langley experimented with compressed air, gas, carbonic acid, electricity, and other means of power, but concluded as a result of his experiments that the answer could still best be found in steam power. With infinite patience and craftsmanship he designed and built a steam engine and flash boiler that was in itself the mechanical marvel of the age. The rig delivered 1 to 1½ horsepower and weighed less than half as much as Stringfellow's prize engine. (It must be remembered that Stringfellow had used much larger and heavier engines in his model airplanes and at the same time that the airplanes themselves had weighed considerably less than Langley's model aerodromes, which tipped the scale at 30 pounds.) The problem of launching came up, of course, and Langley, resolved this by building a catapult launching device on top of what has often been described as a houseboat, as if it were some sort of opulent pleasure palace but which was actually an old scow with a shedlike structure thrown up on it and on top of which was the launching platform. Eventually this elaborate method of launching was to prove the cause of all Langley's troubles, but in the beginning it seemed to serve its purpose well. The aerodromes had dihedral wings and a tail with both horizontal and vertical surfaces, and a contemporary account refers to this as the rudder, and states that by its means the plane could be steered in four directions: up or down, left or right, all "automatically." By this was no doubt meant that the tail could be adjusted prior to flight to steer the plane as desired, and in practice it was set to steer the plane in a giant and rather precise circle around some complicated arms of land along the Potomac River at Quantico, Virginia, so that the model always remained over water on its course.

On May 6, 1896, Professor Langley successfully flew his model aerodrome for over 3,000 feet at a speed of 20 to 25 miles an hour over the Potomac River. It landed safely in the river when its fuel and water supply gave out. The test was immediately repeated, and again the craft flew about 3,200 feet before coming down for a safe landing. Actually, the aerodrome used in this flight was the machine known as No. 5, the fifth basic machine in a series that had been started in 1891, although some of them had been modified considerably from their original construction. Aerodrome

No. 1, built in 1891, was unsuccessful, and was followed by three more models between 1891 and 1894, none of which achieved the desired results. Aerodrome No. 5 was built in 1894 and also failed to fly on its first try. Following certain improvements, however, Aerodrome No. 5 did make a flight of six or seven seconds' duration in 1894.

No further attempts at flight were made until 1896, Langley in the meantime further refining the engine and boiler, thereby producing about the only thing that Rudyard Kipling seems to have found admirable during his stay in the United States in the 1890's. A duplicate model No. 5 was built and also proved unsuccessful. However, on May 6, 1896, the original Aerodrome No. 5, fitted with the improved power plant, made the two successful flights mentioned above. Any contemporary accounts of model airplane flights are scarce, and in view of the historic importance of the events of May 6, 1896, it is worth quoting Professor Langley's own account of his experiences and reactions:

"I had journeyed, perhaps for the twentieth time," he said, "to the distant river station, and recommenced the weary routine of another launch, with very moderate expectation indeed; and when, on that, to me, memorable afternoon the signal was given and the aerodrome sprang into the air, I watched if from the shore with hardly a hope that the long series of accidents had come to a close. And yet it had, and for the first time the aerodrome swept continuously through the air like a living thing, and as second after second passed on the face of the stop-watch, until a minute had gone by, and still it flew on, and as I heard the cheering of the few spectators, I felt that something had been accomplished at last; for never in any part of the world, or in any period, had any machine of man's construction sustained itself in the air before for even half of this brief time. Still the aerodrome went on in a rising course until, at the end of a minute and a half (for which time only was it provided with fuel and water), it had accomplished a little over half a mile, and now it settled, rather than fell, into the river, with a gentle descent. It was immediately taken out and flown again with equal success, nor was there anything to indicate that it might not have flown indefinitely, except for the limit put upon it."

On November 28, 1896, a flight of over 4,200 feet was made at 30 miles an hour by Aerodrome No. 6. This was a machine generally similar to No. 5, but with further slight improvements in the engine, propellers (the Langley models had two propellers, located between the two wings), and wings. After this further success, Langley did nothing materially new for a while; his work was of course dependent upon the authorization of the government. However, when the Spanish-American War was declared in 1898, the possible military use of the aerodrome was brought to the attention of the government, and the Department of War granted Langley $50,000 to continue his experiments and to construct a full-sized aerodrome. Langley sought an assistant, and at the recommendation of Dr. R. H. Thompson of Sibley College of Cornell University, engaged Charles M. Manly, one of his students. Langley planned to power the full-sized aerodrome with an internal-combustion reciprocating engine, which he would have made on the outside, while the remainder of the plane would be built by Langley himself and Manly. As it turned out, Manly proved to be a genius at engine design and construction, and when the outside contractors failed to deliver an engine that was up to the specifications stipulated, took over this end of the work himself. It took some five years to develop the project to its desired goal, an aerodrome with a wingspan of 48 feet, 5 inches, and 52 feet, 5 inches in length and calculated to weigh about 750 pounds with the pilot, who would be Manly. In the course of developing the full-size aerodrome, Langley constructed and flew one more model, a one-quarter-size miniature of the proposed plane, powered by a miniature gasoline engine built by Manly. This model was successfully flown on June 18, 1901. This is accounted by many the first airplane flight of any kind using an internal-combustion reciprocating engine. Information on the model and on the flight or flights made with it appears rather sparse. The model evidently weighed about 58

pounds, and the model radial engine developed about 3 1/5 horsepower.

Curiously, Langley's own full-sized aerodrome of 1903 was not the first attempt to make use of the results of Langley's experiments with models in the building of a man-carrying airplane. In 1901 an Austrian, Wilhelm Kress, completed a twin-propeller seaplane based on Langley practice but with three instead of only two tandem wings and powered by a heavy Mercedes internal-combustion reciprocating engine. Because of poor handling, this plane capsized in the water before an attempt could be made to take off.

Finally on October 7, 1903, the great man-carrying aerodrome was ready for flight and was mounted on a rebuilt launching catapult on the boat. Present were officials of the Smithsonian, observers from the United States Army, reporters and photographers, and the merely curious. The plane was launched, but a guy post stuck in its socket on the carriage and was not released in time and the aerodrome fell into the river, Manly emerging unhurt. The aerodrome was immediately rebuilt and launched again on December 8, 1903. Again the try went wrong, although the front wing took to the air and started to lift the craft skyward, but this time the rear wing caught in something and was damaged and the plane again went into the Potomac River, with Manly again fortunately escaping injury. It was the end of Langley's aerodrome experiments. Although the official report of the military observers clearly specified that the fault was in the launching gear, the government, at peace, declined to appropriate funds for rebuilding the plane and for further experiment. Langley died in 1906, his passing un-

Fig. 234. Three examples of French rubber-powered model airplanes of 1910 sold under the Lux trademark. Note that all models have the rudder located below the tail plane. This appears to have been the line that E. I. Horseman began to import and distribute in the United States in 1910.

G. William Holland

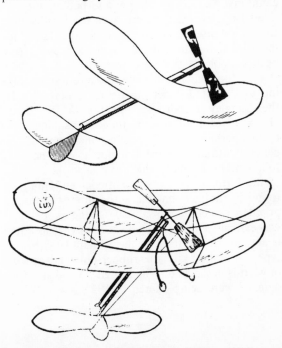

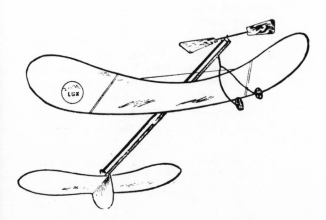

KITES.

FLYING ARTICLES AND FLYING PRICES.

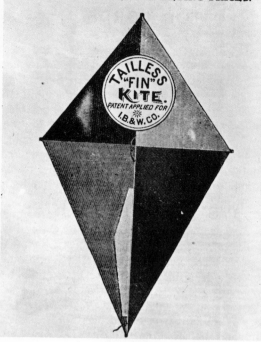

Fig. 235. The Ives, Blakeslee and Williams Company's tailless "fin" kite of the early 1890's. In itself an important development in heavier-than-air models, it is also noteworthy as a product of the most famous and important of all toy and model manufacturers.

G. William Holland

doubtedly hastened by the disappointment, although it should be pointed out that his lasting fame rests not alone on his aeronautical experiments but also on many other highly important and successful scientific achievements.

Poor Langley! In the years after the event, few doubted that he had produced a machine that, except for the accidents in launching, would have proved a complete success. Later the matter became involved in controversy and patent suits. At times Langley, Manley, and even the Smithsonian Institution itself were denounced, the latter for their insistence that the aerodrome would have been capable of sustained free flight. The whole story is too long and in some measure too unedifying to be paraded here in detail. Today, finally, the Langley aerodrome and the Wright Kitty Hawk Flyer both rest in the Smithsonian. Yet oddly, perhaps one of the best measures of the general attitude toward Langley in the decades following his attempt, which were also the decades of the birth of the hobby of model airplaning, is found in the fact that the aerodrome was long a popular prototype for a scale flying model and was evidently regarded by most hobbyists as equal if not superior in fame to the Wright 1903 prototype. Complete kits for rubber-powered models of what is designated "The Langley Tandem Monoplane" were being offered in 1911 by the White

THE STORY OF THE MODEL AIRPLANE

Aeroplane Company and were still being manufactured in the 1920's by the successor, the Wading River Manufacturing Company. It was not until many years later that any model airplane company offered any sort of model of the Kitty Hawk Flyer,* although models of later Wright prototypes were standard from about 1911 on. A number of individual airplane model builders also constructed Langley models; it was for years as much a recognized and accepted prototype as a Blériot or a Curtiss or any other early airplane.

Just nine days after Langley's second attempt to launch the full-size aerodrome, the Wright brothers made their first flight at Kitty Hawk, North Carolina, and, in retrospect, the airplane age had begun, as we now account it. With it also had begun the great model airplane hobby age.

THE MODEL AIRPLANE HOBBY

The years following the Wright brothers' first flight, which also were years of important development in lighter-than-air craft, were exciting and eventful years for toy and model manufacturers, although, as has been seen, aeronautical toys such as helicopters, flying butterflies, and ornithopters had enjoyed a widespread popularity for many years previous. Nevertheless, all this was but as prelude to the demand that burst forth when the public began to be aware of the great developments that were taking place in the sky. From about 1906 on, there was an immense demand for anything in the line of a model or miniature or toy that would fly, or at least in some manner ascend in the air or provide some simulation of flight. In 1909, under the heading "Those Aeroplane Toys," the American toy trade journal *Playthings* commented on the situation, although strangely omitting any reference to the French, who then, as always, were one of the leaders in the production of aerial models and toys and whose creations in this field the same periodical had reported on at length less than a year earlier:

"The day of the reindeer is over! No longer will the small boy lie awake on Christmas eve listening for the tinkle of sleigh bells on Santa Claus' prancing steeds of the North. Rather will he hark to the whirr of the motor and the flapping of the wings of St. Nicholas' modern 'down-to-the-minute' aeroplane, if the promised output of the toymakers marks a trend in the old gift-giver's thought.

---

*The Wright plane of 1903 was not then or at any time since named or renamed the Kitty Hawk as has become widely believed in recent years. The Wrights called their early craft "flyers." The 1903 machine is therefore properly identified as the Kitty Hawk Flyer, or merely as the 1903 Flyer.

Fig. 236. Two 1911 advertisements, addressed to the trade, offering scale model rubber-powered flying model airplanes. The International Aeroplane Company advertisement, which appeared some months after that of the American Aeroplane Manufacturing Company suggests that they may merely have engaged in assembling the latter's models.

"Playthings"

"The persons who cater to young America must keep up to the minute if they hope to flourish, for the younger generation marches conscientiously apace with the times.

"All over the world the toy men are driving their designers to distraction by calling upon them for a nicely behaved, tame and housebroken airship. The retail dealers expect to be fairly swamped with agents explaining their samples of how to fly. In fact, the Christmas market is expected to be choked with flying machines.

"The toymakers are impartial in their selection of the aviator from whom best to get their ideas, and while the Wright brothers and Zeppelin are the most popular, Blériot and Latham have their craft copied freely. It is also safe to say that some of the designs in toy shapes never have graced the mind of any inventor.

"Though the aeroplane is an outdoor toy, several styles have been fitted up so as to fly about at the end of a cord, while there are captive balloons by the score.

"Germans, Swedes, English and Americans are bending every effort to outstrip one another in the race for popular favor. The latest novelty in the German output is a policeman seated astride an aeroplane, with one arm extended in the direction of a fleeing aeronaut whom he is supposed to be pursuing in a sort of 'stop-thief' manner. The other hand is clasping a sword and waving it aloft in a bloodthirsty motion."

If the bright promise of the first paragraph was not to be fulfilled for many years and perhaps has never been completely fulfilled—for ever since this initial craze model airplane popularity has had distinct periods of alternate booming and de-

Fig. 237. Hugo Rosenstein, one of the founders of the Ideal Aeroplane and Supply Company, is No. 7 in this group photograph of leading industry figures taken in 1917. Harry C. Ives of the Ives Manufacturing Company is No. 16.

G. William Holland

Fig. 238. The Ideal Aeroplane and Supply Company, founded in 1911, became one of the most important factors in the business until World War II. This is one of their first advertisements, from December, 1911. At that time, although offering a wide range of parts and materials, they appear to have had only two kits available, a Wright biplane and a Blériot.

New York Public Library

clining popularity in the toy trade, this account nevertheless accurately reflects the contemporary outlook during the first and possibly the greatest boom in model airplanes and other flying craft. As for the French, who supplied many of the models sold on the American market in this period —and, in fact, probably most of the models that were not of domestic production—the earliest account that could be discovered in the time available for gathering and preparing material for the present volume deals with the 1908 exhibition of toys held in Paris in the Tuileries Gardens where "All manner of flying craft were shown . . . single, double and triple aeroplanes, kites and other aeronautical devices, such as metal dirigible balloons which revolved about fixed posts, and others which were suspended by cords and described gradually decreasing circles by the force of their powerful propellers." Some of the airships are described as actually being lighter than air. The display of Monsieur Vallin was noteworthy for his "self-propelling kites," which seem to have been equipped with rubber power and were offered in three sizes, "the smallest being a child's toy, the second to be used for sporting purposes, while the largest was designed for meterological and photographic work."

The exhibit of aeroplanes by Monsieur Mangin, a noted Parisian inventor and designer of toys, was considered especially meritorious, and the operation of his models was described in detail: "These miniature aeroplanes operate in a very simple way. The mechanism, which may be operated by moving a small catch, is driven by the contraction of stretched rubber bands which are wound up about thirty turns by a small crank at the bow. This aeroplane is attached by means of a ring at the top to a long cord, the other end of which is fastened to a hook in the ceiling. The toy itself is set on the floor, and when the catch is freed the mechanism starts and the aeroplane, which is mounted on small wheels, first describes an uncertain course upon the floor, and then rises and circles far into the air."

No reference is made to free-flight model airplanes in connection with this exhibition. Very likely they were present by this date but escaped the observations of the reporter or, if he saw them, did not impress him as much as Monsieur Mangin's captive models. Within two years numerous French model airplanes were being sold in the United States and Great Britain, the Alma and Lux brands of these seemingly achieving very widespread popularity.

THE DAWN OF THE AMERICAN MODEL FLYING MACHINE

Evidently nothing is more fragile and ephemeral than yesterday's flying models themselves, and many of the early manufacturers left behind little tangible evidence of their existence, although in many cases they enjoyed tremendous success for a brief period. At times the product was made or distributed by firms already well established in the toy and model trade, but other companies came into being briefly and solely to manufacture miniature flying machines, and sank into oblivion almost without trace or memory once their brief hours of glory were ended. Aside from kites, the earliest flying device manufactured in the United States appears to have been the variation of the helicopter or aerial top illustrated in Fig. 217, which was made in the early 1890's but whose manufacturer is unknown. As will be seen, it introduced a new mode of launching the propeller by means of rapidly drawing a rod with a spiral twist downward, and may have been the first to have placed a rim around the blades, thus forming a sort of wheel that was sent spinning upward. It has, however, been possible to trace out a fairly good but by no means necessarily complete or definitive history of what appear to have been the first five years of major commerical model and toy airplane manufacture and sale in the United States—the demidecade that carried the product from the status of a mere novelty to the advent of commendable scale models and the establishment of a permanent model airplane industry, 1907 to 1911.

Excepting balloons, the real inception of this era seems to have been marked by the introduction of the "Ladis Flying Cupid" and the "Ladis Flying Airship" in 1907, originally advertised to the trade under the name of Ladis Lewkowicz of Brooklyn, New York. Both of these miniatures flew suspended from a cord, with a pusher propeller powered by means of rubber. The flying cupid, also denominated an "angel," is described as being lithographed in beautiful colors and as having "wings moving gracefully in a lifelike manner," although it is not revealed when and in what Elysian Field the designer had sojourned so as to become an authority on the "lifelike" action of angel wings. The airship was somewhat less ethereal, being simply a model blimp or dirigible, but in case anyone did not know what the miniature represented, it was plainly marked AIRSHIP on the sides. Tastes being somewhat difficult to account for, it appears that the angel was the better seller of the two. Soon after the beginning of 1908 the name of the French American Toy and Novelty Manufacturing Company replaced that of Ladis Lewkowicz as the manufacturer of these two devices, although they still were individually designated as before, and the company also offered a line of equipment for the then frantically booming

Fig. 239. Ideal rubber-powered flying model airplanes of the World War I period available either as kits or as assembled, ready-to-fly models. All described as 3-foot models, the types pictured are, respectively, the Wright biplane, Curtiss flying boat, Blériot monoplane, Nieuport monoplane, Curtiss military tractor biplane, and Taube monoplane.

Howard G. McEntee; G. William Holland photographs

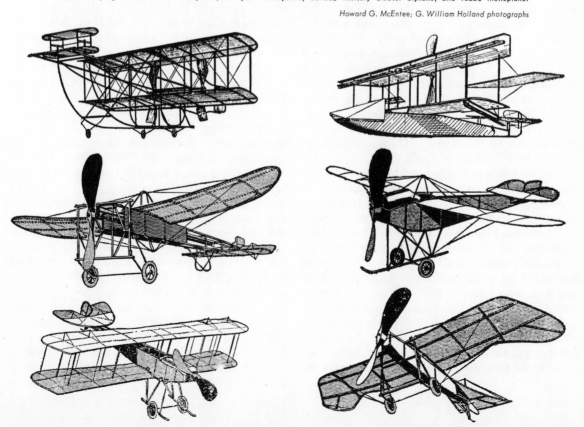

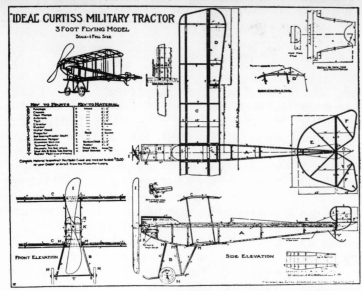

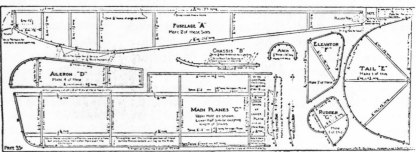

Fig. 240. Ideal Aeroplane and Supply Company plans of 1915 for constructing their 3-foot model of the Curtiss military tractor biplane. The main plans were half the size of the model; the lower illustration shows the full-size forming and assembling drawings.

Howard G. McEntee; G. William Holland photographs

game craze of Diabolo. Yet the most interesting part of the story lies in precisely who Ladis Lewkowicz proved to be. As he himself advertised under that form, it is to be presumed that he regarded it as the preferable spelling of his name in our alphabet, but he also appears in aviation history as Ladis Lewkowiczs and Lydis Lukowitcz. He was a pioneer Russian aviator and one of the first to pilot a Blériot airplane, having been taught to fly by Louis Blériot himself. In 1911 he was competing in aeronautical meets in the United States and is recorded as being "exceptionally experienced and daring in altitude flights." At that time he was flying a Queen monoplane, made in New York, New York, which was a close copy of the Blériot and to whose design Lewkowicz was credited with contributing. As Blériot had not himself flown until 1907 and had not really perfected his monoplane until 1908, it seems unlikely that Lewkowicz had been taught to fly before the latter date and that his miniatures came before his actual flying experience. In any event, it is a most interesting set of circumstances and sidelight on real and model aeronautical history. Lewkowicz must have organized both his own full-size airplane activities and his toy and model interests in the course of trips between the United States and France, and he and Blériot may have had an interest in the Queen Aeroplane Company, who advertised its monoplane as "Queen of Them All." It is to be hoped that more detailed information on these matters eventually will be turned up.

Honors for manufacturing the first actual flying model airplanes in the United States appear to have been divided between the H. J. Nice Company of Minneapolis, Minnesota, makers of the "Aero Miniature Flying Machine," and the Baber Toy Aeroplane Manufacturing Company of Dayton, Ohio, who produced the Lee toy aeroplane. Dayton was, of course, the home town of the Wright brothers, and they had done considerable flying there in 1904 and 1905, which may have inspired some of their neighbors with the idea that a toy airplane would be a good idea; the Baber people noted in 1909 that they had spent several years in experimenting in order to produce "a Toy Aeroplane that does really fly." In any case, both the Dayton and Minneapolis productions were rubber-powered; both boasted of being capable of flights of about 100 feet, and both seem first to have been made and advertised in 1909. Either or both may actually have been on the market a year or more before that date. The 24-inch-wingspan Lee model appears to have been a somewhat conventional tractor monoplane with its rudder below the elevator; the 14-inch-wingspan Aero Miniature definitely was not, at least by today's standards. Nevertheless, the Aero

Fig. 241. Early model airplane manufacture. These photographs were taken in the factory of the Ideal Aeroplane and Supply Company about the time of World War I, and show the assembling of scale flying models (left) and the fabrication and packing of "Bluebird" A-frame racers, which were sold only in assembled form.

Howard G. McEntee; G. William Holland photographs

Miniature—it was not a miniature of anything and the name was shortly changed to the Aero Toy—despite its unusual appearance as revealed in Fig. 219, must have been an extraordinarily satisfactory flyer, for it maintained its popularity over a number of years and evidently was in production as late as 1916, if not even later. It was at times designated a biplane and had two wings,* and it was described as capable of adjustment for either straight or circular flight. It was also said of it that if it were started upside down it would automatically right itself and continue flying. Later ads claimed it was capable of flights of over 150 feet. Its weight is recorded as less than one ounce. For most of its life it was made by the Bing Manufacturing Company of Minneapolis, who took it over from Nice shortly after 1909. The Bing firm was evidently no connection of the famous German toy manufacturer of that name. The Aero Miniature sold for a dollar, while the Lee aeroplane retailed for fifty cents. No trace has been found of the latter after 1910, when the company had been changed simply to Baber Aeroplane Manufacturing Company, and no reference was made to the plane itself being named the Lee. At times both the Aero and the Lee models were described as being capable of flying in circles, with the implication that they would readily return directly to the hands of the launcher somewhat in boomerang fashion.

Also on the market in 1909 was the Aeroplane Flyer, a 25-inch-wing-span, American-flag-

*Technically, the Aero Miniature might more properly perhaps be designated as a semi-biplane. It should be borne in mind that its appearance seemed less unconventional to most at the time it was being made than it does today. In 1909 most people had little idea of what an airplane did or should look like, and those who followed aeronautical affairs closely were aware of the great variety of types that were being experimented with. The wing design of the Aero Miniature was not totally dissimilar to the conformation of some real planes, such as the unsuccessful Blériot biplanes of 1906 and the Robart semi-biplane of 1908. Even the first four Curtiss planes (1908–1909)—more properly, perhaps, the planes of the Aerial Experiment Association—had wings curving toward each other.

bedecked glider, manufactured by F. E. Fuchs of New York, New York, whose factory and what were termed "proving grounds" were located at St. Albans, Queens County, New York. In considering the matter of priority for the manufacture of model airplanes in the United States, it must also be recorded that in 1911 the Goff Aeroplane Company of Chicago, Illinois, advertised that they were not only the largest but also the "oldest manufacturers of MODEL AEROPLANES in America." This firm undoubtedly did make an extensive line of flying models at an early date, but, regrettably, it has not been possible to secure much definite information concerning either the company or its products. Their price list No. 5 was offered in a 1911 advertisement. If it is assumed that one such list was issued each year, this would place their founding in 1907.

The White Aeroplane Company was founded in 1909 in Brooklyn, New York. A few years later they moved to Wading River, Long Island, New York, and thereafter changed their name to the Wading River Manufacturing Company, subsequently moving back to Brooklyn. In the later 1920's, still in Brooklyn, they became the U.S. Model Aircraft Corporation. Wading River was a major factor in the model airplane industry for many years. The 1912 White catalog, which was advertised as ready in the fall of 1911, offers, in addition to a full line of model airplane fittings and materials, construction kits and assembled scale flying models of a Nieuport monoplane, Curtiss hydroaeroplane, Langley tandem monoplane, Blériot monoplane, Wright biplane, and Antoinette monoplane, as well as two A-frame racing models. Most of the scale models were built to a uniform three-foot size, although it is not clear if this represented wingspan or length, and their prices ranged from $3 to $5 in kits and from $10 to $15 in ready-to-fly form. Some of these models represent proto-

Fig. 242. White Aeroplane Company scale rubber-powered flying models of the World War I era: Nieuport biplane, the famed Curtis JN 4B ("Jenny") military biplane, De Haviland 4, Sopwith triplane, Caproni bomber, Handley-Page bomber, Loening monoplane, and Taube. Compare the wing shape of the latter to the Ideal Taube model in Fig. 239.

Howard G. McEntee; G. William Holland photographs

Fig. 243. The Wading River Manufacturing Company's masterpiece, a 4-foot wingspan scale (nonflying) model of the N.C. 4, the first airplane to fly across the Atlantic Ocean (1919). Sold both as a kit and built-up, the latter was probably the most expensive model airplane ever regularly manufactured, retailing for $200.

Howard G. McEntee; G. William Holland photograph

types that were in existence at the time the company was founded in 1909, but it is not clear just when they started to manufacture model airplanes or just where they actually may fit in in the general tabulation of priority of the manufacture of model airplanes in the United States.

White also manufactured a complete line of supplies for full-size gliders, as well as kits and finished gliders; you could purchase a complete glider for $45, or the price of three assembled model airplanes. Gliding was in fact very closely associated with the model airplane hobby in the early years of the hobby, and they seem at times almost to have been considered two facets of the same hobby. Boys were advised at times that though it would be well for them to build and fly model airplanes or man-carrying gliders, and that, while they could probably build a successful full-sized powered airplane, they had best leave the latter alone until they were a little older. One author said that it was all right for a boy to build a full-sized powered airplane as long as he was content with the accomplishment and did not try to fly it himself. White may thus have started with gliders before making model airplanes, as may well have Goff and others. (By 1922 Wading River noted that they had discontinued the manufacture of gliders but could still offer plans for their construction.) It will be noted that neither White nor Goff included the word "model" in their company names. Neither did the Aeroplane Manufacturing Company of Brooklyn, New York, who in 1910 advertised material and directions for building a model airplane for fifty cents, nor the Chicago Aeronautical Supply Company who in the same years offered plans for model airplanes. It will also be recalled that the Baber Toy Aeroplane Manufacturing Company dropped the word "toy" from their name. There was a very close connection between real and model airplanes and gliders at this time, and more than one enterprise that originally expected to engage in the building of full-sized gliders and airplanes may have found it necessary or desirable to produce models—Goff or White, for example. Traces of this connection be-

tween real and model airplane manufacturers may still be found through the 1920's and into the early 1930's when, for example, a line of model airplanes was displayed at the Curtiss-Wright showrooms in New York.

Perhaps the best and most interesting example of this early connection is to be found in an advertisement Carter & Son, who described themselves as "Aviators and Manufacturers," inserted in the trade journal *Toys and Novelties* in 1911. What was primarily being advertised was a kit for a 4-foot-wingspan flying model of a Blériot monoplane at a presumably wholesale price of $2 each. However, if the mood moved the reader to own a real Blériot, Messrs. Carter would build him one for $500, less the engine and propeller! H. G. Carter, who designed the model, was a noted English aviator and parachute jumper, who had built and flown his own airplane.

This lack of any clear demarcation between manufacturers of real and model aircraft and supplies also obtained in Great Britain at this period. Somewhat unlikely as it may appear today, it was far from an illogical conjunction, and in fact indicative of a widespread understanding of the part models had played in aeronautical development up to that time and would continue to play, as well as bearing witness to the widespread acceptance of the conception that model airplanes were truly a scientific hobby and a logical steppingstone toward flight in full-size aircraft.

A DEMAND FOR ANYTHING THAT FLEW

Thus the model airplane arrived on the market. Yet the air was also filled with a variety of other flying toys and models, and the name assigned to a device alone is not always truly indicative of what was being offered and accepted, at least not in the frame of reference of modern terminology. The helicopter took on a renewed lease on life, being in great demand and often regarded as as much of a flying toy or model as a true airplane. The Empire helicopter, looking not

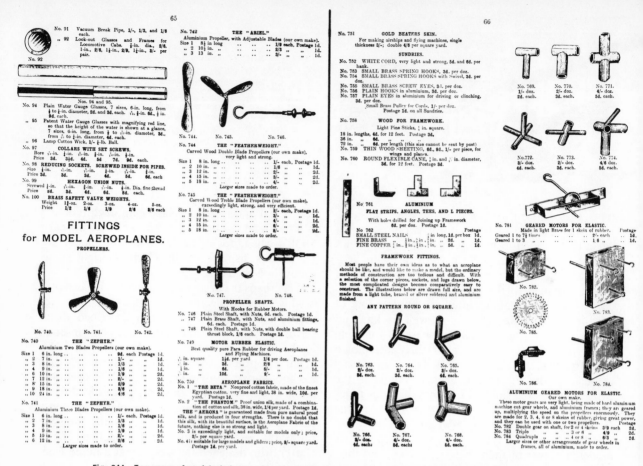

Fig. 244. Two pages of model airplane parts and supplies from a catalog of about 1909 of Stevens's Model Dockyard of London. The assortment includes both aluminum and wooden propellers, flat and tubular construction fittings, and a variety of gearboxes (lower right) for multiplying the speed between the rubber power and the propeller.

G. William Holland

too different from the French helicopters of thirty or more years earlier, except that the propeller had three blades and was encircled by a wheel-like rim (hence the alternate cognomens around 1909 to 1911 of "flying wheel" or "fly wheel") could ascend 200 feet. The "Air-O-Plane" was not an airplane at all, but a hand-projected helicopter, which it was suggested might be employed as a game by flying it from the hands of one player to another. The "Skidoo Butterflies," a 1907 introduction by the large and long-established toy manufacturer E. B. Estes & Sons, who had wooden-toy factories in six states, also was a hand-projected helicopter, and bore no resemblance to a butterfly. It was flown by rapidly revolving the stick between the palms and then releasing it. The name derived from the popular slang brushoff of the day, "Twenty-three, skidoo!" which may be translated into modern English as "Beat it" or "Get lost," and the normal operating procedure no doubt was to launch the helicopter and shout "Twenty-three, skidoo!" as it started to ascend.

Indeed, it appears that almost everyone was endeavoring to get into the flying-machine act between 1907 and 1911, mainly with helicopters,

although in some cases in the absence of illustrations or detailed descriptions it is difficult to determine precisely what was being offered. The Elite Strainer Manufacturing Company of Cleveland, Ohio, produced a helicopter for which extra "fly wheels" were available. The Aerodart Works of New York, New York, had a twenty-five-cent "flyer," further description possibly lost forever, and the Aero Toy Manufacturing Company of Washington, D.C., claimed to produce the cheapest "aeroplane toy" of all intended "For Boys and Girls and Grownups who have 'High Aspirations' "; but despite the use of the word "aeroplane" it is obvious it was only another helicopter, although the "fly-wheels" patriotically were respectively red and blue, as befitted a toy that emanated from the nation's capital. The Goff Aeroplane Company themselves offered something for thirty cents that they called a flying bat but was probably a helicopter.

The Carter Aeroplane, introduced in 1910 by the Carter Manufacturing Company of St. Louis, Missouri, was truly an airplane, even though the manufacturer chose to describe it further as "A self propelled dirigible airship," but what matter? It flew. On the other hand, the Carter Aerostat, which appears much the same as the Carter Aeroplane except that it lacks the wing and underworks, and is a bit smaller to provide "A real flyer for little folks," is revealed as simply a helicopter with a propeller at each end, evidently intended for vertical flight. In 1910 the Aeroflyer Company of Medford, Massachusetts, advertised a Blériot model for a dollar, while the next year the Aeroflyer, indisputably a helicopter that retailed for ten cents, including two "flyers," was offered by the Hamden Toy Company in Westfield, Massachusetts, almost all the way across the Bay State, who depicted it flying over the steeple of a rural New England church. The big-city Buffalo Pitts Company of Buffalo, New York, on the other hand, portrayed their Hi-Flyer, which came out in 1910, soaring over the top of the famous Flat Iron Building in New York, and claimed that aviators used it for testing wind currents before flights. The Hi-Flyer was, in fact, demonstrated at all the major aeronautical events in 1910 and 1911 and was the official souvenir of the Harvard-Boston Aviation Meet in September, 1910. Indeed, all the aviation meets of the period saw numerous hawkers selling helicopters and other flying toys and models. There is one device concerning which it is greatly to be regretted no picture or detailed description survives, or at least has been found up to this writing. This was the "Jersey Skeeter toy aeroplane" manufactured in 1911 by the Lincoln Square Novelty Works of New York, New York, and described as a self-propelled flyer adjustable for use indoors or out. The name derives from the popular designation almost affectionately applied to a supposedly prodigious and by then already semilegendary breed of mosquitoes that inhabited the New Jersey meadows almost immediately west of New York. Anything that could fly like a "Jersey Skeeter" had to be good!

HORSMAN, WHITEHEAD, AND MYSTERY

Into the midst of the dawning craze for flying models stepped Edward Imeson Horsman of E. I. Horsman of New York, a leading figure in the toy and model trade for many years and instrumental in popularizing such things as tennis, bicycling, and amateur photography. From developing and promoting kites on a very extensive scale in the 1890's and early 1900's, which by 1907 he was starting to advertise to the trade as "airships," it was but a short step for Horsman to step full depth into model airplanes and other flying devices. The fact is, as will be seen in a moment, that Horsman

long had known exactly what an airplane was and had rubbed shoulders with the airplane, as it were, a decade earlier. By 1910 Horsman was himself manufacturing the "Air-O-Plane" hand-propelled helicopters, and was representing among others the Bing Manufacturing Company, the Buffalo Pitts Company, and the Carter Manufacturing Company, giving him an extensive and varied line of helicopters and airplanes. In addition, by May, 1910, he was advertising a line of five ready-to-fly rubber-powered model airplanes, which all indications suggest were of French manufacture and very likely the line that was sold under the Lux trademark. The complete list is not without interest. The model numbers also indicated the retail prices, ranging from $0.50 for the little Tabo to $3.50 for the biplane. The prices in the right-hand

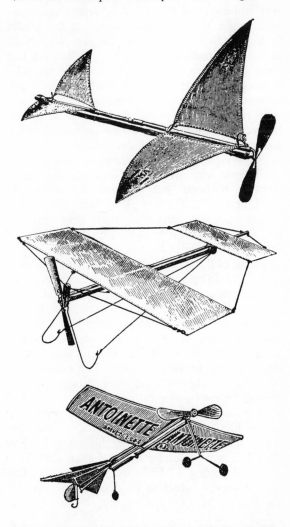

Fig. 245. Three types of elaborate French ready-to-fly rubber-powered model airplanes popular in 1910. The upper model is of the Alma brand, with a wing adjustable to any of several desired angles of incidence. It is 24 inches long; the center model, 31 inches. The Antoinette model was available in four sizes, from 25 inches to a giant 80 inches in length, the latter selling for $30.

G. William Holland

column represent the wholesale price per dozen:

No. 350–Biplane, Rises straight from the
    ground $24.00
No. 250–Monoplane, as shown with boy
    standing   16.50
No. 150–Demoiselle, smaller size than
    No. 250   10.50
No. 100–Mignon, smaller size than No. 150 7.50
No. 50–Tabo, same style, smaller size   4.00

The illustration of the "Boy standing" is reproduced in Fig. 233.

But what of Horsman and his brush with airplane history?

At this point it is necessary to go back a bit and record some remarkable coincidences wherein real and model airplane history were once again intertwined. In 1895 there arrived in the United States one Gustav Weisskopf. Gustave Whitehead, as he soon anglicized his name, is the man that most conventional aviation historians have tried to sweep under a rug and about whom they would be much happier had he never existed, for there is good reason to believe that he built and flew highly successful internal-combustion reciprocating-engine-powered full-size man-carrying airplanes prior to the Wright Brothers.* Whitehead was a native of Bavaria with an interest in flying that dated from his boyhood, and had been associated with the Lilienthal brothers of glider fame for a while in Germany. His credentials must have been impeccable, for almost immediately after he landed in the United States he was engaged by a representative of the staid Boston Aeronautical Society to build a flying machine. He did build two machines, one an only moderately successful glider and the other a completely unsuccessful man-powered ornithopter, although a witness noted that he believed if the latter had been engine-driven it would have gone into flight. At least one of these machines was tested at the Blue Hill Observatory near Boston, where kites were extensively employed for meteorological observations. Blue Hill kites were famous, and the name was a potent one in the kite trade; Horsman then or a little later was to merchandise kites under this name. In 1899 Blue Hill was to send a team of kites aloft for a record-shattering 12,507 feet, almost 2½ miles.

After his failure to produce an airplane for the Boston Aeronautical Society, Whitehead then went to New York, where he entered the employ of none other than E. I. Horsman to design kites and flying machines. Horsman may well have made his acquaintance at Blue Hill. Whitehead's son later recalled that his father demonstrated kites for Horsman and was able to keep as many as fifteen aloft at the same time. However, Horsman obviously did not have to bring Whitehead from Boston merely for the purpose of flying advertising kites, skilled as he may have been in that art. While working for Horsman, Whitehead wrote to the man who had been his assistant in the Boston airplane construction project that he was building an engine for "flying power." Horsman not only probably hired Whitehead to design kites, but it would appear that Horsman at this time was interested in other things besides kites and was undertaking at least some serious experimenting in the line of producing a powered flying machine, although whether as a toy, an advertising device, or with an interest in serious man-carrying flight cannot be determined at present. This would have been about 1897, and Whitehead evidently did build some kind of complete model airplane while in New York. From there he went to Buffalo, New York, and then to Pittsburgh, Pennsylvania, where he built a full-size man-carrying steam-powered airplane, which may or may not have flown. When, in 1900, Whitehead and his Pittsburgh assistant, Louis Davarich, traveled from Pittsburgh to Bridgeport, Connecticut, they stopped off in New York where Davarich (who could not speak English at the time and accordingly was unable to understand the conversation at the establishment) recalled Whitehead had taken him to a building and showed him a display including a model airplane that Whitehead had constructed. This was almost unquestionably at the Horsman showroom on lower Broadway.

According to Whitehead's biographer, he was at that time on his way back to Boston, but for reasons for which there seemed no explanation, Whitehead and Davarich stopped off and remained permanently in Bridgeport, Connecticut.

The late Charles H. Silliman, long the secretary of the Ives Manufacturing Company of Bridgeport, for years the leading toy and model manufacturers in the United States, if not in the world, and employed by Ives from 1890 onward, once related a story that may shed some light on this matter. The then Ives, Blakeslee and Williams Company had already manufactured a notable and revolutionary kite in the early 1890's, the tailless "fin" kite that had a vertical stabilizing fin and was much studied by contemporary aeronautical experimenters. According to Mr. Silliman, Edward

---

*Whitehead's story is effectively told and documented in Stella Randolph's fascinating book *Lost Flights of Gustave Whitehead*, which contains information that complemented material in the present writer's possession. The possibility of Whitehead having flown in 1901 and 1902 is analyzed in Dr. A. F. Zahm's *Early Powerplane Fathers*. Dr. Zahm's conclusions generally support Miss Randolph's thesis that he did.

Fig. 246. A small segment of the exhibit of Maerklin Brothers at the Brussels Exhibition of 1910, showing their trains and a new model airplane being displayed together, along with Steiff plush figures.

G. William Holland

Ives, the president of the company, was quite interested in furthering kite development, and around 1896 or 1897 had undertaken to engage "a German kite expert" to come to Bridgeport to design kites, but business conditions then precluded his carrying out this intention, and the man had gone to work for E. I. Horsman in New York instead. It would seem certain that this "German kite expert" was Gustave Whitehead. Undoubtedly Edward Ives had extolled the merits of Bridgeport, and in the summer of 1900 Whitehead did come to Bridgeport, although not as an employee of Ives. He very likely stopped off in Bridgeport on his way to Boston to see Edward Ives, probably the only man he knew in Bridgeport, and to inquire as to the possibilities of finding employment with him at that time, and and then decided to remain in Bridgeport anyway.

Shortly thereafter Whitehead's family arrived from Pittsburgh, and shipped to him from that city was a large wooden crate which he brought home from the railroad station and engaged a boy, Junius Harworth, to guard until he was through work and able to open it. The box was opened in Harworth's presence and, as he recalled many years later, it was filled with models of a number of types of model airplanes and model airplane engines, as well as drawings, books, and other material on the subject. In 1901 and 1902 Whitehead may well have made several successful flights in his full-size airplanes Nos. 21 and 22. (If Whitehead did not fly at that time, then either a number of witnesses were victims of hallucinations or—and anyone would long hesitate before reaching such a conclusion—knowingly swore false affidavits.) Inasmuch as Whitehead, who was almost always impeded for lack of funds, never could have made twenty-two full-size airplanes between 1895 and 1902, even by transferring major units from one plane to another, it would appear obvious that he counted various model airplanes in his numerical sequence. Probably most of the planes were, in fact, models. As a matter of fact, in an interview published in the *New York Herald* for June 16, 1901, Whitehead stated that he was then building his fifty-sixth airplane. It definitely appears to have been Whitehead's practice first to build models of his proposed gliders and airplanes and test them initially by flying them as kites. Whitehead's flights attracted little attention, although there were reports of them published in Bridgeport, New York, and Boston newspapers and in the aeronautical and scientific press. This, of course, is also precisely what happened in the case of the initial flights of the Wright brothers. It was not until several years later, when a number of airplanes were flying, that the Wrights came forward and vigorously pushed their claims to priority. About this same time Whitehead engaged in building several airplanes and helicopters for other inventors, and for a while was moderately successful as a builder of airplane engines. Later he is said to have become quite embittered and to feel that he had been denied credit for his achievements because of his foreign birth and more particularly because of the anti-German feeling that accompanied World War I. He died, virtually forgotten in aeronautical circles, in 1927.

Unfortunately, a fire in the Horsman factory destroyed their old files and with them any chance that information retained therein might serve to shed more light on Whitehead's work on model airplanes in New York and the unique connection between the man who possibly should rate as the inventor of the airplane and the man who, perhaps as a result of this association, played so important a role in the successful commercial launching of the model airplane in the United States.

MORE PIONEER AMERICAN MODEL AIRPLANE MANUFACTURERS

Reference already has been made to the birth of the model airplane industry in the United States, to the flying devices that were not airplanes, and to some of the earliest actual model airplanes: the

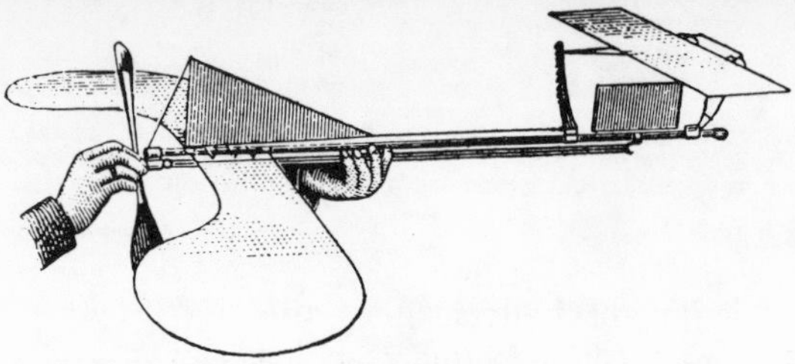

Flying apparata with adjusted Clockworks.

These excellent Aeroplanes, when suspended by a vertical line, are propelled by their own force in safe and steady circular flight.
You can direct them either to the right or left by adjusting the sails accordingly.
Finest original designs.

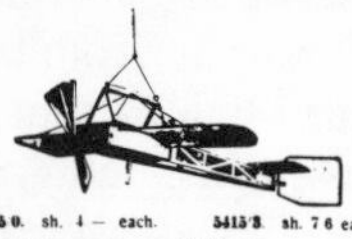

5415/0. sh. 4/— each. 5415/3. sh. 7/6 each.

No. 5415 Monoplane „Blériot".

Long, slender construction; adjustable sails.
Nicely japanned steel plate. Size 3 with celluloid wings. With figure.

No. 5415	0	3
Length . . . inches	10 3/8	14 3/4
Breadth . . . „	9	13 3/4

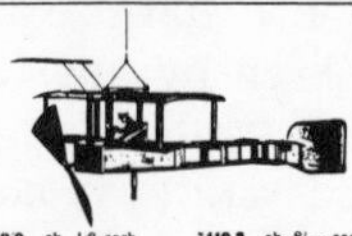

5419/0. sh. 4/8 each. 5419/3. sh. 8/— each.

No. 5419 Biplane „Farman".

Fine and durable make.
Steel plate, finely japanned; size 3 with celluloid wings. With person.

No. 5419/	0	3
Length . . . inches	9 1/8	18 3/8
Breadth . . . „	6 3/4	10 1/4

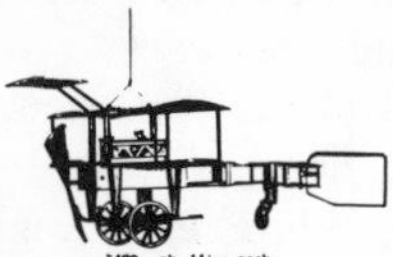

5420. sh. 11/— each.

No. 5420 Biplane „Farman".

Neat and stabile metal framing, planes with colourless celluloid inlays.
Contrivances both for flight and running on the floor. With figure 1 main propeller, adjustable sails.

Length . . . 15 3/4 inches	Breadth . . . 12 3/4 inches

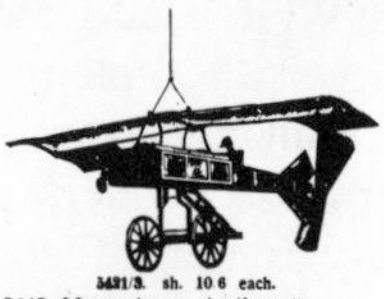

5421/3. sh. 10/6 each.

No. 5421/3 Monoplane „Latham".

Unequalled, precise construction.
Carved framing, planes with celluloid inlay.
Contrivances both for flying and running on the floor. With person.
1 main propeller. 2 air propellers.

Length . . . 11 1/8 inches	Breadth . . . 12 1/8 inches

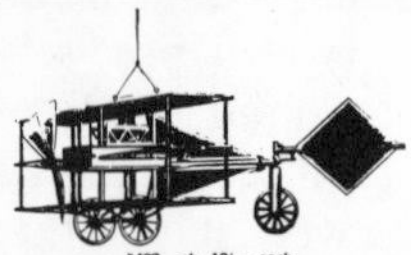

5422. sh. 12/— each.

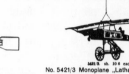

No. 5422 Three plane „Grade".

Best workmanship; perfect precision model.
Steel plate, finely japanned; celluloid planes and sail; adjustable wheel framing, with person.

Length . . . . . 17 inches	Breadth . . . . 12 3/4 inches

Aëroplane on rotary framing, with opposite clockwork.

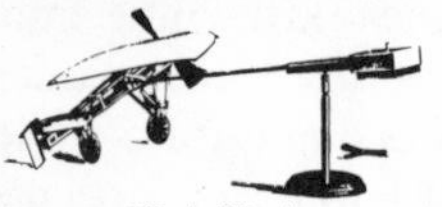

5460. sh. 13/6 each.

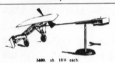

No. 5460 Aëronaut's Training apparatus.

Ingenious representation of full fledged aeroplane flying.
A rotary shaft, mounted on a post, carries the clockwork at one end, the monoplane „Blériot" at the other. The shaft transmits its revolutions to the aëro, which propells itself in circular flight.

Length of the monoplane	12 3/8 inches
Diameter of the circle of flying	15 „
Height of post	6 3/8 „

Free flyers with spring starters. Protected.

To play with most flying apparata "tops, aeroplanes, balloons" is to a certain extent waste of time, energy, skill and even dangerous. More perfect in every respect is the free flyer operated by the force of the spring starter, acting on the propelling screw of the flyer, the rotating of which propells the flier through the air.

9131 GL 3. sh. 1/4 each.

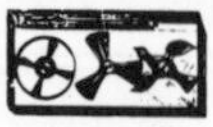

9131 GV 3. sh. 1/6 each.

9131 1	2	3	4	5	6
each 2 d.	2 d.	2 d.	2 d.	2 d.	2 d.

9131 G 6. sh. 2/— each.

No. 9131 Air tops, operated by spring starter. Made of colored celluloid.

For indoor use. Cross pin in the center to be set in the tube of the winder.
Nicely embossed and stamped air-propeller-tops, taking pretty flight through the air, when set rotating by the spring starter.

Single No. 9131	1	2	3	4	5	6
	Top	Screw	Star	Star	Dragon Fly	Swallow
Diameter inches	2 1/2	2 1/8	2 3/8	3	2 1/8	3 1/8

Set No. 9131 GL 3.
Spring starter 9131 S, with 3 Flying tops 9131 2, 3, 5.
In fine cardboard box. Size of box 8 1/8 × 4 1/8 × 1 inches

Set No. 9131 GV 3.
Spring starter 9131 S, with 3 air tops 9131 1, 4, 6.
In strong cardboard box. Size of box 8 1/8 × 4 1/8 × 1 inches.

Set No. 9131 G 6.
Spring starter 9131 S, with 6 air tops 9131 1, 2, 3, 4, 5, 6.
In strong cardboard box. Size of box 8 3/8 × 6 1/2 × 1 inches.

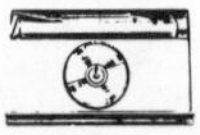

9132 GK. sh. 1/4 each.

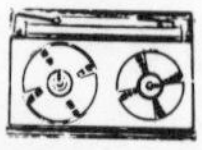

9132 GK 2. sh. 1/8 each.

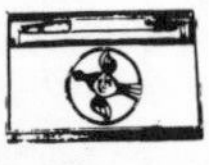

9132 GV. sh. 1/10 each.

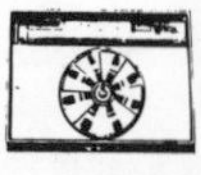

9132 GR. sh. 1/10 each.

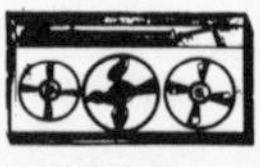

9132 G 3. sh. 2/3 each.

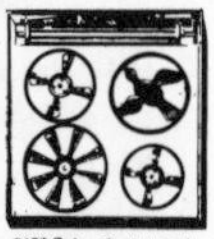

9132 G 4. sh. 2/8 each.

9132 1	2	3	4
sh. each —/3	—/3	—/4	—/5

No. 9132 Air tops.

Nicely japanned metal. Screw propeller with cross pin, fitting on te spring starter. (Same system as 9131).

Single No. 9132	1	2	3	4
	Screw	Screw	Bird	Screw
Diameter . . . inches	2 1/2	3	3 1/8	3 3/4

Set No. 9132 GK.
Spring starter 9133 S. 1 air top 9132 1.
In colored cardboard box.
Size of box . . . . . 6 3/8 × 3 3/8 × 1 inches

Set No. 9132 GK 2.
Spring pistol 9133 S, 2 air tops 9132 1, 2
In colored cardboard box.
Size of box . . . . . 6 3/8 × 4 1/2 × 1 inches

Set No. 9132 GV.
Spring pistol 9132 S, 1 Bird 9132 3.
In colored cardboard box.
Size of box . . . . . 7 × 5 1/2 × 1 inches

Set No. 9132 GR.
Spring pistol 9132 S, 1 top 9132 4.
In colored cardboard box
Size of box . . . . . 7 1/2 × 5 1/2 × 1 inches

Set No. 9132 G 3.
Spring pistol 9132 S, 3 air tops 9132 1, 2, 4.
In colored cardboard box.
Size of box . . . . . 10 × 5 1/8 × 1 inches

Set No. 9132 G 4.
Spring pistol 9132 S with 4 air tops 9132 1, 2, 3, 4.
In colored cardboard box.
Size of box . . . . . 9 × 8 × 1 inches

Free Flyers.

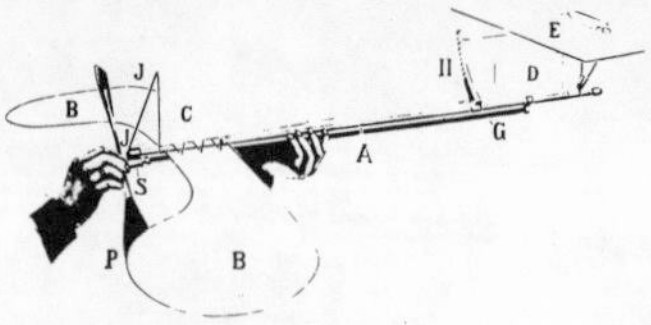

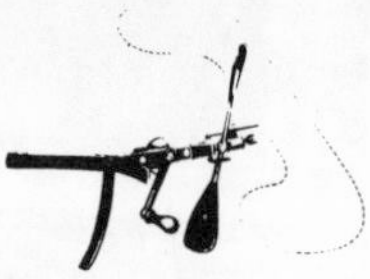

No. 5470 Free flyer "Dragon-fly".

The best existing self propelling aëro suitable for the use as a toy and for scientific demonstration.
Made of light, but undestructable aluminium and steel wire, with beautiful silk planes, adjustable.
Genuine Para rubber, propelling to the longest distance attainable.

Main construction parts:

A	Shaft	G	Rubber strings
B	Carrying planes	H	Set lever
C	Back sail	J	Hook
D	Front sail	P	Propeller
E	Height sail	S	Screw nut for the propeller.
F	Wire hook		

Single No. 5470/	1	2	3	4
Length . . . . inches	21 1/4	27 1/4	33 1/4	41
Breadth . . . „	26 3/8	29 1/2	31 1/2	34 1/4
Price of each . sh.	9/6	12/—	17/—	21/—
Set with winding up apparatus 5469. No. 5470 G/	1	2	3	4
Size of cardboard box inches	[illegible]	[illegible]	[illegible]	[illegible]
sh. each.	10/8	13/6	18/6	22/4

No. 5469 Winding up apparatus

for Flying machines with rubber propulsion.

Permits easy stretching of the rubber strings by turning the crank of the winding apparatus.
Solidly made of iron with metal garniture.
Suitable for all apparata 5470.
Price sh. 1/4 each.

Single adjusting parts for Free flyers:

Suitable for 5470	1	2	3	4
Aluminium tubes 5470 R/	1	2	3	4
Outward diam. . . . inches	3/16	1/4	9/32	5/16
Price p. yard . . . sh.	—/8	—/10	1/—	1/4
Fixing-sockets 5470 UR/	1	2	3	4
with little tubes . . . Width inches	3/16	1/4	9/32	5/16
Price each . . . sh.	—/1	—/1	—/1	—/1
Propeller, 2 wings 5470 P/	1	2	3	4
Length . . . inches	10	10 1/2	10 3/4	11
Price each . . . sh.	/4	—/4	—/6	—/6

Propeller-Bearing 5470 PL: Shaft, Hook. Nut. Bearing and socket. 3 d. each.	Steel-wire, tinned 5470 SD. Diam. 1/32, 3/64 [illegible]	Rubber string 5470 G ☐ Diam. 3/16 inches Best Para. p. yard 6 d. each

Post with Clockwork, propelling Flying apparata.

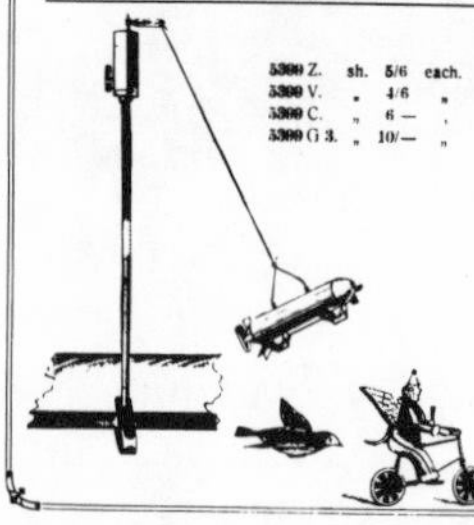

5399 Z. sh. 5/6 each.
5399 V. „ 4/6 „
5399 C. „ 6/— „
5399 G 3. „ 10/— „

No. 5399 Propelling Frame

with Clockwork and swinging Flying apparata.

Adjustable post, with cramp to fix on tables etc., fitted with clockwork with driver and wire to fasten and swing the flyer.
Height of the post 23 3/8 inches.

No. 5399 Z.	Propelling Frame with Zeppelin airship with 4 air propellers. Length of the airship 7 1/2 inches
No. 5399 V.	Propelling Frame with Bird. Length of bird 5 1/8 „
No. 5399 C.	Propelling Frame with Clown on Bicycle with propeller wheels. Length of flyer 5 1/8 inches
No. 5399 G/3.	Propelling Frame with air ship, bird and Clown. Size of cardboard box 14 1/4 × 8 3/8 × 2 3/8 inches

Free flying Aeroplanes with Spring starters. Protected.

Surprising efficiency by spring starters, which set rotating the propellers and hereby effect the smooth and pretty fight of the aeroplans.

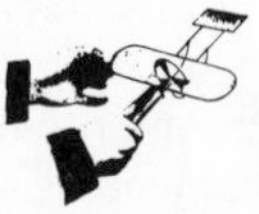

9133 G. sh. 2/10 each.

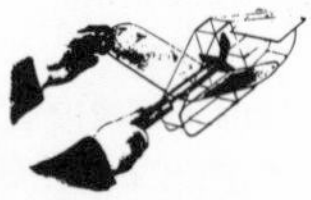

9134 G. sh. 5/6 each.

Free flying Monoplanes, started by spring pistol.

Wire skeleton and silk wings.
Propeller to be inserted on the spring starters.

Single. No. 9133. Free flying Monoplane.
Length . . . . 6 3/4 inches | Breadth . . . . 9 inches
Set. No. 9133 G. Free flying Monoplane. with spring starter 9133 S.
In pretty cardboard box Size of box 9 1/2 × 7 1/8 × 3 inches

Single. No. 9134. Free flying Monoplane.
Length . . 11 7/8 inches | Breadth . . 16 1/2 inches
Set. No. 9134 G. Free flying Monoplane. with spring starter 9132 S.
In pretty cardboard box. Size of box 12 1/4 × 5 1/8 × 5 1/2 inches

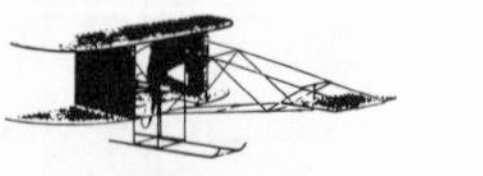

9135 G 4. sh. 10/— each.

Free flyer Biplane operated, spring starter by push.

Tinned wire skeleton and silk sails.
Propeller axle with crosspin, to be inserted in the notches of the little tube projecting on top of the push starter.
Rotating of the propeller and flying off of the biplane is effected by mere pressing on the trigger of the starter.

Single. No. 9135. Free flyer Biplane.
Size . . . . . 16 1/2 × 14 1/2 × 5 1/8 inches
Set. No 9135 G/4. Free flyer Biplane 9135, spring push starter 9135 S, 2 bird tops 9132/3.
In pretty cardboard box with colored picture.
Size of box . . . . . 16 1/2 × 14 1/2 × 5 1/2 inches

Mixed sets of free flyers with spring starters.

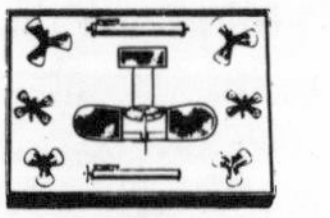

9133 G 9. sh. 6/— each.
9133 G 15. „ 7/— „

Set No. 9133 G/9 containing 9 pieces:

Monoplane 9133, Spring starter 9133 S
6 Celluloid tops 9131/2, 4, 5, Spring starter 9131 S.
In pretty cardboard box. Size of box 16 3/4 × 11 1/8 × 3 3/8 inches

Set No. 9133 G/15 containing 15 pieces:

Monoplane 9133, Spring starter 9133 S.
12 Celluloid tops 9131/2, 3, 5, 6, Spring starter 9131 S.
In pretty cardboard box. Size of box 19 3/4 × 14 3/8 × 3 3/8 inches

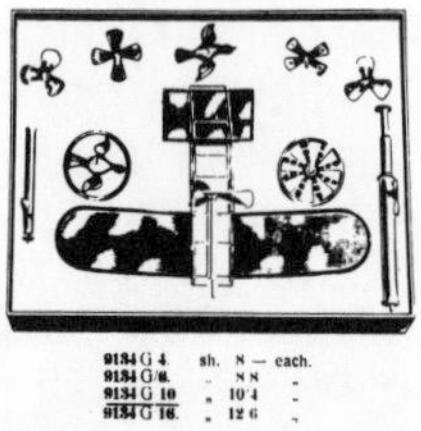

9134 G 4. sh. 8/— each.
9134 G 6. „ 8/8 „
9134 G 10. „ 10/4 „
9134 G 16. „ 12/6 „

Set No. 9134 G/4 containing 4 pieces:

Monoplane 9134, 2 tops 9132/2, Spring push starter 9135 S.
In pretty cardboard box. Size of box 17 3/8 × 13 3/8 × 5 1/2 inches

Set No. 9134 G/6 containing 6 pieces:

Monoplane 9134, 4 tops 9132/2, 3, Spring push starter 9135 S.
In pretty cardboard box. Size of box 17 3/8 × 13 3/8 × 5 1/2 inches

Set No. 9134 G/10 containing 10 pieces:

Monoplane 9134, 2 tops 9132 3, 4, spring push starter 9135 S
5 Celluloid tops 9131/2—6, Spring starter 9131 S.
In pretty cardboard box. Size of box 21 3/8 × 16 1/8 × 5 1/2 inches

Set No. 9134 G/16 containing 16 pieces:

Monoplane 9134, 5 tops 9132 3, 4, Spring push starter 9135 S.
8 Celluloid tops 9131/3—6, Spring starter 9131 S.
In pretty cardboard box. Size of box 25 3/4 × 17 × 5 1/2 inches

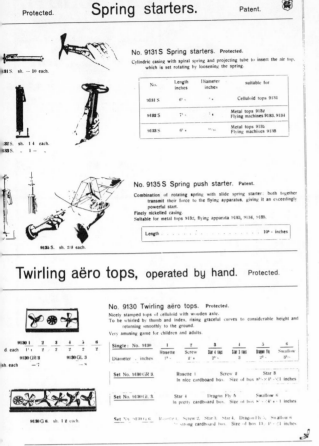

Spring starters.

Protected.   Patent.

No. 9131 S Spring starters. Protected.
Cylindric casing with spiral spring and projecting tube to insert the air top, which is set rotating by loosening the spring.

No.	Length inches	Diameter inches	suitable for
9131 S	6"		Celluloid tops 9131
9182 S	7"		Metal tops 9182 Flying machines 9183, 9184
9133 S	6"		Metal tops 9133 Flying machines 9138

No. 9135 S Spring push starter. Patent.
Combination of rotating spring with slide spring starter; both together transmit their force to the flying apparatus, giving it an exceedingly powerful start.
Finely nickelled casing.
Suitable for metal tops 9132, flying apparata 9183, 9184, 9185.

Length	10" inches

Twirling aëro tops, operated by hand. Protected.

No. 9130 Twirling aëro tops. Protected.
Nicely stamped tops of celluloid with wooden axle.
To be whirled by thumb and index, rising graceful curves to considerable height and returning smoothly to the ground.
Very amusing game for children and adults.

	Single : No. 9130		1 Rosette	2 Screw	3 Star 4 rays	4 Star 5 rays	5 Dragon Fly	6 Swallow
Diameter	inches		1"	2"	3	2"	3"	3"
	Set No. 9130 GR 3.		Rosette 1	Screw 2	Star 3			
			In nice cardboard box. Size of box 8"×1"×1 inches					
	Set No. 9130 GL 3.		Star 4	Dragon Fly 5	Swallow 6			
			In pretty cardboard box. Size of box 8"×1"×1 inches					
	Set No. 9130 G 6.		Rosette 1, Screw 2, Star 3, Star 4, Dragon Fly 5, Swallow 6					
			In strong cardboard box. Size of box 13"×1"×1 inches					

Fig. 247. Maerklin flying toys and models of 1910 and 1911. Above left is their "Dragon Fly," a rubber-powered free-flying model airplane made in four sizes, along with translated nomenclature from the 1910 catalog and a winding handle. Other catalog pages show a line of suspended clockwork model airplanes, and spring-launched airplanes and helicopters, hand-launched helicopters, and other devices.

G. William Holland

Aero and the Lee, the Goff and White enterprises, and to the models promoted by Horsman. This in turn led to the interesting and historically important examination of the connection between Horsman and Whitehead, and thence to the latter's story, related above. Other developments leading up to the establishment of a definite model airplane industry in the United States followed swiftly around 1910 and 1911. One of the first companies to manufacture a line of flying model airplane kits in the United States was the American Aeroplane Manufacturing Company of New York. By 1911 they were offering kits that retailed at $2 each for building 2-foot-wingspan rubber-powered flying models of Wright, Blériot, Farman, Santos-Dumont, Antoinette, Langley, and what they spelled "Curtis" prototypes, or for $5 each they would supply built-up models of the Blériot, Antoinette, or Santos-Dumont ships for window display. No reason is given as to why only these three were offered in assembled form. Presumably

they were the simplest and easiest to put together; they were the standard monoplanes in the line. This is somewhat confirmed by the fact that later in 1911 the prices of all the kits except the Curtis (*sic*), Wright, and Farman were dropped to $1 each.

The advertisements of another New York firm, the International Aeroplane Company, also appeared later in 1911. They offered finished model airplanes only, 2-foot wingspan models of "Curtis" (again!), Wright, Santos-Dumont, or Blériot planes for $10 each for window-display purposes; nothing is said in their advertisements as to these being flying models. There is a strong suspicion, buoyed by their repetition of the Curtiss misspelling, that they may have been engaged in assembling the kits made by the American Aeroplane Manufacturing Company rather than in manufacture on their own, but this is admittedly speculation. Likewise in 1911 appeared the Aeroplane Model Company of New York. They did not manufacture kits but offered a single ready-to-fly, rise-off-the-ground $2 model of what they termed the Blériot Monoplane Flyer. Their advertising suggested that not only could any man or boy derive pleasure from flying their model but that inasmuch as airplanes were then only in their infancy, a fortune might await anyone who worked out an improvement in real airplanes by studying their model in flight.

It does not appear that any of these three above-mentioned concerns were for very long important factors in the model airplane industry. However, in 1911 there also was founded the Ideal Aeroplane and Supply Company, for many years probably the leading factor in the industry, who were to make model airplanes, kits, and parts for thirty-four years. This well-known and with the possible exception of the White—Wading River—U.S. Model Aircraft concern, probably most important of the early manufacturers was established by William Kramer and Hugo Rosenstein. Their factory, originally on West Broadway in New York, New York, included a retail counter where individual hobbyists could make purchases of needed parts and materials. In the memory of many older model airplane enthusiasts, the Ideal factory was long the only place in New York where supplies for building model airplanes could readily be obtained. Many years later, George McLaughlin, then editor of *Aero Digest,* was to recall it as a "shop . . . run by a man named Kramer in lower Manhattan," which while an interesting recollection was by no means an accurate picture of the size and scope of the activities of this notable pioneer firm. Among the first Ideal kits were 3-foot flying models—as with White, they do not specify if this represents wingspan or length—of a Wright biplane, Blériot, and Nieuport monoplane. The next models were a Curtiss military tractor biplane, a Taube monoplane, and a Curtiss flying boat. These were sold both as kits and in assembled form. They also produced a variety of A-frame racing models. They also soon offered kits for 6-foot models of the Nieuport monoplane and the Curtiss military tractor. Then, as now, there were certain prototypes that were particularly popular among model builders or particularly suitable for scale flying models, and the Ideal and Wading River lines tended to develop along very similar lines. As a matter of fact, in at least two instances the identical cuts appear in both the Ideal and Wading River catalogs—a dual-propeller winder and a multiple-gear assembly—indicating that the two companies either were exchanging at least some parts or else buying from a common supplier.

There is no reason to believe that the connection between the two firms was any closer than this, however. Wading River's masterpiece and incidentally probably the most expensive model airplane ever offered commercially in the United States was their 48-inch-wingspan model of the famous N.C. 4, the first airplane to fly across the Atlantic Ocean, in May, 1919. Three United States Navy planes undertook this flight, the N.C. 1 and the N.C. 3 being forced down at sea, but the N.C. 4 braved through from New York to Plymouth, England, with stopovers at Nova Scotia, Newfoundland, the Azores, and Portugal. (The first nonstop crossing of the Atlantic by air of course took place less than a month later when the British pilots John W. Alcock and Arthur Whitten Brown flew from Newfoundland to Ireland.) The Wading River model of the N.C. 4 was strictly a nonflying display model. The company noted that their engineering department, headed by J. F. McMahon, had devoted much time to unsuccessful experiments in an effort to develop a flying model of the N.C. 4 "but at last came to the conclusion that it was absolutely impossible to produce a model that would fly and justly be called the N.C. 4." Accordingly they produced a scale exhibition model, detailed down to the fully working controls, and brought out the kit in 1920. The kit sold for $25 as a unit, or it could be purchased in three sections for slightly more. It was the price of the assembled model, or the "Built model," as Wading River termed it, that was record-breaking—initially $200 and later reduced to $175. This model was built to order only, and furnished, according to the catalogs, "An important medium for School lectures on Aeronautical Technology, excellent for Store Window display, Home, Office or Club Decoration."

Fig. 248. Left, Maerklin spring-launched parachutes of 1911; right, bow-and-arrow-launched parachutes of the same year, made by the American Toy Manufacturing Company of Salem, Massachusetts.

G. William Holland
"Playthings"

It is not certain when Wading River's successor, the U.S. Model Aircraft Corporation, left the scene. Although Ideal continued in the model business until 1964, and retained the original name, it did not manufacture any model airplanes after 1945. No reference to this famous company would be complete without mention of the long-popular model-industry figure David Newmark, who entered the firm in 1924 and later became its president.

There might well be considerable interest in a detailed account of the model airplane manufacturing business in the United States down through the years since 1911. However, the limitations of space preclude the inclusion of such a full history in this volume. Yet at the same time the subject cannot be passed by without mentioning at least some of the better remembered firms—some of their successors still are active—that played a substantial part in the growth of the industry. A few are discussed in some detail later. There were, for example (some underwent variations in name and changes in location), the Broadfield Toy Company, Incorporated (Broadfield Billings), of Hempstead, New York; the Selley Manufacturing Company (Armour Selley) of Brooklyn, New York; the Flying Model Airplane Corporation of West Cheshire, Connecticut; the Lawrence Airplane Model and Supply Company of Chicago; the Scientific Model Airplane Company (John D. Frisoli) of Newark, New Jersey; Madison Model Air-

Fig. 249. Five other early Maerklin aeronautical models. The suspended airplane and the smaller dirigible date from about 1908; the large dirigible and the dirigible traveling game were made in 1910. Shown also is a combined model railroad and airplane item introduced by Maerklin in 1911: a dismantled airplane mounted on a railroad flatcar.

G. William Holland

planes, Incorporated, of Brooklyn; the Cleveland Model and Supply Company (Edward Packard) of Cleveland, Ohio; the Ritchie-Wertz Company of Dayton, Ohio; the Peerless Model Airplane Company of Lakewood, Ohio; Hawk Model Airplanes of Chicago; the National Model Aircraft and Supply Company of New Rochelle, New York; the Kingsbury Manufacturing Company of Keene, New Hampshire; the Grant Aircraft Company (Charles Hampson Grant) of Chester, Vermont; Majestic Model Airplanes of Brooklyn; the G.H.Q. Model Airplane Company of the Bronx, New York; Paul K. Guillow of Wakefield, Massachusetts; the Tropical Model Airplane Company of Miami, Florida; the Lindberg Model and Supply Company of Chicago; the Bunch Model Airplane Company of Los Angeles, California; the Comet Model Airplane and Supply Company of Chicago; Megow's Model Airplane Shop of Philadelphia; Berkeley Model Supplies (William L. Effinger, Jr.) of Brooklyn; the Burd Model Airplane Company of Baltimore, Maryland; the Crescent Model Aircraft Corporation of Brooklyn; the Hub Model Airplane and Supply Company of the Bronx; and the Universal Sales Corporation of Detroit, Michigan—the list might be extended almost indefinitely. Possibly the foregoing enumeration will seem a little tedious to those who have

but lately come to the hobby, but it will certainly touch many chords of recognition and nostalgia among those whose experiences in model airplane building go back a little way. It might also be observed—for the point is frequently remarked by old-timers in the hobby—that for a time there was much to give the impression that from some unusual set of circumstances, the commercial model airplane industry in the United States long centered in Brooklyn, New York.

PIONEER BRITISH MANUFACTURERS

Concerning pioneer British model airplane manufacturers, an American must naturally speak with somewhat less assurance. Some of the best-remembered firms, such as Bonds O' Euston Road, Limited; A. W. Gamage, Limited; and A. E. Jones, Limited, all of London, appear to have been primarily dealers and suppliers rather than manufacturers themselves, although Gamage's may have controlled certain lines exclusively, and a 1925 catalog offers to build scale model airplanes to order. So too did the custom model-building department of Holtzapffel and Company, Limited, a London company that was founded in 1794, and its successor, Walkers and Holtzapffel (Retail), Limited. Particularly well remembered and with a worldwide reputation were the model airplanes and kits manufactured by Warneford Flying Aircraft of London. Outstanding also were Wm. E. Appleby (N/c) and Company of Newcastle-on-Tyne who manufactured or sold a very extensive line of model airplanes and kites, kits, and components of all types in the 1920's, including some printed-cardboard rubber-powered model airplanes that, unlike many of their type that came later, were quite realistic looking, and successful flyers. Appleby issued model aircraft catalogs of well over 100 pages in the 1920's but obviously included many lines not actually of their own manufacture.

Gamage was active in the field quite early, and was issuing extensive catalogs fairly early in the 1900's. T. W. K. Clarke and Company, "Aeronautical Engineers," of the Crown Works, Kingston-on-Thames, were one of the leading British manufacturers of both stock and custom model airplanes at a comparatively early date. In 1910 they advertised a model list comprising 160 items, and a series of rubber-powered models known as Clarke's Flyers, which were extremely popular and evidently came off with honors at many contests. The list is worth reprinting in full:

Model	Length	Weight	Average Distance Flown	Price s. d.	Postage, Packing, etc.
B	Folds up	¾ oz.	100 feet	1 0	By post 1/2
C	1 foot	1 "	120 "	2 6	" 3/-
*D	2 ft. 4 in.	1 "	550 "	3 0	" 3/6
E	1 ft. 6 in.	3 "	220 "	6 6	" 7/6
F	2 feet	½ lb.	350 "	10 0	" 11/-
G	3 "	1¼ "	450 "	17 6	Crate 6d. carriage forward by rail.
I	5 "	3 "	500 "	42 0	Crate 2/6 (returnable by rail).

The asterisk next to Model D was no doubt intended to call the prospective buyer's attention to the fact that this model (whose specifications were printed in boldface type) had made the longest flights. Other manufacturers and purveyors of model aeronautical equipment were J. Bonn and Company, Limited, of London; S. Summerfield of Melton Mowbray, who advertised "Models & Parts made True to Scale and Weight"; and C. G. Spencer and Sons of London, although the latter seems to have concentrated mainly on lighter-than-air equipment, ranging from passenger balloons to toy balloons. This company offered hydrogen in tubes for lighter-than-air enthusiasts. There were also then, or a little later, the Warmley

Fig. 250. Miscellaneous imported flying toys and models of about 1910–1914, including a balloon with parachute, two clockwork suspended model airplanes, a suspended flying clockwork pigeon ornithopter, and a clockwork dirigible carousel.

G. William Holland

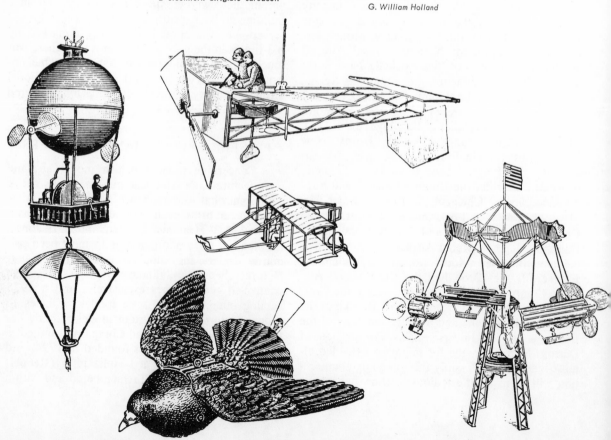

Fig. 251. An inexpensive stamped-metal rubber-powered suspended
model airplane as advertised to the trade in 1909. This model, with a
geared propeller drive, is undoubtedly of European manufacture.

"Playthings"

Fig. 252. Two views of another inexpensive European stamped-metal
suspended model airplane of the 1909-1915 period, this one clockwork-
powered, fitted with an adjustable elevator of questionable practical
value, and with virtually no wingspan beyond the width of the fuselage
itself.

G. William Holland

Aeroplane Company of Warmley, Bristol, who
made Brookley model airplanes and parts and advertised themselves as "the premier Model Aeroplane Firm in Great Britain," and the "Birmac"
Aeroplane Company of Tottenham, London, who
produced a variety of interesting flying models.

Special note should be paid to the extensive
line of model airplane parts and fittings offered
from a date beginning well before 1910 by
Stevens's Model Dockyard of London, a company
established in 1843, and especially well known
among model enthusiasts throughout the world for
their ships and yachts and fittings, steam engines
and live-steam model locomotives. Stevens's (the
firm always used this form of the possessive)
produced a complete range of wooden and aluminum propellers (up to 24-inch diameter) and a
great variety of tubular metal angle and joint fittings, as pictured in Fig. 244, that greatly simplified the construction of model airplanes based on
pre–World War I prototypes. (A similar but far
more limited range of such fittings was made in the
United States by the White Aeroplane Company.)
Stevens's, who did not make any sort of complete
kits, also cataloged a series of covering materials,
some of which were real airplane fabrics being
offered for model use. There was "The Beta,"
made of Egyptian cotton; "The Phantom," proof
union silk made of a combination of cotton and

silk—both of these available in 38-inch width
only; and the "Aerona," which was made from
pure natural proof silk. The lightest grade of the
latter was noted as suitable for models only; the
next heavier grade was suitable for larger models
and gliders. Stevens's Model Dockyard still offered
a few model airplane parts in the mid-1920's, but
it is obvious that their great days in this field were
prior to World War I when many both real and
model airplanes were somewhat glamorously
naïve.

Without question there were many other important firms active in model aeronautics in Great
Britain at fairly early dates, and it is to be hoped
that their history will be chronicled in detail at
some future date.

EARLY CONTINENTAL EUROPEAN
MANUFACTURE

A certain amount already has been related
concerning early French model airplanes. It may
be reiterated that French-built flying model airplanes were extremely popular in the American
market in the early years of model aviation as a
hobby, as they likewise were in Great Britain.
The cheaper French model airplanes had wings
covered with gauze, the more expensive models
with silk. All the early models appear to have been

rubber-powered, and most of them were tractor types, with the rudders located below the elevators. The largest and most elaborate French model that seems to have been widely sold in the United States around 1910 and 1911 was a fine replica of the Antoinette, made in four sizes. Lengths rather than wingspans are provided in catalog listings; the 80-inch-long Antoinette retailing for the very considerable price of $30 ready-to-fly in 1911 probably was the finest model available on the market at that time. All the French models sold during that period seem to have been offered in assembled form only, as indeed appears to have been the case with most of the Continental models. At least no trace has been found thus far of kits originating in France or elsewhere on the European Continent being offered in the United States or Great Britain in this early period.

As a matter of fact, little can be ascertained concerning Continental manufacture outside France, a condition that possibly accurately reflects a prevailing feeling at that time and down to the present time that France was to a large measure the heart and center of early European airplane development and aeronautical interest in general. At least a few flying models were manufactured in Germany at a fairly early date. Advertising in 1927, the "Aeroplane Model Works" of R. & G. Pause of Pasing-Munich, Germany, boasted of fifteen years' experience, which would date their flying model airplanes back to 1912. A number of Pause rubber-powered model airplanes are found in the catalogs of the 1920's of the British manufacturer and dealer Appleby. Pause also manufactured model gliders and parachutes.

Considerable material exists on the wide range of model airplanes and flying devices made by Maerklin Brothers of Goppingen, Württemberg, already well established in the early 1900's as one of the largest toy and model manufacturers. While Maerklin may have made a few clockwork-powered model airplanes and dirigibles designed for use suspended from a cord or wire a little earlier, in 1910 they appear to have suddenly blossomed

out with a rather extensive line of model airplanes and other "Flying apparata," and to at least some extent to have featured them in their prizewinning display at the International Exhibition at Brussels in that year. They had a complete line of seven clockwork-powered suspended models; some were also arranged for running as clockwork toys on the floor, reproducing in modified metal forms suitable for the toy trade Blériot and Latham monoplanes, Farman biplanes, and a Grade triplane. They also introduced a free-flying canard type (the name applied to designs that fly tail first), the "Dragon-fly," available in four sizes from a 26⅜-inch wingspan, 21¼-inch-long model to the largest with a 34¼-inch wingspan and 41 inches in length. These rubber-powered models were made of aluminum and steel wire, with silk-covered wings, and were termed "The best existing self-propelling aero suitable for use as a toy and for scientific demonstrations." They also offered a complete line of replacement parts for these models. As the illustrations in Fig. 247 indicate, the "Dragon-fly" was of somewhat complex and unusual design. It is also interesting to observe that at this time Maerklin endeavored to transfer the existing and well-established system of designating European model railroad gauges to model airplane usage and to indicate the relative sizes of various models by the gauge numbers 0, 1, 2, 3, and 4. Maerklin also made some model airplanes and dirigibles operating from center posts, as well as a Zeppelin travel game.

More interesting from a standpoint of model airplane history, however, was another type of free-flying model airplane introduced by Maerklin in 1910. These were designed to be used with spring starters, a unit entirely independent of the model airplane and used to set the propeller rotating at speed before the model was released. The spring starters themselves were made in several styles and were also suitable for use with a wide variety of "air tops" or helicopters made by Maerklin. A free-flying spring starter model airplane was, in fact, as the illustrations in Fig. 247

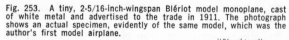

Fig. 253. A tiny, 2-5/16-inch-wingspan Blériot model monoplane, cast of white metal and advertised to the trade in 1911. The photograph shows an actual specimen, evidently of the same model, which was the author's first model airplane.

"Playthings"
G. William Holland

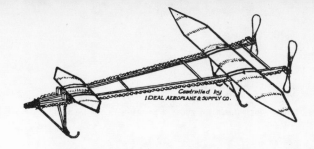

Fig. 254. An advertisement from a 1911 airplane-meet program offering Francis A. Collins's two books on model airplanes, the first two books on the subject published in the United States.

G. William Holland

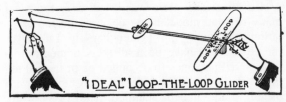

"IDEAL" LOOP-THE-LOOP GLIDER

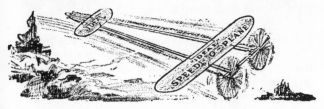

Fig. 255. Five A-frame twin-pusher racing model airplanes manufactured by the Ideal Aeroplane and Supply Company about the time of World War I. The model at the upper right is the famous Cecil Peoli racer, and under it the Ideal improved racer of 1915. Both of these three-foot models were available either as kits or built-up; the following three smaller models were sold only in assembled form, the Speed-O-Flyer, the Blue Bird, and the Speed-O-Plane. Also shown is the Loop-the-Loop slingshot launched glider.

Howard G. McEntee; G. William Holland photographs

will reveal, simply the adaptation of a lightweight model airplane with wire frame and silk-covered wings to the familiar old helicopter launching method. Maerklin's varied line of model airplanes does not seem to have been manufactured over a very long period of time, but the "air tops" with their spring starters remained in production well into the 1930's. In 1910 Maerklin also introduced some hand-launched "twirling aero tops" as well, but these did not achieve the popularity of their spring starter launched devices, however. In 1911 Maerklin also brought out a spring-starter-launched parachute and adapted the spring-starter idea to various other spinning toys that have no re-

lation to aeronautics. Interesting as indeed are the spring-starter models, and particularly the model airplanes, it is a little difficult to understand the statement made in the 1910 supplementary catalog that announced their introduction to the effect that "To play with most flying apparata 'toys, aeroplanes, balloons' is to a certain extent waste of time, energy, skill and even dangerous. More perfect in every respect is the free flyer operated by the force of the spring starter, acting on the propelling screw of the flyer, the rotating of which propels the flier [*sic*] through the air." It is possible to concede that improperly used, some aerial toys and models might be dangerous—it is impossible, for example, to

Fig. 256. The Pierce Manufacturing Company of Philadelphia, Pennsylvania, was operated by Percy Pierce, a pioneer model airplane enthusiast and designer. This 1920 advertisement features his Loop-O-Plane slingshot-launched glider, a popular seller at the time.

G. William Holland

repress a shudder at the thought of the amount of explosive hydrogen gas used over many years by model balloon builders—but conceding Maerklin's obvious enthusiasm for spring-starter-launched "free flyers," it is necessary to question Maerklin's assertion that most other contemporary model airplanes and other flying devices were a "waste of time, energy, skill."

In 1911 Maerklin also introduced a combined model airplane and railroad item that has become rather well known over the years and whose manufacture continued into the 1920's. This was a model railroad flatcar, made in both O (1 1/4-inch) and No. 1 (1 3/4-inch) gauge loaded with a partially dismantled Blériot model airplane.

Model airplane interest, of course, manifested itself in this early period, as it still does today, in many toy and model flying devices and representations of heavier- and lighter-than-air craft. Over the years, there have been all sorts of nonmotorized model airplanes to be pulled or pushed along the floor. In the earliest period such models were usually made of light stamped metal or of white metal castings; later there were also very popular models of cast iron and steel in the 1920's and 1930's. Many of the early tin models were made in Europe, while most of the cast replicas were products of American factories. Around 1909, as well as later, there were a number of tin rubber- or clockwork-powered models that flew suspended from a cord or wire, as well as numerous other often inexpensive and sometimes quite ingenious miniatures that to some extent imitated an airplane or airship in movement through the air but did not actually fly. Aviation interest showed itself in various other ways in the early days: one could play a tune on the German "Aero Band" harmonica that pictured a Zeppelin, launch parachutes with a bow-and-arrow outfit (this was an American product), and even obtain what was known around 1910 as an "Air-Ship Cannon," which was not a piece of airborne artillery, as the name might suggest, but rather a toy cannon used to shoot arrows at a balloon target. Unfortunately, space does not permit a detailed treatment of the almost countless number of widely varied devices of this type, all of which it might well be argued have to some extent a definite bearing on and place in model aeronautical history.

THE DAWN OF THE MODEL AIRPLANE HOBBY

Interesting as would be a detailed discussion of such sidelines, both in themselves and for their broader implications, it is desirable to confine this study to the main line of development as it relates to the model airplane hobby. So far the story of model aviation has been viewed first from the standpoint of the actual airplane experimenters in their use of models and then, following the advent of the realized airplane, in terms of the commercialization of the model airplane and the birth of the model airplane industry. No model hobby ever attains notable success and truly widespread popularity without such commercialization, intrepid and important as may be the activities of many individual pioneers. In almost every model hobby it is possible to find traces of, if not conflict, then at least a differing of opinion as to the relative importance of the manufacturer and the individual experimenter. Sometimes these differences are carried to extremes, at least by some of the enthusiasts involved. Great roles were played in the birth of the model airplane hobby by individuals who in their enthusiasm were willing to give endlessly of their time and efforts, such as Edward Durant; by authors such as Francis A. Collins,[*] Charles M. Miller, and George A. Cavanagh in the United States and by V. E. Johnson and W. G. Aston in Great Britain; by the numerous newspapers in the United States, Great Britain, and

[*]Francis Arnold Collins, author of the first two model airplane books published in the United States, *The Boys' Book of Model Aeroplanes* (1910) and *The Boys' Second Book of Model Aeroplanes* (1911); the model airplane expert for *St. Nicholas* magazine should not be confused, as he often is, with A. Frederick Collins, the author of many boys' and popular scientific books. The latter also wrote a model airplane book or, more exactly, a combined model and real airplane book, *Aviation and All About It* (1929).

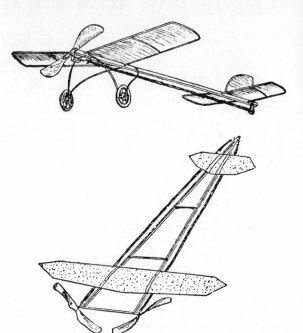

Fig. 257. Three A-frame twin-pusher rubber-powered racing models from the White Aeroplane Company catalog of 1912. Also shown (upper left) is a tractor monoplane. Some of these White racers, and similar models made by Ideal, were manufactured through the 1920's.

Howard G. McEntee; G. William Holland photographs

France that reported and sponsored model airplane activities, starting in the second half of the first decade of the twentieth century; by actual aeronautical organizations; by virtually all the real airplane magazines in the United States and Great Britain that were for many years a primary source of model airplane news and plans, and, of course, above all, by the efforts of the individual model airplane builders themselves.

It is neither practical nor necessary to weigh each of these factors individually and attempt to assign each of them a proportionate importance in the establishment of the model airplane hobby. Suffice it to say that there was no one force behind or wholly responsible for the birth of the hobby. Francis A. Collins once pictured the model airplane as wholly a boy's invention—the hobby literally springing full blown within a few months' time from a spontaneous effort of boys all over the United States—and by implication, the world—suddenly setting to work to build their own flying models. This is an attractive-enough picture and, like many generalizations, has a certain element of truth in it, but the fact is that to a large extent the model airplane hobby rose to its initial widespread popularity because it was deliberately promoted and nurtured, often for differing reasons, by the many elements enumerated in the preceding paragraph, and by others as well. In the first edition of *The Boys' Book of Model Aeroplanes,* published in 1910, Francis A. Collins noted that any boy would feel disgraced if he were to attempt to fly a model airplane that he had not built himself. This was rather unfair to the boy or parents who could afford to purchase a commercial model

airplane and by way of being at least a mild slap at the then dawning model airplane industry. Little lasting trace of this outlook can be found. Mr. Collins's purpose may well have been primarily to demonstrate how democratic a hobby was model airplane building and flying. If, as it seems, he was afraid that the young man with a commercial ready-to-fly model would invariably hold an advantage in competition over his fellows with homemade jobs, he was completely in error. In many cases the mass-produced models could not keep pace with advancements in model airplane designs as perfected almost month by month by individual hobbyists. Similarly, as individual builders created superior models, their designs often were taken over by model airplane manufacturers, and enthusiastically accepted either in kit or ready-to-fly form by a host of hobbyists. At least three American boys' names became virtually household words in model aviation circles through such a process as reflected in the Percy Pierce Flyer, the Cecil Peoli Racer, and the Lauder Racing Model, Not only that, but Peoli and Lauder also gave their names to propeller designs that long figured in model airplane supply catalogs cheek by jowl with Langley and Wright types. Well through the 1920's, long after more sophisticated models had been developed, the magic of their names and fame kept these models in the forefront of popularity. Even today the names of Pierce and Peoli especially maintain a sort of semilegendary aura in American model airplane circles as, evidently for somewhat similar reasons, does that of Fleming-Williams in Great Britain.

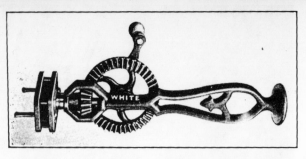

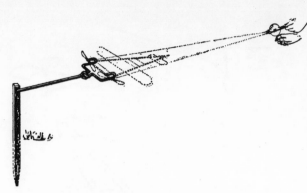

Fig. 258. Winding devices for early rubber-powered model airplanes. At the top is a White eggbeater-type winder for winding two propellers at once. At the right is the Ideal winding rig, allowing for one man winding by holding the model airplane to the stake driven into the ground.

Howard G. McEntee; G. William Holland photographs

To many early model airplane builders, the model airplane supply houses were thought of not as makers of ready-to-fly models or even of kits—seldom if ever designated by that name in the early period, but more generally as outfits, sets of parts, construction sets, K.D. (knocked-down) sets, or unassembled sets or models—but of individual parts and materials. Many boys, of course, built their models entirely from materials they could obtain from any handy sources—cane, reed, or rattan; cigar-box wood, and so on. The more knowing or more fortunate secured at least some of their materials, particularly propellers or blanks from which to carve propellers, from the model airplane companies. Balsa wood, while neither unfamiliar to nor unused by a few model airplane builders prior to World War I, was to remain to most hobbyists for some time a rather mysterious and obscure material whose qualities and advantages were little known or understood, and was not really to come into its own or become readily available until the 1920's. Even then its acceptance was quite gradual on the part of many hobbyists and manufacturers. In 1922 the Wading River Manufacturing Company was to catalog only a few sizes of balsa and to note that they used it for making "flying boats, pontoons, stream line struts, etc." Spruce was at first considered the most desirable wood for model airplanes because of its great strength in proportion to its weight, just as spruce was considered the favored wood for full-size airplanes, but the somewhat less-expensive basswood also soon came into favor. Another popular early material was split bamboo, furnished in flat strips, which was much favored for skids, ribs, and shock absorbers, and was often used for other components. Besides spruce and basswood, a number of other woods were regularly offered in early model airplane supply catalogs, such as poplar, maple, white holly (which could be easily steamed to any desired curve), and birch. At least some of these woods seem to have met with comparatively little general acceptance, and the principal woods of model airplane making were spruce, basswood, split bamboo and, later, balsa wood. Though ob-

scured by the seemingly ubiquitous use of balsa wood in subsequent years, spruce continued to be readily available for model airplane builders up to World War II, along with reed and bamboo. Basswood, of course, has always been and continues to be easily obtainable in a wide range of sizes, and even today there are a number of builders of larger model airplanes who use woods heavier than balsa for various applications.

Pre–World War I catalogs of model airplane supplies offer a wide range of materials: steel wire for guy wires, sheet aluminum and other metals in tube and rod forms, stamped metal and built-up wire spoke wheels, silk and bamboo paper for covering materials and, of course, the all-important rubber strands. In addition there were also a great many finished parts, including an astounding variety of propeller types and sizes in wood and aluminum. Mahogany, spruce, and poplar were the favored woods for propellers, with pine later attaining considerable popularity. While some smaller propellers were available, the usual range of sizes was from 5 to 24 inches. No reference was made to pitch, size, and the type of propeller —Langley, Wright, Antoinette, White, Ideal, Cecil Peoli, and so on, being the sole descriptive factors for finished propellers, although the factor of pitch clearly was understood by the manufacturers. Inasmuch as a propeller blank from which the hobbyist would himself carve his propeller usually cost from about a fourth to an eighth as much as a finished propeller, a great many enthusiasts naturally undertook to carve their own from such blanks, some attaining great success in the art, while others, of course, found that even if they built every other part of a model airplane themselves they would have to rely on ready-to-use propellers. It is interesting to note that almost from the earliest days of the model airplane industry ball-bearing propeller shafts were available and apparently quite popular. A number of enthusiasts evidently optionally undertook to construct their own ball-bearing assemblies, for separate steel balls were offered for this purpose.

Repeatedly winding a large rubber-powered

Fig. 259. An early custom-built exhibition model airplane by the White Aeroplane Company, an example of fine scale modelmaking work prior to 1912. This evidently is a nonflying display model with the propeller powered by an electric motor built into the fuselage between the wings.

Howard G. McEntee; G. William Holland photographs

Fig. 260. Crowds gather around a large model airplane (left foreground) at the First Exhibition of the Aeronautic Society of New York at Morris Park, the Bronx, New York, on November 3, 1908. This may be the model known to have been built by Percy Pierce and displayed at this event.

Russell Holderman; G. William Holland photograph

model airplane naturally was a tedious business, and an eggbeater type of winder appeared on the market at an early date and long remained popular. Usually they were designed so as to simultaneously wind the two rubber motors of twin propeller models if desired, not only saving time and effort but assuring that each motor had been wound exactly the same number of turns. Similar winders are still used today, but curiously, this once-standard device seems to have disappeared from the market in recent decades, and the present-day model airplane hobbyist who desires a winder is in the rather peculiar position of having to make his own version—usually by converting an eggbeater or a hand drill—of something that was readily available commercially at a very early date in the hobby's history.

Space unfortunately does not permit a more detailed analysis of the many commercial model airplane components and materials that were provided for hobbyists in what may be considered the great pioneer period: chain and sprocket drives, gears and gearboxes for propellers, propeller hangers in a wide variety of forms, and so forth. It obviously was an era of great ingenuity and much experimentation, a time of considerable trial and error, and after the passage of more than half a century a romantic and nostalgic air perceptibly hangs over these pioneer years that no one who examines them in any great detail can escape noting. It is possible—and it is to be hoped—that increasing interest in these bright morning years of the model airplane hobby may eventually warrant the reproduction of some of the old catalogs *in toto,* as has occurred with early model railroad catalogs, for to a certain extent only in their pages can much of the raw excitement of these early years be recaptured. At the time they were issued, even to the boys and men who could not avail themselves of commercial parts, much less complete kits or ready-to-fly models, the catalogs and lists of the suppliers played an important role in

promoting model airplane building, indeed even in providing evidence and needed assurance of the existence of a widespread model airplane hobby. To the young man who, in 1912, for example, questioned or was questioned as to the worthiness of his interest in model airplanes, it was comforting to read in the foreword of the White catalog that this company had by that time some 52,000 names on their mailing list of enthusiasts who were interested in model airplane supplies and in gliders. Thus, even if in a somewhat indirect manner, the industry played a role in awakening interest and enthusiasm in model airplanes, even among those who might never actually be customers. It is certain that many a young man sent in for a free Goff or Ideal or White catalog who was never in a position to purchase their materials but who was nonetheless inspired by this literature to undertake the construction of a model airplane, or whose total investment in the commercial circles might never extend beyond buying a plan, a propeller, or some rubber strands.

THE KITE INFLUENCE

Lastly, in assessing some of the factors that inspired many to participate in the hobby in its early period, it is important that the kiting tradition and influence, already touched upon, be neither ignored nor underestimated. Undoubtedly there long had been a limited number of amateur airplane enthusiasts and model builders. In the 1890's and early 1900's there assuredly were vast numbers of ardent kite builders and flyers, many of whom slipped automatically into being model airplane hobbyists in whole or at least in part in the early years of the twentieth century. There was in fact a widespread feeling in these years that the airplane had evolved more or less directly from the kite and particularly from the box kite. From the vantage point of today it is possible to punch many holes in this belief, although the con-

Fig. 261. Pioneers in real and model aviation. At upper left is George A. Page, Jr., subsequently Director of Engineering for Curtiss-Wright and Aeronca and designer of over a hundred airplanes, with one of his models in 1912. At upper right is Russell Holderman, pioneer pilot, shown in 1952 with a plaque (top) marking his fifty years as a pilot and a plaque won in 1911 for first prize in a national. model airplane contest. Both Mr. Holderman and Mr. Page are still (1966) active in aviation. Below are medals and trophies for model airplanes won by Mr. Page, 1911–1912. At the left center is a compressed-air model airplane engine he designed and built in 1912.

George A. Page, Jr.
Russell Holderman
G. William Holland photographs

cept still retains a certain element of validity. As already noted, one of the first results of the birth of the actual airplane was greatly to increase kite interest and sales: one dealer upon placing an extra-large order for box kites in 1908 was quoted by *Playthings* as being heard to remark that "the experiments of Wright and other famous aeronauts were responsible for an increase in the demand for kites," and we have seen how about this same time Horsman promoted kites as "airships." It was not long, however, before a definite distinction became noticeable in some quarters, but the linking of kites and model airplanes long continued in others, and some residual traces can still be found even today.

If some writers such as Francis A. Collins clearly perceived at a comparatively early date that the model airplane hobby was essentially a different one from kiting, others cannot be faulted from the standpoint of today's knowledge if they for some time almost automatically continued to link the two. It was an accurate reflection of a widespread prevailing state of mind. Charles M. Miller of the Los Angeles schools entitled his book, published in 1914 but written in 1912, *Kitecraft and Kite Tournaments* without seeing any incongruity in devoting about a fourth of it to a fairly comprehensive treatise on model airplanes. The present governing body for model aeronautics in Great Britain, the Society of Model Aeronautical Engineers, Ltd., was founded several years prior to World War I as the Kite and Model Aeroplane Association, merging in 1922 with a newer body known as the London Model Aeroplane Association, formed in 1920, to become the SMAE.* The original title of Kite and Model

*In the late 1920's the governing body in the United States under National Aeronautics Association sponsorship was the Airplane Model League of America, which was financed by *The American Boy* magazine, published in Detroit, Michigan, and the Detroit Board of Commerce. In 1931 they found it impossible to continue this support, although a 1931 National contest was finally held in Dayton, Ohio. After a period of confusion and uncertainty, the present governing body in the United States, the Academy of Model Aeronautics, was established in 1934, to a large extent through the efforts of Lieutenant H. W. Alden, USN, and Irwin and Nathan Polk. The AMA accordingly counts the present United States Nationals as dating only from 1934.

Fig. 262. A group of members of the New York Model Aero Club photographed at Van Cortlandt Park, the Bronx, New York, in the summer of 1910. About half of these young men soloed in real airplanes within the next six years. Left to right, rear row, are: unidentified, Edward Durant, the club's mentor; Harry Herzog, Percy Pierce, H. Walter Maass, George A. Page, Jr., unidentified, Harry Adler, Russell Holderman, Harry D. Graulich, Ernest Kothe; center row: Stuart Easter, Jean Roché, Ralph S. Barnaby, Charles Ragot; front row: Rudy Funk, unidentified, unidentified.

Russell Holderman; G. William Holland photograph

Aeroplane Association speaks for itself in reference to the situation under discussion.

SCALE VERSUS PERFORMANCE MODELS

Very early in the game, almost as soon as organized competitions for model airplanes were set up based on the distance flown and/or on the duration of flight, it became apparent that there was to be an important division between scale flying models based on actual prototype airplanes and on free-lance models that gave, as working miniatures, superior performance. Much original flying was done indoors as actual races between a number of model airplanes that were started at once, but a great deal of outdoor flying also was undertaken at an early date and became more and more popular as distance flights increased. When good flights were measured in terms of 100 or 150 feet or so, there was much that could be said in favor of the flying qualities of scale models, but as individually designed models rapidly topped these distances and flights became measured in terms of hundreds and then of over a thousand feet and finally in thousands of feet, it became obvious that the scale flying model as such was hardly suitable for competition except in events limited to this type of model. It was to be many years, well into the 1920's and even into the 1930's, before the scale flying model was to reach a new stage of development where it once again could compete successfully. Within only a few years of the start of model airplane contests it

was quite obvious to almost everyone that the scale flying model as such simply was not "in" it, and was, if not perhaps a curiosity, at least a thing apart from the mainstream in which competitive model aeronautics was traveling. Curiously enough, of the scale models generally seen in the 1908–1918 era—Wright biplanes, Curtiss hydroplanes, Nieuports, Blériots, Antoinettes, and so on—the best flying scale models seem to have been miniatures of the Langley aerodrome, which were capable of flights of over 400 feet.

The newspapers of the United States and Great Britain were filled with news of model airplane events and contests, in many cases sponsored by the papers themselves. It must be emphasized that these contests were not confined to very young boys. In fact, in many cases the majority of contestants were young men or adults; in 1907, for example, A. V. Roe won the *London Daily Mail*'s competition, and two years later had produced the first of the famed Avro full-size airplanes, a triplane. A flight of almost 200 feet was still news in 1910. One such newspaper account may well serve for all of them, in conveying the flavor and the interest of the day. It appeared in the *New York Herald* for Sunday, January 16, 1910, under a fair-sized two-column headline, "Model Aeroplane Makes Flight of Nearly 190 Feet," and a subheading, "New Records Made in Contest Flights at the Grounds of the Y.M.C.A.":

"New records were made in yesterday's contest for flights by model aeroplanes at the armory of the Twenty-second regiment, at Broadway and Sixty-eighth street, under the auspices of the edu-

Fig. 263. More members of the pioneer New York Model Aero Club. At left, as guests of the Witteman Brothers, airplane and glider builders, at Oakwood Heights, Staten Island, New York, in October, 1912, are: Norman McQueen at the tail, Ralph S. Barnaby, now Captain U.S. Navy (Ret.), who was to become the Navy's glider expert, in the glider; George A. Page, Jr., wearing derby, between struts at the right; and Andrew Surini at extreme right. Right: before a Galledaut "Flying Coffin," are, left to right: Andrew Surini, Harry Adler, George Cavanagh, George McLaughlin, Russell Holderman, Harry D. Graulich, Courtland Parker, and Frank A. Schober. Louis Fennouliet is in the plane.

cational department of the West Side Y.M.C.A. in connection with their lecture courses on aeronautics. In the contest for men and youths more than eighteen years of age Dr. C. Dederer won with a new record of 189 feet 8 inches, the previous best, his own, being 163 feet. In the contest limited to boys less than eighteen the winner was F. M. Watkins, aged fifteen, whose machine flew 111 feet 5 inches.

"Machines of all shapes, sizes, models, materials and descriptions were flown. The winner of the men's event described his model as a bi-tandem monoplane of the modified Langley type, while the winner of the boys' contest said he didn't know what his was called, but he had made it like it was because he thought that a machine belonging to one of his friends would go better the wrong way round and that an extra propeller would give it more power. When he tried it his expectations were exceeded, and during the afternoon his model made several very graceful flights.

"The contest was the second of a series by which the ownership of two cups is to be decided on. In both classes, men's and boys', the first to win three events takes the prize. Dr. Dederer has now a clear lead of two victories in the men's class. Yesterday's winner in the boys' class was a newcomer in the field. His score is equal to that of last week's winner, Ralph G. [sic] Barnaby,* whose best yesterday was 71 feet 7 inches. Other machines in the men's class were owned by Messrs. W. M. Sage, second; W. Picella [sic],† third; W. P. Talmage, F. S. Crocker and A. Armstrong. In

the boys' class H. Hiller, A. W. Macqueen, John Carisi and A. Halpine also flew machines."

The reference to Frederick Watkins in the preceeding account is especially interesting because it suggests that the soon standard A-frame racer or duration model, usually believed to have been invented in Great Britain, may also have been independently created in the United States. (In 1914 Fred Watkins held the American record for rise-off-ground models with a distance of 1,761 feet.) In any event, it was the birth and rapid acceptance of the A-frame twin-pusher model that spelled the doom of the fantastic modeling efforts of "all shapes . . . and descriptions" and definitely put the scale model into the background for many years. Consequently, the fact is that about this time American hobbyists found their records being pushed sadly aside by the then seemingly fantastically long flights being accomplished in Great Britain. In 1909 the American record was held by Percy Pierce with a flight of a little over 200 feet, but the British record and the world record was set by England's C. Fleming-Williams. There could be little argument in the face of such results, although there were naturally adherents of scale models—then more often known as scale reduction models, scale facsimile models, or simply as facsimile models—who, not without some merit to their case, argued that a model airplane must be a model of some actual prototype and that the new free-lance types were admittedly good miniature flying devices but not model airplanes. They prophesied the quick demise of the "freak distance flyer" that was so simple in design that construction of such "frail and homely machines" should certainly not properly bring any credit upon their builders. As has been said, they had a case, but in the face of the records being run up by the A-frame racers they were voices crying in the wilderness. Even most other free-lance designs gave

*Actually Ralph Stanton Barnaby, now (1966) Captain, United States Navy (Retired), some of whose aeronautical exploits are related shortly.

†Undoubtedly a misprint for William Piceller, an active aero modeler and a pioneer pilot who was taught to fly early in 1912 and received Pilot License No. 116, April 12, 1912. He was killed in the crash of his Wright Model B on October 2, 1914, at Hempstead, New York.

Fig. 264. A rubber-powered A-frame twin pusher built by Charles W. Meyers of the New York Model Aero Club about 1912. This model won a rise-off-ground duration record of 178 seconds. The lower photograph shows a Meyers model on pontoons.

Charles W. Meyers

way, until the establishment of separate categories for different types, before the A-frame twin-pusher, a simple model with stick fuselage shaped like a letter A, with the top of the A forming the front of the airplane and twin pusher propellers at the base of the A. In 1911 Cecil Peoli wrote his name forever large in model aviation history when his A-frame design made official records of 1,691 feet for distance and 48 4/5 seconds for duration at meets at Van Cortlandt Park in the Bronx, New York. In 1912 an English schoolboy, R. F. Mann, chalked up a flight of almost half a mile with an A-frame twin pusher he had designed. In 1913 Armour Selley of the New York Model Aero Club flew his design 2,800 feet; in 1915 Wallace Lauder of the Summit (New Jersey) Model Aero Club set a new record of 3,537 feet for distance and over three minutes for duration; in 1916 Thomas Hall of the Illinois Model Aero Club flew his model 5,337 feet. Still the A-frame twin pushers went on and on. The final record of all seems to have been made in 1924 when Robert V. Jaros of the Illinois Model Aero Club (an organization whose members by this time were racking up championships with an almost monotonous regularity) flew his A-frame job 7,920 feet. His duration record was 10 minutes and 14.2 seconds. The latter has long since been surpassed, for A-frames were noted for their powered flight, not for their subsequent sustained gliding characteristics. Mr. Jaros's distance has, however, never since been equaled in a rub-

ber-powered model. (These are all records for hand-launched models.) Today A-frame models still occasionally turn up and are demonstrated at model airplane meets, but purely as antiquarian curiosities.

All this is not to imply that the A-frame twin-pusher monoplane was the only type of model widely built and flown in the early period once it had been developed, although it was rapidly recognized as the best performer. There were also biplane pushers and monoplane and biplane tractor types (a tractor model is one with the propeller or propellers in front of the main lifting surface), with competition classes for these as well as for flying boats or hydroaeroplanes.* Hydroaeroplanes originally were urged as ideal for seashore or country vacations, so that the model airplane enthusiast did not have to abandon his activities while away for the summer, although this precise thinking may be granted to be somewhat specious, as anyone could as obviously fly a landplane model from a beach or country road as in a city park. However, with the development of the successful hydroaeroplane by Glenn Curtiss in 1911, a great deal of enthusiasm arose for this type, to be further whetted consider-

*Early real and model aviation writers were careful to distinguish between the hydroaeroplane and the hydroplane, the latter properly being a form of boat with steps on the bottom. Today few people make any distinction, and the term "hydroplane" frequently is heard applied to aircraft. There also was an intermediate name of hydro-airplane or hydroairplane used at times in the late 1920's and early 1930's.

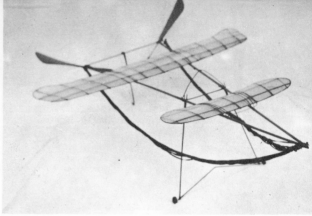

Fig. 265. Two rubber-powered models built by members of the Summit Model Aero Club of Summit, New Jersey, about 1912-1914. The model at the top left was built by Wallace A. Lauder and the one at the top right by Curtis B. Myers. The plane at the bottom is the Lauder champion model of 1915 that was subsequently marketed by White and its successors through the 1920's.

Carter Tiffany
Howard G. McEntee; G. William Holland photographs

ably in 1914 when Curtiss mounted the original 1903 Langley aerodrome on pontoons and successfully flew it from a lake at Hammondsport, New York. Many model airplane fans flew substantially the same and in some cases identical models both as landplanes and as hydroaeroplanes, merely substituting or adding pontoons or floats for the latter applications. Of course, in actual practice it was almost impossible successfully to launch a model from the rough surface of the ocean, and in practice model hydroaeroplanes usually were launched from quiet lakes and swimming pools; sometimes, at competitions, from special shallow tanks of water.

Most A-frame twin pushers were consistently good flyers—there were numerous minor variations in design, but models of this type could almost always be counted on to give a fairly satisfactory performance. This was the main reason for their popularity: the design was sound. This often was not true of other types, and particularly in the early days with tractor models, although as more and more real tractor airplanes appeared efforts were continually being made to produce satisfactory tractor miniatures. It was long, however, a hit-and-miss game, for there was little scientific study and reasoning behind the designing process, and few people understood to any degree the prin-

ciples involved in their successful creation until Charles Hampson Grant conducted the most lengthy and detailed experiments, and gradually made his findings available, at first in personal contacts and later, in the 1930's, in a long series of articles in *Model Airplane News*. It was his findings that to a large measure spelled the doom of the A-frame twin pusher by making tractor models practical in the 1920's and 1930's and thus, by the same token, bringing back to popularity what were essentially scale flying models.*

The Percy Pierce Flyer was an eminently satisfactory single-propeller canard pusher, which although it too gave way before the A-frames, established Pierce's name in model airplane history. Pierce was long active in model aviation, building his first model airplane in 1906, when twelve years of age, and in 1908 he exhibited a 6-foot rubber-powered model biplane at the first exhibition of the Aeronautic Society of New York held at Morris Park, the Bronx, New York. He is reported to

---

*Mr. Grant's material was finally collected in his book *Model Airplane Design and Theory of Flight,* published in 1941. Anyone interested in seeing just how much serious study, including a mass of mathematical computations, went into the perfecting of this material should examine this classic, which unfortunately has been out of print for some years. The present writer has also been privileged to be given copies of some of Mr. Grant's experimental data sheets from 1919. The depth of this research is truly fantastic.

Fig. 266. Some members of the Summit Model Aero Club at a meet with their friends of the New York Model Aero Club, about 1912-1913. Left to right in the group, standing, are: Walter A. Phipps, Harry Herzog, Carter Tiffany, Edward Durant, Wallace A. Lauder, Curtis B. Myers; stooping in front, Percy Pierce. At top right is Carter Tiffany launching a model; at lower left, Wallace Lauder launching; at lower right, Percy Pierce launching.

Carter Tiffany

have built five out of a total of thirty-five models entered in an exhibition at Boston in 1910. Around this time his Percy Pierce Flyer was becoming famous; like so many other young men interested in model aeronautics, he soon became a pilot of real airplanes and gliders. He served as First Lieutenant in the Engineering and Information Service of the Army Air Service during World War I and produced a standard manual on aircraft rigging. After the war he formed the Pierce Manufacturing Company of Philadelphia and turned out a ten-cent "airplane," the Loop-O-Plane, actually a slingshot-launched glider. While a reasonably satisfactory seller in the toy marts, the Loop-O-Plane was by no means a sensational development, being quite similar to the Loop-the-Loop glider manufactured by Ideal. Pierce, however, was one of the few pioneer model airplane builders who long kept up a very active interest in model aeronautics. In 1929 he was one of the organizers of the Philadelphia Model Airplane Association and was directing model airplane meets in the 1930's.*

*There is an interesting volume, *Model Aircraft Yearbook,* 1936 Edition (although actually published in 1937 and covering events into that year), by Philip Zecchitella, who evidently conceived, wrote, and published it as a labor of love. What the author recorded as early history at the time is to a considerable extent inaccurate and useless, but what he reported as current or recent news of the day is now of substantial historical value for this period.

Another of the famous early model airplane enthusiasts to enter the business of making model airplane kits and supplies, although on a vastly broader and longer-lasting basis than Pierce, was Armour Selley of Brooklyn, New York. In 1913 Selley held not only the American but the world's records for hand-launched distance and duration, and rise-off-ground distance. Two other Americans, Curtis Myers and George A. Cavanagh, held the world's records respectively for rise-off-ground duration and rise-off-water duration, and Selley had held the latter record, too, in 1912. Armour Selley was regarded as primarily responsible for at last giving the United States its place in the sun in worldwide model aviation, for Great Britain had been preeminent until the spring of 1912. Selley seems to have had no particular "secret" for his consistently successful models other than scientific study and application, although they were noted, recalls Harry D. Graulich, for their extremely, high-pitched propellers and gossamer-wing loadings. *Aircraft* for May, 1913, noted of "that remarkable model flyer from Flatbush, Brooklyn," Armour Selley, that "All of his record-breaking models are different in construction, each of them having been designed for the particular contest that they were entered. In addition, none of his records are flukes, as he has made many

Fig. 267. Charles A. Arens, a member of the Illinois Model Aero Club, with a rubber-powered A-frame twin-pusher model he designed and built at Cicero Field, Chicago, in 1913. Mr. Arens shortly thereafter became a pilot and later developed and manufactured the famous Arens Control System for airplanes.

Charles A. Arens

flights, very closely approaching each of his best marks." Selley's "secret" therefore appears to have been primarily an early grasp of the fact that models should differ according to the type of event in which they were to compete and that there was not necessarily an all-around "best" model. Selley subsequently formed the Selley Manufacturing Company, Incorporated, of Brooklyn, for many years a leading factor in the model airplane business, eventually expanding into model boat and railroad parts and being one of the pioneers in the die casting of small metal parts for models. The firm is still in existence, although long out of the model airplane kit business.

Pierce and Selley, along with many of the other early record holders mentioned in this section, were all members of the famous New York Model Aero Club, where they came under the influence of a remarkable old gentleman, Edward Durant.

THE REMARKABLE NEW YORK MODEL AERO CLUB

The earliest history of model airplane clubs in the United States remains a bit obscure and even somewhat contradictory. At least two of the pioneer authors, A. Hyatt Verrill and George A. Cavanagh, specify the date as 1907—Verrill says the winter of 1907—and there is no disagreement among them or other sources that the place was New York, New York, and that the club was founded by Miss E. L. Todd. However, an even more contemporary report, the magazine *Fly* for March, 1909, recounts that Miss Todd formed the Junior Aero Club of America, which was under the sponsorship of the Aero Club of America, in June, 1908. Verrill makes a brief reference to the Junior Aero Club of America and thereby implies

that it was a separate effort from the organization founded in 1907, while earlier referring to the exhibition at Madison Square Garden in New York in December, 1908, which is known to have been an endeavor of the Junior Aero Club of America as an accomplishment of the group formed in 1907. It is possible that even as early as 1913, when Verrill wrote, there was some confusion on this point and that three years later Cavanagh took his cue from Verrill; it is also possible that Miss Todd had formed an earlier and possibly more local group in 1907.* In March, 1909, one of the members of the Junior Aero Club of America, W. H. Phipps,† reported that they had fifty-one members representing thirteen states, that no one was eligible for active membership who was over twenty-one, and that all members must construct models. The objects of the club, as set down in its constitution, were "to promote interest in and encourage the study of aerial science among young people and to hold exhibitions and contests of apparatus designed and made by the boys."

The exhibition held at Madison Square Garden in December, 1908, was no doubt a part of the general aeronautical exhibition held there at that time. *Playthings* recorded that it included model airplanes, airships, and kites, and *Fly* noted that the youngest member of the club, nine-year-old Charles Whittlesey, displayed an 8-foot long dirigible of remarkable workmanship. In his 1910 book, Francis A. Collins noted (seemingly writing

---

An Epitome of the Work of The Aeronautic Society from July, 1908, to December, 1909 states that "Among those who have built machines elsewhere than at Morris Park are Miss E. L. Todd, the only lady member." Miss Todd presumably was thus a member both of the Aero Club of America and of The Aeronautic Society of New York, and had caused some sort of flying machine to be built for her by the end of 1909. Unfortunately, this does not help to clarify the matter of the early model airplane club or clubs.

†Phipps had become Assistant Editor of *Aircraft* by 1912. Between 1910 and 1915 he also was active as a dealer in model airplane supplies.

in 1909) that some fifty medals had been distributed among members of the New York Junior Aero Club, thereby introducing still another name, although possibly he may have meant the organization formed in 1907, or may have been referring to the Junior Aero Club of America. There were also a number of model airplane clubs set up in the schools of New York and elsewhere, and in New York the West Side Young Men's Christian Association became interested in real and model aeronautics and began holding model airplane contests, of the type alluded to in the article previously quoted from the *New York Herald* of January 16, 1910. The Aeronautic Society of New York also held model airplane and kite contests in 1909, awarding a number of trophies and medals, although far more of the competitions were for kites than for model airplanes, with first, second, and third prizes given in such categories as the highest flight of a kite, the greatest length of kite string in a flight, the least pull on a kite string during flight, and the most novel kite.

All these things—and some of them continued for some years—interesting and valuable as they might be, were merely preliminary skirmishings that preceded the establishment of the New York Model Aero Club.

Accounts and recollections of the exact sequence of events that brought this about vary somewhat and are not necessarily contradictory. All agree that the mainspring was Edward Durant and that such formal preliminary organizational discussions as transpired took place at the residence of Louis Ragot, whose two sons, Charles and Henri, were to become enthusiastic members of the organization. H. Walter Maass, the first Secretary-Treasurer of the club, has provided the present writer with a more detailed account than he has found in print elsewhere and places the date definitely as late 1909, following the return of Glenn Curtiss after his winning of the Gordon Bennett Trophy at the first great airplane races held at Rheims, France, in August of that year.

(Some accounts cite 1910, which probably represents the date of the club starting to hold their famous outdoor meets at Van Cortlandt Park in the Bronx, New York.) When Curtiss won the race, the *New York Herald* published plans of his Herring-Curtiss *Golden Flyer*. The appearance of these plans inspired the teen-ager to construct an excellent model of the plane, which in turn came to the attention of the Aero Club and was exhibited at their banquet for Curtiss at the Hotel Plaza upon his return. Maass was then advised that the model was desired for display at the *New York World* building, and upon taking it there he met Edward Durant who had done publicity work on Curtiss's activities. The conversation led from one thing to another, and the results were the meetings at the Ragot home at Twenty-seventh Street and Lexington Avenue and the formation of the New York Model Aero Club.

Durant, who was born in 1858, appeared quite an elderly gentleman to most of the boys. He was the son of Charles Ferson Durant (1805–1873), the famous nineteenth century American balloonist and scientist. Probably no single individual did as much to lay the initial groundwork for the model airplane hobby in the United States as Mr. Durant,* as he was respectfully called by most of the boys and young men. Only a few of the members of the club appear to have been aware that he should more properly be addressed as Professor Durant. This dignified-looking individual was evidently a gentleman of many talents and interests in addition to his hereditary enthusiasm for aviation: a noted scientist, an expert on sunspots and on the gyroscope, an experimenter and inventor and associate of Sperry in the development of the gyroscope and automatic pilot. At the Aeronautical Show at the Grand Central

---

*In their model airplane books both Verrill (1913) and Cavanagh (1916) mention him as having been involved with Miss Todd's 1907 endeavors. It is possible that Professor Durant was connected with these activities at their inception; it is certain he was connected with the Junior Aero Club of America by 1910, at about the same time he was launching the New York Model Aero Club.

Fig. 268. A hydroairplane competition of the Illinois Model Aero Club, held at Calumet Lake, Illinois, on June 21, 1914, where the club members were the guests of Charles Dickinson, president of the Aero Club of Illinois. Starting about this time and extending through the 1920's, members of the Illinois Model Club accumulated an amazing number of records.

Charles A. Arens

Palace in New York in May, 1912, he demonstrated the gyroscope and explained its influence and application in aeronautics. Twenty-five years later, when he was almost eighty, he read a notable paper before a scientific body in New York entitled "The electronic significance of disastrous explosions of chemicals and gases caused by increased electrostatic generation due to sunspot influence" in which he included his contention that the effects of sunspots had caused the explosion of the United States Battleship *Maine* and other notable disasters.

In any event, what is essential, and beyond peradventure true, is that no name is more fondly remembered over the years, no memory greener in the hearts of those who participated in early model airplane activities around New York than that of Edward Durant. He is recalled as their mentor and inspiration, their "wonderful old friend" who was possessed of a seemingly uncanny ability to find them a place to fly at almost any time, by countless boys and young men who were achieving remarkable success with flying models at the time and who went on to carve notable careers in real aviation for themselves. "That gentleman can never be given enough praise and credit to the untiring efforts that he put forth for us. He was a leader in every respect, in our meetings using and teaching us procedures, as well as guiding in some of the mysteries of aerodynamics as well as design, structures etc. To me there is not enough to be said in his praise. He was a big help to me." So writes Charles W. Meyers, a pioneer American pilot who entered the Royal Flying Corps in 1916, as did many of this countrymen, and went on to design such famous airplanes as the Waco Ten, the Waco Taper Wing, the Great Lakes Trainer, the Meyers Midget, and the Meyers Commercial.

This is, in fact, the great point and meaning of the memorable New York Model Aero Club, part of which is due, of course, to the fact that it was organized and flourished at precisely the right time for such results. It perhaps means but little to the modern reader to hear that Page's model beat Pierce's or that in turn Page's record was superseded by that of Peoli. Instead, let the reader look at one or more of the photographs of the New York Model Aero Club or its associated or successor bodies. Almost inevitably there was the moment when the boys—mostly young men, actually—lined up with their model airplanes for a formal photograph, and a number of these pictures fortunately have survived. When we look at one of these pre–World War I pictures—the intense, enthusiastic faces; the models that now appear so archaic and strange—we cannot escape a

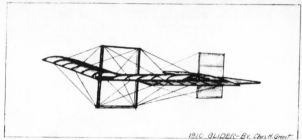

Fig. 269. At top, in 1910 fifteen-and-a-half-year-old Charles Hampson Grant carries parts of his homemade glider preparatory to taking off in the first heavier-than-air flight in the State of Vermont. The drawing shows the completed glider. The lower two photographs are from 1913, and show the takeoff and landing approach of a second Grant glider built in 1911.

Charles Hampson Grant; G. William Holland photographs

Fig. 270. Two views of Charles Hampson Grant's first successful rubber-powered contest model, constructed mainly of bamboo strips tied together with thread. A tractor model, a type with which Grant was to attain particular success, it flew 128 feet rise-off-ground in May, 1909. The landing-gear struts curved up into the wings to become the wing spars. The wings were "gulled" and about 28 inches in span.

Charles Hampson Grant

feeling that the camera has preserved a time and a place and a spirit that portended much and whose like assuredly will never quite come again, no matter how ardent an interest the youth of later years have and will continue to display in model aeronautics. When it is possible to identify some of the boys in these photographs and trace their later histories, this impression is confirmed; they were pioneers not only of model flight but of full-size aviation as well. Take the subsequent histories in aviation of some of those whose faces peer out at us from the old New York Model Aero Club photographs. Among them are Captain Ralph Stanton Barnaby, United States Navy (Retired), who entered Navy aviation in 1917 and helped prepare the NC flying boats for the first transatlantic flight in 1919; glider expert, in charge of the Navy's experiments in launching unmanned target gliders from blimps in the early 1920's, and, in 1930, the first man to pilot a glider launched from the dirigible *Los Angeles;** Vincent J. Burnelli, who was engineer and factory superintendent in the construction of the Lawson airliner, America's first big transport plane (eighteen passengers), of 1919; Harry D. Graulich, pioneer pilot and airplane designer; Russell Holderman, a World War I aviation instructor, one of the first airmail pilots, and for many years chief pilot for the Gannet Newspapers, who now operates his own air service; George A. Page, Jr., designer of some 100 airplanes, Director of Engineering for Curtiss-Wright and later for Aeronca; in 1966 still active as a consultant for Aeronca; and Jean Alfred Roché, designer of the Aeronca and president and chief engineer of the Aeronca Company (Captain Barnaby, who went through high school and college with Roché, test-flew some of the first Aeroncas for him in 1929) and for over thirty-five years a

civilian aeronautical engineer for the United States Army and Air Force. Allusion has already been made to the aeronautical achievements of club members Charles W. Meyers and Percy Pierce. What a crew to fly with!

Besides the eight members mentioned in the preceding paragraph, at least eight others of what may be more or less considered the original members of the New York Model Aero Club soloed before the end of 1916. Six of these—Luis de Florez, Arthur C. Heinrich, George F. McLaughlin, George B. Post, Frank Schober, and Andrew Surini—became, along with the eight above, members of the Early Birds of Aviation, Incorporated, the pioneer pilots' organization, whose membership is limited to those who soloed before December 17, 1916, the thirteenth anniversary of the Wrights' first successful flight. (Several others probably also soloed before this date but never joined the Early Birds or died before its formation in 1928.) At least two of the original club members died prior to 1916 in the crashes of planes they were piloting. One was Cecil Peoli, whose modeling exploits already have been chronicled. Peoli learned to fly at a very early age, and achieved considerable fame as the "boy aviator." In 1913 A. Hyatt Verrill cited him as the "mere boy" who had made over 400 flights in a single season, and in fact bracketed him with the Wright brothers, Captain Tom Baldwin, and Glenn Curtiss as examples of the safety of flying, and noted that neither serious accident nor death had attended the flights of "these famous aviators." In retrospect the paragraph gives the reader a strange sensation. Peoli was, in fact, a protégé of Captain Baldwin and was flying by 1911 and became one of Baldwin's exhibition flyers, flying the Baldwin "Red Devils." In 1915 he designed and built an airplane of his own that he hoped to sell to the United States Army—Captain Barnaby describes it as a more or less conventional Curtiss-type pusher biplane—and was killed in it on his first flight at

---

*The idea was to launch a mooring officer from a dirigible to the ground to take charge of the landing. The experiment was successful—Captain Barnaby made a 13-minute glide before landing (January 31, 1930)—but the basic idea was given up, and only one other glider launch was made from the *Los Angeles.*

Fig. 271. Charles Hampson Grant in 1910, age fifteen, with his eighth successful model airplane, in this case a rubber-powered A-frame twin-pusher type that flew 1300 feet. This picture was taken at Peru, Vermont, where, a few months later, Grant built and flew his first full-size glider.

Charles Hampson Grant; G. William Holland photograph

Fig. 272. An experimental all-balsa-wood rubber-powered tractor bi-plane, built by Charles Hampson Grant while a lieutenant in the Air Corps station at Dayton, Ohio, in 1918-1919. The remarkable performance of this and similar models attracted the attention of local businessmen and led to the production of a Grant-designed line of model airplanes in 1919.

Charles Hampson Grant; G. William Holland photograph

College Park, Maryland. In describing the Cecil Peoli Racer in their catalogs after his death, Ideal noted that the designer "has since given his life in the cause of aeronautics" and that "this Model will ever remain as a silent tribute to the early work of this true American Hero."

The other New York Model Aero Club member who died even before the arrival of the date that was to determine eligibility for membership in the Early Birds was William Piceller, mentioned earlier. Unfortunately, the date of his death has, as will be seen, an important bearing in establishing the time of an event of major importance in model airplane history, the date of the first gas model competition in the United States. Piceller was born on November 18, 1883, and accordingly was almost thirty when he learned to fly in the spring of 1912. One of his closest friends was Andrew Surini, another member of the New York Model Aero Club, and one of a group that, according to Harry D. Graulich, practically lived at the hangars at the Mineola, New York, flying field so that they could fly at the crack of dawn when the wind was right. Piceller usually would wake Surini with a jovial "C'mon Andy, get up, we might get killed today." On October 2, 1914, while flying alone at Hempstead, New York, the right-wing warping line of his Wright Model B broke in the air; Piceller lost control and the plane crashed. As Piceller lay in the Garden City Hospital later that day, he turned to Surini and said, "I'm so glad that I didn't

take you on this flight with me. . . ." and died a few minutes later. The only reason Surini had not gone on that flight was that Piceller could not get the engine up to the proper number of revolutions per minute and was unable to carry a passenger.

We are told that Ruth Law, one of the first American women to fly and to give stunt exhibitions, purchased the wreckage of the Piceller plane.* Such was the spirit of the era.

No reference to the New York Model Aero Club would be complete without mention of Mr. Durant's associate and assistant, evidently in business as well as in his model airplane club activities, Mr. Uncle or Unkle, a contemporary of Mr. Durant's in years. He too put his heart and soul into furthering the interests and activities of the model club and, like Mr. Durant, occupies a cherished place in the memories of the members.

OTHER EARLY MODEL AIRPLANE CLUBS

Competitions were conducted on a rather broad basis in the earliest days, and at first there was little interclub rivalry. Members of one club evidently freely competed as individuals in events

---

*Harry D. Graulich advises that the plane was the third Wright "B" built by the Wright brothers and that Piceller had purchased it from the publisher, Robert J. Collier, who owned stock in the Wright Company. Harold E. Morehouse, however, has a contemporary magazine account that states the machine was a locally built 'B' type and "was in distressingly bad shape."

Fig. 273. Four examples of "Right Fliers" designed by Charles Hampson Grant and manufactured by the Ritchie-Wertz Company of Dayton, Ohio, in 1919. The upper two models are tractor monoplanes, while below are two A-frame twin pushers. This was the first line of commercial model airplanes to make extensive use of balsa wood.

Charles Hampson Grant; G. William Holland photographs

sponsored by other organizations; often the same hobbyists' names are found in accounts of events sponsored by clubs, the YMCA, newspapers, and others who were either interested in model aviation as such or who saw a potential spectator sport in the new-found hobby. A number of early model airplane flying contests were held in conjunction with athletic meets where, recalled H. Walter Maass in a 1939 broadcast of "The Model Airplane Club of the Air," they provided "a sort of Roman entertainment where the fans would cheer every time a model cracked up, our own hearts breaking as we thought of the hours of toil ahead to reconstruct the precious but frail machines."

Mr. Maass related a personal experience that took place at the Greek American Games which were held at the armory at Broadway and Sixtyeighth Street in New York during the winter of 1910. He had built a model especially for this contest "that was to fly across the armory in a sort of ocean wave effect," with goldbeater's skin for the wing covering. "After attaching these delicate skins to the frame," he said, "I would moisten them slightly which caused them to shrink, tightening up like the top of a drum. The backbone of the fuselage was made of half inch dowel and the rubber for the motive power was supplied by hundreds of rubber bands about one inch long and knitted together to make about twenty thirty-six-inch strands. My elevator was adjusted carefully to change the level of the flight. The day of the event

I spent the entire afternoon in the armory adjusting the ship to get the best results and I was certain of victory when the fatal hour arrived. So as to run everything off on schedule we had appointed starters who would give the signal when to let go. Not being ready was the cause for disqualification. This particular event was started by Ralph Barnaby who had no plane entered for it.

"I gave my propeller a few extra turns for good luck, which was fatal, the backbone strained against the terrific pull of the tightly knitted rubber bands, but something delayed Barnaby's signal for a few seconds and then BANG—with a report that probably was heard outside the armory, the backbone broke and my pride and joy, hours of toil, was wound into a mass of rubber bands, goldbeaters' skin, splintered wood and bamboo. The crowd roared its delight and I was about the most miserable kid in the world at that moment."

Many of the early contests were held indoors, in armories, which of course presented an entirely different set of flying conditions than in the outdoor meets. For a while it seems to have been the practice to hold the contests indoors during the winter and outdoors in the warmer seasons. In time, distance flights became so long that it was impossible any longer to hold contests even in the enormous Kingsbridge Road Armory in the Bronx, New York, the largest armory in the United States. In a number of cases model airplane contests were sponsored by department stores. At one time Gim-

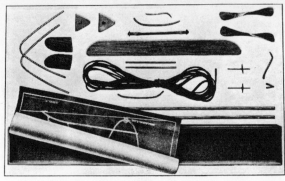

Fig. 274. All the Grant-designed 1919 model airplanes were sold in assembled form, and a few as kits or "Knocked Down" sets as well. Shown here are two of the kits, one as packed in the box, and the other—for an A-frame twin pusher—with the components spread out.

Charles Hampson Grant; G. William Holland photographs

bel's in Philadelphia turned over an entire vacant floor to such an event every Saturday and between 3,000 and 4,000 boys came each week, and the L. Bamberger Department Store of Newark, New Jersey, was consistently interested in promoting the hobby over several decades, and sponsored a contest at the New Jersey National Guard Armory in Newark as early as 1911. In 1912, however, they were forced by the increased length of flights to hold the contest in the open at East Orange, New Jersey. From a purely commercial standpoint, it has been long well understood that model airplanes have attained several waves of enormous enthusiasm interleaved with somewhat slacker eras— wherein they remained staple sellers—but it is doubtful if, proportionately at least, the initial enthusiasm of a few years prior to World War I ever has been equaled.

Around New York, the favorite outdoor flying ground for model airplanes was Van Cortlandt Park in the Bronx. A number of other competitions within the city were held at the Oakwood Heights Flying Field on Staten Island, where Captain Tom Baldwin had the headquarters of his flying circus and the Wittemann brothers—who would have the club over as their guests at times— constructed their airplanes and gliders (Gustave Whitehead built some of their engines for the Wittemanns), or at what were known as the Rugby Flying Grounds in Brooklyn. At times other events and demonstrations were held at the old Mineola Flying Field at Mineola, Long Island, or at other airports located on what were then generally known as the Hempstead Plains. The program for the International Aviation Tournament held at the Nassau Boulevard Aerodrome, September 23 to October 1, 1911, announced that an "Exhibition of Model Flying" would be made during the meet by "Messrs. Deoli [*sic*] and Pierce, the present champion model-flyers of the world."

Until Cecil Peoli's then amazing flight of 1,691 feet, and 6 inches on August 19, 1911, at Van Cortlandt Park, model airplane flying distances had been measured off with ordinary tape measures. The Peoli flight was measured off by George A. Page, Jr., whose own record Peoli had

just outdone, with a 50-foot tape and some help from others. He then went home and designed a wheel-type measuring device that would save the labor of measuring out distance by hand. To his surprise he soon found that the wheel-type measuring apparatus was a standard surveyors' tool and could readily be purchased in finished form from purveyors of surveyors' equipment. From that point on, these wheeled measurers, either home-fabricated or of the commercial surveyors' models, became virtually standard equipment at all model airplane meets, and can be observed in many of the photographs of early model airplane activities.

The Summit (New Jersey) Model Aero Club was formed shortly after the New York Model Aero Club by Carter Tiffany, Curtis B. Myers, and Wallace Lauder, whose models were to attract much attention. They were joined later by Guido Foster and others. Tiffany had built his first model airplane in 1909 when he was thirteen, but it was not a success, and he notes, "After trying to copy airplanes from pictures of them I gave up copying and began designing models that would fly." The Summit club soon joined in friendly competition with the New York Model Aero Club "under the fatherly guidance of Mr. Durant... the official measurer of duration and distance of model flights." The Long Island Model Aero Club was formed in 1911, and another New York club, the Bay Ridge Model Aero Club of Brooklyn, came into being about the same time or shortly thereafter. This put four clubs in the New York area, and in the spring of 1913 the handsome silver "Collins Interclub Trophy" was offered by Francis A. Collins for the winning club on a point basis spread over five separate competitions held at two-week intervals. The first of these, held on April 6, was won by the New York Model Aero Club through the flights of Harry Herzog, an upcoming name as a champion model flyer and designer; J. Billings, and George A. Page, Jr. It was the last appearance in a model airplane contest for Page, the future airplane designer, for he reported for flight training on April 18 at the school conducted by Heinrich Brothers ("No charge for breakage," they advertised in a phrase that a present-day

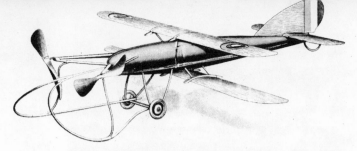

Fig. 275.   Ritchie-Wertz's 1919 masterpiece, the Charles Hampson Grant twin-propeller biplane. It had a 30-inch wingspan, was 38 inches long, had 9½-inch-diameter propellers, and weighed 13 ounces. It sold for $20.70 ready-to-fly. Elaborately twining combination skids and propeller guards protected the propellers from damage in the event of a bad landing.

Charles Hampson Grant; G. William Holland photograph

Fig. 276.   Charles Hampson Grant, pioneer pilot and real and model airplane designer whose activities have done so much to promote the model airplane hobby, which he has always looked upon not so much as a hobby but as a science. He is still (1966) active in real airplane design work.

Charles Hampson Grant; G. William Holland photograph

advertising agency might suggest deleting as too suggestive of potential aerial misfortunes) at Baldwin, Long Island. The Summit Model Aero Club came in second best that same day, with flights by Carter Tiffany and Wallace Lauder, with Curtis Myers failing to qualify. Like so many other boys and young men of the day, the Summit members also were interested in real gliders, several being built as joint projects by Tiffany and Myers at this time. "The last one, for which Curt was mostly responsible, was successful in that it got off the ground," recalls his associate in these ventures. Tiffany became a pioneer pilot, served in World War I, and after the war became active in a number of aviation enterprises, including an association with A. H. G. Fokker, the famed Dutch airplane builder. Tiffany was appointed by Queen Wilhelmina of the Netherlands to handle all Dutch aviation assets in the United States during World War II.

The 1913 competitions among the four clubs were the first serious attempt at organized interclub contests. At the time, *Aircraft* magazine advocated that clubs in other parts of the country combine with the New York group in arranging such interclub meets, seemingly the first time the idea was broached of model airplane competitions on a national basis. If no local club existed, then let the enthusiasts in the area come together and form one. *Aircraft* estimated that even as few as five interested hobbyists were sufficient to form the basis of a club, for it was the spirit that counted more than mere numbers. By 1916 there were at least twenty-five model airplane clubs active in the United States. The activities of the New York Model Aero Club had by then been absorbed by a new organization in the area, the Aero Science Club, still under the guidance of the redoubtable Edward Durant. The Aero Science Club was evidently at once a local New York club and at the same time an endeavor to affiliate clubs in other parts of the country in a single overall body. In 1915 the Aero Club of America organized the First National Model Aeroplane Competition. The prime mover in this action was Major Augustus Post, famed balloonist and pioneer pilot. It was at this event that Wallace Lauder's model starred, with a distance record of 3,537 feet and a duration record of 195 seconds. A second competition was held in 1916, but the coming of World War I evidently caused the series to be broken off and they were not resumed after the war. In the 1920's, Major Post was the instructor in aviation at Dan Beard's Outdoor School, with courses that involved the construction of model airplanes, and throughout his life retained his enthusiastic belief that the hobby of model airplanes was an ideal steppingstone toward an understanding of and careers in full-size aviation.

THE ILLINOIS MODEL AERO CLUB

It obviously is impossible to recount in detail the history of each of the early model airplane clubs. One other club, however, does merit special reference, the Illinois Model Aero Club, based in Chicago. Founded in 1911, it is the oldest model airplane club in the United States, and for a period that must have seemed depressingly long for contestants from other areas, its members dominated most of the events in organized model aviation, roughly from World War I until 1930 when the parent organization, the Aero Club of Illinois, was unable to continue to finance the member's trips to various distant competitions.

Donald Lockwood, who joined the club in 1922 at the age of eleven and is now the club sponsor, attributes the rise of the club and its great success to the efforts and interest particularly of three men, Charles Dickinson, Joseph J. Lucas, and Walter L. Brock. Charles Dickinson was a wealthy seed merchant who became interested in

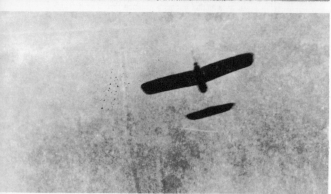

Fig. 277. About 1912. Left to right, Charles W. Meyers, Wallace A. Lauder holding a compressed-air-powered model and the bicycle pump needed for its operation, ——— Thiel, Robert King, and Edward Durant holding another compressed-air model. The other two photographs show a compressed-air model built by Frank A. Schober, in repose and in flight.

Charles W. Meyers

aviation at an early date and financed many aeronautical activities; a pilot himself, he was one of the organizers of the Early Birds, although he had not soloed in time to qualify for actual membership in the organization. Aviation became Mr. Dickinson's dedicated purpose in life, and he sparkplugged the Aero Club of Illinois and, in turn, the Illinois Model Aero Club. Joseph J. Lucas was an early member of the club, and kept up his activity in promoting and publicizing the club over many years; in the 1920's he was to become the model airplane authority for *Boys' Life* magazine, and many of the model designs he published were originated by the members of the Illinois Model Aero Club. Walter L. Brock was a mechanical engineer who first came in contact with aviation in 1906 when he met a former associate of Sir Hiram Maxim in the building of Maxim's aeroplane who was interested in the Elmore Automobile Company of Clyde, Ohio, and who engaged Brock to work for Elmore. He then became associated with Augustus M. Herring in airplane building and subsequently went to Europe, where he obtained his pilot's license and won fame as an air racer until the outbreak of World War I. He then returned to the United States, where he became a protégé of Mr. Dickinson's. In such free time as he had between making exhibition flights and helping to train American World War I pilots, he acted at Mr. Dickinson's request to devote himself to work-

ing with and teaching the boys and young men of the Illinois Model Aero Club, with the result that the club members soon were accumulating a seemingly unaccountable number of model airplane championship records. In fact for years the Illinois Model Aero Club seems to have engaged in a definitely thought-out and long-range continuing process of creating champions, spotting and encouraging likely future winners at an early date so that they would be ready to move up and occupy the positions held by the older and current champions when they in turn were ready to move out into the full-size airplane field. It had in fact some of the aspects of a baseball team, with likely rookies in reserve waiting to be brought up from the minors at the appropriate moment, all accomplished with the financing of Mr. Dickinson, the enthusiasm and promotion of Mr. Lucas, and the know-how of Mr. Brock, who was the practical mainspring of the whole endeavor.

Like the New York Model Aero Club, the Illinois Model Aero Club in its earliest days sent a surprising number of members into aviation, such as Emil M. (Matty) Laird, whom even as early as the World War I period the club cited as an outstanding example of practical aeronautical success "won through work with models." In 1912 he designed and built a small 12-horsepower biplane in which he taught himself to fly and in which he later flew exhibitions through the Midwest, subse-

Fig. 278. This photograph taken in 1915 shows two members of the New York Model Aero Club with elaborate model airplane power plants. Left, Frank A. Schober with a steam engine and boiler, and, right, Rudy Funk with a compressed-air engine and cylindrical tank assembly.

G. William Holland

quently going into the designing and construction of airplanes that ranged from outstanding small private planes to mail planes and Bendix trophy winners. Another member and Early Bird, Charles A. Arens, worked in various aircraft factories and subsequently developed and manufactured the famed Arens Control System, which was used in almost all airplanes and made it possible to transmit push-and-pull motions through any degree of arc. George (Buck) Weaver, who died in 1925, another Illinois Model Aero Club alumnus, became a civilian flying instructor for the Army Air Corps at Waco, Texas, during World War I. After the war he was for a while a member of a barnstorming team with Charles W. Meyers and E. P. Lott, both of whom had come out of the old New York Model Aero Club. (It occurs that there may be many younger readers to whom the term "barnstorming" may be unfamiliar. "Barnstorming" was the term applied to pilots who, in the 1920's, would travel around the country giving flying exhibitions, often at rural county fairs before audiences that often included many people who had never yet seen an airplane. Many World War I pilots became barnstormers, and many of the barnstormers subsequently became among the first of the commercial pilots as commercial aviation began to make real headway.) Weaver later formed the Weaver Aircraft Company, which in turn developed into the famous Waco Aircraft Company, although Weaver had himself left before this change was made and was associated with Laird at Wichita, Kansas, during the time of the production of the Laird Swallow and until his death. Others who came out of the Illinois Model Aero Club and into actual aviation at an early date included Ellis Cook, Lindsay Hittle, Harry Wells, Willis Hitt, William Courtney, Thomas Hall, Ward Pease, Donald Cornell, Charles Laird, and Arthur E. Nealy. The process continues to this day.

CHARLES HAMPSON GRANT

However, this progression from an interest in model aviation to a career in the real thing was by no means limited to those who lived in or near the large cities where the earliest clubs were functioning. An interest in real and model aviation often manifested itself in less thickly populated portions of the country and might turn up anywhere. In the summer of 1910, in the little Vermont village of Peru, a fifteen-and-a-half-year-old boy, Charles Hampson Grant trundled the parts for a home-designed and homemade glider up a hill to his home. After a few preliminary test hops were made on a gentle slope, he boldly climbed to the top of the roof of the house and galloped down the slope to the edge and into space. The description conjures up what seems to be a familiar scene from an old motion picture about a boy who became a World War I ace; in the movies the boy invariably falls to the ground as his homemade flying machine fails. Instead, in this real life occurrence the boy sailed buoyantly out into space, airborne, and made a successful landing in a broad meadow for the completion of what has been officially recognized as the first heavier-than-air flight in the State of Vermont.

Young Grant had already built and flown a number of successful model airplanes, even journeying to New York and competing in some of the contests of the New York Model Aero Club. He was a keen scientific observer and noted that rise-off-ground models exhausted much of their power in the act of taking off, and accordingly set himself the task of designing quick-takeoff models. One of these set a record in 1911 by taking off in only two-fifths of a second and flying 421 feet. By the summer of 1910 the exploits of the Wrights, Curtiss, and others had fired his desire to fly to a fever pitch, but not so feverish but that before attempting to build a glider he did not set to work gathering all the information and design data on which he could lay his hands and analyzing it carefully—a procedure that was to characterize all his work. He decided that Santos-Dumont's Demoiselle airplane design held the greatest possibilities for adaptation as a simple glider, and then started designing and constructing his machine with great care. For example, he tested the tapered spruce spars with superimposed weights before assembly. The resulting glider had 47 square feet of doped muslin covering and weighed 30 pounds, the young pilot weighing 105 pounds at the time. Grant subsequently built and flew a second and larger glider, studied engineering at Princeton and

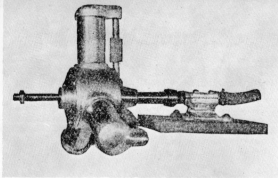

Fig. 279. Two commercial compressed-air engines of the World War I era, the Nomie three-cylinder (available as early as 1911 at least) and six-cylinder engines. Only the engines themselves are shown here; in addition, a pressure tank to hold the compressed air was required.

G. William Holland

the Massachusetts Institute of Technology, and became an Early Bird pilot, always retaining his interest in model aeronautics and laying the background for the tremendous job of research and study in the field of models mentioned earlier in this chapter.

It is rather remarkable that two cousins, Charles Hampson Grant and Harry C. Grant, contributed so much to the pioneer development work in two of the most important and popular model-building hobbies: model airplanes and model railroads respectively. Charles Hampson Grant, it should be noted, constantly approached and always considered model airplanes as essentially a science, not as a toy or even a hobby. "Actually it is," says Mr. Grant, "one of the greatest means for training and acquiring aviation knowledge (and mathematical knowledge) that has ever been devised." He feels strongly that the youth of America were equipped for the demands to be put upon them for quickly establishing United States airpower in World War II because of this properly scientific approach to model airplanes that was imposed upon the boys in the 1920's and 1930's and that much of this important element is missing in today's easy-to-build and easy-to-fly model airplanes (although much of this sureness and simplicity is in fact based on the results of his model aeronautical studies that he published in the 1930's and 1940's). The great-grandfather of Charles Hampson and Harry C. Grant was John Hampson, an English engineer who came to the United States and first attained fame in connection with the *DeWitt Clinton* locomotive, later becoming foreman of locomotives on the old Camden and Amboy Railroad and other railroads. He was regarded as one of the foremost locomotive men of the earliest period of railroading in America. (His son, Edward P. Hampson, was in turn a steam and electrical engineer.) One of John Hampson's great-grandsons, Charles Hampson Grant, became a real and model aeronautical pioneer. Another great-grandson, his first cousin,

Harry C. Grant, together with J. Lionel Cowen, founded the Lionel Manufacturing Company in 1901, Grant being the partner primarily responsible for the electrical and mechanical design of the product. Thus, as noted, the two cousins played their respective major roles in the development of the hobbies of model aviation and model railroading.

While Charles Hampson Grant was serving as a lieutenant in the Air Service at Dayton, Ohio, in 1918, he continued his model-building and flying activities whenever time was available to him. The remarkable performance of these models, and particularly his tractor models, attracted the attention of some of the business interests of that city, and in 1919 a line of Grant-designed ready-to-fly model airplanes and kits was put into mass production by the Ritchie-Wertz Company of Dayton. The models were known in 1919 as "Right Fliers" and in 1920 as "Riteflyers," plays on the aeronautical connotating name Wright. The 1919 line consisted of models selling for from $3.75 to a deluxe $20.70 model. "To gain strength and flexibility, a very rare and light wood has been used, overcoming the necessity for constructing of tissue paper or silk," the catalog noted. The wood, of course, was balsa, which was for the first time being brought into its own in model aviation, although a few modelers had used it a decade earlier. While Ritchie-Wertz manufactured some standard A-frame pusher types, their most interesting and attention-getting models were their tractor monoplanes and biplanes. For the first time manufactured tractor models were made available that were uniformly capable of sustained stable flight. The Ritchie-Wertz models, which were demonstrated by being taken to the top of a building and launched out over some city to convince dubious toy buyers that they really would fly, sold like the proverbial hot cakes, some $250,000 worth in two years. The factory turned out about 1,000 models a day, a hitherto unheard-of quantity, using special machinery designed by Mr. Grant. However, busi-

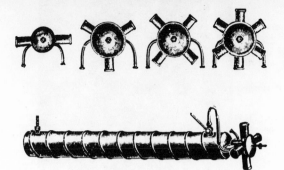

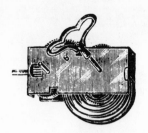
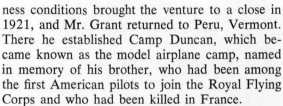

Fig. 280. Two-, three-, four-, and six-cylinder rotary compressed-air engines cataloged both before and after World War I by Stevens's Model Dockyard of London, England. Also pictured is a complete assembly with wire-wound compressed-air tank and a four-cylinder engine.

G. William Holland

Fig. 281. A clockwork mechanism especially designed for model airplane use and available in four sizes is shown at the left. At the right is an electric motor for model airplanes. Both units are reproduced from Stevens's Model Dockyard pre–World War I catalogs.

G. William Holland

ness conditions brought the venture to a close in 1921, and Mr. Grant returned to Peru, Vermont. There he established Camp Duncan, which became known as the model airplane camp, named in memory of his brother, who had been among the first American pilots to join the Royal Flying Corps and who had been killed in France.

Model airplane building and flying played a major role in the activities of the boys who attended Camp Duncan, one of whom was Howard G. McEntee, one of today's major names in model aeronautics. In 1928 he established the Grant Aircraft Company at Chester, Vermont, to manufacture a new line of model airplanes he had designed, including the famous "Silver Arrow" models, with fuselages made of precisely stamped 6/1000-inch-thick medium-hard aluminum. Despite the Ritchie-Wertz venture, ready-to-fly models and particular tractors still retained a poor reputation in many quarters.

The success of the Grant models came to the attention of the Kingsbury Manufacturing Company of Keene, New Hampshire, well-known toy manufacturers—and they arranged to take over the manufacture of the "Silver Arrows" with Mr. Grant moving his factory to Keene. This was in 1929, and almost as if following a script the earlier sequence of events at Dayton, Ohio, was repeated. Over $300,000 worth of the model airplanes were sold the first year, but again a depression necessitated the curtailment of the operation. In 1931 Mr. Grant became editor of *Model Airplane News,* the first model airplane magazine in the United States, which had been started in July, 1929, a position he held until 1942 when he was called upon to bring his talents into play in the design of military equipment, the glide bombs of World War II being to a large extent the result of Mr. Grant's earlier scientific studies and experiments with model aircraft.

As a matter of fact, Mr. Grant had been involved in the engineering and design of real aircraft ever since World War I, particularly in the field of airplane wings and flaps and controls, on which he holds a number of patents. At the time of this writing, he is still actively engaged in airplane engineering work, and the Grant Vertawing, which he developed between 1954 and 1962, appears destined to play a vital role in the vertical takeoff aircraft of the future. In any event, no man appears to have writ his name quite as large or as brightly in the dawning sky of the model airplane era as Charles Hampson Grant.

ENGINE-POWERED MODEL AIRPLANES

Until the comparatively recent advent of startlingly inexpensive miniature internal-combustion reciprocating engines, rubber remained the main powering force for model airplanes built for hobby use. However, there were other forms of power used in the early 20th century.

In most cases, a model engine that will operate on compressed air will also operate on steam or carbon dioxide. The use of the latter, however, involved generating the gas, with the attendant danger that it would turn into dry ice or carbonic acid snow, as it is known in Great Britain. Some CO_2-powered model airplanes were successfully flown in the 1890's and early 1900's, but little seems to have been done with them after World War I—although there was still considerable discussion concerning their possibilities in the 1920's —until an attempt was made to revive the form in the 1930's, which met with some but no substantial acceptance. The preceding remarks, of course, refer to the use of carbon dioxide to power a reciprocating engine. Today CO_2 is available in cartridge form and at times is used as a means of providing jet propulsion.

The use of steam for power involved the carrying of a boiler on the model aircraft, and those who attempted to employ this form of power ran into all the problems of boiler design and weight that had confronted experimenters from the days

Fig. 282. In 1887 Gustav Trouvé built what was regarded as the lightest electric motor constructed up to that time, fitted it with a propeller, and demonstrated its lifting power on the special test device pictured here.

Warshaw Collection of Business Americana

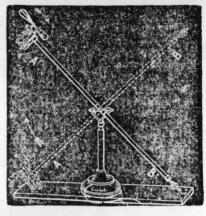

Fig. 283. Electrically powered models of 1909. The Pioneer Airship (left) flew in tethered flight around the pole. The device at the right is a monorail elevated railroad from which is suspended an electrically powered pusher-type triplane.

"Playthings"

of John Stringfellow onward. Despite these problems, a few commendable steam-powered model airplanes were built and flown by individuals in the early days of the hobby. A good deal more development work in this direction appears to have been done in Great Britain than in the United States, notably by H. H. Groves, V. E. Johnson, and G. Harris. Mr. Groves built several models, one of which flew over a thousand feet in 1912. One psychological hazard that confronted most early experimenters with steam-powered model airplanes is that they constantly held before themselves the image of Professor Langley's three-quarter-mile flight in 1896 and, seldom pausing to take into consideration the differences in size, weight, and wing loading between their models and Langley's comparative giant, often tended to regard their own creations as somewhat less successful than they actually were. For some reason the best of Groves' flights was not generally known in the United States for some years, Cavanagh mentioning only an earlier flight the same day that measured 450 feet. The steam-powered model airplane continued to be a favorite subject of conversation and theoretical calculation in certain model aeronautical circles after World War I, but very little seems to have been done in the way of practical experimentation. No attempt appears ever to have been made to attempt to introduce a commercial steam engine and boiler for model airplanes.

COMPRESSED-AIR AND OTHER ENGINES

The compressed-air engine, on the other hand, has had a long and honorable career in model aviation. As already recorded, Lawrence Hargrave of Australia built and flew a number of successful compressed-air-powered semiornithopters and airplanes; his best distances with the two types of models were 368 feet and 128 feet respectively. The compressed-air engine attracted a great deal of attention in the first decade of model airplanes as a hobby and was second in popularity only to rubber, but its overall use proportionately was infinitesimal. There is considerable disagreement among early writers as to the country where the greatest amount of development and use was done. Francis A. Collins attributed it to France (for in 1910 he viewed rubber power as but a makeshift) and noted that some believed it would solve the model airplane power problem, although he himself at the time pinned his best hopes to springs and clockworks. Cavanagh regarded Great Britain as the home of compressed-air power, although in 1910 Britain's V. E. Johnson had dismissed it as a snare and a delusion with copious calculations to prove that nothing better could be brought about with a "bicycle pump" than could be had at far less expense with rubber. By 1922 he was somewhat more sanguine. What must be remembered in connection with compressed-air

Fig. 284. Two electrically powered Blériot monoplanes manufactured in the World War I era by the A. E. Rittenhouse Company. These models took off, flew, and landed in tethered circular flight, the two tether lines serving to carry electric current to the motors. The larger model (left) is the first unit in the line, introduced in 1913.

G. William Holland

power is that, regardless of its difficulties, cost, and not necessarily superior results, it did provide a model airplane with a real reciprocating engine, thereby to a certain measure at least following prototype practice, and this was regarded by many model enthusiasts as an accomplishment of very substantial merit.

In point of fact, compressed-air engines became fairly popular in Great Britain at an early date, and the first mass-produced engines seem to have been made in that country. As much interest in the use of such commercial engines and as much individual experimentation and home building of the engines seem to have held in the United States as in Britain, although such engines do not seem to have been manufactured in the United States until after World War I. Several members of the New York Model Aero Club, notably Rudy Funk— noted for his method of making propellers by bending pieces of birch veneer over an alcohol flame instead of carving them from a block—John McMahon (later editor of *Aero Digest*), and Frank Schober, attained considerable success with their homemade compressed-air engines, as did a number of other early model airplane enthusiasts. Others had less luck. Many of the engines had interesting constructional details, for often they were built by hobbyists who had no machine tools whatsoever available to them. More often than not the engines would run perfectly, but the drawback to successful flying lay in the amount of air that could safely be compressed into the tank that had to be carried on the model, the tank itself often forming the main member of the fuselage. The air tank, in fact, often presented more problems than the engine itself, for it was necessary to combine optimum lightness of weight with sufficient strength safely to withstand the high pressure of the air compressed within it. Frequently the tanks were externally wound with piano wire for added safety, somewhat similar to the manner in which the boilers of early steam automobiles were wound. Homemade engines were either of the rotary type

wherein the entire engine, to which the propeller was fastened, turned around a central fixed shaft, or of the opposed cylinder type; all the production engines appear to have been rotary engines.

The first compressed-air engine sold in the United States seems to have been the Nomie three-cylinder engine, which was available by 1911 from the Goff Aeroplane Company, who advertised themselves as exclusive agents for the Nomie Engine Company Limited ("Sole Mfrs Chicago"); but from the form of the company name it is to be suspected that the engine manufacturer was a British enterprise and the engines were actually produced in England. The three-cylinder Nomie was advertised in 1911 as developing ¼ horsepower at 2,500 rpm and weighing 6¼ ounces, being capable of being operated on compressed air, carbonic acid gas (a further clue to British origin), or steam. It was intended primarily for use on compressed air, high-pressure air tubes were supplied, with the engine weighing 16 ounces, and charged with 1,176 pounds of air. Extra tubes were $0.75 each, or an empty tube could be returned and exchanged for a new charge for $0.15. The engine and one cylinder of compressed air sold for $15.00, and there must already have been other such engines on the market, for the advertisements cautioned against imitations. The name Nomie was a takeoff on the name of the actual Gnome rotary engines of full-size aviation.

About the same time or shortly thereafter, Stevens's Model Dockyard of London introduced a line of much less expensive rotary compressed-air engines in two-, three-, four-, and six-cylinder models, sold separately or in combination with what they termed an air chamber. These air tubes or cylinders were also available separately. By this time it was the custom to furnish the air cylinder empty and for the hobbyist to pump them up with a bicycle pump. The usual working pressure for compressed-air engines was about 60 pounds per square inch, although some hobbyists talked loftily of the possibilities of running pressures up as high

Fig. 285. A single-cylinder internal-combustion reciprocating model airplane engine weighing 7 pounds, made by W. A. Gamage of London, England, in 1910. It was actually a modification of a previous design, manufactured in 1909 or even earlier.

Warshaw Collection of Business Americana

as 300 pounds per square inch or more! In 1916, flights of over 200 feet in length or over 40 seconds' duration were considered excellent achievements for compressed-air-powered model airplanes. From a purely mathematical standpoint these figures could be far surpassed by rubber-powered models (which were of course much lighter and usually smaller), but these lacked the appeal, so important in some enthusiasts' eyes, of having a real engine. A ½ horsepower 6-cylinder Nomie engine was brought out a little later, and both of the Nomie engines were sold in the form of kits of unmachined parts as well as assembled. By the end of World War I the prices for Nomie engines in the United States were $10 and $15 in kit form, with the air tanks $5 and $7 additional respectively, or $25 and $50 (presumably without the tank) completely assembled and ready to run.

The Wading River Manufacturing Company also offered two- and four-cylinder compressed-air engines and parts about this time. The engines were advertised as built on special order only and, with air tank, sold for $15 and $22 respectively. They sold blueprints and parts for the two-cylinder model separately, and also showed a special compressed-air-driven monoplane for their two-cylinder engine, with the frame largely built of steel. The kit, without engine, sold for $6, and special propellers also were offered for use with the compressed-air engines.

Concerning clockwork and other spring-powered model airplanes there is comparatively little that can be said. Prior to World War I Stevens's Model Dockyard offered a series of four sizes of lightweight clockwork mechanisms especially designed for model airplanes, with a propeller shaft extending at one end at right angles to the winding stem and the axles of the gears. These were evidently simply adaptations of clockwork mechanisms for model locomotives, probably of Continental European manufacture, with a crown gear —or contrate wheel, as it is known in Great Britain—placed on the last stage axle to drive a pinion on the propeller shaft. Some hobbyists evidently built and flew model airplanes powered with these mechanisms (as some nineteenth-century aeronautical experimenters had driven models), but virtually no references can be found to them either in American or British sources other than Francis A. Collins's statement in 1910 that some interesting models had been equipped with clockwork motors. World War I marked the end of any commercial offerings of mechanisms of this type, although somewhat surprisingly the power form evidently was still under some discussion in the late 1920's and early 1930's, and Irwin S. Polk reports that the original AMA contest rules were written broadly enough to encourage experimentation with forms of power other than rubber and that spring power was one of the means they definitely had in mind at the time.

In view of the present interest in model rocketry it might be interesting to trace the history of rockets to their beginnings many centuries ago, but model rocketry itself is a comparatively modern hobby and it is desirable to confine this discussion to rockets only as they were applied to model airplanes, particularly as model rocketry as such should be considered as a thing entirely apart from fireworks rockets. There had been some proposals for and experiments with jet propulsion of airplanes in the nineteenth century. (The conception of the Saxon army officer Werner Siemens, in 1847, however, was not for a rocket-powered airplane, as it sometimes stated, but for an ornithopter driven by a gunpowder engine.) In the early days of the model airplane hobby several enthusiasts experimented with rocket-powered model airplanes. In 1922 V. E. Johnson published plans for a rocket engine not too dissimilar in its internal configuration from modern Series II rocket engines. As early as 1909, Jean A. Roché, the future creator of the Aeronca, attempted to build a rocket-engine model airplane

Fig. 286. In 1913, or a year or two earlier, the British firm Stuart Turner Limited introduced single- and two-cylinder model internal-combustion reciprocating engines for model use, each being made both air- and water-cooled. The single-cylinder engine pictured here is water cooled; the air-cooled models, of which the two-cylinder model shown here is an example, customarily were used for model airplanes.

G. William Holland

Fig. 287. As far as can be ascertained, the first internal-combustion reciprocating model airplane engine manufactured in the United States was the Baby Engine, a ½-horsepower design weighing 3¾ pounds, and equipped with an 18-inch aluminum propeller. This advertisement is reproduced from a 1911 airplane-meet program, wherein it occupied a full page.

G. William Holland

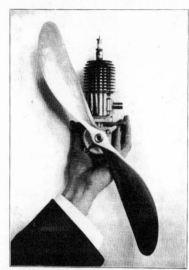
—which he actually regarded as a powered glider because of the absence of a propeller—but was unsuccessful and gave up after a few tests indoors. In 1911 the Co-operative Aero Association of Muncie, Indiana, advertised a device they termed an internal-combustion turbine for model airplanes, describing it as a complete power plant weighing half a pound and delivering 1/8 horsepower. The price, $2, indicates clearly that this could not have been any kind of reciprocating engine, and in combination with the name, suggests that it was some sort of jet-propulsion device. Despite the paucity of definite reports, some American and British enthusiasts must have met with fair success in powering model airplanes with rockets, for Francis A. Collins later spoke of it as an accomplished fact. In the 1920's, Wm. E. Appleby (N/c) and Company of England cataloged their "Super Aeroplane," a 52-inch wingspan rubber-driven tractor monoplane, as also being fitted with a rocket apparatus. In this case the rockets, which were mounted in the landing gear, presumably were used primarily to provide thrust to assist the model in quickly becoming airborne.

ELECTRICALLY POWERED MODEL AIRPLANES

It is obvious that electricity commended itself at an early date to a number of model airplane hobbyists. It is important in this connection to distinguish carefully between offerings of electric motors for actual flying models and the cataloging of electric motors intended simply to operate the propellers of nonflying display models. In 1912 the White Aeroplane Company cataloged a Lionel New Departure Type B electric motor* "for exhibition models" (this was evidently about as near as Harry C. Grant ever came to model aviation), and White's successors continued to offer various small electric motors for this same purpose through the 1920's, noting "Designs Not Guaranteed," which evidently did not refer to the performance of the motors being questionable but rather that in the 1920's they shipped whatever make and pattern was readily available to

---

*The White catalog pictures a Lionel Type BS motor with an off-on switch, but it is clear from the price of $1 quoted that they actually were selling the switchless Type B.

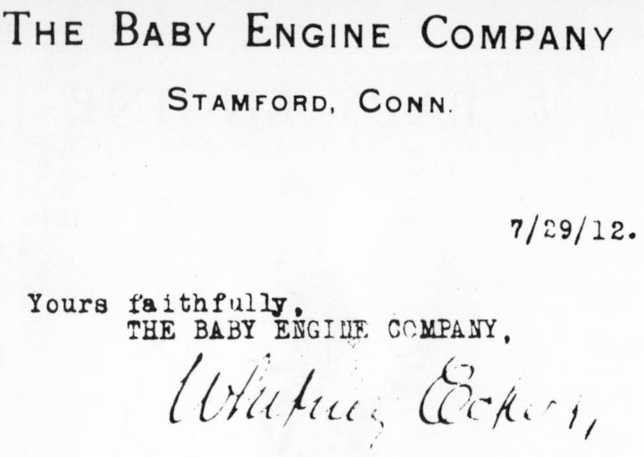

THE BABY ENGINE COMPANY

STAMFORD, CONN.

7/29/12.

Yours faithfully,
THE BABY ENGINE COMPANY,

Whitney Eckert,

Fig. 288. Letterhead and conclusion of a letter from the Baby Engine Company of Stamford, Connecticut, in 1912. Whitney Eckert, who signed the letter, was one of two brothers who operated this venture that produced the first American internal-combustion reciprocating model airplane engine.

Stamford Historical Society

them at the time. In Great Britain, however, what were specifically designated "Aeroplane Electric Motors" were offered a few years prior to World War I, along with small batteries, or "accumulators," as the British term them, with the evident implication that they might be used in flying models. However, in both 1910 and 1922 V. E. Johnson warned rather dogmatically that under no circumstances should anyone attempt to use electric motors for model airplanes, and undertook to prove his point mathematically, pointing out that while one might get about three ounces of static thrust from an electric motor and batteries weighing a pound, a thrust of pounds, not ounces, could be obtained from a pound of rubber.

The idea of not carrying batteries themselves in the airplane does not seem to have occurred to him or to other British experimenters. Nonetheless, in California in 1910 there was serious talk of carrying a storage battery around on a wheel on the ground, with light wires running to the flying model airplane. One boy, whose name is not recorded, actually built and flew a model airplane using a Kendrick and Davis "Ajax" motor, a familiar design of stationary electric motor that weighed about one pound, connected to a storage battery he carried under his arm!

As a matter of fact, the idea of powering flying models electrically goes back at least to 1887 when Gustav Trouvé, who had built the cartridge-powered ornithopter in 1870, constructed what was regarded as the lightest electric motor built up to that time, weighing only two ounces. He mounted a propeller to the motor and successfully demonstrated the lifting power of the electrically powered propeller mounted on the arm of a special testing stand. What he produced was in essence an electrically powered model helicopter that rose in an arc. He displayed this device before French scientific bodies in 1887 and 1888 but evidently did not attempt to carry the idea much further, and in 1891 returned to his ornithopter proposal, although he had in the interim since its original conception devoted much time and effort to scientific studies of propellers and is credited with establishing that the pitch of an air screw should be equal or close to the diameter, as opposed to marine engineering practice, which was at the time accepted by many aeronautical experimenters. Trouvé should also evidently be credited with the inception of the idea of powering an electrically operated flying device by means of a power source that itself did not become airborne with the model, an idea that was later to find considerable favor in the United States but which does not seem to have been followed up in other countries.

The first commercial fruition of this idea occurred in 1909, with the introduction of a toy known as the Pioneer Airship (Fig. 283) whose great feature was specifically acclaimed as the fact that it was operated by electricity rather than by clockwork and that it was fitted with a special regulating device. When the model airship swung out too far under the pull of centrifugal force, this device automatically broke the circuit to the motor and restored the power only when the airship swung in to its normal position again. The model operated on three dry cells. It was undoubtedly a "novel toy" and quite possibly also a "splendid toy," to use two of the terms by which it was described, but unfortunately it also to this day remains somewhat of a mystery, as it has not been possible definitely to ascertain by whom it was manufactured. It was evidently made in the United States, a deduction reached not by the presence of the American flags—for European manufacturers frequently decorated their products with these banners when they were to be exported to the United States—but rather from details of the construction and the style of the drawing. A sort of negative identification may be made by noting that investigation indicates it was not made by any of the companies that readily come to mind as producing electric toys and novelties at the time: Carlisle and Finch, Empire, Ives, Ken-

Fig. 289. The first model airplane contest in the United States involving internal-combustion reciprocating engines took place in the fall of 1913 and was sponsored by the Baby Engine Company, who supplied the engines for use in planes built by members of the New York Model Aero Club. These photographs show the tractor monoplane built and entered by John Carisi. Sitting behind the model are, left to right, William Piceller, a pioneer pilot; John Carisi, and Henry Ragot. Russell Holderman, wearing a cap, is standing at the extreme right. The second photograph shows the Baby Engine running in the Carisi model. Left to right are Henry Ragot, William Piceller, and John Carisi.

Capt. Ralph S. Barnaby, USN (Ret.)

drick and Davis, Knapp, Lionel or Voltamp, and the successors to the A. E. Rittenhouse Company, express doubt that it is of their manufacture. Perhaps some reader will be able to shed further light on this and on the model described in the following paragraph.

Fig. 283 illustrates another 1909 electrically powered model that can only be described as a truly fantastic conception. It embodies an electric railroad, not an ordinary railroad, but a suspended monorail system, on which runs a wheeled carriage covered by what may well be intended to represent the envelope of an airship. From this is suspended a foreshortened triplane containing an electric motor driving a large pusher propeller that evidently drove the whole affair around the circular track. Electric current reached the motor through the two separate rails that, together with their insulated connecting pieces, formed the monorail track. The track is in fact of a type not otherwise seen until the electric monorail model trains made by the Leland Detroit Manufacturing Company of Detroit, Michigan, in 1933. The picture was presented in 1909 as an illustration to an article on a suggested system of combining airplanes and trains on a regular railroad, and had no relation whatsoever to the device described in the accompanying article. The pictures was captioned simply "Model of Aeroplane Toy," which if interpreted with pre-

cision is, of course, something quite different from a "Model Aeroplane Toy" and which may indicate this was simply a sample model of something that had been displayed to the trade but was not then in actual production and which may in fact never had gone into manufacture. Certain features of the model, however, including the formed round railheads, indicate that if this were a mere sample it was a most elaborate one for the day and that it is not at all impossible that the picture is of a model that actually was manufactured and sold.

THE RITTENHOUSE ELECTRIC AIRCRAFT

The great producer of early electrically powered model airplanes—actual flying model airplanes—was the A. E. Rittenhouse Company of Honeoye Falls, New York. Their models, although they were always out of the mainstream of model airplane development, attained considerable popularity between their introduction in 1913 and the termination of production about twenty years later. The Rittenhouse electric airplanes, although substituting metal for wood and fabric, actually flew. They would take off and fly in a circle by a combination of centrifugal force and the lifting power of the wings, although tethered to a revolving ceiling fixture by means

Fig. 290. Another entry in the 1913 internal-combustion reciprocating engine model airplane contest, a canard-type model whose builder is unknown. The competition, probably the first of its kind in the world, was held at the old flying field at Mineola, Long Island, New York.

Capt. Ralph S. Barnaby, USN (Ret.)

of the two light wires that completed the electrical circuit to and from the special series-wound "Aero Motor" in the airplane. The heart of the system was the special swiveling counterbalance mounted on a screw hook that was to be inserted in the ceiling of the room where a model was to be flown. The models operated on 6 to 12 volts a.c. or d.c. and could be operated from dry cells, a storage battery, or alternating or direct house current by means of a transformer or direct current reducer. Rittenhouse soon also made a full line of transformers for use with the airplanes, model trains, or other electrical toys. The size of the circle that the airplane would describe in flight would be regulated either by adjusting the length of the wires that fed the current or by increasing or decreasing the speed of the motor. When the current was shut off, the model airplane would circle down to a perfect landing.

The first model airplane introduced by Rittenhouse in 1913 was a 22-inch-wingspan commendable-looking model of a Blériot that could be flown in a circle 5 to 100 feet in diameter and would attain an actual speed of 12 miles per hour on 8 dry cells, although it would fly on the power of as few as 4 dry cells. It was completely equipped with struts, stays, and a wheeled landing gear (which Rittenhouse termed the "Alighting Gear"), and had a 9½-inch-diameter aluminum propeller. This model immediately attained substantial popularity after its introduction in the spring of 1913, both as a device for individual use and as a show-window attraction. Rittenhouse felt that it soon proved itself to be "the most popular Electric Toy manufactured," which may be open to some question, particularly as the era was precisely that during which electric-train sales were booming beyond all expectations each successive year, but the sales certainly were sufficient to induce Rittenhouse to start a gradual expansion of the line, which was to continue to grow into the 1930's. By 1915 two more airplanes had been added, a smaller, 16-inch-wingspan Blériot monoplane, which would fly in circles up to 50 feet in diameter, and a still smaller model of a Curtiss biplane that would travel in circles of 3 to 25 feet in diameter. The initial prices of the No. 1 and No. 2 Blériot outfits, including the suspension device, were $9 and $7.50, which were later increased to $12 and $10 with the little No. 3 Curtiss biplane selling for $8.

Swiveling counterbalances (there were two models, for airplanes weighing one to two pounds and for those weighing two to three pounds), motors, and propellers were sold separately, and it is obvious that a number of hobbyists built their own model airplanes around these parts; but the prices both of complete airplane outfits and components were beyond the reach of many of the vast army of boys who were interested in flying model airplanes. The line gradually was increased, with more modern designs of monoplanes in the 1920's and a dirigible around 1930, as well as illuminated hangers and airfield marker lights and revolving beacon towers. The great drawback was, of course, the necessity for boring a hole in the ceiling to suspend the swiveling counterbalance, although no doubt a number of ingenious owners worked out substitute methods by which they could suspend the apparatus from a chandelier. In the late 1920's Rittenhouse worked out an alternate system whereby the airplanes or dirigibles were powered through and suspended by a flexible steel rod that rose out of the center of the roof of an airplane or dirigible hanger, and by the early 1930's this method—although more expensive, involving as it did the acquisition of a miniature hanger instead of the ceiling fixture—had entirely supplanted the older ceiling suspension method. It is quite clear that Rittenhouse envisioned a complete system of working electrical air toys and accessories, and had proceeded a good ways toward this end in the early 1930's when the depression dictated a cessation of the aeronautical line (although the company continued in business). In the then burgeoning climate of commercial aviation development, a few more years of the survival of the line might have crowned it with far greater popularity than it had ever previously realized.*

INTERNAL-COMBUSTION RECIPROCATING ENGINES

The great historical epic of powered model airplane development lies, however, in the realm of the saga of the miniature internal-combustion reciprocating engine, for it is not only these engines that most closely mirror the power plans of real airplanes but that the developments of recent years have made them at least the almost equal rival, if not the master in popularity, of rubber power. Despite the widespread present-day use of model engines of this type, no greater void generally exists than that concerning their origins and history. With the exception of a small, al-

---

*Many hobbyists familiar with the electrically powered model aircraft of the 1930's tend to bracket the Rittenhouse models with the electrically powered model airplanes manufactured from 1935 to 1939 by the Lionel Corporation (with whom Harry C. Grant had long since severed his connection). This is due to a misconception, for while the Lionel units did present some interesting control features simulating the control stick of a real airplane, there were no motors in the model airplanes themselves and they did not truly fly, becoming airborne by means of what might best be described as a whipping action on the part of the supporting motorized rods.

Fig. 291. A surviving specimen of the Baby Engine. This particular unit has been fitted with an adapter insert for the spark plug, to take the hole down to accept a smaller-thread plug, and the original induction system has been replaced by a homemade intake and exhaust assembly.

Victor G. Didelot

Fig. 292. The Midget Engine, manufactured by the Aero Engine Company of Boston, Massachusetts, was manufactured around 1913–1916. Like the Baby Engine, it was a ½-horsepower engine and of about the same size as the Baby, but slightly lighter in weight. It was equipped with an 18-inch-diameter aluminum propeller.

New York Public Library

though steadily growing, number of enthusiasts of model engine history, there is a strong, indeed an almost universal tendency in both the model airplane hobby and industry to recall the Brown Junior engine, first marketed in 1934 by the Junior Motors Corporation of Philadelphia, Pennsylvania, as the first of such engines. A few older or more sophisticated individuals in the business may cite the Loutrel engine (first advertised by Louis P. Loutrel of Brooklyn, New York, but actually deriving from the M. L. Weiss engine that was on the market for about three years previous), the Knight engines made by the Power Model Boat and Airplane Company of Chicago, or various other engines that were made about the same time, or the Gil engines of the Gil Manufacturing Company of Chicago, some of which were on the market by 1922 at the latest. Actually, there has been no time since almost the earliest days of the model airplane era when commercially made internal-combustion reciprocating engines specifically designed for model airplanes were not readily available.

Francis A. Collins noted this availability in 1910, and stated that the smallest of the engines available was a ½ horsepower model that weighed 7 pounds and would run for 15 minutes, the latter presumably referring to its capacity on one tank of gas. In 1912 the California author Charles M. Miller noted that two firms "in the east" were advertising small gasoline engines for model airplanes. One of these undoubtedly was the Baby Engine Company of Stamford, Connecticut, who had introduced their ½ horsepower Baby Engine weighing 3¾ pounds—about half the weight of the smallest engine mentioned by Collins—by July

of 1911 at the latest. The second engine noted by Miller may have been what David Newmark described to the writer as a 1-horsepower motorbike or motorcycle engine with a 24-inch wooden propeller cataloged by the Ideal Aeroplane and Supply Company in 1912. (The idea of a motorbike engine being used for model aircraft need not be too startling; in 1937 Edward Roberts, the president of the Junior Motors Corporation, reversed the procedure and demonstrated the power of his engines by riding around at model airplane contests on a bicycle powered by one of his Brown Junior engines. For the most part, however, the internal-combustion reciprocating engines offered for model airplanes were from the beginning especially designed for this purpose. Most of them were about ½ horsepower and made use of 18-inch cast-aluminum propellers.) It is not too important to ascertain if the second of the engines Miller took note of was Ideal's; there were others available as well, made both in the United States and in Great Britain. In 1924, *The Modelmaker* recorded that the first small model gas engine commercially made in the United States—although not necessarily a model airplane engine—was marketed by a Mr. Hopkins, but did not specify any date* As early as 1909, A. W. Gamage of London advertised and cataloged a one-cylinder engine that weighed 7 pounds, which probably was the engine referred to by Francis A. Collins, as well as a second engine of somewhat different

*In 1924 *The Modelmaker* indicated they were speaking of the status of modelmaking in the United States "thirty years ago," which would be 1894, but they mentioned the names of several individuals and firms who were not in business at that date, or even until well after 1900, and Mr. Hopkins may well have been among this group.

design, available ready to run or in the form of a set of castings, which was not sold under the Gamage name and whose manufacturer cannot be determined.

In 1910 Gamage cataloged the slightly modified design of their earlier engine illustrated in Fig. 285. In the spring of 1911, and for an undetermined length of time prior to that date, A. Melcombe of Bedford, England, manufactured a 1/3 horsepower air-cooled (as were all the early model airplane engines) engine weighing 4 pounds, and advertised it in Great Britain and the United States. The American price in 1911 was $20 ready to run (about £4) or $6 in casting form. Furthermore, by 1913 at the latest, the well-known British firm of model engine makers, Stuart Turner, Limited, was manufacturing in assembled and kit form the four-stroke cycle "Stuart Model Petrol Motor" in a ¼ horsepower single-cylinder design and a ½ horsepower two-cylinder model. Each size was made in both an air-cooled and a water-cooled version. These engines were supplied fitted with flywheels but it was noted that "Where used for model or experimental Aeroplanes and Dirigibles the flywheels may be omitted." The Stuart engines sold in 1913 for £7 10s. 0d. ($37.50) and £12 12s. 6d. ($63.13) for the single- and double-cylinder models in ready-to-run form respectively. Shipping charges and customs duties would have made the cost of these engines substantially higher delivered in the United States. These engines were continued in production by Stuart with only slight modifications in the 1920's, although at that time they were cataloged only in form of sets of parts, materials, and drawings. Another production British engine of this period was the Bonn-Mayer, a two-cylinder V-type that is variously described as being introduced in 1912 or 1914, and is said to have been made by or for A. E. Jones, Limited.

It is quite obvious that there was no lack of availability of miniature internal-combustion reciprocating engines for model airplane use from an extremely early date onward. Nor was there any difficulty in securing suitable carburetors, and small spark plugs and ignition coils, although the smallest spark plugs and ignition coils of the pre-World War I era were by no means the miniatures that were to be developed later. In the United States what were then rated as extremely minature coils and spark plugs were manufactured by the Connecticut Telephone and Electric Company; in Great Britain substantially similar devices were produced for model engines by Fuller and Company and possibly others. Each engine manufacturer produced his own design of carburetor, sometimes simple drip designs with wicks, sometimes quite elaborate, as for instance the early Stuart Turner carburetors, which had jets, metal floats, and air and throttle controls. There was, however, one almost completely insuperable obstacle to the widespread use of internal-combustion reciprocating engines in model airplanes, and that was their high cost. The Baby Engine might be complete with "commutator, special spark plug, aluminum carburetor, gasoline tank and 18-inch aluminum propeller"—"commutator" evidently refers to the timer—for $35 but where were the customers to be found at this price? George A. Page, Jr., recalls that during his last model flying years at Van Cortlandt Park—this would be about 1911 or 1912—"some older men came around and exhibited a ½ h.p. engine—air-cooled for model airplanes and water-cooled, copper jacketed for model boats and canoes. Personally I marveled, but paid no further attention. . . . I'm sure no N.Y.M.A.C. member could have afforded to purchase same." These undoubtedly were Baby Engines, as a 1912 account speaks of the company manufacturing both air- and water-cooled types of one-, two-, and four-cylinder design from ½ to 2 horsepower, depending on the number of cylinders. At that time the company presented the engines as suitable for model airplanes and boats, and even for small electric lighting outfits.

THE BABY ENGINE

The Baby Engine is probably the earliest of the engines put into production in the United States and without question the most interesting. As with most of the earliest engines, it was of the two-stroke cycle type. In fact the design is in all its essentials substantially similar to the miniature internal-combustion reciprocating model airplane engines of today. Several who have examined the material gathered on the Baby Engine have remarked that model airplane engine design has shown virtually no change or improvement since 1911, a thought that is perhaps rather unfair to the carefully studied and thought-out numerous refinements that a great number of trained engineers and designers have incorporated into model airplane engines in the decades that have passed but that nevertheless has a kind of basic validity. The Baby Engine was advertised as developing a full ½ horsepower at 2,300 rpm; the standard cast-aluminum propeller supplied with it was of 18-inch diameter and 13-inch pitch, and the price of the complete engine was $35 in 1911. The earliest reference to the Baby Engine is in the July, 1911, *Aircraft,* and there was a full-page advertisement, reproduced in Fig. 287, in the "Official Program of the 1911 International Aviation Tournament at the Nassau Boulevard Aerodrome," and it is evident they anticipated that an eagerly awaiting public would seize upon the opportunity to purchase model airplane engines —many other advertisers, such as the Goodyear Tire and Rubber Company, contented themselves with half-page or even smaller advertisements. Nor is there any visible evidence that the Baby Engine Company may have secured some special concession in the placing of their advertisement. Everything points to their enthusiastic belief that they were launching something for which the aeronautical world was waiting.

It might well be noted here, in connection with the Baby and similar engines, that the thought sometimes is expressed that while such early engines were available, they must have proved themselves extremely poor in design and workmanship, and probably failed to achieve success because of this. There is no reason to accept this theory. Victor G. Didelot, a long-time model airplane engine expert, kindly analyzed Baby Engine Serial Number 117, which was available to him, and reported that the overall height is 7 inches, not counting the spark plug; that the cylinder is cast iron with 12 fins machined in (the photograph in the 1911 advertisement, evidently of a sample or an early model, shows 11 fins); that the engine is of the conventional sideport type with both intake and exhaust on the same side (the left, facing the engine—the advertising photograph indicates the right side); that the crankcase is cast of aluminum in two halves and has bronze bearings; that the piston is of cast iron with three rings (two compression and one oil), the connecting rod is a bronze casting, the crankshaft is, except for the counterblances, which are two machined weights, one piece, and the timer body and the bypass cover (which provides the nameplate on its external surface) are aluminum castings. The shaft is tapered and keyed for the cast-aluminum propeller, which is held on by means of a threaded bolt that is run into a hollow shaft, in a manner very similar to that used on many modern small engines. There are, however, a number of unusual and commendable special points of construction employed within the engine. The spark plug size is ⅝ inch—18 thread. The bore and stroke are both 1½ inches, and the indicated displacement is about 2.67 cubic inches (or a little more than three times that of the largest internal-combustion reciprocating model airplane engines acceptable under present-day AMA rules), this representing swept volume exclusive of the domed combustion chamber.

Mr. Didelot notes: "One of the things which impressed me the most in taking this engine apart was the general refinement in the internal machined parts. For an engine that looks pretty rough externally, it is very well machined internally. The crankcase halves, for instance, do not have a gasket between them; both halves are ground and then fitted together. The timer is pretty primitive, but the present owner tells me he has run the engine, and it runs quite well. Enough to throw a prop, anyway! There are signs that the casting technique might not have been all it might have been, as the piston has some open spots on the top where casting obviously wasn't up to snuff, and there are a few visible open spots on the cylinder internal surfaces where there are pits."

In short, a well-designed, good, working, competent engine, displaying first-class machine work, flawed only by some slight deficiencies in the work done by a foundry with probably limited experience in making small iron castings of the caliber designed for a miniature engine. Mr. Didelot notes that his father also owned a Baby Engine which, prior to his death, he was planning to employ to propel a canoe.

Another Baby Engine was reported on by John G. Steenken, who advised that it and the original "buzzer type" spark coil (which carried a serial number to match that of the engine) bore the variant name of the Baby Aero Engine Company of Stamford, Connecticut. He also describes it as a well-made and competent engine.

The Baby Engine Company was operated by Whitney Echert and his brother of Stamford, Connecticut. The company itself is unlisted in any of the Stamford city directories for the period, but researches by Alfred W. Dater, Jr., of the Stamford Historical Society indicate that it was more than a mere basement enterprise and that they maintained a sort of experimental shop and probably assembly plant at what would now be approximately 52 Pulaski Street on the upper harbor. The machine work on the engines appears to have been farmed out to the shop of George Muench at 52 Garden Street. It has not yet been possible to ascertain the name of the foundry that produced the castings or the first name of the other Echert brother. The Stamford City Directory for 1914 lists Whitney Echert as having removed to the West. Mr. Dater was able to locate several residents of Stamford who remembered the Baby Engine Company and its product, but virtually nothing concerning the proprietors. Harry D. Graulich, who originally supplied the name of the Echert brothers and who had one time had a considerable portfolio of printed matter on their model

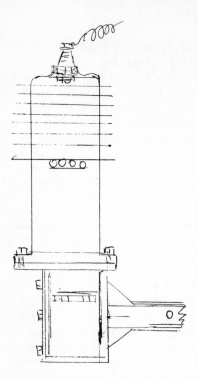

Fig. 293. Harry Wesley Aitken, pictured here in 1960, devoted much time and effort between 1906 and 1913 to perfecting a working internal-combustion reciprocating engine for model airplanes. At the right is a sketch of his engine, which was subsequently commercialized as the Midget Engine, especially prepared by Mr. Aitken in 1966 for use in this book.

H. W. Aitken

engine, recalls the Echert brothers as deeply interested in aviation and as building, at Oakwood Heights, Staten Island, New York, about 1912–1913 a successful tractor biplane powered with a Franklin automobile engine in which they made a number of flights. Of the Baby Engine itself, Mr. Graulich recalls that it ran well but was difficult to start. He names John Carisi, Cecil Peoli, and Percy Pierce as having made flights of several hundred feet with model airplanes powered by Baby Engines.

THE FIRST GAS-MODEL MEET IN AMERICA

Before the date of his moving to the West late in 1913 or early in 1914, which presumably marked the demise of the Baby Engine Company, Whitney Echert and his brother engaged in what was evidently a final promotional effort to advertise and put across the model engine. If the engine was beyond the means of most of the successful young model airplane builders of the day, they would demonstrate its ability by lending engines to builders of model airplanes who would compete in a gas-model meet! They offered to furnish an engine on this basis to any member of the New York Model Aero Club who would build a model airplane to receive it, and provided the members with drawings and mounting layouts so that they could construct their model airplanes ready to receive the engine. This was the first gas-model-powered model airplane meet in the

United States, and probably the first in the world. The meet was held at the old Mineola Flying Field at Mineola, Long Island, New York (by coincidence the factory of a present-day plastic model airplane manufacturer is located close by the very spot), and the meet *was* held—Captain Barnaby has supplied photographs he took at Mineola on the day of the contest, shown in Fig. 289 and 290, but *when* exactly was the meet held? This is one of the prime mysteries of model airplane history, for it has not yet been possible to ascertain the exact date of this all-important pioneer event. Even the year is not yet known for certain. Harry D. Graulich dates in 1910–1911; Jean A. Roché recalls it as 1911; Captain Barnaby about 1911 or 1912. It is at this point that the death of William Piceller on October 2, 1914, takes on its tragic significance, for Piceller was one of the approximately eighteen members of the New York Model Aero Club who built a model airplane to compete for the prize offered by the Echert brothers for the best flight made by a model powered by one of their engines, and appears in two of Captain Barnaby's photographs.* The prize was to be permanent possession of the Baby Engine.

The meet must therefore have taken place prior to October 2, 1914, at the very latest. As

---

*An added note: these may be the only pictures of Piceller extant. Harold D. Morehouse, the aviation historian who is endeavoring to compile biographies of all the pioneer pilots, with their photographs, had long searched unsuccessfully for a photograph of Piceller until he learned of the existence of Captain Barnaby's pictures through correspondence with the present writer.

the Stamford City Directory for 1914 was presumably based on information obtaining or gathered in late 1913 or early 1914, by which time Whitney Echert is recorded as having moved to the West, it is likely that the meet took place before 1914. The mean date of 1911 that can be arrived at as a consensus from the recollections noted above seems probably too early. One important point is that George A. Page, Jr., did not compete in the event and does not recall ever hearing of it—if he had he would certainly have entered—which he can account for only by the fact that it took place after he gave up his model airplane activities in April, 1913, to begin his flight training. On this basis is may be concluded that the meet took place between the spring and winter of 1913, and from the clothing seen in the photographs it seems logical to conclude that the event actually took place in the fall of 1913.

Captain Barnaby has actually found a note from Jean Roché reporting on a meeting of the New York Model Aero Club that the captain apparently missed, and referring to the models for the contest: "Nothing particular at meeting. Both Mr. Echerts were there but no more models were brought. Carisi's is finished." Unfortunately, the note is not dated! No construction work was ever done at the meetings of the New York Model Aero Club in the quarters furnished them by the Engineers Club at 250 West Fifty-fourth Street, New York, New York. This was simply a meeting room where the club met each Saturday evening with Mr. Durant, preparatory to their flying meets each Sunday.

Among the members of the New York Model Aero Club who built models for this event and eagerly carried them to Mineola for the installation of the Baby Engines that were awaiting them courtesy of the Echert brothers were Vincent J. Burnelli, John Carisi, Cecil Peoli, William Piceller, Percy Pierce, Jean A. Roché, Frank Schober, and Andrew Surini. Curiously, the remainder of the story is rather anticlimactic. No one is able to recall who was the winner of the event. Jean A. Roché reports that his 6-foot wingspan monoplane cracked up on its first flight, and that no contestant made a flight good enough to win the prize engine. In fact the creator of the Aeronca enters a dissenting opinion on the merits of the Baby Engine—"It was a model wrecker" (from excessive vibration) writes Mr. Roché. Captain Barnaby, who did not have an entry of his own but worked with Roché on his notes, says that in his recollection none of the models made really successful flights. On the other hand, Harry D. Graulich, who was also present but not competing, recalled the afore-

mentioned flights of several hundred feet by Carisi, Peoli, and Pierce and writes that "at that particular contest there were more than a dozen entrants and the meet stopped because of darkness." Probably the prize was offered not merely for the best flight, but for the best flight *over* a certain preset distance or duration, and none of the contestants was able to complete the requirement. There is a reference that at the time the Baby Engine was introduced its makers had claimed the gas tank would contain fuel sufficient to fly a 6- to 8-foot wingspan model for twenty minutes. In view of this, likely the qualifying performance established for the contest was more than a few hundred feet, or the comparatively few seconds it would take to fly such a distance. It must also be remembered that the contestants were accustomed to building and flying rubber-powered models, and the circumstances under which the contest was held, with the engines being installed at the flying field almost immediately prior to flight, gave them no opportunity to familiarize themselves with the characteristics of the engines or the requirements of designing model airplanes for them. Regardless, in all probability this was the world's first organized gas-model competition, and as such one of the major landmarks in the history of model aeronautics.

OTHER EARLY ENGINES

Harry Wesley Aitken of Philadelphia, Pennsylvania, was a boy with great mechanical interests and ability. He had constructed model steam engines, and built and flown rubber-powered model airplanes when in 1906, at the age of sixteen, he conceived a great desire to build a working miniature internal-combustion reciprocating engine capable of flying a model airplane. With great single-mindedness of purpose, he devoted a substantial amount of time over the next seven years to this effort, although the endeavor had to be suspended for a while for lack of funds following the Panic of 1907. Aitken, although possessed of great skill in designing, preparing drawings, and patternmaking, had no machine-shop facilities; every part required had to be made at local foundries and machine shops. He considered his endeavors realized in 1913 when he finally got his Elf Motor, as he termed it (there is no connection of course between this and the Elf line of model airplane engines that appeared on the market in the 1930's), to "sing at last," even though he recalls that the 18-inch propeller "nearly broke my finger when kicking." The engine was a ½-horsepower job with 1⅜-inch bore and 1⅜-inch stroke, bronze connecting rod, aluminum crank-

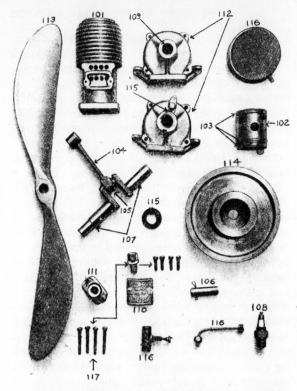

Fig. 294. This photograph, from a 1919 Chicago dealer's catalog evidently shows the Baby Engine in dismantled form, although the engines being offered for sale in the listings under this picture at that date apparently were of a different make and did not correspond in all details to the old illustration that was still being used.

G. William Holland

case, wrist pins and shaft of cold rolled steel, and one piston ring. The ⅜-inch American Society of Mechanical Engineers thread spark plug and the ignition coil were secured from the Connecticut Telephone and Electric Company, Incorporated, of Meriden, Connecticut. Shortly after completing the fully developed engine Mr. Aitken secured a position working on real airplane engines with the B. F. Sturtevant Company of Hyde Park, Massachusetts, near Boston. Mr. Aitken thereupon sold the entire outfit for the manufacture of his engine, including all the patterns, to a group of individuals who formed the Aero Engine Company of Boston and put the engine into production under the name of the Midget Gasoline Motor.

In his 1916 book *Model Aeroplanes and Their Motors*, George A. Cavanagh describes the Midget Engine as weighing 2½ pounds complete with carburetor, spark plug, and ignition coil, which is more than a pound less than the Baby Engine, although both were 7 inches high. The Midget was said to develop various speeds of from 400 to 2,700 rpm, reaching ½ horsepower at the latter, and to have an 18-inch diameter and 13-inch pitch propeller. P. C. McCutchen of Philadelphia is reported to have made a number of highly successful flights with an 8-foot wingspan model of a Voisin

biplane using an engine of this design. Mr. Aitken recalls visiting Mr. McCutchen when the latter offered to show off the running of the engine in his cellar, but it made such a terrific amount of noise that the others in the house called down and demanded he stop; during the time he was developing the engine Mr. Aitken was able to test run it only when people were out of the adjacent apartments.

The identities and histories of the Baby Engine and the Midget Engine are clear, although it is to be hoped further data concerning them can eventually be turned up. There is also the matter of the so-called Weiss Engine which has been listed and erroneously dated 1911 on some engine checklists compiled by collectors, and in the absence of knowledge of the Baby and Midget Engines thereby regarded as the first commercial American engine. Mel Anderson, one of the great names in model airplane engine design, who ascribes the dawn of his interest in miniature internal-combustion reciprocating engines to having received the Weiss literature, definitely dates it on the basis of concurrent events as 1915 or 1916, and recalls he learned of it through advertisements in *Popular Mechanics*. The following classified advertisement appeared in that periodical from late 1914 into the middle of 1916 under the heading of "AERONAUTICS" which covered both real and model products: "LIGHT Weight Gasoline Engines, 2½ lbs. Guaranteed ½ H.P. The Weiss Co., Torrington, Conn." This confirms Mr. Anderson's recollections but in the absence of further evidence for which a search continues, does not establish whether a Weiss engine was manufactured at this time or whether the advertisements were simply those of a dealer who was selling Midget Engines. It will be noted that the weight and horsepower specified in the Weiss advertisements are identical with those of the Midget Engine, and that the Midget Engine was evidently the only American-made production engine known to Cavanagh at the time of his 1916 book.* In 1919 R. E. McAdams of Springfield, Ohio, advertised blueprints for $1.50 of a ½-horsepower, 2½-pound model airplane engine. Possibly he would also supply completed engines, but the absence of any reference to this suggests that it may represent a latter-day spinoff from the

*In any event there does not appear to have been any connection between the engine sold by the Weiss Company in 1914-1916 and the M. L. Weiss engine of the late 1920's (which subsequently became the Loutrel) and in the account of his engine M. L. Weiss did not make mention of any efforts on his part at such an early date. Around 1916 there was also a Wise engine, a 5-cylinder rotary compressed air engine. It is not clear from Cavanagh's book, where this engine is described and illustrated, if this was a production engine or an individual hobbyist's homemade effort, although the impression is conveyed that the latter was the case.

Midget Engine in the form of drawings made up by an owner of one of those engines.

In 1919, too, the Modern Engine and Supply Company of Chicago, who claimed to manufacture some of their goods but who obviously were primarily distributors of and dealers in a wide variety of products, cataloged (along with Nomie compressed-air engines) a ½-horsepower internal-combustion reciprocating engine for small power models, including "model aeroplane work." Casting sets and drawings sold for $7; the completed engine, including spark plug and coil, for $32.50. The dimensions given are 8½ inches high, 1½-inch bore, and 1½-inch stroke, with the total weight 6½ pounds. The illustration that accompanied this offering showed the parts of a dismantled engine (Fig. 294) that has positively been identified as being those of the Baby Engine, with the nameplate possibly deliberately mutilated to prevent its being read. The greater weight of the 1919 engine over the known weight of 3½ pounds of the Baby Engine suggests that the later engine may have been manufactured by the Chicago company itself; in any event it is clear that the engine sold in 1919 was an entirely different proposition and must remain for the moment at least somewhat of a mystery engine. While the weight of the engines offered by the Chicago firm* was considerably greater than those of the equally powerful Baby and Midget engines, it might be noted solely as a matter of interest—not in any sense as an extenuation—that at the time anything less than 40 pounds was considered a good light weight for a ½-horsepower stationary internal-combustion reciprocating engine. The height of 8½ inches given for the 1919 model airplane engine may have included the spark plug. In any case the greater weight indicates that the engine was substantially less efficient than the earlier Baby and Midget engines.

INDIVIDUALLY MADE ENGINES

A number of individually crafted internal-combustion reciprocating model airplane engines were made in both the United States and Great Britain from a comparatively early date; perhaps the first was Manly's miniature engine for Langley's gasoline-powered model of 1901. In Great Britain the individually crafted engines of D. Stanger particularly attracted much attention at an early date. He built a four-cylinder V-type

*In the 1921 catalog of the same company, the old illustration is again used and the engine weight given as 10 pounds. There are, however, two models listed, one of cast iron and one "all Aluminum for airplane work." (We are at approximately the point of the popular transition in the United States from "aeroplane" to "airplane.") Ten pounds may have represented the iron model and 6½ pounds the aluminum version. The price of the aluminum engine in 1921 was $11.50 in the form of rough castings and $40.00 assembled. The indicated speed was 700 to 1,500 rpm.

engine in 1908 that weighed 5½ pounds and delivered 1¼ horsepower at 1,300 rpm. It powered a semibiplane of about 8-foot wingspan. A particularly interesting feature was a clockwork-operated timer similar to modern timers, that automatically stopped the engine after a predetermined time had elapsed. The model airplane was displayed at an aeronautical exhibition at Agricultural Hall, London, in 1908 and had a propeller of 29-inch diameter and 36-inch pitch. It is not clear if the plane was flown at the time in 1908 or a little later, but it did fly. Stanger subsequently built other engines (including a two-cylinder V-type in 1910) and other planes, and in 1914 established the first official record for mechanically powered rise-off-ground models with a flight of 51 seconds' duration, although some of his models had previously made longer flights. It was announced that a class for mechanically driven models would be included in the Second National Model Aeroplane Competition in the United States in 1916, but it is not clear if such a special event for power other than rubber was held and, if so, the results. Another noted early British model engine was a one-horsepower, 7½-pound design four-cycle opposed two-cylinder model developed by W. G. Jopson of the Manchester Model Aero Club. It is not certain if this engine eventually was commercialized, even if in a very small way, but it appears very similar if not identical to the engine used in a 5-foot wingspan model built by T. W. K. Clarke, and Jopson is said to have patented the special variable-pitch propeller he designed for the engine.

With the exception of the ardent Cavanagh, and partially at least for reasons already explained, few early writers on model aviation showed much enthusiasm for internal-combustion reciprocating engines, and particularly for single-cylinder engines, a form that was obviously the best for inexpensive production. They professed to fear excessive vibration in a single-cylinder model, although Johnson noted in 1910 that the problem was not insuperable. Nevertheless, it was not generally appreciated to what extent engine designers could and did counteract this by proper counterbalancing. In 1922 Johnson substantially repeated his earlier remarks except that he omitted the reference to the problem not being insuperable and added a statement to the effect that he did not believe success would ever attend such efforts. A similar opinion was expressed in 1921 in the model section of the first issue of the American magazine the *Aeronautical Experimenter*. Whatever the conscious or subconscious intention behind such remarks, they served only to dampen enthusiasm and progress in this direction. As noted before, such an outlook was understandable but regrettable. Fortunately, there were always enough individuals who did not read these advices, or who did not believe what they read, that internal-combustion engines for model airplanes were able to make an almost continual progression from several years prior to 1910 onward.

As a matter of fact, by 1910 Thomas R. Arden of New York, New York, was repeatedly making successful internal-combustion engine-powered flight up to almost a mile in length with a model airplane powered by an engine of his own design and making. This was the same Ray Arden who, starting in 1948, was to effect a rapid revolution in model engine ignition by introducing the glow plug, which was swiftly to replace the spark plug almost entirely. One day in 1910 Arden sent his plane into flight. Following it to its landing place some thousands of feet away he found a young lady who was just about to take home the unusual object that had come out of the sky and landed at her feet. Shortly thereafter she became Mrs. Arden in a romance the *New York Evening Telegram* chronicled under the headline "He First Conquers the Air, Then Wins a Maiden's Heart."*

For those interested in such details, the model seems to have been a biplane of about 6-foot wingspan. Arden was to become famous as a designer and manufacturer of small internal-combustion reciprocating model airplane engines—the smaller, the better in his eyes. Though his production engines set new standards of miniaturization, they were as nothing to what he accomplished individually for experimental purposes and his own amusement. Working under powerful magnifying lenses and using special drills, dies, taps, and other tiny tools he constructed for the purpose, he turned out an amazing series of tiny working engines. Some of his working spark plugs were no larger than the head of a match, and his smallest complete working engine weighed but twenty-three grains! It was Arden's pleasure to carry around a conventional snap-cover eyeglass case, which he would open on occasion to reveal its contents of some half-dozen perfect miniature working internal-combustion reciprocating engines!

All this, however, lay long years ahead of Arden in 1910, although his object evidently almost from the beginning was to construct the smallest, lightest engines possible. Arden was originally inspired by a meeting with Augustus M. Herring when Arden was in his late teens; he was born in 1890. Some time around 1907 or 1908 a friend took Arden to what he later described as a sportsmen's show at Madison Square Garden, but which most probably was the December, 1908,

aeronautical exhibition. There, Herring was displaying a model biplane, powered by a miniature internal-combustion engine. Arden, who had already built many rubber-powered model airplanes and marked himself as seriously inventive, was completely enthralled by Herring's miniature engine. Seeing the youth's interest, the aeronautical pioneer devoted some time to explaining the model and internal-combustion reciprocating engines in general. Arden is reported to have told Herring, "Someday I will make the smallest engine ever built!" but in the light of future events this story sounds apocryphal. Arden is also said to have told Herring that the two-stroke cycle engine, which Herring advised, was too elementary for his tastes.

In any case, Arden shortly thereafter began to design and build his first internal-combustion reciprocating engine. Arden did not immediately invent and fly with glow-plug engines, as some believe. His first model engines were of the spark ignition type. The glow plug as such did not develop for many, many years. However, the hot-wire or hot-bulb system of engine ignition was then well known and was applied to many real and to some model engines. What Arden seems to have done initially was to create spark ignition engines with a jump spark that frequently missed at high speed (Arden had already worked in a New York spark coil factory) and he decided to supplement the spark plug, which he retained, with an additional hot-wire system incorporated in the same engine. Obviously, if the meeting with Herring inspired Arden to make model engines, and the meeting did not take place until December, 1908, as seems probable, Arden did not first build and fly engines of any type in 1907 or 1908 as sometimes is reported; likely the date should be 1909. In any event, he certainly did not fly anything that properly can be described as a glow-plug engine at any such early date. A particularly interesting point that emerges from the story is that Herring was an early builder of working model engines.

Thus the story of the model airplane, of the models that foretold the real thing and of the models that mirrored it during the pioneer period of its practical reality. It has not been easy to determine exactly when the pioneer period of model aviation itself should logically be determined to have ended. As already noted, the Early Birds of Aviation, Incorporated, after much thought, decided that the close of the pioneer period of piloting should be marked as December 17, 1916, the thirteenth anniversary of the Wrights' first successful flights. Upon due consideration it appears best to accept the same date as marking the end of the pioneer era of model aviation, and this boundary has accordingly been adopted here.

---

*Quoted from an article about Arden by William Winter that appeared in 1948 in *Air Trails* (now *American Modeler*) and was reprinted in the same year in the British publication *Aero Modeller*.

APPENDIX I

Governing Bodies and National Associations

Listed below are the principal model aircraft organizations in the United States and the governing bodies in other countries. In many cases model aeronautical events are under the direct control of the regular national aeronautical club representing the Fédération Aéronautique Internationale. In other countries the aeronautical club has delegated the authority covering models to a special group, as happens to be the case in the listings below. In other countries, information concerning the governing of model aircraft events can be obtained by writing to the national body representing the FAI. Listed below under the United States are the two national governing bodies, the AMA and WAM, the rocketry group, two organizations devoted to collecting old model engines and flying old types of model aircraft, and a lighter-than-air group. The latter is included because it appears to be the only organization presently active in promoting the building of lighter-than-air models, and in sponsoring hot-air balloon races.

UNITED STATES

ACADEMY OF MODEL AERONAUTICS, 1025 Connecticut Avenue. N.W., Washington, District of Columbia, 20036

MODEL ENGINE COLLECTORS ASSOCIATION, 21306 Lopez Street, Woodland Hills, California 91364

NATIONAL ASSOCIATION OF ROCKETERY, 1239 Vermont Avenue, N.W., Washington, District of Columbia 20005

SOCIETY OF ANTIQUE MODELERS, 11801 Stanwood Drive, Los Angeles, California 90066

WESTERN ASSOCIATED MODELERS, 228 Culp Avenue, Mayward, California 94544

WINGFOOT LIGHTER-THAN-AIR SOCIETY, 1210 Massillon Road, Akron, Ohio 44315

CANADA

MODEL AERONAUTICS ASSOCIATION OF CANADA, 101 Normandy Boulevard, Toronto 8

GREAT BRITAIN

SOCIETY OF MODEL AERONAUTICAL ENGINEERS, 10A Electric Avenue, London SW 9

IRELAND

MODEL AERONAUTICS COUNCIL OF IRELAND, C/O Department of Transport and Power, Kildare Street, Dublin

APPENDIX II

Radio-Control Licensing Authorities

The following list provides the names and addresses of various national radio-control authorities in charge of licensing radio-control apparatus and from whom information may be obtained regarding the special regulations and requirements obtaining in each country. In the United States and in Great Britain, this licensing is handled by the central authority in Washington and London respectively. In Canada inquiries should be directed to the Regional Director of Air Services of the Department of Transport nearest to the place of residence of the applicant.

UNITED STATES

FEDERAL COMMUNICATIONS COMMISSION, Washington, District of Columbia 20025

CANADA

REGIONAL DIRECTOR, AIR SERVICE, DEPARTMENT OF TRANSPORT, at the nearest of the following offices:

739 West Hastings Street, Vancouver 1, British Columbia

9820 107th Street, Edmonton, Alberta

Winnipeg General Post Office Building, 266 Graham Avenue, Winnipeg 1, Manitoba

26 St. Clair Avenue East, Toronto 7, Ontario

Regional Administration Building, Montreal International Airport, Dorval, Province of Quebec

Federal Building, Post Office Box 42, 1081 Main Street, Moncton, New Brunswick

GREAT BRITAIN
GENERAL POST OFFICE, RADIO SERVICES DEPARTMENT, Headquarters Building, St. Martins-le-Grand, London, E.C. 1

IRELAND
DEPARTMENT OF TRANSPORT AND POWER, Kildare Street, Dublin

APPENDIX III

The Literature of the Model Aircraft, Spacecraft, and Rocket Hobbies

A substantial number of books have been published on model aeronautics, including several early and long-out-of-print volumes that are now quite difficult to obtain but of considerable historical interest. Many other books, not necessarily devoted to real aeronautics, but including a number of such works, have proved of value in preparing the historical section of the present book. There are currently available a number of model aeronautical books, particularly specialized treatments of such topics as radio control, that many readers will probably find of substantial interest and value. Residents of the United States and Canada may obtain a catalog of many of the model airplane and related books presently available by sending fifteen cents to Hobby Helpers, 1543 Stillwell Avenue, Bronx, New York 10061.

The following is a list of magazines published in the United States and Great Britain that are devoted to model airplanes or that contain material pertaining to the subject. Within the country of origin, sample copies often can be purchased at newsstands or hobby shops. If copies cannot be located in this manner, it is suggested the reader write directly to the publisher, enclosing a self-addressed stamped envelope. In addition to the periodicals listed below, some of the organizations listed in Appendix I also publish their own magazines or bulletins, and supply them to members as one of the privileges of membership.

AERO MODELLER, 38 Clarendon Road, Watford, Herts, England

AMERICAN MODELER, 1012 14th Street N.W., Washington, District of Columbia, 20005, U.S.A.

AVIATION COLLECTOR'S NEWS, P.O. Box 5036, Camp Curtin Station, Harrisburg, Pennsylvania 17110.

ENGINE COLLECTORS' JOURNAL, P.O. Box 15162, Lakewood, Colorado 80215, U.S.A.

FLYING MODELS, 215 Park Avenue South, New York, New York 10003, U.S.A.

GRID LEAKS—MODEL AIRCRAFT WORLD, P.O. Box 301, Higginsville, Missouri 64037, U.S.A.

MODEL AIRPLANE NEWS, 551 Fifth Avenue, New York, New York 10017, U.S.A.

MODEL RACING BUYERS' GUIDE, 505 Park Avenue, New York, New York 10022, U.S.A.

RADIO CONTROL MODELER, P.O. Box 1128, Laguna Beach, California 92653, U.S.A.

RADIO CONTROL MODELS AND ELECTRONICS, 38 Clarendon Road, Watford, Herts, England

SCALE MODELER, 7376 Greenbush Avenue, North Hollywood, California, U.S.A.

INDEX